Forensic Interven
and Rehabilitatioı

CW00796796

Forensic Interventions for Therapy and Rehabilitation: Case Studies and Analysis provides an up-to-date overview of the latest therapeutic ideas being used for forensic service users and prisoners in both custodial and community settings.

The field of forensic work is increasingly being recognised for its importance, both in terms of the value of the work in reducing reoffending and in terms of the salience given to it by the media, the public, and politically. This text reflects current policy and practice, and furthermore considers the therapeutic encounter from a broad perspective, which incorporates individual, group, and systemic interventions. *Forensic Interventions for Therapy and Rehabilitation* includes chapters on a range of therapeutic models, issues pertinent to specific groups of people with criminal convictions, and discussion on the various contexts in which interventions take place.

Forensic Interventions for Therapy and Rehabilitation is essential reading for all students of Forensic or Clinical Psychology, as well as practitioners in the field.

Belinda Winder is a Professor in Forensic Psychology, Chartered Psychologist and Research Director of the Centre for Crime, Offending, Prevention & Engagement (COPE) in the School of Social Sciences at Nottingham Trent University. Belinda is a co-founder of Safer Living Foundation, a charity set up in 2014 to conduct and evaluate initiatives that help to prevent further victims of sexual crime.

Nicholas Blagden is an Associate Professor in Forensic Psychology, Chartered Psychologist and head of the Sexual Offences, Crime and Misconduct Unit at Nottingham Trent University. He has worked and researched within the criminal justice system and HM Prison Service extensively and is a co-founder and trustee of the Safer Living Foundation charity.

Laura Hamilton is a Consultant Forensic Psychologist and Senior Lecturer at Nottingham Trent University. She has worked in a range of prison and forensic psychiatric settings for almost 20 years, providing assessment, formulation, and treatment services to a broad spectrum of individuals with criminal convictions.

Simon Scott is a Senior Researcher in the Centre for Crime, Offending, Prevention & Engagement (COPE) in the School of Social Sciences at Nottingham Trent University. He has previously been a Trustee of the Prisoners' Education Trust which supports the education in prisons.

Forensic Interventions for Therapy and Rehabilitation

Case Studies and Analysis

Edited by Belinda Winder,
Nicholas Blagden, Laura Hamilton,
and Simon Scott

Routledge
Taylor & Francis Group

LONDON AND NEW YORK

First published 2022
by Routledge
4 Park Square, Milton Park, Abingdon, Oxon OX14 4RN

and by Routledge
605 Third Avenue, New York, NY 10158

Routledge is an imprint of the Taylor & Francis Group, an informa business

British Library Cataloguing-in-Publication Data
A catalogue record for this book is available from the British Library

Library of Congress Cataloging-in-Publication Data
Names: Winder, Belinda, editor.
Title: Forensic interventions for therapy and rehabilitation : case studies and analysis /
    edited by Belinda Winder, Nicholas Blagden, Laura Hamilton, and Simon Scott.
Description: Abingdon, Oxon ; New York, NY : Routledge, 2022. | Includes
    bibliographical references and index.
Identifiers: LCCN 2021032732 (print) | LCCN 2021032733 (ebook) | ISBN
    9780367205362 (pbk) | ISBN 9780367205355 (hbk) | ISBN 9780429262074 (ebk)
Subjects: LCSH: Forensic psychology. | Prison psychology.
Classification: LCC RA1148 .F549 2022 (print) | LCC RA1148 (ebook) | DDC
    614/.15—dc23
LC record available at https://lccn.loc.gov/2021032732
LC ebook record available at https://lccn.loc.gov/2021032733

ISBN: 978-0-367-20535-5 (hbk)
ISBN: 978-0-367-20536-2 (pbk)
ISBN: 978-0-429-26207-4 (ebk)

DOI: 10.4324/9780429262074

Typeset in Bembo
by Apex CoVantage, LLC

This book is dedicated to Dr Ruth Mann, a mentor, friend and colleague who inspired others and who had a profound impact on rehabilitative interventions, particularly for men with sexual convictions. Her compassion, intelligence and genuineness transformed how we think and work with individuals within prison, both in the UK and internationally. The range and scope of Ruth's influence on forensic practice are breath-taking. For a more thorough and fitting celebration of Ruth's work and life, please read Travers, Williams and Willis (2020) – it is a must read!

I first met Ruth in late 2010 when she examined my PhD thesis and following that we began to work collaboratively on projects. I was always struck with how generous Ruth was with her time and how much she promoted and championed the work of those in junior positions. She had a genuine desire to help develop and bring on others, and was always receptive to others' ideas, even if they challenged established viewpoints. During the ATSA conference in Vancouver in 2018 she told me how important it was to encourage others, especially those early-career, and that it was important to make time and support them. I walked with her as she went to every poster in every session, she asked thoughtful questions, gave encouraging feedback and listened to them intently about their research.

Ruth was an innovator, a pioneer and the moral compass of interventions for people with sexual convictions for many years. Her work moved the field forward and often challenged established practice, from rethinking cognitive distortions (Maruna & Mann, 2006), victim empathy (Mann & Barnett, 2013), psychologically meaningful risk factors (Mann, Hanson & Thornton, 2010), accepting responsibility (Ware & Mann, 2012) or working positively and strength-based with men with sexual convictions (Ward & Mann, 2004; Ward, Mann & Gannon, 2007). Ruth was a beacon of hope for those working in correctional settings. For instance, her Twitter feed would often highlight good and innovative practice at a local and national level. It was a much needed rebuttal to overly negative criticism of rehabilitative work in prisons. I do miss her posts. She promoted positivity and was passionate about evidence-informed practice. Her later work focused on rehabilitative culture, procedural justice, humane relationships and rehabilitative leadership (showing the way) (Mann et al., 2019; Tate, Blagden & Mann, 2017). This work was influential in shaping the focus of rehabilitative culture, and she developed a model which outlined the evidence-based features of a rehabilitative culture in prison (Mann et al., 2019; Travers et al., 2020).

Ruth is perhaps best known, in terms of research and practice, for leading the design and implementation of the CORE SOTP programme. A recent research evaluation of this programme found that the programme was generally associated with little or no changes in sexual and non-sexual reoffending (Mews, Di Bella & Purver, 2017). The question as to whether treatment can work with men with sexual convictions in prison remains contested (see e.g. Gannon, Olver, Mallion & James, 2019; Lösel et al., 2020), and although the robust evaluation had flaws, Ruth accepted the results. In a time where people are defensive and hostile to negative feedback, Ruth exuded grace and dignity, using the lessons of the evaluation for self-reflection, to promote the importance of being evidence-led and to try and make prisons places of hope. In her words "we all want to believe that treatment works. Don't stop believing – but remember to keep up those checks on confirmation bias" (Mann, 2018 cited in Travers et al., 2020, p. 146). Her ATSA keynote in 2018 was one of the most inspiring talks I have been to. It highlighted the risk of confirmation bias, outlined the principles of effective intervention, the importance of context within intervention e.g. prison climate and how we must be evidence-led (even though it's hard).

For me, Ruth was a mentor and friend, she had a profound impact on my life in terms of shaping my thinking, values and perspective on working with others. I'm grateful to have known her and to have learnt from her. I'll miss the cocktails at conferences, her shouts of "Dr B" when we spoke on the phone and I'll never forget her kindness, warmth or humour. They say people remember you for how you make them feel. Ruth made people feel valued, gave them self-belief – even if they were plagued with self-doubt; she displayed such compassion for others and inspired confidence in those she worked with. She genuinely wanted the best for people, is there a better legacy than that? I'll remember her insights and wisdom. On behalf of all of us, thank you, Ruth.

Contents

Contributor list

Honorary Professor Dr Geraldine Akerman is a chartered and HCPC-registered Forensic Psychologist, Euro Psych and Associate Fellow of the British Psychological Society. She has worked for the prison service since 1999 assessing risk and providing treatment to men convicted of violent and sexual offences and complex needs. Geraldine is Chair of the Division of Forensic Psychology Executive Committee and a member of the Professional Practice Board, National Organisation for the Treatment of Abusers Research committee and a clinical member of ATSA, and member of the International Association of Forensic Psychotherapists. She is a Trustee for the Safer Living Foundation. Geraldine has published articles and book chapters in peer-reviewed journals on the subjects of offence paralleling behaviour, managing deviant sexual fantasies, sexual interests, sexual offending, and ex-service personnel in prison and edited a book on enabling environments, managing problematic sexual interests, and therapeutic communities. Geraldine currently works as a therapy manager at HMP Grendon and completed a PhD at the University of Birmingham (UK). Geraldine is a visiting lecturer at the University of Birmingham and Cardiff Metropolitan University.

Mark Andrews (PhD) is a Senior Lecturer in the Department of Psychology at Nottingham Trent University. There, he specializes in teaching statistics and data science at all levels from the undergraduate to PhD level. Currently, he is the Chair of the British Psychological Society's Mathematics, Statistics, and Computing section. Dr Andrews's background is in computational cognitive science, particularly focused on Bayesian models of human cognition. He has a PhD in Cognitive Science from Cornell University and was a Postdoctoral Researcher in the Gatsby Computational Neuroscience Unit at UCL and also in the Department of Psychology at UCL.

Lee Bacon is a Clinical Nurse Practitioner and Radically Open-Dialectical Behavioural Therapy (RO DBT) treatment lead. He is currently working within a high-secure mental health hospital. He has over 19 years' experience of working in secure settings in the fields of mental health and personality disorder. He has extensive experience delivering DBT treatment and Boundary See-Saw training and has been involved in the clinical development and implementation of RO DBT within a forensic setting for the last six years.

Dr Nicholas Blagden is a co-founder and Trustee of the Safer Living Foundation, Associate Professor in Forensic Psychology, Chartered Psychologist, and head of the Sexual Offences Crime and Misconduct Research Unit. He has worked and researched within criminal justice and prison settings for over 15 years. He has taught undergraduate and postgraduate courses in psychology, forensic psychology, and criminology. He has also trained police officers. His work has been funded by the HMPPS, and he is currently engaged in numerous collaborative forensic projects with NTU; HMPPS; Institute for Mental Health, Ontario, Canada; and Correctional Services Australia. He sits on NOTA's policy and practice committee. He has led programme evaluations, has a track record of high-quality research, and has disseminated his work widely in international journals conferences.

Imogen Byrne previously worked as a Research Assistant for the Sexual Offences, Crime and Misconduct Research unit at Nottingham Trent University. Imogen conducted outcome and process evaluations of projects aimed at rehabilitating people who had sexually offended on behalf of the Safer Living Foundation, a charity established to reduce sexual (re)offending. Imogen now works for the NHS as a Higher Research Assistant in Liaison Psychiatry.

Dr. Laura Hamilton is a Registered and Chartered Forensic Psychologist and Senior Lecturer. Working in forensic practice for 20 years, she has specialised in the assessment and treatment of trauma and personality disorder with individuals who have convictions. She is an innovative practitioner, often working at the cutting edge of clinical practice and seeking new ways of enhancing forensic interventions. She conducted the first trials of Radically Open-Dialectical Behavioural Therapy (RO-DBT) with forensic service users and was part of the development team which trialled cognitive analytic therapy (CAT). Laura is trained in a range of treatment modalities, including CAT, dialectical behavioural therapy, RO-DBT, EMDR, and sensorimotor psychotherapy. As an academic she developed postgraduate courses for forensic psychologists in-training and delivers specialist teaching, supervision, and workshops on a range of applied clinical forensic issues. Her research interests are in applied boundary studies, overcontrol, and trauma.

Dr Kerensa Hocken is a Registered Forensic Psychologist. She has worked with people convicted of sexual offences for 20 years and has a lead role in Her

Majesty's Prison and Probation Service based in the Midlands region of the UK. In 2016, she was the winner of the prestigious Butler Trust award for excellence in correctional services, presented by Princess Anne. Kerensa is a Trustee and co-founder of the Safer Living Foundation (SLF), a charity to prevent sexual abuse by working with those who have offended or are at risk of committing a sexual offence. Kerensa is a member of the Compassionate Mind Foundation and co-founder of the CFT forensic special interest group.

Victoria Hodierne is the Coordinator for the Safer Living Foundation's Apollo project, seconded to the charity from Her Majesty's Prison and Probation Service. She has held various roles at prisons within the Midlands region, most recently delivering individual and group-based interventions to adult males convicted of sexual offences at HMP Whatton. Victoria is a member of the Association for Contextual Behavioral Science and in addition to her role with Apollo is a part-time facilitator with the Safer Living Foundation's Aurora Project – an acceptance and commitment therapy and compassion-focused therapy–based intervention for adults experiencing unhealthy sexual thoughts and feelings.

Lucy Justice (PhD) is a Senior Lecturer in the Psychology Department at Nottingham Trent University where she teaches statistics and research methods to undergraduate students. Her academic interests include using statistical models to explore human behaviour and best practices for teaching statistics/coding. Dr Justice has a PhD in Cognitive Psychology from the University of Leeds and spent a number of years working in the private sector as a statistician.

Rachael Lee is a Registered and Chartered Forensic Psychologist who works for Her Majesty's Prison and Probation Service. She has 20 years' experience, specialising in the assessment and treatment of men who commit sexual offences. Rachael has previously worked at Interventions Services within HMPPS Headquarters as a National Specialist Lead for the Healthy Sex Programme (HSP), during which time she led the re-design of the programme in 2013. Rachael currently works for the East Psychology Service and is the Regional Lead for Practice Relating to Men Convicted of Sexual Offences, as well as providing the management and clinical oversight of the psychology services delivered at HMP Bure and HMP Littlehey.

Dr Rebecca Lievesley is a Senior Lecturer in Psychology at Nottingham Trent University. She has conducted research within the criminal justice system since 2008, with projects including an investigation of reoffending and desistance in those serving short sentences, the evaluation of anti-libidinal medication for individuals convicted of a sexual offence, and help-seeking prior to committing a sexual offence. She was also one of the co-founders of the Safer Living Foundation charity.

Emma Longfellow is a Consultant Forensic Psychologist in the National Learning Disability Service. Her clinical practice has specialised in working with sexually harmful behaviour, complex trauma, and neurodevelopmental disorders. Emma is trained in a range of therapy models, including DBT, EMDR, schema, and ACT. She is an advocate of neurodiversity and ensuring equitable assessment and therapy. Her passion is innovative practice and developing an evidence base for complex populations, which contributed to her being part of the first forensic RO-DBT trials and piloting a specialist version for intellectual disability. As an academic Emma provides workshops on forensic psychology and arousal assessments. Her research interests are sexual thought, developmental trauma, overcontrol, and autism.

Dr Ruth E. Mann was the Lead for Rehabilitative Culture across Public Sector Prisons North within Her Majesty's Prison and Probation Service. Ruth worked in and with prisons for over 30 years, and for the major part of her career was responsible for the Prison Service's Sex Offender Treatment Programme. Ruth authored over 70 research articles and book chapters related to sexual offending and rehabilitation in prison.

Dr Naomi Murphy is a Consultant Clinical and Forensic Psychologist who has worked in secure hospitals, prisons, and community forensic settings. She was involved in establishing the first mental health in-reach team in an English prison and an early court diversion scheme. In 2003, she co-developed the first specialist treatment programme in prison for people considered to experience "psychopathy" as part of the high-profile Dangerous and Severe Personality Disorder initiative. This trauma-focused service emphasises the therapeutic milieu and prioritising psychological safety and emotional authenticity for staff and residents; it was later absorbed into the Offenders with Personality Disorder Pathway. She is the author of several chapters and journal articles on themes of using trauma-focused treatment with people in the criminal justice system and creating services characterised by psychological safety and enabling treatment to be accessible to people with a history of trauma. She is co-host of *Locked Up Living*, a podcast devoted to exploring barriers to well-being for those who live and work in secure environments and finding ways to promote resilience and enable growth.

Helen O'Connor is a BPS-chartered and HCPC-registered Forensic Psychologist employed by HM Prison and Probation Service (HMPPS) since 2007. She has worked with a range of prisoners convicted of sexual and violent crimes in both risk assessment and intervention capacities, specialising in working with men with learning disabilities and challenges (LDC). Her interest in using different communication methods drew her to working with prisoners who are

Deaf. She helped design and deliver the first group intervention for prisoners who are Deaf and have been convicted of sexual offences in 2012. She has continued to be involved in the delivery and supervision of interventions with this population. She also provides consultancy for psychologists, probation services, and operational staff working with Deaf clients and has authored national policy for psychological services within HMPPS, advising on working with and risk assessing this population. She has presented at numerous conferences regarding her clinical work with this population and has published in the *Prison Service Journal* on the topic. Helen was involved in the accreditation of the first Deaf Aware prison by the Royal Association for Deaf people (RAD). She won a Butler Trust award for her work in this area in 2015.

Nicola Payne is a BPS-chartered and HCPC-registered Forensic Psychologist. She has been employed by HM Prison and Probation Service (HMPPS) since 2005, and her current position is as a Senior Forensic Psychologist. Nicola has worked with both males and females who have been convicted of sexual and violent crimes and in more recent years has worked with individuals convicted of terrorism-related and stalking-related offences. Her experience includes both risk assessments and bespoke intervention work. Nicola's interest in Deaf individuals who have committed sexual offences developed when she conducted an evaluation of the first group-based intervention for this population in 2013. Nicola went on to complete risk assessments for Deaf prisoners and provides supervision to colleagues in their completion of such assessments. In addition to her establishment-based role, she has been a guest lecturer at a university where she has shared her knowledge and experience of working with Deaf prisoners.

Dr Jon Taylor is a Consultant Forensic Psychologist and Psychotherapist who has worked in a range of prison, secure hospital, and community forensic settings for almost 30 years. Jon was one of the original team who developed the TC+ model for men and women with an intellectual disability that received accreditation in 2010. With a keen interest in developing a rich understanding of the role of trauma, adversity, and oppression in the lives of those who develop offending behaviours, Jon is committed to promoting and modelling a compassionate and cooperative approach to all aspects of forensic service provision. Jon is a member of the Compassionate Mind Foundation and co-founder of the CFT forensic special interest group.

Michael Underwood is a Research Associate with the Centre for Crime, Offending, Prevention and Engagement at Nottingham Trent University. The focus of his work is on those who have served long prison sentences and how they take their place in society once released from custody.

Dr Jamie S. Walton is Cluster Psychology Lead at Midlands Psychology Services in HM Prison and Probation Service (HMPPS). He is a Registered Practitioner Psychologist (forensic) with the Health and Care Professions Council (HCPC), a Chartered Psychologist, and an Associate Fellow of the British Psychological Society (BPS). Since 2006, Jamie has worked in prison and healthcare settings as well as HMPPS headquarters, designing accredited offending behaviour programmes, and supporting the implementation nationwide. His research interests include the biopsychosocial understanding of human behaviour, causes of paraphilia and sexual offending, and the evaluation of clinical interventions aimed at reducing sexual recidivism.

Foreword

Following in the footsteps

This book aims to explore innovative and new directions in working with people with convictions. Ruth's work challenged established practice and paved the way for new humane and effective intervention. This edited book captures some of the spirit of that work and focuses on approaches that push boundaries and emphasise collaboration, sense-making, and compassion. Chapter 1 focuses on the cross-fertilisation of knowledge, techniques, and theory between prison and healthcare settings and the implications this has for effective practice. Chapter 2 is an important and critical examination of statistical analyses used in intervention studies within forensic psychological services. Chapter 3 outlines the development of a fantasy modification programme designed to integrate skills to manage inappropriate sexual or violent fantasies within a democratic therapeutic community. Chapter 4 focuses on boundaries and boundary setting in forensic clinical practice. The chapter highlights how boundaries and their management play a crucial role in forensic interventions. Chapter 5 outlines how Radically Open-Dialectical Behaviour Therapy (RO-DBT) has integrated with an existing DBT-standard service to produce specialised undercontrolled and overcontrolled treatment pathways for men identified as having significant personality difficulties which are functionally linked to their offending behaviour. Chapter 6 focuses on a biopsychosocial understanding of paraphilia and an overview of the Healthy Sex Programme (HSP) delivered in HM Prison and Probation Service for adult men with offence-related paraphilia. The chapter emphasises working compassionately and collaboratively with men with sexual convictions. Chapter 7 reviews the evidence base for intervention with men who categorically deny responsibility for their sexual crimes. Specifically, the chapter unpacks the ambiguities in definition and conceptualisation, reviews the context and function of denial, the impact on identity and self-presentation, and explores the evolutionary basis for denial. Chapter 8 discusses the interventions HMP Whatton offers for prisoners who are Deaf. Chapter 9 argues that an exploration of the traumatic and adverse events that underpin the development of criminogenic need is necessary to address risk when working with people who harm others. It proposes compassion-focused therapy for working with such individuals. Chapter 10 focuses on mindfulness and mindful intervention within UK-accredited offending behaviour programmes. The final chapter, Chapter 11, outlines a new intervention for young people displaying sexually harmful behaviour. Underpinned by acceptance and commitment therapy, Apollo takes a holistic, strengths-based approach to supporting young people who have needs in relation to managing emotions, urges, and developing a pro-social identity.

It is vital that we continue to learn and develop new innovative and compassionate responses within forensic interventions, that we follow the blueprint that Ruth has laid out for us to strive to make correctional interventions evidence-informed, humane, compassionate, and effective.

Nicholas Blagden, Belinda Winder,
Laura Hamilton, Simon Scott

References

Gannon, T. A., Olver, M. E., Mallion, J. S., & James, M. (2019). Does specialized psychological treatment for offending reduce recidivism? A meta-analysis examining staff and program variables as predictors of treatment effectiveness. *Clinical Psychology Review*, *73*, 101752.

Lösel, F., Link, E., Schmucker, M., Bender, D., Breuer, M., Carl, L., . . . & Lauchs, L. (2020). On the effectiveness of sexual offender treatment in prisons: A comparison of two different evaluation designs in routine practice. *Sexual Abuse*, *32*(4), 452–475.

Mann, R. E. (2018). Being evidence-based. Keynote presentation at 37th Annual Research & Treatment Conference. Association for the Treatment of Sexual Abusers, Vancouver, BC, October.

Mann, R. E., & Barnett, G. D. (2013). Victim empathy intervention with sexual offenders: Rehabilitation, punishment, or correctional quackery? *Sexual Abuse*, *25*(3), 282–301.

Mann, R. E., Barnett, G. D., Box, G., Howard, F. F., O'Mara, O., Travers, R., & Wakeling, H. (2019). Rehabilitative culture in prisons for people convicted of sexual offending. In N. Blagden, B. Winder, K. Hocken, R. Lievesley, P. Banyard, & H. Elliott (Eds.), *Sexual crime and the experience of imprisonment* (pp. 1–33). Palgrave Macmillan.

Mann, R. E., Hanson, R. K., & Thornton, D. (2010). Assessing risk for sexual recidivism: Some proposals on the nature of psychologically meaningful risk factors. *Sexual Abuse*, *22*(2), 191–217.

Maruna, S., & Mann, R. E. (2006). A fundamental attribution error? Rethinking cognitive distortions. *Legal and Criminological Psychology*, *11*(2), 155–177.

Mews, A., Di Bella, L., & Purver, M. (2017). *Impact evaluation of the prison-based core sex offender treatment programme*. London: Ministry of Justice.

Tate, H., Blagden, N., & Mann, R. (2017). *Prisoners' perceptions of care and rehabilitation from prison officers trained as 5 minute interventionists: Analytical summary*. Ministry of Justice.

Travers, R., Williams, F., & Willis, G. M. (2020). Recognising a trailblazer; celebrating a colleague; thanking a friend. *Journal of Sexual Aggression*, *26*(2), 145–150.

Ward, T., & Mann, R. E. (2004). Good lives and the rehabilitation of offenders: A positive approach to sex offender treatment. *Positive Psychology in Practice*, 598–616.

Ward, T., Mann, R. E., & Gannon, T. A. (2007). The good lives model of offender rehabilitation: Clinical implications. *Aggression and Violent Behavior*, *12*(1), 87–107.

Ware, J., & Mann, R. E. (2012). How should "acceptance of responsibility" be addressed in sexual offending treatment programs? *Aggression and Violent Behavior*, *17*(4), 279–288.

Acknowledgements

The editors would like to thank all the chapter authors for their contributions, their patience, and their hard work. We would also like to thank all those people who have lived and worked experience of the interventions that are discussed in this text.

We would also like to thank Nottingham Trent University – it is a brave and progressive place that helps us in our mission to change the world and create a better, more humane place for everyone, including those amongst us who have previously been convicted of a criminal offence. All adults in society have committed a criminal act, some minor, some extremely serious. We are all human beings, all part of society. It is our responsibility not just to punish people for a criminal act but also to support that person in understanding how and why they came to commit the act and help them to change, develop, and move forward. We need to understand these are not 'other' but they are us, part of us, part of our shadow side, sadly acting out the darker aspects that many of us keep contained and managed.

Finally, this book would not have been possible (probably) without some key figures in our life: Jumble Griffon, Sunny, Beau, Somnium, Sloggi, Om, Dylan, Jake, Tony, and Phil Banyard – you have all played your part in helping us manage a work–life balance (the publishers might think perhaps too much!).

Belinda Winder

Nicholas Blagden

Laura Hamilton

Simon Scott

1
Health meets justice

Transformation in forensic practice

Naomi Murphy and Michael Underwood

Introduction

Forensic practice is broadly defined as the scientific field pertaining to courts and the law; it extends into both the prison and health systems, as well as the work of those in non-custodial settings such as community forensic teams or approved premises (under section 13 of the Offender Management Act, 2007). Anyone working within these settings might describe their work as being encompassed within forensic practice. However, the scope of forensic *interventions* is more restricted. For many years, it has been most closely associated with prisons, where forensic interventions aimed to change "the thinking, attitudes and behaviours which may lead people to re-offend . . . to help people develop new skills to stop their offending . . . (and) . . . to encourage prosocial attitudes and goals for the future" (GOV.UK, 2021).

Whilst those working in secure hospitals or approved premises could legitimately define their work as forensic in nature, there was inconsistency in how practitioners incorporated attention to the individual's risk of re-offending into their therapeutic endeavours. Undoubtedly, it is assumed that some individuals' risk of violence would diminish if medication addressed some of the symptoms of their poor mental health; thus, risk reduction was often not directly addressed. Other practitioners in health settings used models such as psychodynamic psychotherapy and schema-focused therapy. Still, they varied in the degree to which, during the course of treatment, they focused on those factors empirically identified as underpinning physical and sexual violence. At times, risk reduction probably wasn't clearly expounded upon in end-of-treatment reports as practitioners tried to balance the dual requirements of alleviating distress whilst reducing risk.

DOI: 10.4324/9780429262074-1

However, practitioners working in the health system also tended to address causal factors underpinning risky behaviour rather than just targeting the manifest behaviour (which was perceived as a "symptom" of underlying distress). Consequently, the language in reports generated within the health service perhaps masked the endeavour to reduce risk that drove much hospital-based treatment. Indeed, "interventions" is in itself language that is synonymous with the work of prison-based staff; those working within the health sector are more inclined to talk about "therapy". Thus, it was assumed for many years that "forensic interventions" were available predominantly within the criminal justice system, as they lacked visibility within health contexts.

Forensic psychological interventions and the dominance of accredited offending behaviour programmes

Most interventions within the UK's criminal justice system (CJS) have been based on the risk–needs–responsivity model (Andrews & Bonta, 2010) and predominantly draw on cognitive behavioural approaches, which were argued to be the most effective (Landenberger & Lipsey, 2005; McGuire, 2002). Typically, these offending behaviour programmes (OBPs) are delivered in a standardised fashion to ensure programme integrity and provide psychoeducation to target problem-solving (McGuire, 2002), help participants recognise and define maladaptive patterns, and then plan and execute solutions (McMurran, Egan, Blair & Richardson, 2001). Hospitals sought to import these programmes into their services in an attempt to ensure they were more explicitly addressing risk; sometimes, these were adapted to take into account the individual's differing mental health needs; at other times, delivery was consistent with a prison format to maintain programme integrity, but with little or no adaptation to accommodate the mental health needs of patients. When delivered following the successful treatment of mental health conditions, this might have been appropriate, but this requirement was not uniformly applied to their application.

In the UK government's Offending Behaviour Programmes and Interventions (2021) documentation depicting the work they commission to help individuals reduce their risk, the omission of any explicit reference to relationships or emotion and affect is symbolic of the neglect of these domains in the types of interventions that have been delivered. Affect is the visceral feeling which occurs in every moment (interoception); emotion is a more complex construction that includes, amongst other things, attribution and physiological and expressive changes (Panksepp & Biven, 2012; Russell, 2003). The UK government's documentation also fails to suggest that work on an individual's self-concept and the social context within which their offending originated might be relevant. The emphasis upon improving left-hemisphere, rational brain functioning to reduce thinking errors and cognitive distortions can be really useful. It can help people "analyse what went wrong and identify situations which may make them vulnerable to offending" (Murphy, 2017). Whilst OBPs in prison do include reference to emotion, e.g., the CALM programme (Controlling Anger and Learning how to Manage it), they tend to be predominantly concerned with anger and to be focused (since they derive mainly from cognitive behavioural theory [CBT]) on recognising one's thoughts and enhancing control over one's emotional state in order to reduce the likelihood of offending behaviour. There is very little attention to the felt visceral affect that is incorporated within our concept of emotion. As Murphy (2017) points out,

> many people who commit violent crime aren't in a rational state of mind when offending. Instead, they find themselves overwhelmed by strong affect that restricts their capacity to think logically, their ability to draw on the intellectual knowledge they may have about themselves and their functioning or think rationally about the consequences of possible behaviours.
>
> (p. 181)

Lynch (2018) also observes that for some people, too much self-control can be as problematic as too little and highlights the relationship of overcontrol to personality dysfunction. Contact with forensic populations indicates that a significant proportion of the population relies on maladaptive over-control to manage their emotions. Hamilton, Winder, Norman and Baguley's (submitted for publication) systematic review found 50% of patients in secure hospitals and one in three prisoners could be identified as overcontrolled. Placing such individuals on programmes to bolster their self-control is likely to be iatrogenic. These ideas are explored more in Chapter 5 of this book, together with a potentially new intervention offered to address the needs of this population.

Additionally, Drennan, Cook and Kiernan (2015), Knight (2014) and Rossner (2013) conclude that the neglect of emotion has been a significant deficit in conceptualising criminal behaviour and thus devising appropriate interventions to more effectively reduce risk. The work of Canton (2017), Knight (2014) and Murphy and McVey (2010) goes further by drawing attention to the reduced impact of rehabilitation efforts when staff are unable or unwilling to authentically discuss their own emotional reactions to the person they're working with and the person's violent and/or sexual offending. Knight (2014), in particular, highlights how emotion and emotional literacy (the ability to work actively with emotion) is undervalued within the criminal justice sector and may thus impact the delivery and quality of interventions aimed at enhancing emotional regulation. She suggests this may be a consequence of the preponderance of men in the senior power structures of the prison system. However, Fox (2010) discusses prison service culture as one in which operational staff understood they were tasked with maintaining control to ensure there were no crises.

One could argue that within such a culture, emotion and the expression of affect might be perceived as more dangerous than a culture in which emotion *appeared* relatively absent. Thomas (1972) observes that prison officers are often perceived as agents of punishment and barriers to change. It is likely that the anxiety that generally accompanies change would be perceived as possibly signalling impending crisis and thus stifled before it could become out of hand. Within such a context, it is perhaps unsurprising that a somewhat repressed, "macho" culture prevailed for many decades, which perhaps made it very difficult for emotion, affect, and relationships to be discussed or expressed.

The culture of an organisation tends to be fairly stable over time without an intentional strategy and resources to implement systematic change and "unlearn" elements of the existing culture (Hanna, 1988; Moos & Moos, 1974; Schein, 1990). Whilst many staff who didn't fit the cultural norm would have worked within the prison system during this period (e.g., staff labelled "civilian" such as probation officers, forensic psychologists, and primary care nurses), they were in a small minority and would have found it hard to resist the human tendency to assimilate in order to belong. Gelfand (2020) suggests that individuals tend to desire increased autonomy when they feel safe but that a sense of threat increases their propensity to conform, so it is perhaps unsurprising that affect, emotion, and relationships have been so neglected. Similarly, operating within such a threat-conscious system is not conducive to the free expression of individual staff members, so it seems unremarkable that developers of OBPs have been so little preoccupied with facilitating the expression of an authentic self.

Both McMurran (2002) and McGuire (2013) acknowledge that relationships have an influential effect on the success of interventions. In particular, they highlight the benefits of staff members' role-modelling of prosocial attitudes and behaviour through their interpersonal skills, but initially, the What Works movement and its "adherence to a prescriptive programme manual for a time shifted the emphasis away from the significance of the relationship in promoting engagement and change" (Knight, 2014). More recently, the risk–needs–responsivity model has emphasised the importance of "collaborative relationships between clinicians and offenders" (Andrews & Bonta, 2010) and, in the organisational principles, give value to being human and having respect for the person. They continue to say that effectiveness is "enhanced when delivered by therapists and staff with high-quality relationship skills", and Serran, Fernandez, Marshall and Mann (2003) also highlight how programme facilitators who exhibited "empathy, warmth and being directive and rewarding" encouraged greater beneficial changes in participants. Despite this, such values, particularly respect for the person, have been observed to be more widely lacking in criminal justice settings (Hulley, Liebling & Crewe, 2012), and in general, much less attention has been given to relationships beyond those with the immediate programme facilitators. The absence of a milieu in which OBPs were embedded will perhaps inevitably also have reduced the capacity of OBPs to focus on elements over which course facilitators will have had little control, such as the wider culture of the criminal justice sector.

Therapeutic communities (TCs), such as HMP Grendon, represented a divergence from most standard OBPs and are often cited as exceptions to the earlier observation since they prioritise the importance of social relationships and the community as a vehicle for change (Bennett & Shuker, 2018). The approach adopted has produced "extraordinary outcomes" (p. 48), including increased self-esteem and a reduction in anxiety (Shuker & Newton, 2008), improved psychological health and well-being (Gunn & Robertson, 1982; Newton, 1998), improved relating (Birtchnell, Shuker, Newberry & Duggan, 2009), and reduced offending levels (Taylor, 2000). Working therapeutically in this manner promotes autonomy, emphasises the value of relationships and of the person, and assists "the residents" in reconfiguring their identity into a more prosocial one whilst dealing with trauma in a proactive way (Bennett & Shuker, 2018). Perhaps significantly, this relationally focused work proved possible in TCs because several of the staff were trained as psychological therapists and specifically in models that attended to the transaction between patient and therapist, such as psychodynamic or psychoanalytic psychotherapy. This is unlike other forms of OBPs, which are based on cognitive behavioural treatment where affect, emotion, and relationships tend to be less of a priority. There have been calls for emulation of the democratic therapeutic community as a model for other parts of the prison estate (Her Majesty's Inspector of Prison reports, 2004, 2009, 2014; Cretenot, 2013).

Additionally, many of the individuals delivering OBPs did not have formal training as therapists, which may have made it more difficult to prioritise the kind of idiosyncratic adaptations that are necessary when working with visceral feelings and relationships. Those trained in psychodynamic and psychoanalytic therapies are also required to undergo therapy as part of their training, which could be argued to give the therapist a different perspective on the importance of emotions, the relationship, and power than one might have if trained in other models with different priorities. Perhaps of most importance is that TCs employed staff to act as therapists, which meant expecting them to use their own clinical judgement and tailor the delivery to the various people they happened to be working with. This was in distinct contrast to OBPs, which had strict adherence procedures designed into the system to enable elimination of variability as part of the means of maintaining interventions of a certain quality. Services that are delivered by accredited therapists can, to some degree, be assured of competence due to the need for the therapist to maintain their professional registration, and this enables flexibility of delivery. However, OBPs could not rely on this assurance due to the variability in experience and knowledge of the staff delivering the intervention and so needed to ensure that safeguards against threats to the integrity of the programme were built in. Whilst this had advantages for the mass scale of delivery of these programmes (such as ensuring participants received programmes delivered to a reasonable standard), it may have had the unfortunate effect of stymying the creativity of some of the more experienced and skilled professionals delivering these programmes. Crucially, the success of TCs may have proved possible because an emphasis upon visceral affect, emotion, and relationships was something the whole prison had agreed should be a priority; the task of the operational staff was therefore extended beyond maintaining control, and they were given tacit permission to develop therapeutic relationships with prisoners and talk explicitly about feelings. This approach may reduce role conflict and role-model other ways of relating within large group settings.

Similar to their neglect of relationships and emotion, offending behaviour programmes did not prioritise the ecological context within which offending behaviour had originated and been maintained. Undoubtedly, many practitioners would have seen the relevance of a significant lack of material resources, lack of safety, lack of societal acceptance, and so on as significant factors in the development and perpetuation of offending behaviour throughout much of the participants' lives. However, OBPs tend to be primarily focused on assisting the individual in making internal changes rather than recognising that if a person adapts their way of functioning, not only will they not fit back into their original environment as they did previously (desired), but they will also need help adjusting to being accepted and living within a more prosocial one. The situation in hospitals often mirrored that within prisons; interventions tended to be focused on the individual level rather than prioritising the creation of communities where feeling safe would be prioritised and where prosocial behaviour could be repeatedly rehearsed. Again, TCs (in both hospitals and prisons) were almost unique in the consistency with which they gave the ecological system attention to ensure safety and to encourage participation and preparation for living among a community once at liberty. TCs also prioritised enhancing the strengths of those who participated in their groups by explicitly asking participants to share some responsibility for therapy, rather than only addressing deficits as was characteristic of OBP. The TCs shared this in common with hospital settings, which frequently employed occupational therapists who contributed reflections on strengthening capabilities and growing self-efficacy in multi-disciplinary discussions.

A further obstacle to successfully reducing the risk of those people in prisons was the lack of attention to the high prevalence of mental health problems among this population and, therefore, a lack of attention to how mental health may interface, drive, and aggravate offending behaviour. This is unsurprising, given that staff working in prisons are not usually mental health professionals and therefore are not trained to recognise or address these issues. There are no accurate figures documenting the exact number of people with serious mental health problems in UK prisons (National Audit Office, 2017). Estimates of the prevalence of formal mental health conditions are problematic and range from a third of people who are imprisoned (Hassan et al., 2011) to as high as 90% of the population (Andrews & Bonta, 2010; Singleton et al., 1998), depending on the definition of mental health condition that is utilised. Comorbidity appears to be "the rule rather than the exception" (Göbbels, Thakker & Ward, 2016). Tyler, Miles, Karadag and Rogers (2019) found that almost 50% of people screened met the criteria for two or more mental health conditions, which would suggest that complexity of presentation might also be an issue. Those working within the system recognise that a history of complex trauma and its subsequent impact on emotional regulation is ubiquitous. It is therefore perhaps unsurprising that substance misuse is also rife (Hodgins, 2000), since many find themselves incarcerated as a consequence of activities related to the acquisition of illicit substances, and substance misuse is associated with attempts to regulate affect (Wills, Simons, Manayan & Robinson, 2017).

Cognitive behavioural–based interventions such as most OBPs (and like low-intensity contact delivered under the Improving Access to Psychological Therapies [IAPT] initiative, which commenced within the community in 2008) are at their best and work well when applied to people with discrete problems who have good interoceptive awareness (the ability to sense how we are feeling inside our bodies) and an ability to engage in metacognition (reflect on their thinking). That Her Majesty's Prison and Probation Service (HMPPS) has managed to consistently deliver OBPs on such a large scale to so many prisoners and with such limited financial resources is an achievement (the cost of treating someone within a high-secure hospital is estimated to be approximately double the cost of treating someone within a high-security prison). However, given the context within which most OBPs have been delivered, it is perhaps unsurprising that large segments of the prison population were considered unsuitable for these interventions or were unable to benefit sufficiently to have effectively reduced their risk. Perhaps because of the long-standing involvement and influence of psychiatrists who had trained in psychoanalytic psychotherapy, TCs have often included staff with mental health training and experience and thus have been able to tolerate a degree of mental distress and disruptive behaviour that could not be managed within OBP. However, those with more significant needs, such as those with more marked instability, including the use of aggression within the prison setting, and those who required psychotropic medication would often also find themselves precluded from treatment in TCs as well as from OBPs by virtue of their psychopathology.

Finally, despite the complex needs that most people in prison have, almost all treatment available within the CJS until 2000 (including within TCs) has been delivered in a group format when some (Völlm et al., 2018) have suggested that assessment and treatment might at times have been better individually tailored. Individually tailored interventions enable treatment planning that can cater for idiosyncratic risk-related treatment needs; additionally, it can be easier to engage individuals who are fearful of others in treatment when they only have to manage their anxiety in relation to one other person (Murphy & McVey, 2010) rather than a whole group of others and can be offered work that directly targets the therapy-interfering behaviour that derives from this anxiety. This might be important, particularly when thinking about the notion of "treatment readiness", which in its broadest sense can be considered the willingness to overcome the barriers to change that exist within the individual and therapeutic context.

Within the individual, generating or nurturing a sense of agency and a belief in one's autonomy is essential. Believing that one can shape one's life (even if with the support of another) is a precursor to embarking on the road towards a changed future, but a sense of agency is dependent upon a sense of the self as a coherent being with an ability to master the environment. Davidson and Strauss (1992) and Hodge and Renwick (2002) note that for many people with mental health problems who offend, this sense of coherent self, and thus a sense of one's agency and ability to act with autonomy, has to be re-established. This might be particularly important for those recovering from chronic and enduring mental health conditions, such as experiencing psychosis (Synofzik, Vosgerau & Voss, 2013). Belief in the possibility of change, the perception that one can steer it, and identifying oneself as prepared to do so are therefore crucial. But though acknowledged that it may be necessary to modify an intervention to maximise engagement (e.g., McGuire, 2013), this is often harder with manualised programmes where consistency, and thus *rigidity*, is built into the system.

In manualised programmes, there are limited opportunities to target the idiosyncratic needs of many individuals, and the skills of facilitators may vary enormously. The Reasoning and Rehabilitation Programme was adapted successfully to take into account those with more complex needs (Young, Chick & Gudjonsson, 2010), which led to a higher completion rate and significant treatment effects on follow-up (Rees-Jones, Gudjonsson & Young, 2012; Young & Ross, 2007), but this process requires resources and time. It also still requires a certain threshold of entry and for the individual not to have other significant needs that serve as a barrier to treatment. Crucially, addressing individual responsivity runs counter to the prison service's commitment to run programmes in a uniform way, which is arguably an artefact of the accreditation process for CBT-derived interventions.

The common use of the phrase "there should be equivalence of care" that accompanied reflections on the paucity of attention to mental health in prisons (Forrester, Till, Simpson & Shaw, 2018) indicates that better care was evident beyond the CJS in hospitals and community settings. The lack of attention to mental health is perhaps unsurprising, given the prison service had no remit to improve the mental health of those who passed through it and thus rarely employed mental health professionals directly. Instead, its chief priority was to reduce risk. The absence of mental health expertise in many parts of the CJS may have served to mask the huge need of this population. So long as the system lacked the knowledge, skills, and expertise that would be required to adequately identify those with outstanding mental health needs, it was unlikely that appropriate therapeutic interventions would be delivered or that existing OBP would be adapted to incorporate the needs of those whose mental health difficulties played a role in their offending. The exception to this was awareness of intellectual disability, which led to some OBPs being adapted for those with additional needs. There was also some work adapting interventions for people with hearing impairments in prison (see Chapter 8 of this book).

Beyond this, neglect of mental health had emerged as part of the inferior service that people in prison received for their overall health when providers within prisons were dislocated from wider National Health Service (NHS) values, culture, and norms (Bradley, 2009). That the inadequacies of the system were tolerated for so long might speak volumes about societal values towards those who have infringed societal norms by offending. Poor mental health carries association with vulnerability, and Canton (2017) discusses the populist attitude towards those who've offended, which can pose a barrier to progressing with any improvements in the conditions for those in prison.

Blending NHS treatment values with the priorities of criminal justice

Around the turn of the century, there was a real sea change in the approach to forensic psychological interventions, perhaps enabled by two major initiatives that were designed to improve the experience of people with mental health problems who also offended. Firstly, there was a major strategic change to create therapeutic opportunities for people meeting diagnostic criteria for personality disorder, who had often found themselves denied access to treatment

(DoH, 1999). Secondly, there was a recognition that more attention needed to be devoted to ensuring that those with serious mental illness were appropriately located in hospitals rather than prisons and received some parity of care when they continued to be appropriately imprisoned rather than diverted to hospital (DoH, 2001).

The Fallon Inquiry (Fallon, Bluglass, Daniels & Edwards, 1999) into events at Ashworth Hospital concluded in 1999 and made a number of recommendations that significantly impacted both the prison and health services. A previous inquiry into Ashworth in 1992 by Blom-Cooper (Blom-Cooper, Committee of Inquiry into Complaints about Ashworth Hospital, Great Britain & Department of Health, 1992) had described a punitive, authoritarian regime, and the hospital was required to implement a period of countermeasures within a short space of time. This resulted in a pendulum swing from which emerged a culture of lax boundaries and permissiveness, with staff appearing to lack control over events within the hospital. This culture was characterised by misuse of alcohol and drugs, financial irregularities, the availability of pornographic material, and shockingly, a child being groomed for paedophilic activity on one of the wards. The Fallon Inquiry escalated the concern that there were a group of people who were not adequately catered for within either hospitals or prisons. Fallon made a number of recommendations, including that hybrid services were developed for those who met diagnostic criteria for a personality disorder to ensure the creation of cultures where both security and therapeutic needs were given equally adequate consideration and weighting. The government chose not to invest in a recommended third strand of services like the TBS ("*terbeschikkingstelling*", which literally means "making a person available for psychiatric treatment") hospitals in the Netherlands (van Marle, 2002) for prisoners who had psychiatric treatment needs. However, service providers became aware of the necessity to cater to needs that had hitherto been neglected for those populations who had committed serious violent offences but also had significant mental health issues. Fallon's recommendations added momentum to a view that was increasingly articulated; those who met diagnostic criteria for personality disorder were more likely to find themselves in secure facilities in either the justice or health system (even if primarily located there due to mental illness), and therefore greater attention needed to be given to personality psychopathology in both health and justice settings.

The increased attention to the role that personality psychopathology may play in offending raised by Fallon impacted both the NHS and the CJS and led to the creation of four pilot sites (two in each sector) known as pilot units for the treatment of people who were considered dangerous by virtue of severe personality disorder (DSPD pilot projects, documented within MOJ/DoH, 2002) to address those who presented with complex personality psychopathology, including psychopathy. The first of these units opened in the high-security prison, HMP Whitemoor, in 2000. Each of these services was aimed at those who were believed to experience psychopathy, as defined using the Hare's Psychopathy Checklist Revised (Hare, 2003).

The change within hospital or other NHS-provided services may have been less dramatic. In addition to the creation of specialist services at Rampton and Broadmoor for those considered psychopathic, the inquiry strengthened recognition that adequate resources and attention needed to be allocated to explicitly address people's offending behaviour rather than assuming that offending behaviour would diminish along with the symptoms of mental ill health. Thus, there was an increased acceptance that poor mental health was not in itself an explanation for offending behaviour. This led to imports of OBPs into healthcare settings (either with or without adaptations to incorporate attention to mental health) and the broader employment of forensic psychologists. Over time, these programmes began to be adapted to accommodate needs that had not been explicitly considered when originally designed, such as becoming more sensitive to neurodiversity or intellectual disability, but ultimately strengthened the commitment that health service–based staff had to consider how offending behaviour was explicitly rather than tangentially addressed. It also led to creative adaptations of mainstream psychotherapeutic approaches, for example, schema-focused therapy (Murphy, McVey & Hopping, 2012) and Radically Open-Dialectical Behaviour Therapy (Hamilton, Bacon, Longfellow & Tennant, 2018; Hempel et al., 2018), to more explicitly address offending behaviour in those who were also identified as in need of psychotherapeutic assistance.

Within prisons, the creation of two specialist high-secure units for the treatment of personality disorder meant a radically different approach to the standard OBPs emerged. This was out of necessity, as the population these services were intended to treat had hitherto been excluded due to the perception they were "psychopathic" or were considered unresponsive to OBPs. These innovative programmes represented a major shift in approach from accredited behaviour programmes (Murphy & McVey, 2010; Saradjian, Murphy & McVey, 2010). Each programme not only incorporated attention to relational ways of working as a key implement of change but prioritised the milieu to ensure there was an emphasis on psychological safety and to ensure affect and emotion could be spoken of authentically. Crucially, operational staff were encouraged to broaden their role to play an active part in delivering treatment, as the way in which they related to prisoners was seen as instrumental in enabling people to find new, more prosocial ways of being (Fox, 2010). Fox highlights how this extension of their role may at first have been unwelcome, but over time officers were "won over" as they began to recognise that "control" sometimes reinforced an individual's psychopathology, whilst treatment approaches such as discussing feelings might at times prevent an escalation in conflict. This is reflected in Hamilton's concurrent work on boundaries at the Rampton DSPD site, which concluded that consistent boundary management was a dynamic relational process that sought a synthesis between the care and control imperatives (Hamilton, 2010).

The emergence of these approaches in prison was amplified by the recognition that those who received treatment would benefit from a continued pathway of care, influenced by the treating principles mentioned earlier. This also corresponded with the landmark publication in 2003 of "Personality Disorder: No Longer a Diagnosis of Exclusion" (NIMH(E), 2003), which acknowledged the systemic failings of statutory services for people who met the diagnostic criteria for personality disorder and outlined a range of proposals to ensure services were provided in health as well as justice settings. This culminated eventually in a network of services spanning health and justice settings known as the Offenders with Personality Disorder Pathway (OPDP) for those who had committed violent offences, as well as other community initiatives. This was jointly funded by the Ministry of Justice (MoJ) and NHS England, with the latter party contributing the larger financial share. This rollout of OPDP services across the CJS (in both prisons and community settings) had a dramatic impact on the types of interventions that became available. It was possibly relevant that most of these services included a significant number of staff who were employed by the NHS and roles that had not previously been common in prisons, such as clinical psychologists, occupational therapists, and mental health nurses. These staff were often firmly rooted within NHS culture as opposed to those employed directly by HMPPS with no background training in mental health. Perhaps more significantly, whilst the number of civilian staff working in prisons remained a minority, for the first time, their numbers were significantly boosted (to about 20% of the staff group in these services), and they included experienced staff who were confident in their roles and who crucially were not working in isolation.

This influx of NHS-employed staff was further boosted by the impact of the clinical improvement partnership between the NHS and Her Majesty's Prison Service (HMPS) designed to achieve equivalence to community provision in the range and quality of prison-based healthcare. This was expressed via three important policy documents: National Service Framework for Mental Health (DoH, 1999), which emphasised the need to improve mental health services in prisons through close partnerships between NHS and prisons at a local, regional and national level; the Future Organisation of Prison Healthcare (Joint Prison Service and National Health Service Executive Working Group, 1999), which focused on identifying prisoners with mental health problems and planning an appropriate care pathway; and Changing the Outlook (DoH, 2001), which provided direction to enable prison mental health reform with an emphasis upon local planning. This partnership between the NHS and HMPS led to healthcare budget and commissioning responsibilities being transferred to the NHS and the creation of mental health in-reach (MHIR) teams for prisoners with serious mental illness (DoH, 2001). It planned for the deployment of 300 NHS-employed clinicians to work across the prison estate by 2004. These latter teams were originally intended to divert the seriously unwell into hospitals, but increasingly found themselves providing a service to a broader range of people with serious mental health needs; role modelling good practice; and delivering training, consultancy, and advice to prison-employed personnel (Ricketts, Brooker & Dent-Brown, 2007).

The significant increase in the number of staff working within prison and probation settings with clinical training inculcated in NHS philosophy and with experience of mental health assessment and treatment had a significant effect on what is available within the CJS. Ricketts et al.'s (2007) study of the impact of MHIR teams found that staff working within these teams believed that the quality and continuity of care for those with mental health problems in prisons had significantly improved as a consequence. They also found there had been a beneficial effect on prison staff's ability to deal with prisoners with mental health needs. This despite the MHIR's primary focus upon severe and enduring mental illness, which "for all its headline-grabbing potential, is not the main issue" (Bartlett & Alam, 2011). Additionally, the development of specialist personality disorder services brought staff whose main focus was personality disorder rather than mental illness and with a greater emphasis upon talking therapy skills than within MHIRs. Arguably, the presence of staff working across both strands of mental health service delivery has not only strengthened pre-existing good psychotherapeutic practices within the justice system. It also broadened awareness; increased understanding and identification of mental health problems (including the long-term consequences of childhood trauma); and led to changes, adaptation, and innovation in treatment that would perhaps not otherwise have occurred or would have occurred at a significantly slower pace. Perhaps significantly, boosting the number of non-operational staff has allowed the prevailing cultural priority of control to be challenged more effectively than previously and facilitated a treatment attitude that explicitly wished to facilitate personal growth.

Prior to 2000, despite the limited number of mental health professionals employed within these services, the TCs perhaps represented an attempt to meet prisoners' psychological needs in a manner that most fitted with services available within forensic health settings. Somewhat ironically, given the intervention is delivered in a group, the attention to systems thinking, process, and defence mechanisms allowed for a more individualised understanding of each prisoner's needs and utilised their strengths to effect change at both a group and individual level that was more typical of clinical services than the manualised CBT-based programmes. The further arrival of staff who were used to considering the importance of a milieu and reflecting on the process and defence mechanisms in health settings strengthened awareness beyond TCs that prisoners are more complex and their needs more nuanced than standard forensic OBPs might imply.

Like the two initial DSPD services, many of the services on the OPDP are, or at least were initially, residential in nature. In addition to a number of treatment services, OPDP commissioned a number of Psychologically Informed Planned Environments (PIPEs) (Turley, Payne & Webster, 2013) that were designed to provide a supportive milieu in which prisoners would live post-treatment without access to any further formal intervention in order to consolidate their treatment gains and demonstrate that their change was sustainable. Thus, there has been a significant commitment to "ecological resilience" (Ungar, 2018). Resilience is perhaps most succinctly summarised for the purposes of this chapter as the "dynamic process encompassing positive adaptation within the context of significant adversity" (Luthar, Cicchetti & Becker, 2000). This is most easily achieved when the system supports and enables positive adaptation (Ungar, 2011). Although PIPEs did not initially offer treatment, they were frequently located in institutions that did (and at times were run by the same NHS staff) and were expected to benefit from the support of the NHS staff within the nearby treatment services. Over time, some of these PIPEs have begun to offer interventions within them, likely influenced by their proximity to the associated treatment service.

Entry to the two DSPD services required diagnostic criteria for a personality disorder to be met, which led to much greater awareness of the "symptoms" of these conditions. It is now palatable to talk of these conditions as a consequence of significant childhood adversity, abuse, and neglect, but this was not the case at the turn of the century. Around 2000, being identified as having a mental health condition as opposed to a *predictable reaction to adversity* enabled access to services tied to significant funding. Similarly, MHIR teams were considering whether those referred to them experienced significant mental illness. So clinical staff discussed whether individuals they assessed for their services met diagnostic criteria and also discussed alternative or concurrent conditions. These discussions were not only held within clinical services but with referrers, and efforts were devoted to raising the general awareness of mental health conditions in prisons so that prison personnel might be able to make appropriate referrals. Prison staff also sought advice from these groups of clinical staff about how to manage prisoners whose behaviour they found problematic; all of these discussions raised the level of awareness within the CJS about the presence and presentation of mental health conditions among prisoners.

The ethos of clinical psychologists, who began being present in significant numbers in the CJS, brought an emphasis on the skill of formulation and being curious about "what happened" to understand and explain presenting problems in adulthood. Coupled with their training in attachment theory and neuroscience, which helped make sense of these problems as adaptive responses to adversity, this led to significant numbers of staff within the justice system talking openly about the traumatic histories of those they work with. Inevitably, this created an increasing recognition of the need to prioritise relational ways of working to engage meaningfully with patients who were understandably reluctant to trust authority figures. Whilst those studying CBT for a protracted period to become an accredited therapist do spend time reflecting on what it means to work relationally, the focus on relational working in this approach is arguably less developed than within other schools of therapy. A further limitation of CBT as utilised in OBPs was that many of those delivering them had no formal training as therapists; instead, the principles of CBT were used to develop manualised programmes that could be delivered by people with very limited experience of "therapy".

Within CBT, consideration of relational working tends to be restricted to an emphasis upon the importance of a therapeutic alliance. Gaston (1990) summarises the alliance as the incorporation of a bond in treatment between a therapist and patient, which is affected by the patient's ability to work in therapy and the therapist's ability to empathically understand, and the pair's ability to agree on goals and tasks. Murphy and McVey (2010) discuss the inadequacies of the therapeutic alliance as a vehicle for change when working with people with profound interpersonal difficulties, such as fear of rejection and abuse, and advocate for emotionally intimate relationships instead. They summarise these as ones that

> feature understanding or knowing whereby the two parties 'get' each other; within the therapeutic relationship, connectedness between the client and therapist requires the therapist to endeavour to find a way to meet the client in the logical world he or she inhabits and to find a way to make their own logical world apparent to the client. Emotionally intimate relationships are also characterised by the two parties tolerating the strong emotions that inevitably arise as the relationship deepens. For the client, this includes overcoming the fear of being hurt, shamed or rejected by the clinician; the clinician must in turn have a willingness to know and accept the many aspects of the client and to remain connected even when those aspects make him or her feel deeply uncomfortable. Finally, emotionally intimate relationships involve an ability to communicate clearly despite the idiosyncrasies of the relating parties; within the therapeutic relationship this involves the clinician finding a way to create a channel of dialogue that is clear and transparent and where opportunities for misinterpretation are thus minimised.
>
> (p. 91)

As a consequence of the need to prioritise relational ways of working, many practitioners in forensic health services have looked beyond CBT to other approaches such as mentalisation-based therapy (Bateman & Fonagy, 2016; Fonagy & Bateman, 2006; McGauley, 2017), cognitive analytic therapy (Shannon & Pollock, 2017), eye movement desensitisation and reprocessing (Ricci & Clayton, 2017), compassion-focused therapy (Chapter 9 of this book; Gilbert, 2017), acceptance and commitment (Brillhart, 2017; Hayes et al., 2011; Zurita Ona & Harris, 2020), schema therapy (Keulen-de Vos & Bernstein, 2017; Murphy et al., 2012), Radically Open Dialectical Behavioural Therapy (Hamilton, this volume), personal construct therapy (Needs & Jones, 2017), and sensorimotor psychotherapy (Murphy, 2017). These interventions are transdiagnostic treatments aimed at core latent psychological constructs. Thus, they ensure the therapeutic relationship is given adequate attention and that treatment impacts not only on cognition but on a person's ability to process and manage their emotions. This has allowed for opportunities of increasing diversity of approaches in CJS interventions and increasing access to opportunities for formulation-driven therapy at both an individual and group level. It has also led to the cross-fertilisation of ideas as psychologists employed by HMPPS increasingly pursue training as therapists and find creative ways to merge robust therapeutic skills with knowledge of offending. This book includes some innovative representations of these approaches, which have extended the breadth of interventions available to people in contact with the justice system and enabled people to grow and develop in ways not so readily achieved by approaches overly focused on cognition.

Another key feature of all services involving NHS staff has been the rollout of clinical supervision and reflexive practice. Clinical supervision is an essential requirement for mental health professionals and is explicitly endorsed by the National Institute for Health and Care Excellence guidelines (NICE, 2009) for working with patients who meet diagnostic criteria for personality disorder. Thus, clinical staff observed that prison officers would also benefit from the opportunity to reflect on the emotional burden of their work, gain support, learn more complex skills, identify their own treatment-interfering behaviours, and take action to protect themselves and the people they work with from boundary violations through reflection in relational supervision (Sneath, 2010). Different services had different levels of success in introducing a very different way of working, but there were undoubtedly services such as Fens at HMP Whitemoor, where relational supervision for officers was running from about 2005 (Sneath, 2010), and for nurses in the DSPD Unit at Rampton from a similar time (Davies, Tennant, Ferguson & Jones, 2004). This relationally oriented supervision focused on understanding oneself in relation to the person one was working with rather than focusing primarily on technical treatment delivery per se, as was more common in OBP.

The increasing emphasis on relational ways of working beyond the TCs dramatically shifted the role of prison officers within these services (Fox, 2010). Fox highlights how within one DSPD service, officers were expected to be "much more 'emotionally engaged' than typical staff" (p. 230) and assume the role of "quasi treatment specialist" and assimilate knowledge and skills from conversations and formal training with their NHS colleagues. Prison officers became increasingly able to hold conversations with staff in other parts of the prison service and at conferences and networking events with health professionals, where their own knowledge of mental health, formulation, and systemic processes was clearly evident. Relational supervision for prison officers thus amplified the voice of health professionals within the system as these officers became increasingly able to competently participate in team discussions about prisoners' responses to treatment. The intentional upskilling of prison officers had a concomitant effect on qualified clinicians, creating pressure on them to focus on the more specialist and complex parts of direct trauma-focused treatment and other advanced therapeutic skills.

Although still very early in its evolution, the voice of people in prison has also begun to become more powerful outside the TCs. Whilst secure hospitals have had a Recovery College and a Patients' Council, their endeavours have tended to lag behind other psychiatric services in terms of involving those with lived experience in co-production of interventions and practices. Within the health sector, this imperative has existed for quite some time, and services are used to employing and consulting those with lived experience to be more responsive. Whilst secure hospitals still have a considerable way to go, they have been far more willing to engage with service users, listen to their feedback, and adapt elements of service in response than has yet to be seen in prisons. However, those services delivered within prisons by health service employees have made efforts to enable their services to incorporate the feedback of those with lived experience. As yet unpublished research for the OPDP has suggested that when prisoners are asked about their experience of this network of services, access to different models of treatment and relational ways of working are greatly appreciated. Again, it is likely that the voice of those receiving the service amplifies the benefits of working in ways beyond CBT in their own conversations throughout the system.

What does the future hold? Challenges, tensions, and opportunities

Broadening what is available within the system has not come without its challenges. Some HMPPS-employed psychologists have grasped the nettle, broadened their own training, and created innovative, adaptive approaches to addressing the needs of those in contact with the justice system in more holistic ways. A good outcome of this might be that the NHS staff working within the CJS are able to shift their priorities and contribute further towards creating mental health services within prisons that genuinely offer parity with the community. However, this shift towards a more therapeutic role challenges that of the prison psychologist as an "agent of the state", which might undermine the relationship between forensic psychologists and other parts of the justice system. A further danger is that other factors such as the impact of a global pandemic, the inevitable increased financial squeeze as a consequence, the emergence of a more conservative, punitive approach to justice, and the discomfort of accommodating different ways of working may lead to push-back at these approaches and a shrinking of influence. It is also possible that forensic psychologists (who are increasingly employed within the NHS and third sector) may retreat from an environment that is not the easiest to navigate to one which affords them different options and where they are able to share their skills and knowledge with teams within which they are integrated.

The growth of NHS influence within the CJS also appears to have corresponded with a reduction in the influence of the educational sector. It may be that this is entirely coincidental, but one wonders whether an investment in mental health has come at the expense of investment in education when there is a need for both. Human beings thrive when they are enabled to grow, and both therapy and education have the capacity for this, and both are surely necessary.

Forensic services are, by their nature, often very conservative institutions that are slow to change. The chapters in this book represent many interesting and innovative approaches to the delivery of forensic interventions. It will be interesting to see how many of these manage to thrive within prisons. However, it is important to recognise that forensic interventions are provided in many other places, and as these become increasingly routine in other settings, they will create pressure for prisons to also keep apace of treatment modernisation.

References

Andrews, D. A., & Bonta, J. (2010). *The psychology of criminal conduct*. Elsevier Science.

Bartlett, A., & Alam, F. (2011). The health status of prisoners is the real challenge. *The Psychiatrist*, *35*(9), 355–355. https://doi.org/10.1192/pb.35.9.355

Bateman, A., & Fonagy, P. (2016). *Mentalization-based treatment for personality disorders: A practical guide* (1st ed.). Oxford University Press.

Bennett, J., & Shuker, R. (2018). Hope, harmony and humanity: Creating a positive social climate in a democratic therapeutic community prison and the implications for penal practice. *Journal of Criminal Psychology*, *8*(1), 44–57. https://doi.org/10.1108/JCP-06-2017-0030

Birtchnell, J., Shuker, R., Newberry, M., & Duggan, C. (2009). The assessment of change in negative relating in two male forensic therapy samples using the person's relating to others questionnaire. *Journal of Forensic Psychiatry and Psychology*, *20*(3), 387–407.

Blom-Cooper, Committee of Inquiry into Complaints about Ashworth Hospital, Great Britain, & Department of Health. (1992). *Report of the Committee of Inquiry into Complaints about Ashworth Hospital*. H.M.S.O.

Bradley. (2009). *The Bradley report: Lord Bradley's review of people with mental health problems or learning disabilities in the criminal justice system*. House of Lords. The Bradley Report. Retrieved from iriss.org.uk

Brillhart, D. (2017). Acceptance and commitment therapy. In J. Davies & C. Nagi (Eds.), *Individual psychological therapies in forensic settings: Research and practice*. Taylor & Francis.

Canton, R. (2017). *Why punish?: An introduction to the philosophy of punishment*. Macmillan International Higher Education.

Cretenot, M. (2013). *From national practices to European guidelines: Interesting initiatives in prison management*. Rome: European Prison Observatory. Retrieved from www.prisonobservatory.org/upload/EPOinterestinginitiatives.pdf

Davidson, L., & Strauss, J. S. (1992). Sense of self in recovery from severe mental illness. *British Journal of Medical Psychology*, *65*(2), 131–145.

Davies, J., Tennant, A., Ferguson, E., & Jones, L. (2004). Developing models and a framework for multi-professional clinical supervision. *The British Journal of Forensic Practice*, *6*, 36–42. https://doi.org/10.1108/14636646200400018

DoH. (1999). *National service framework for mental health: Modern standards and service models (executive summary)*. Department of Health.

DoH. (2001). *Changing the outlook: A strategy for developing and modernising mental health services in prisons*. Department of Health.

Drennan, G., Cook, A., & Kiernan, H. (2015). The psychology of restorative practice in forensic mental health recovery. *The Psychology of Restorative Justice: Managing the Power Within*, 105–120.

Fallon, P., Bluglass, R., Daniels, G., & Edwards, B. (1999). *Report of the Committee of Inquiry into the Personality Disorder Unit, Ashworth Special Hospital* (Vol. 1). HM Stationery Office.

Fonagy, P., & Bateman, A. W. (2006). Mechanisms of change in mentalization-based treatment of BPD. *Journal of Clinical Psychology*, *62*(4), 411–430. https://doi.org/10.1002/jclp.20241

Forrester, A., Till, A., Simpson, A., & Shaw, J. (2018). Mental illness and the provision of mental health services in prisons. *British Medical Bulletin*, *127*(1), 101–109. https://doi.org/10.1093/bmb/ldy027

Fox, S. (2010). The role of the prison officer (dangerous and severe personality disorder in the prison system). In N. Murphy & D. McVey (Eds.), *Treating personality disorder: Creating robust services for people with complex mental health needs* (pp. 220–238). Routledge/Taylor & Francis Group.

Gaston, L. (1990). The concept of the alliance and its role in psychotherapy: Theoretical and empirical considerations. *Psychotherapy: Theory, Research, Practice, Training, 27*(2), 143.

Gelfand, S. (2020). The Nocebo effect and informed consent: Taking autonomy seriously. *Cambridge Quarterly of Healthcare Ethics, 29*(2), 223–235.

Gilbert, P. (2017). Exploring compassion focused therapy in forensic settings. In J. Davies & C. Nagi (Eds.), *Individual psychological therapies in forensic settings: Research and practice.* Taylor & Francis.

Göbbels, S., Thakker, J., & Ward, T. (2016). Desistance in offenders with mental illness. In J. Winstone (Ed.), *Mental health, crime and criminal justice: Responses and reforms* (pp. 67–90). Palgrave Macmillan.

GOV.UK. (2021). *Offending behaviour programmes and interventions.* Retrieved from www.gov.uk/guidance/offending-behaviour-programmes-and-interventions

Gunn, J., & Robertson, G. (1982). An evaluation of Grendon prison. In J. Gunn & D. Farrington (Eds.), *Abnormal offenders, delinquency and the criminal justice system.* Wiley.

Hamilton, L. (2010). The boundary seesaw model: Good fences make for good neighbours. In A. Tennant & K. Howells (Eds.), *Using time, not doing time* (pp. 181–194). John Wiley & Sons, Ltd.

Hamilton, L., Bacon, L., Longfellow, E., & Tennant, A. (2018). Not everything is as it seems: RO DBT and overcontrolled disorders in forensic settings. *The Behavior Therapist, 41*(3), 157–160.

Hamilton, L., Winder, B., Norman, C., & Baguley, T. (submitted for publication). *The perils of high self-control: A systematic review of maladaptive overcontrol and offending.*

Hanna, D. P. (1988). *Designing organizations for high performance* (Vol. 12693). Prentice Hall.

Hare, R. D. (2003). *The Hare psychopathy checklist-revised manual.* Multi-Health Systems.

Hassan, L., Birmingham, L., Harty, M. A., Jarrett, M., Jones, P., King, C., . . . & Senior, J. (2011). Prospective cohort study of mental health during imprisonment. *The British Journal of Psychiatry, 198*(1), 37–42.

Hayes, S. C., Strosahl, K., & Wilson, K. G. (2011). *Acceptance and commitment therapy, second edition: The process and practice of mindful change.* Guilford Publications.

Hempel, R. J., Booth, R., Giblin, A., Hamilton, L., Hoch, A., Portner, J., . . . & Hunt, K. (2018). The implementation of RO DBT in clinical practice. *The Behavior Therapist, 41*(3), 161–173.

HM Inspectorate of Prisons. (2004). *Report on full announced inspection of HMP Grendon, 1–5 March 2004.* HMIP.

HM Inspectorate of Prisons. (2009). *Report on full announced inspection of HMP Grendon, 2–6 March 2009.* HMIP.

HM Inspectorate of Prisons. (2014). *Report on full announced inspection of HMP Grendon, 5–16 August 2014.* HMIP.

Hodge, J. E., & Renwick, S. J. (2002). Motivating mentally disordered offenders. In M. McMurran (Ed.), *Motivating offenders to change* (pp. 221–234). John Wiley & Sons, Ltd.

Hodgins, S. (2000). The etiology and development of offending among persons with major mental disorders. In S. Hodgins (Ed.), *Violence among the mentally Ill: Effective treatments and management strategies* (pp. 89–116). Springer. https://doi.org/10.1007/978-94-011-4130-7_7

Hulley, S., Liebling, A., & Crewe, B. (2012). Respect in prisons: Prisoners' experiences of respect in public and private sector prisons. *Criminology & Criminal Justice, 12*(1), 3–23. https://doi.org/10.1177/1748895811423088

Joint Prison Service and National Health Service Executive Working Group. (1999). *The future organisation of prison healthcare.* Retrieved from https://webarchive.national archives.gov.uk/20110504020423/www.dh.gov.uk/prod_consum_dh/groups/dh_digitalassets/@dh/@en/documents/digitalasset/dh_4106031.pdf

Keulen-de Vos, M., & Bernstein, D. P. (2017). Schema therapy. In J. Davies & C. Nagi (Eds.), *Individual psychological therapies in forensic settings: Research and practice.* Taylor & Francis.

Knight, C. (2014). *Emotional literacy in criminal justice: Professional practice with offenders.* Springer.

Landenberger, N. A., & Lipsey, M. W. (2005). The positive effects of cognitive-behavioral programs for offenders: A meta-analysis of factors associated with effective treatment. *Journal of Experimental Criminology, 1*(4), 451–476. https://doi.org/10.1007/s11292-005-3541-7

Luthar, S. S., Cicchetti, D., & Becker, B. (2000). The construct of resilience: A critical evaluation and guidelines for future work. *Child Development, 71*(3), 543–562.

Lynch, T. R. (2018). *Radically open dialectical behavior therapy: Theory and practice for treating disorders of overcontrol.* New Harbinger Publications.

McGauley, G. (2017). Mentalisation based treatment. In J. Davies & C. Nagi (Eds.), *Individual psychological therapies in forensic settings: Research and practice.* Taylor & Francis.

McGuire, J. (Ed.). (2002). *Offender rehabilitation and treatment: Effective programmes and policies to reduce re-offending.* J. Wiley.

McGuire, J. (2013). "What works" to reduce re-offending: 18 years on. In L. A. Craig, L. Dixon, & T. A. Gannon (Eds.), *What works in offender rehabilitation: An evidence-based approach to assessment and treatment* (pp. 20–49). Wiley Blackwell. https://doi.org/10.1002/9781118320655.ch2

McMurran, M. (2002). *Motivating offenders to change. A guide to enhancing engagement in therapy*. John Wiley Sons.

McMurran, M., Egan, V., Blair, M., & Richardson, C. (2001). The relationship between social problem-solving and personality in mentally disordered offenders. *Personality and Individual Differences, 30*(3), 517–524.

Moos, R. H., & Moos, R. H. (1974). *Evaluating treatment environments: A social ecological approach*. Wiley-Interscience.

Murphy, N. (2017). Sensorimotor psychotherapy. In J. Davies & C. Nagi (Eds.), *Individual psychological therapies in forensic settings: Research and practice*. Taylor & Francis.

Murphy, N., & McVey, D. (2010). *Treating personality disorder: Creating robust services for people with complex mental health needs*. Routledge.

Murphy, N., McVey, D., & Hopping, G. (2012). Using ST principles to increase the therapeutic efficacy of the forensic care team's interactions with personality disordered clients. In M. van Vreeswijk, M. Nadort, & J. Broersen (Eds.), *The Wiley-Blackwell handbook of schema therapy* (pp. 569–578). John Wiley & Sons, Ltd. https://doi.org/10.1002/9781119962830.ch43

National Audit Office. (2017). *Mental health in prisons*. National Audit Office. Retrieved from www.nao.org.uk/report/mental-health-in-prisons/

Needs, A., & Jones, L. (2017). Personal construct psychotherapy. In J. Davies & C. Nagi (Eds.), *Individual psychological therapies in forensic settings: Research and practice*. Taylor & Francis.

Newton, M. (1998). Changes in measures of personality, hostility and locus of control during residence in a prison therapeutic community. *Legal & Criminological Psychology, 3*(2), 209–223.

NICE. (2009). *Overview | Borderline personality disorder: Recognition and management | Guidance | NICE*. NICE. Retrieved from www.nice.org.uk/guidance/CG78

NIMH(E). (2003). *Personality disorder: No longer a diagnosis of exclusion* (Gateway Ref: 1055). Retrieved from http://personalitydisorder.org.uk/wp-content/uploads/2015/04/PD-No-longer-a-diagnosis-of-exclusion.pdf

Panksepp, J., & Biven, L. (2012). A meditation on the affective neuroscientific view of human and animalian MindBrains. *From the Couch to the Lab: Trends in Psychodynamic Neuroscience*, 145–175.

Rees-Jones, A., Gudjonsson, G., & Young, S. (2012). A multi-site controlled trial of a cognitive skills program for mentally disordered offenders. *BMC Psychiatry, 12*(1), 1–11.

Ricci, R. J., & Clayton, C. A. (2017). Eye movement desensitisation and reprocessing with sexual offenders. In J. Davies & C. Nagi (Eds.), *Individual psychological therapies in forensic settings: Research and practice.* Taylor & Francis.

Ricketts, T., Brooker, C., & Dent-Brown, K. (2007). Mental health in-reach teams in English prisons: Aims, processes and impacts. *International Journal of Prisoner Health, 3*(4), 234–247. https://doi.org/10.1080/17449200701682428

Rossner, M. (2013). *Just emotions: Rituals of restorative justice.* Oxford University Press.

Russell, J. A. (2003). Core affect and the psychological construction of emotion. *Psychological Review, 110*(1), 145.

Saradjian, J., Murphy, N., & McVey, D. (2010). Delivering integrated treatment to people with personality disorder. In N. Murphy & D. McVey (Eds.), *Treating personality disorder: Creating robust services for people with complex mental health needs.* Routledge.

Schein, E. H. (1990). *Organizational culture* (Vol. 45, Issue 2). American Psychological Association.

Serran, G., Fernandez, Y., Marshall, W., & Mann, R. (2003). Process issues in treatment: Application to sexual offender programs. *Professional Psychology: Research and Practice, 34*, 368–374. https://doi.org/10.1037/0735-7028.34.4.368

Shannon, K., & Pollock, P. (2017). Cognitive analytic therapy. In J. Davies & C. Nagi (Eds.), *Individual psychological therapies in forensic settings: Research and practice.* Taylor & Francis.

Shuker, R., & Newton, M. (2008). Treatment outcome following intervention in a prison-based therapeutic community: A study of the relationship between reduction in criminogenic risk and improved psychological well-being. *British Journal of Forensic Practice, 10*(3), 33–44.

Singleton, N., Coid, J., Bebbington, P., Jenkins, R., Brugha, T., Lewis, G., & Farrell, M. (1998). *The national survey of psychiatric morbidity among prisoners and the future of prison.* The Stationary Office.

Sneath, E. (2010). Issues and challenges for the clinical professional. In N. Murphy & D. McVey (Eds.), *Treating personality disorder: Creating robust services for people with complex mental health needs.* Routledge.

Synofzik, M., Vosgerau, G., & Voss, M. (2013). The experience of agency: An interplay between prediction and postdiction. *Frontiers in Psychology, 4*, 127.

Taylor, R. (2000). *A seven-year reconviction study of HMP Grendon therapeutic community.* Home Office Research, Development and Statistics Directorate.

Thomas, J. E. (1972). *The English prison officer since 1850: A study in conflict.* Routledge & Kegan Paul.

Turley, C., Payne, C., & Webster, S. (2013). *Enabling features of psychologically informed planned environments.* National Offender Management Service.

Tyler, N., Miles, H. L., Karadag, B., & Rogers, G. (2019). An updated picture of the mental health needs of male and female prisoners in the UK: Prevalence, comorbidity, and gender differences. *Social Psychiatry and Psychiatric Epidemiology*, *54*(9), 1143–1152. https://doi.org/10.1007/s00127-019-01690-1

Ungar, M. (2011). The social ecology of resilience: Addressing contextual and cultural ambiguity of a nascent construct. *American Journal of Orthopsychiatry*, *81*(1), 1.

Ungar, M. (2018). Systemic resilience: Principles and processes for a science of change in contexts of adversity. *Ecology and Society*, *23*(4), art34. https://doi.org/10.5751/ES-10385-230434

van Marle, H. J. (2002). The Dutch Entrustment Act (TBS): Its principles and innovations. *International Journal of Forensic Mental Health*, *1*(1), 83–92.

Völlm, B. A., Clarke, M., Herrando, V. T., Seppänen, A. O., Gosek, P., Heitzman, J., & Bulten, E. (2018). European Psychiatric Association (EPA) guidance on forensic psychiatry: Evidence based assessment and treatment of mentally disordered offenders. *European Psychiatry*, *51*, 58–73. https://doi.org/10.1016/j.eurpsy.2017.12.007

Wills, T. A., Simons, J. S., Manayan, O., & Robinson, M. K. (2017). Emotion regulation and substance use disorders in adolescents. In *Emotion regulation and psychopathology in children and adolescents*. Oxford University Press. Retrieved from www.oxfordclinicalpsych.com/view/10.1093/med:psych/9780198765844.001.0001/med-9780198765844-chapter-11

Young, S., Chick, K., & Gudjonsson, G. (2010). A preliminary evaluation of reasoning and rehabilitation 2 in mentally disordered offenders (R&R2M) across two secure forensic settings in the United Kingdom. *The Journal of Forensic Psychiatry & Psychology*, *21*(3), 336–349. https://doi.org/10.1080/14789940903513203

Young, S., & Ross, R. R. (2007). *R&R2 for ADHD youths and adults: A prosocial competence training program*. Cognitive Centre of Canada.

Zurita Ona, P., & Harris, R. (2020). *Acceptance and commitment therapy for borderline personality disorder: A flexible treatment plan for clients with emotional dysregulation*. New Harbinger Publications.

2

Statistical analysis of intervention studies in forensic psychology

Mark Andrews and Lucy Justice

Introduction

In an intervention study in psychology or related fields, a sample of participants is given a *treatment* and then their value on some *outcome* variable is measured. As an example from forensic psychology, the participants might be currently serving prisoners who were convicted of sexual offences, the treatment that they are given might be a cognitive behavioural group therapy programme, and the outcome variable might be whether the prisoner commits another sexual offence during a follow-up period after their release from prison. As a related example, the participants might again be prisoners who were convicted of a sexual offence and the treatment might be a cognitive behavioural therapy programme, but the outcome variable might be the prisoner's score on a psychometric scale that measures their sexual knowledge and attitudes, which might be assumed to be causally related to the propensity to commit sexual offences. In any intervention study, the aim is to establish whether the treatment will reliably change the outcome variable by an amount that is deemed to be of practical or clinical significance. This requires establishing that any observed changes in the outcome variable are in fact due to the treatment itself and not to some other factor. It also requires establishing that these observed changes will generalise beyond the particular sample of participants used in the study.

Many types of study designs are used to evaluate intervention studies. These may be classified according to different criterion, such as whether a control group is used for comparison with the treatment group or whether participants are assigned to the treatment or the control group by the investigator. These designs

DOI: 10.4324/9780429262074-2

are usually presented as a hierarchy, with studies higher in the hierarchy defined as providing more definitive evidence in favour of the nature of the treatment's effect on the outcome (see, for example, OCEBM Levels of Evidence Working Group, 2011).

Studies lower in the evidence hierarchy include *case series*. These are where participants who are given the treatment are monitored over time and their responses or behaviours, particularly with respect to the outcome variables, are recorded. Case series are of limited evidential value, primarily because they do not compare to a group that did not receive the treatment. Given that any observed change in the outcome in the treatment group may be due to countless factors other than the treatment itself, the presence of a comparison group is a necessary, though not sufficient, method to determine if the treatment is the causal factor that is affecting the outcome variable.

Higher in the evidence hierarchy are *cohort studies*. These are similar to case series but usually have more participants and, more importantly, are typically defined by having both a treatment and no-treatment group, or at least groups that received different levels of the treatment. However, even including a comparison group is not itself sufficient to establish the efficacy of a treatment. If the treatment and control groups differ in terms of other relevant variables, these other variables, and not the treatment itself, may be responsible for any observed differences in the outcome variable. For example, in an intervention study of people with a sexual conviction, if those receiving the treatment had higher scores on measures of sexual deviance than those in the control group, then a difference in recidivism between the treatment and control group may be due to this variable and not the treatment itself.

Higher still in the evidence hierarchy is a *matched and controlled non-randomised* study. In these studies, both the control and treatment group are matched in terms of many, or even all, variables that are assumed to be causally linked to the outcome. By controlling for these variables, if a difference in the outcome variable between the treatment and control group is observed, this may be attributed to the effect of the treatment and not some other variable. A variant of these studies are (matched and controlled non-randomised) *before and after* studies. In these studies, values of the outcome variable before and after the treatment, or non-treatment in the case of the control group, are obtained. The "before" scores can then be used to further match the participants in the two groups. Although they are deservedly higher in the hierarchy, these types of studies are not without serious shortcomings too. In practical terms, matching for all relevant variables may be very challenging. It may, for example, be practically impossible to find one participant for the control group with identical scores of any given relevant variable to those in the treatment group. It may even be practically challenging to ensure that the two groups are similar on average on these variables. Moreover, this matching process assumes that all potentially causal variables are known. This is rarely the case. There may be many unknown variables along which the treatment and control groups differ that could potentially affect the outcome variable. Given that the two groups are, by definition, non-randomly assigned to their groups, it must be the case that they differ in some non-random ways, which may not all be known and which may affect the outcome.

High on the evidence hierarchies are *randomised controlled trials*, ideally *double-blind randomised controlled trials*. In these studies, there are two groups, the treatment and the control group, and participants are randomly assigned to one of these groups. If the study is double-blind, neither the investigators nor the participants themselves know what group the participant is assigned to. By randomly assigning the participants to the groups, all known and unknown variables are distributed evenly between the two groups, assuming sufficiently large sample sizes. As a consequence, the two groups differ only in terms of the treatment variable, and so if a difference in the outcome variable between the two groups is observed, this can be attributable to the effect of the treatment variable alone. Despite being regarded as the gold standard for intervention studies, randomised controlled trials are practically challenging to administer in comparison to observational studies. For example, it is much easier to monitor volunteers in a cognitive therapy programme and then compare these volunteers to participants not in the programme that are matched in terms of key characteristics than to design a concurrent placebo control programme and randomly assign participants to one programme or another. In addition, randomised controlled trials are not always possible to conduct for ethical reasons. For example, it might be unethical, or at least irresponsible, to withhold a potentially effective treatment from half of the study's participants.

In this chapter, we consider some of the statistical issues that arise in the analysis of intervention studies. We will assume that these analyses are being applied to study designs that are higher up the evidence hierarchy. In particular, we will assume that there is a treatment and control group and that at least some key *covariates* related to the outcome variable are known. Likewise, we will assume that before and after scores of the outcome are available, assuming that they are possible to obtain. The analyses we consider will in fact be equally applicable to randomised controlled trials as well as non-randomised designs, such as cohort studies or matched and controlled non-randomised studies of the kind described earlier. While the methods we describe can be applied or extended to almost any kind of outcome variable, we will primarily consider continuous and normally distributed outcome variables, as well as the special case of reoffending behaviours, given their prominence in intervention studies in forensic psychology.

Analysing controlled interventions with baseline and follow-up

Here, we will consider how to analyse intervention studies that have *baseline* and *follow-up* scores on the outcome variable from a *treatment* and a *control* group. We will assume that the outcome variable is normally distributed. In an intervention study in a forensic psychology context, an example of an approximately normally distributed outcome variable might be the score on a psychometric scale that measures attitudes related to sexual offending. For simplicity, in the examples we discuss here, we will assume that the variability of the outcome variables scores is the same at baseline and at follow-up. In other words, if there is an effect in either the treatment or control group, this leads to a shift to the left or right in the mean of the normal distribution over the outcome variable, such as is illustrated in Figure 2.1. We will also assume, again for simplicity, that the variability in the outcome variable scores are the same in both the treatment and control group. These assumptions of equal variability in the outcome variable from baseline to follow-up in both the treatment and follow-up groups are not necessary, but they do simplify the explanation of the required statistical analysis. These assumptions are also likely to hold true in practice: when participants in the treatment and control groups are measured on the same variable at two points in time, it is

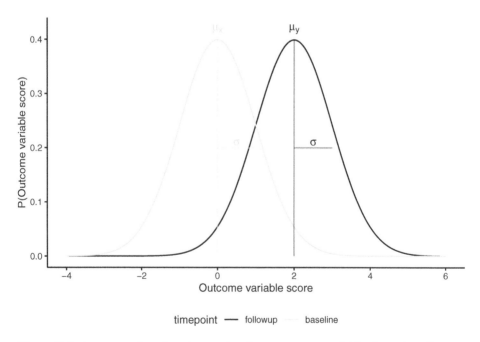

Figure 2.1 An example of a change in the outcome variable from baseline to follow-up where the standard deviation of the outcome variable does not change.

reasonable to expect the variability in the scores in both groups and on the two occasions will be approximately the same.

Another important assumption that we will make is that follow–up scores are *positively correlated* with baseline scores and that this is the case in both the treatment and control groups. In other words, participants who score higher than average at baseline will be more likely to be higher than average at follow–up, while those who are lower than average at baseline will be more likely to be lower than average at follow–up. This is, in fact, a very reasonable and conservative assumption. Given that the same participants are being measured on the same variable at two points in time that are usually not far apart, it is difficult to conceive of any situation where there would be zero correlation between follow–up and baseline scores. Given the similarity of the treatment and control participants and that they are both being measured on the same outcome variable, it is also reasonable to assume that the correlation between follow–up and baselines scores is the same in the treatment and the control group.

In an intervention study that has the characteristics just outlined, the *treatment effect* is defined as the difference between the expected score in the treatment group and that of the control group, assuming a fixed constant value at baseline in both groups. Put another way, holding constant the baseline score in both the treatment and control group, the treatment effect is the difference between the expected follow–up score in the treatment group and that of the control group. For example, if we have two individuals, one in the treatment group and one in the control group, who have identical scores at baseline, the treatment effect is the difference between their expected scores at follow–up.

We will now consider three different possible analyses of an intervention study of this nature. First, we will consider an analysis based on just the follow-up scores alone. Next, we will consider an analysis that uses *change scores*, which are the difference between the baseline and follow–up scores. Finally, we will consider an analysis of covariance (ANCOVA) approach. Our aim will be to show that both the analysis of follow–up scores and the analysis of change scores lead to biased estimates of the treatment effect, while the ANCOVA leads to unbiased estimates.

Datasets

To illustrate these analyses, we will use simulated datasets that have been drawn from distributions with known population parameters. Doing so allows us to know what the true treatment effects in the population are, and this allows us to demonstrate how biased estimates of the treatment effect will occur in some analyses and not others. In particular, in the main dataset that we use, the population difference between the mean baseline score in the treatment group and the mean baseline score in the control group is equal to 3.0, the population treatment effect is equal to 10, and the correlation between the baseline and follow-up scores in both the treatment and control groups is $r = 0.7$. An illustration of these data is shown in Figure 2.2, and some descriptive statistics are shown in Table 2.1.

A sample of ten rows of the data are shown in Table 2.2. It is important here to note the format of the data. The first column 'Group' contains the condition to which an individual was assigned (control or treatment), 'Baseline' contains the baseline score of the individual before the intervention, and 'Follow-up' contains the score of the individual following the intervention. When analysing intervention studies, it is therefore important to include the baseline and follow-up measurements in separate columns and to have each row corresponding to exactly one individual participant.

Method 1: analysis of follow-up scores

In order to determine the treatment effect, we might first consider analysing individuals' scores following the intervention in order to see if the follow-up scores are meaningfully different between the treatment and control groups. This analysis can be run using a general linear model, with 'follow-up' score as the outcome variable and 'group' as the binary predictor, coded 0 for control and 1 for treatment. We could write this model formally as follows:

$$y_i = \beta_0 + \beta_1 x_i + \epsilon_i, \text{ for } i \in 1 \dots n, \tag{1}$$

where y_i is the follow-up score of individual i, x_i is the binary indicator variable that indicates if the condition to which individual i is assigned is control $(x_i = 0)$ or treatment $(x_i = 1)$, ϵ_i is normally distributed random noise, and n is

Table 2.1 The sample means of baseline and follow-up scores, and their difference, in control and treatment in the simulated data

Measurement Time	Treatment	Control	Difference
Baseline	3.15	−0.09	3.24
Follow-up	3.31	−0.08	3.38

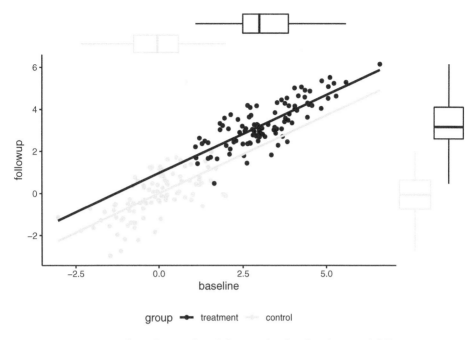

group ●— treatment   ─── control

Figure 2.2 A scatterplot of a simulated dataset that has baseline and follow-up scores in both a treatment and a follow-up group. The Tukey boxplots show the distribution of scores at baseline and follow-up in the two groups. These data were generated by assuming that the difference (in the population) between the treatment and the control group at baseline is exactly 3.0 and that the true value of the treatment effect is exactly 10.

Table 2.2 Structure of intervention data

Group	Baseline	Follow-up
Control	1.46	1.25
Control	0.63	0.79
Control	−0.77	−0.48
Control	−0.23	−0.44
Control	0.08	1.16
Treatment	2.12	2.11
Treatment	1.46	2.41
Treatment	3.87	4.17
Treatment	3.51	3.07
Treatment	4.43	4.30

the total number of participants in the study (i.e., in the treatment and control groups combined). The value of β_0 is the average value of the follow-up score in the control group, and β_1 is the difference in average value of the follow-up scores between the treatment and control groups. The results of this model applied to the data described earlier are shown in Table 2.3.

According to this model, the estimated average score of individuals in the control group following the intervention is −0.08 and the difference in the follow-up scores between the control and treatment is 3.38. That is, the estimated follow-up score of treatment is −0.08 + 3.38 = 3.3. Recall, however, that the true value of the treatment effect in the population is exactly 1.0. As such, the results from this model do not approximate this true value. Specifically, this model estimates the treatment effect to be 3.38, which is a large overestimation of the known true treatment effect of 10. Furthermore, this true value of 10 is not even included in the 95% confidence interval of the treatment effect in this model.

One of the major problems with analysing treatment effects by only using follow-up scores is that this analysis does not take into account differences in the individuals' scores prior to the intervention. The estimates of the treatment effect will therefore be biased if there are differences in baseline scores between the treatment and control groups. Furthermore, it can be shown that the strength of the correlation between the baseline and follow-up scores also introduces bias in the estimate of the treatment effect. We can illustrate the biasing effect of baseline differences and correlations between baseline and follow-up using some more simulated datasets. Here, we simulate four datasets, labelled A, B, C, and D. Each one is generated according to different population baseline differences, treatment effects, and baseline/follow-up correlations. These population parameter values are shown in Table 2.4, and the resulting data are visualised in Figure 2.3. All four datasets were analysed using the follow-up scores model defined in Equation 1.

As can be seen in Table 2.4, only simulation A, which had zero baseline differences and a moderate correlation between baseline and follow-up (of −.60), provided a reasonable estimate of the population treatment effect, with the 95% confidence interval containing the known population treatment effect of 10.

Table 2.3 General linear model parameter estimates in the analysis of follow-up scores

Parameter	Coefficient	SE	CI	CI_low	CI_high	t	df_error	p
(Intercept)	−0.08	0.11	0.95	−0.29	0.14	−0.71	198	0.48
grouptreatment	3.38	0.15	0.95	3.08	3.68	22.19	198	0.00

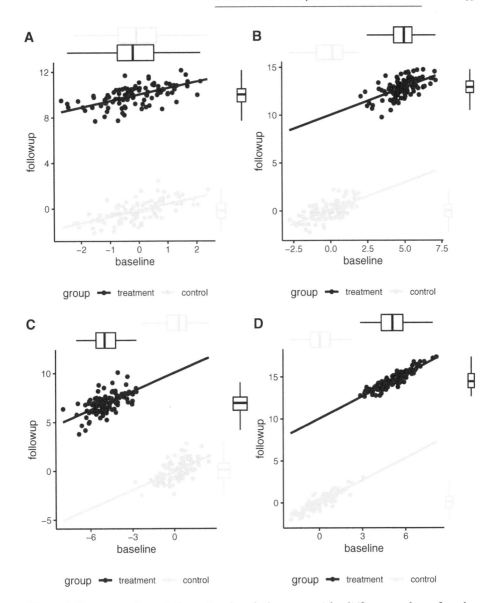

Figure 2.3 Scatterplot of four simulated datasets with different values for the differences between the treatment and control group in the average scores at baseline and different correlations between baseline and follow-up.

Table 2.4 Summary of estimated treatment effects using follow-up score analysis
with simulated data

Simulation	Population Baseline Difference	Population Correlation	Population Treatment Effect	Estimated Treatment Effect	Estimated Treatment Effect 95% Confidence interval
A	0	0.60	10	10.11	9.86, 10.36
B	5	0.60	10	12.76	12.49, 13.03
C	−5	0.60	10	6.85	6.56, 7.15
D	5	0.90	10	14.43	14.14, 14.72

We see in simulation B that the estimate of the treatment effect is overestimated
when the treatment baseline scores are higher than the control baseline scores.
On the other hand, from simulation C, we see that the treatment effect is underestimated when the control baseline scores are higher than the treatment scores.
Finally looking at simulation D, which includes baseline differences and a strong
correlation between baseline and follow-up scores, we see the estimation of the
treatment effect may be overestimated by nearly 50% of the true effect. Note,
too, that for simulations B, C, and D, none of the 95% confidence intervals contain the known population treatment effect. Although not shown here, the closer
the correlation of baseline and follow-up scores is to zero, the less bias it will
introduce into the model. However, as mentioned earlier, it is difficult to conceive of a situation that would lead to zero correlations when the same individuals are measured on the same variable at two points in time that are not far apart.

Method 2: analysis of change scores

In the previous section, we illustrated the problems with analysing treatment
effects in terms of the difference in follow-up scores between the treatment
and control group. A frequently employed attempted solution to the problem
of baseline differences is to analyse differences in *change scores*, which are the
differences between the baseline and follow-up scores. The change scores for
some of the participants from the main dataset are shown in Table 2.5, and the
distribution of change scores in the treatment and control group are shown in
Figure 2.4. Analysing differences in change scores is sometimes also termed a
difference in differences (DiD) analysis (see, for example, Bertrand, Duflo & Mullainathan, 2004). In this approach, it is usually believed that baseline differences

Table 2.5 Structure of intervention data, including change scores

Group	Baseline	Follow-up	Change
Control	1.46	1.25	−0.21
Control	0.63	0.79	0.16
Control	−0.77	−0.48	0.29
Control	−0.23	−0.44	−0.22 ·
Control	0.08	1.16	1.08
Treatment	2.12	2.11	−0.01
Treatment	1.46	2.41	0.95
Treatment	3.87	4.17	0.29
Treatment	3.51	3.07	−0.44
Treatment	4.43	4.30	−0.13

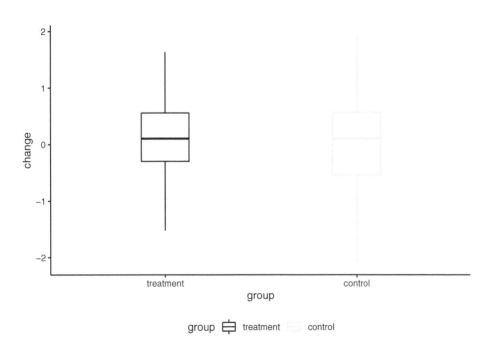

Figure 2.4 Tukey boxplots of the change scores in the treatment and the control group in the mains simulated dataset.

between the treatment and control groups have been controlled, given that analysis uses only differences between baseline and follow-up. However, as we will show through simulations, DiD analysis also provides biased estimates of treatment effects in intervention studies.

In a change score analysis, we assess whether there is a difference in the change scores, rather than the follow-up scores, between the treatment and control groups. Just as with the analysis of follow-up scores, we can run this analysis using a general linear model with **group** as a binary predictor coded 0 for **control** and 1 for **treatment**, but where our outcome variable is the change score. We could write this formally as follows:

$$y_i^1 - y_i^0 = \beta_0 + \beta_1 x_i + \epsilon_i, \text{ for } i \in 1 \dots n, \tag{2}$$

Here, y_i^0 is the score of participant i at baseline and y_i^1 is their corresponding score at follow-up. In the general linear model, the value of β_0 represents the average change in the control group and β_1 represents the difference of the change scores between the treatment and control groups.

Applying this model to our main dataset leads to the results shown in Table 2.6. The results show that the estimated change in scores between baseline and follow-up for the control group is approximately 0.01 and that the difference of the change in scores between the treatment and control groups is 0.15. In other words, scores of individuals assigned to control changed by around 0.01, and scores of individuals in treatment changed by around $0.01 + 0.15 = 0.16$. Recall, however, that this dataset was generated with a population treatment effect of 1.0. In other words, this model estimates the treatment effect to be 0.16, which is a drastic underestimate of the known population effect. Furthermore, the associated 95% confidence interval does not come close to this known population value.

From the analysis we have just conducted, we can see that just like follow-up score analysis, change score analysis can also lead to biased estimates of the treatment effect. This occurs despite the fact that change score analyses are widely

Table 2.6 General linear model parameter estimates in the analysis of change scores

Parameter	Coefficient	SE	CI	CI_low	CI_high	t	df_error	p
(Intercept)	0.01	0.08	0.95	−0.14	0.17	0.19	198	0.85
grouptreatment	0.15	0.11	0.95	−0.07	0.37	1.32	198	0.19

assumed to control for any biasing effects of baseline differences between the treatment and control groups. We can further illustrate the biases that arise in change score analyses using the same simulated data as shown in Figure 2.3 but instead analysing the data using the change score model, outlined in Equation 2. Estimates and 95% confidence intervals of the treatment effect are shown in Table 2.7.

From these analyses, we see slightly less over- and underestimation of the treatment effect compared to the results based on the follow-up scores analyses. However, just as in the case of the analysis of follow-up scores, only the confidence interval for simulation A (which had a zero baseline difference and a moderate correlation between baseline and follow-up) contains the true population treatment effect. Once we introduce differences into the baseline scores in simulations B and C, we see biasing of the treatment effect. This time, the bias is in the opposite direction to that seen in the follow-up scores analysis. In general, it can be shown that when baseline treatment scores are greater than baseline control scores, the treatment effect will be underestimated by a change score analysis. Conversely, when baseline control scores are greater than baseline treatment scores, the effect will be overestimated. Finally, in simulation D, we observe a slight reduction in bias due the stronger positive correlation between baseline and follow-up scores. Even in this case, however, the treatment effect is still underestimated and the 95% confidence interval does not contain the known population effect.

Method 3: analysis of covariance

As has been shown using the simulations in the previous sections, contrary to popular belief and practice, analysis of change scores does not provide suitable

Table 2.7 Summary of estimated treatment effects using change score analysis with simulated data

Simulation	Population Baseline Difference	Population Correlation	Population Treatment Effect	Estimated Treatment Effect	Estimated Treatment Effect 95% Confidence interval
A	0	0.6	10	10.2	9.97, 10.43
B	5	0.6	10	7.87	7.62, 8.12
C	−5	0.6	10	11.98	11.72, 12.23
D	5	0.9	10	9.38	9.25, 9.51

models for analysing intervention studies, as they, too, are prone to the same biasing effects due to a difference in baseline scores and the correlation between the baseline and follow-up scores. However, a statistical model that leads to unbiased estimates of the treatments and that is not affected by differences in baseline scores, nor correlations between baseline and follow-up, is the ANCOVA model. In an ANCOVA analysis, we analyse differences in follow-up scores for the treatment and control groups whilst controlling for the baseline scores. In other words, we add the baseline scores into the model as a *covariate*. Accounting for, rather than ignoring or subtracting, baseline scores means we avoid the biases due to differences at baseline and due to the correlation between baseline and follow-up scores. In the ANCOVA model, like the analysis of follow-up scores, we specify the follow-up score as the outcome variable, the treatment group variable as a binary predictor coded 0 for control and 1 for treatment, and now also include each participant's baseline score as an additional predictor.

The ANCOVA is a simple extension of the previous models we have used. Despite its name relating to ANOVA-like (analysis of variance) analysis, it is more helpful to think of ANCOVA as a general linear model with a categorical and continuous predictor. We can specify this formally as follows:

$$y_i^1 = \beta_0 + \beta_1 x_i + \beta_2 y_i^0 + \epsilon_i, \text{ for } i \in 1 \ldots n, \tag{3}$$

where, as earlier, y_i^0 is the score of participant i at baseline, y_i^1 is their corresponding score at follow-up, and x_i is a binary indicator variable indicating whether participant i was in the control group ($x_i = 0$) or the treatment group ($x_i = 1$). In this model, β_0 is the average effect of the follow-up scores of the control group, assuming baseline scores are held constant. Likewise, β_1 is the difference in the effect on follow-up scores between the treatment and control groups, assuming baseline scores are held constant. Finally, β_2 is the average change in follow-up scores for every one-unit change in baseline scores in both the treatment and the control groups.

The results of this model applied to the main simulated dataset are shown in Table 2.8. The results show us that if the baseline scores are equal to 1.0, the

Table 2.8 General linear model parameter estimates of the ANCOVA model

Parameter	Coefficient	SE	CI	CI_low	CI_high	t	df_error	p
(Intercept)	−0.01	0.07	0.95	−0.15	0.14	−0.11	197	0.91
grouptreatment	0.97	0.19	0.95	0.59	1.35	5.07	197	0.00
baseline	0.74	0.05	0.95	0.65	0.84	14.95	197	0.00

estimated follow-up scores of individuals in the control group (which is coded by the value of 0) is $-0.01 + 0.97 \times 0 + 0.74 \times 1.0 = -0.01 + 0.74 = 0.73$. On the other hand, when the baseline score is 1.0, the estimated follow-up scores of the treatment group (which is coded by the value of 1) are $-0.01 + 0.97 \times 1 + 0.74 \times 1.0 = -0.01 + 0.97 + 0.74 = 1.7$. The difference between the scores of control and treatment in these two cases is therefore $1.7 - 0.73 = 0.97$. Indeed, this difference between the scores of control and treatment, assuming any fixed constant value, of the baseline scores is always β_1, which in this case is 0.97. Finally, according to this model, we see that for every one-unit increase in baseline scores, follow-up scores increase by 0.97, and this occurs in both the treatment and control groups equally. It is important to note here that this estimate of the baseline scores need not be statistically significant. Our key reason for including baseline scores as a covariate is not to find a statistically significant relationship between the baseline and follow-up scores, but rather to statistically control for the effect of the baseline scores in the follow-up scores. When it comes to deciding if there was a significant treatment effect, we can simply look at the 95% confidence interval and p-value for the group (β_1) term. This shows that the difference between the treatment and control group in the follow-up scores is statistically significant when adjusted for baseline scores. Again, given we are using simulated data with known population parameters, we can see that this model provides a good estimate of the treatment effect, with the 95% confidence interval of the group containing the known population treatment effect of 1.0. Note that this model is the only model of the three analyses we have used to accurately estimate this effect.

To further illustrate that in ANCOVA the treatment effect is not biased by the differences in baseline scores or the correlations between baseline and follow-up scores, we run analyses using the four simulated datasets shown in Figure 2.3, using the ANCOVA model outlined in Equation 3. Estimates and 95% confidence interval of the treatment effect of the analyses are shown in Table 2.9.

As can be seen in Table 2.9, all simulations provide good estimates of the treatment effect. All estimates are close to the true population effect of 10, and the 95% confidence intervals of all simulations contain this value.

Analysing longitudinal intervention studies

In the previous section, we established that the ANCOVA model was the ideal method of analysing the efficacy of an intervention study of the prototypical kind that we described, which was, amongst other details, where there was one treatment and one control group and both groups were measured at baseline and follow-up. By using the standard options available to us when using general

Table 2.9 Summary of estimated treatment effects using ANCOVA analysis with simulated data

Simulation	Population Baseline Difference	Population Correlation	Population Treatment Effect	Estimated Treatment Effect	Estimated Treatment Effect 95% Confidence interval
A	0	0.6	10	10.16	9.96, 10.36
B	5	0.6	10	9.94	9.41, 10.48
C	−5	0.6	10	10.08	9.45, 10.72
D	5	0.9	10	9.99	9.66, 10.31

linear models, such as using treatment or contrast coding for categorical variables, the ANCOVA method can be immediately applied to the case of more than two groups. For example, when two or more treatment groups are being compared to a single control group, we can use treatment codes in the ANCOVA to assess the treatment effect of each individual treatment, or use contrast codes to assess the treatment effect of the average of all treatments. However, for other intervention study designs, the basic ANCOVA method per se cannot used, and extensions are necessary. One common situation for which ANCOVA must be extended is when the study has measurements at more than just baseline and follow-up. For example, there may be baseline and follow-up measurement times, but also an intermediate measurement time between baseline and follow-up. In this scenario, we can now assess the treatment effect occurring between baseline and the intermediate time and between the baseline and follow-up times. In general, we may extend this design to have any number, and not just one, intermediate measurement time. In order to analyse the treatment effect in intervention studies of this nature, it is necessary to use a longitudinal extension of ANCOVA, known as a *longitudinal analysis of covariance* (LANCOVA) (see, Twisk et al., 2018, for details and discussion).

The LANCOVA model is specified similarly to the ANCOVA model: post-baseline scores are set as the outcome variable, the treatment group is a binary predictor coded 0 for control and 1 for treatment, and each participant's baseline score is included as a covariate. However, LANCOVA includes two additional terms: the interaction between the treatment group and a binary variable indicating whether the post-baseline measurement occurred at the intermediate or follow-up times and a random effect of participation. The structure of data needed for a LANCOVA analysis with baseline, intermediate, and follow-up scores is shown in Table 2.10. In more detail, in LANCOVA, the value of the dependent outcome of participant i at baseline, intermediate, and follow-up can be denoted, respectively, by

$$y_i^{t=0}, y_i^{t=1}, y_i^{t=2}.$$

In other words, the $t \in \{0,1,2\}$ superscript indicates the timepoint of the outcome variable measurement, and the $i \in 1...n$ subscript indicates the participant. If we assume that there is just one treatment and one control group, then we can use $x_i \in \{0,1\}$, as earlier, to indicate if participant i is in the treatment ($x_i = 1$) or control group ($x_i = 0$). For the intermediate time (i.e. $t = 1$) and follow-up time ($t = 2$), the value of the outcome variable can be modelled as follows[1]:

$$y_i^t = \beta_0 + \beta_1 x_i + \beta_2 y_i^0 + \beta_3 z_i^t + \beta_4 z_i^t x_i + \zeta_i + \epsilon_i^t \text{ for } i \in 1...n \qquad (4)$$

Here, $z_i^t \in \{0,1\}$ is another binary indicator variable: if $t = 2$ then $z_i^t = 1$, and if $t = 1$ then $z_i^t = 0$. The error terms ζ_i and ϵ_i^t are both normally distributed with means of 0 and standard deviations of τ and σ, respectively. The ϵ_i^t term is the residual variation from timepoint to timepoint and from participant to participant and plays an identical role to the ϵ_i terms in Equations 1 to 3. On the other hand, the ζ_i term, which is a *random effect* term, is specific to participant i and accounts for the intra-participant correlation between the values of the dependent variable at times $t = 1$ and $t = 2$. In other words, this term allows us to account for the fact that participants' responses at times $t = 1$ and $t = 2$ may be correlated. For example, participants who are above (or below) average at time $t = 1$ may also be above (or below) average at $t = 2$, and we may model these by participant-specific effects that may be positive (or negative).

This LANCOVA model effectively tells us how the outcome variable at the intermediate time ($t = 1$) and the follow-up time ($t = 2$) vary as a function of the treatment group, indicated by x_i, while controlling for each participant's baseline value $y_i^{t=0}$. There are two key parameters of interest in this model: β_1 and β_4. The value of β_1 gives the treatment effect at the intermediate time ($t = 1$). In other words, β_1 is the difference between the average of the control and treatment groups on the outcome variable at the intermediate time after controlling for baseline values. To see why this is the case, note that, as mentioned earlier, whenever $t = 1$, then $z_i^t = 0$, and so by substituting $t = 1$ and $z_i^t = 0$ into Equation 4, we obtain the following:

$$y_i^1 = \beta_0 + \beta_1 x_i + \beta_2 y_i^0 + \zeta_i + \epsilon_i^1, \text{ for } i \in 1 ... n.$$

With the exception of the two sources of random variability, this is identical to the ANCOVA model presented in Equation 3, and so β_1 identifies the treatment effect from baseline to the intermediate time.

We can estimate the effects of scores at follow-up by noting that whenever $t = 2$, then $z_i' = 1$, and so substituting $t = 2$ and $z_i' = 1$ into Equation 4, we obtain the following:

$$y_i^2 = \beta_0 + \beta_1 x_i + \beta_2 y_i^0 + \beta_3 + \beta_4 x_i + \zeta_i + \epsilon_i^2, \text{ for } i \in 1 \dots n,$$

From this, we see that this model is also identical to an ANCOVA model, and so the value of $\beta_2 + \beta_4$ gives the difference between the average of the control and treatment groups on the outcome variable at the follow-up time, after controlling for baseline values. Finally, note that the value of β_4 itself indicates the difference between the treatment effects from baseline to intermediate and from baseline to follow-up.

In Figure 2.5, we illustrate data from a simulation of an intervention study with one intermediate and one final follow-up measurement time. From this simulation, the population treatment effect at the intermediate timepoint is 1.0, and the population treatment effect at the follow-up timepoint is 2.0. A LANCOVA analysis estimates these two effects as 1.37 and 2.18, respectively. By contrast, as is apparent from Figure 2.5b, if we were to run an analysis of change scores, as outlined in Method 2, we can see that the differences in change scores both at the intermediate time and follow-up are misleading. The difference in the

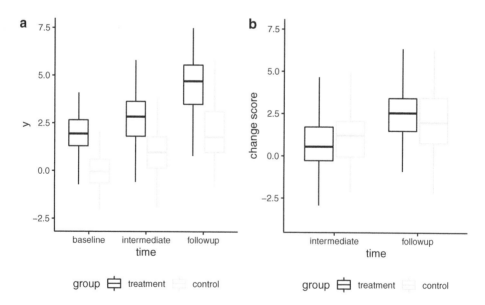

Figure 2.5 a) Boxplots of outcome variable scores for a treatment and control group at three points in time. b) The change scores from baseline and the intermediate and final timepoints.

Table 2.10 Example of some data to illustrate the necessary structure of the data for a LANCOVA.

ID	Group	Baseline	Measurement Time	y
98	Control	0.15	Intermediate	1.49
98	Control	0.15	Follow-up	1.65
99	Control	−0.42	Intermediate	0.42
99	Control	−0.42	Follow-up	−0.45
100	Control	−1.38	Intermediate	1.54
100	Control	−1.38	Follow-up	3.48
101	Treatment	1.16	Intermediate	3.34
101	Treatment	1.16	Follow-up	6.13
102	Treatment	3.57	Intermediate	1.63
102	Treatment	3.57	Follow-up	4.38

Note: The ID is the subject identifier, and each subject's data occur on multiple rows, one for each measurement time after baseline (e.g. intermediate and follow-up). The outcome variable at these times is denoted here by y.

change scores between treatment and control at the intermediate time is −0.37. In other words, the change from baseline is higher in the control group than in the treatment group. The difference in the change scores between treatment and control at the follow-up time is 0.44. Clearly, change scores at both timepoints badly underestimate the true population effect, and hence LANCOVA is the most appropriate model to use in longitudinal intervention studies.

Analysing interventions measured by recidivism rates

In the preceding sections, we discussed the analysis of prototypical intervention studies. In these analyses, the major features were that there was a treatment and a control group, measurements were obtained at two or more timepoints, and the outcome variable was approximately normally distributed. It is clear that not all of these features will occur in all intervention studies. When the outcome variable is not normally distributed, there are usually some immediately available alternatives. For example, if the outcome variable is an ordinal variable, such as a risk factor with levels *low*, *medium*, and *high*, it would be straightforward to extend the ANCOVA and LANCOVA models to their generalised linear model counterparts, such as ones based on ordinal logistic regression. All the major issues we discussed in the previous section would still hold in this case. However, in some other cases, the extension is not as straightforward. One very important example of this in forensic psychology is the analysis of recidivism rates. Typically, when analysing recidivism, there are no baseline rates to compare to subsequent rates: there is simply whether and when a prisoner reoffends in a follow-up period after being released from prison. The outcome variable is also of a special nature. It is time after release from prison up to the end of the follow-up period, which may be a long duration but is nonetheless still finite, when the reoffending event occurs. If the reoffending event does not occur for a particular individual before the end of the follow-up period, the data for that individual are said to be *right censored*. Data of this nature are in fact typical in other contexts too. For example, time to recurrence of a cancer in patients after their treatment ends or time to death of patients who undergo a medical treatment is ultimately of the same kind of data. The field of statistics that deals with analysis of data of this kind is known as *survival analysis*. In this section, we provide a brief introduction to how survival analysis can be applied to recidivism data and can be used to evaluate whether recidivism rates change with a treatment variable.

The data that we will use is from Rossi, Berk and Lenihan (1980), which investigated whether a randomly assigned financial aid package affected whether each of 432 individuals were arrested in the 52 weeks after their release from prison. For each prisoner, there is the week number when they were arrested, if they were arrested within the year-long follow-up period. For those not arrested at all, their arrest data are listed as right censored at 52 weeks. We can estimate the *survival function* for these data using a non-parametric method known as the Kaplan-Meier estimator. This method is used to estimate the proportion of individuals who have not been arrested yet for each of the 52 weeks in the follow-up period. We plot this survival function in Figure 2.6. In this plot, we see that by 52 weeks, approximately 75% of individuals have not yet been arrested. However, we see that the probability of a non-arrest is lower (or the probability of rearrest is higher) for those individuals who did not receive the treatment.

A widely used statistical analysis method of this data is *Cox regression*, also known as a *proportional hazards* model. This is a type of regression analysis, related to a logistic regression, specifically applied to survival data. In brief, it models how the *hazard* function, which gives the probability of an event happening at any given time, varies by a constant factor that is a function of predictor variables. For our data, it allows us to model the probability of a non-arrest as a function of time and how this changes depending on whether the individual is in the treatment group or not. Applying the Cox model to these data leads to an estimate of the treatment effect of 0.69. This tells us that the hazard function for an arrest changes by a factor of 0.69 as we go from the non-treatment to the treatment group. In other words, the risk of rearrest is reduced by approximately $(1 - 0.69) = 31\%$ in the treatment group. The Cox model assumes that this change in risk is constant over time.

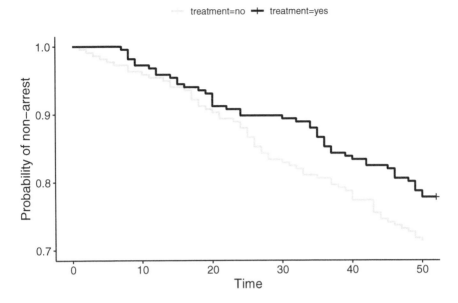

Figure 2.6 The Kaplan-Meier estimated survival function of the Rossi et al. (1980) recidivism data. This plot shows the probability of not yet being arrested in each week of the 52-week follow-up period after being released from prison for individuals in a treatment versus control group.

Like any other regression model, the Cox model can take any number of covariates. For the analysis of recidivism data, this allows us to statistically control for other variables that may also affect the probability of being arrested. For example, in the Rossi et al. (1980) data, for each individual, we have their age, race, marital status, previous work experience, number of prior convictions, whether they released on parole, and their educational level. Potentially, any or all of these variables could affect the probability of being rearrested, and so we can control for them in the Cox model to focus on the main treatment effect. Doing so now leads to an estimate of the treatment effect of 0.70. This tells us that if age, race, marital status, work experience, amount of prior convictions, parole status, and education level are the same between individuals, there is a 30% reduction in the probability of being arrested as a result of the treatment.

Conclusion

Intervention studies in forensic psychology and elsewhere aim to identify if a change in a given variable, which is known as the treatment variable, leads to a change in an outcome variable of interest. In general, an intervention study involves participants in one group being given a treatment and then their scores on a relevant outcome variable are measured. Preferably, the scores on the outcome variable are also measured before the treatment is applied in order to identify the change from baseline values that occurs as a consequence of the treatment. Likewise, it is of considerable evidential value to have a comparison group that does not get the treatment, but that is also measured at a baseline and follow-up time in order to demonstrate that the change in scores on the outcome measure is causally related to the treatment and not to any other factor.

In this chapter, we have considered the best method of analysis of intervention studies of this kind. In these studies, the *treatment effect* is defined as the difference between the expected score in the treatment group and that of the control group, assuming equal value at baseline in both groups. We initially showed that analysis of differences between treatment and control at follow-up only can lead to biased estimates of these treatment effects. More importantly, we showed that analysis of change scores, which are differences between the treatment and control group in differences between baseline and follow-up, can also lead to biased estimates of treatment effects. This is noteworthy, as differences in change scores are widely used and seemingly widely believed to correct for any biasing effects of baseline differences. From this, it is apparent that widely used methods of analysis of intervention studies will routinely lead to considerable overestimates or underestimates of treatment effects. By contrast, in the scenarios we have considered, the ANCOVA method we described will lead to unbiased estimates of the treatment effect. We also showed that ANCOVA is a practically and conceptually simple extension of the other widely used methods, so there are no practical reasons why it should not be more widely employed for the analysis of intervention studies. We then showed how ANCOVA can be easily extended to multiple measurement timepoint intervention studies.

Finally, we briefly considered the analysis of intervention studies that assess effects on recidivism rates. These require special statistical tools, specifically survival analysis. One of the survival analysis methods we considered, the Cox proportional hazards model, can be understood as an extension of the generalised linear model. It can therefore allow us to model the effect of a treatment variable on the probability of an event over time, such as the occurrence of reoffending. It can easily be used to control for covariates, and thereby statistically control for any difference between a treatment and control group that might otherwise affect the outcome.

Note

1 In this version of LANCOVA, we are assuming the correlation between baseline and intermediate is the same as the correlation between baseline and follow-up. This

assumption is not necessary and can be easily avoided by the inclusion of an extra interaction term, specifically for the interaction of x_i and y_i^0.

References

Bertrand, M., Duflo, E., & Mullainathan, S. (2004). How much should we trust differences-in-differences estimates? *The Quarterly Journal of Economics, 119*(1), 249–275.

OCEMB. Howick, J., Chalmers, I., Glasziou, P., Greenhalgh, T., Heneghan, C., Liberati, A., Moschetti, I., Phillips, B., and Thornton, H. *Explanation of the 2011 Oxford Centre for Evidence-Based Medicine (OCEBM) Levels of Evidence (background document)*. Oxford Centre for Evidence-Based Medicine. https://www.cebm.ox.ac.uk/resources/levels-of-evidence/ocebm-levels-of-evidence

Rossi, P. H., Berk, R. A., & Lenihan, K. J. (1980). *Money, work and crime: Some experimental results*. Academic Press.

Twisk, J., Bosman, L., Hoekstra, T., Rijnhart, J., Welten, M., & Heymans, M. (2018). Different ways to estimate treatment effects in randomised controlled trials. *Contemporary Clinical Trials Communications, 10*, 80–85.

3
Therapeutic communities and facilitating change

Geraldine Akerman

Context of the programme

HMP Grendon is a Category B prison, housing up to 230 adult male prisoners. It runs entirely as a democratic therapeutic community (DTC) and is described extensively elsewhere (e.g. Akerman, 2019; Akerman & Mandikate, 2018; Shuker & Sullivan, 2010). A DTC within a prison provides an environment where a range of behaviours (including those exhibited in the build-up to their offending) can become apparent and therefore open to assessment and change. The DTC works on the principle that society can be the agent of change. Examples of residents' fantasies, thoughts, feelings and behaviour are discussed in the thrice-weekly small therapy groups and the twice-weekly community meetings. Their behaviour in all other places where residents spend their time is integrated into their therapy. It provides an opportunity to practice and refine skills learned in other offending behaviour programmes in a living-learning environment.

HMP Grendon comprises five discreet communities. One community is for induction and assessment, and there are four communities in which men live together and participate in intensive therapy for an average period of eighteen months to three years. One community houses men who have committed offences with a sexual motivation or whose behaviour within prison leads to some concern in this area; however, the wings are not segregated; the residents mix throughout the day, for instance, at the gymnasium, chapel or in education. One community is for men with learning difficulties, which adheres to the accredited DTC model but is adjusted to meet the needs of those residents (see Akerman & Jamieson, 2020, for further details).

DOI: 10.4324/9780429262074-3

Sexual offence paralleling behaviour

While dilemmas are involved in considering whether to attempt to amend an individual's sexual interests, for some they are problematic, and this has led them to seek tools to manage them (see Akerman, Perkins & Bartels, 2020). Due to the intimate nature of the sexual interests, it is important to explore the role of sexual offence paralleling behaviours (SOPBs) in relation to risk assessment and risk reduction in those who have committed sexual offences. SOPB can be difficult to identify by its very nature and due to the increased use of detection evasion skills (DESs) in this domain. It is acknowledged that much is invested in terms of comfort, pleasure, relief and so forth, much of which is unconscious, and so it will be difficult to give this up (Akerman & Beech, 2013). Sexual interest will be defined as the fantasies, thoughts, ideas or preferences that individuals find sexually attractive, and arousal is defined as the resulting response. Previous research (Hanson & Bussière, 1998) concluded that sexual deviance was a significant factor in sexual recidivism. Further, meta-analytic reviews (Hanson & Bussière, 1998; Hanson & Morton-Bourgon, 2004) consistently show that deviant sexual interests (for example, sex with children, or to include adult sexual coercion) are the strongest predictors of future offending. Therefore, a thorough understanding of current sexual interest is important in order to assess risk of further offending. However, it can be very difficult for residents to discuss such personal interests. Therefore, alongside the need to provide the optimal conditions in which therapy can occur, a thorough functional analysis of sexual offending behaviour is required, reflecting the complex nature of offence-related sexual arousal. Offence paralleling behaviour (OPB) is described by several authors (for example, Genders & Player, 1995; Shine & Morris, 2000). Jones (2004, p. 38) described it as 'any form of offence related behaviour (or fantasised behaviour) pattern that emerges at any point before during or after an offence. It does not have to result in an offence; it simply needs to resemble, in some significant respect, the <u>sequence</u> of behaviours leading up to the offence'. What this emphasises is the importance of the 'sequence' of behaviours rather than an individual behaviour, such as acting in an aggressive manner. In terms of SOPB, the role of fantasy may be important, and in a custodial setting may indicate on-going risk. A fuller discussion about the role of sexual fantasy in offending is beyond the scope of this chapter, so for further information please refer to Akerman and Beech (2011); Flak, Beech and Fisher (2007); Kahr (2007); and Ryan (2004). Flak et al. (2007) noted that 'fantasy is being seen as important in the acquisition and maintenance of deviant interest' (p. 75). However, Stinson and Becker (2008) comment that respondents may feel more able to discuss historical offences or sexual fantasies, but not as willing to acknowledge current ones out of fear of their level of risk being affected. Williams, Cooper, Howell, Yuille and Paulhaus

(2009) suggested that the term sexual fantasy should include all imagined forms of sexual activities, whether they are deliberate or unintentional.

How does sexual fantasy relate to risk?

As stated, fantasy may serve a number of functions: to plan an offence, select the victim, stimulate sexual arousal, increase sexual activity, regulate the offender's mood state, escape reality, feel in control over threats and stimulate grandiosity and omnipotence (Carabellese, Maniglio, Greco & Catanesi, 2010). A large body of research has demonstrated that people who have never participated in sexually deviant behaviour are likely to engage in atypical sexual fantasies (Leitenberg & Henning, 1995). Bartels (2020) describes how sexual fantasies can be used to assess risk. Consideration is given to the terms 'deviant' (which carries negative connotations) and 'atypical', which is not as so morally laden. The term is used in the literature, but more recently thought has been given to the use of language so as not to be pejorative. In this context the terms are used to describe fantasies and behaviour which would be outside the usual accepted standards, as defined in the Oxford Dictionary.

Ryan (2004) completed a comprehensive review of men who had committed sexual offences (date rape, marital rape, gang rape, serial rape, rape–murder and homosexual rape), including sexual thoughts from a non-offender sample of college students. She stated, 'Fantasy appears to have a significant role in rape, although there is very little research on some populations (e.g., date and marital rapists)' (p. 589). Her review looked at rape myths, hyper-sexuality and sexually deviant thoughts and found that the men convicted of rape had masturbated more, used more pornography, enjoyed sex less and had higher levels of sexual preoccupation. She questioned whether a major difference between men who rape and men who do not rape is in their willingness to manage their own sexual fantasies.

Ryan (2004) also discussed 'scripts' which seem to be thought-out scenarios, plots and actors, which may serve as plans of offending. She discusses the environmental and maybe unconscious cues and suggested scenarios such as parties where there are drugs and alcohol, the victim being scantily dressed, seeing a previous sexual partner, using pornography, having a sexually explicit conversation or being in isolated places as examples of this.

Gee, Devilly and Ward (2004) noted that those who have committed offences report diverse types of fantasies at various stages of the offence chain, and they should recognise their content as a further method of assessing their emotional state and therefore a measure of current risk. So, if fantasies could be openly discussed, they could provide an indication of current sexual interest. So, it is not clear if having the fantasy is enough evidence of possible offending and whether masturbating to the fantasy increases the likelihood of offending, but masturbating, and particularly if paired with orgasm, increases arousal (Laws & O'Neil, 1981). Furthermore, Gannon, Olver, Mallion and James (2019) concluded that treatment was most effective when inappropriate sexual interest was tackled. The premise of this work is not to be judgemental of the content of the sexual fantasy, but rather to help those for whom it is a problem.

Aim and premise of the Fantasy Modification Programme

The Fantasy Modification Programme (FMP) was devised because although there is a fantasy modification programme within the Sex Offender Treatment Programmes (SOTPs), i.e. the Healthy Sexual Functioning Programme (HSFP), this is not available, as HMP Grendon is not an SOTP site. Some residents found their sexual interests, preoccupation or fantasies intruding on their ability to work effectively in therapy. Their options would be to transfer to another establishment and join a waiting list for the HSFP and to return at a later date or leave therapy. Therefore, a viable alternative was devised specifically for this setting. One major difference is that the HSFP is run on a one-to-one basis and the work at Grendon is carried out in groups. As such, residents are used to discussing their offence-related fantasies in a group setting and managing the feelings evoked. In the past they have used offence-related fantasy as a means of escaping discomfort but recognise that this is not appropriate. Therefore, the FMP was developed to teach alternative means of managing the feelings. The need for fantasy modification techniques was identified through discussion with residents. One of the underlying principles of the HSFP is that sexual arousal should be discussed alongside another intervention, and so the fantasy modification techniques are applied when the sexual arousal problems are current. Therefore, the residents can participate on the FMP whilst at Grendon and be assessed for suitability for the HSFP later in the sentence should it still be required.

The aim of this programme is to help residents manage inappropriate sexual or violent fantasies as and when they occur and to develop robust relapse prevention plans. Residents throughout Grendon are invited to apply to complete the programme, and in line with DTC principles, they seek group, wing and staff backing. Backing to participate would be dependent on risk and need.

Theory underpinning the FMP

In order to meet the standards suggested by the 'What Works' literature (Andrews & Bonta, 1998; McGuire & Priestly, 2000) for effective programme design, a programme must be based on current theory supported by empirical backing. Further, programmes which take a risk–need–responsivity (RNR) approach have been found to be the most effective (Hanson, Morton-Bourgon, Helmus & Hodgson, 2009). The programme is underpinned by seeking to enhance pro-social goals through incorporating the development of a Good Lives plan (Andrews, Bonta & Wormith, 2011; Ward & Stewart, 2003a) and thus reduce risk. The Good Lives model indicates that all people strive for goals, but that those who have offended could have sought these through ineffective means, i.e. sexual violence. As such, there needs to be a treatment plan to account for individual strengths and necessary resources to achieve these goods. The application of the model to fantasy modification was described by Akerman (2005). That paper described how Good Life goals were developed alongside teaching fantasy modification techniques so that the need satisfied by fantasy was met through pro-social goals. The FMP is based on the risk, need, and responsivity principles and designed to be applied when a treatment need is identified. It was piloted on one wing with men who had volunteered to participate. It has since been run with further groups as and when required.

There are a number of theories and models underpinning the FMP. In short, these include the following.

The Good Lives Model (GLM)

The GLM posits the need to teach participants to strive for approach-focused goals and add to their skills, rather than remove a problem, leaving what Ward and Stewart (2003a) described as a 'pinhole'. The DTC works on a holistic strengths-based model, as suggested by Ward and Mann (2004), and so the FMP dovetails with this approach. The FMP considers the role sex has in the wheel of needs as highlighted by the GLM. It considers how sex can be used to serve a number of purposes, such as soothing emotion, relieving tension, a distraction from difficulties and so forth. So, the FMP aims to suggest alternative ways to manage these so that sex can hold a more proportionate role in functioning. Mahendren and Wilson (2015) found that research suggests that treatment focused on the attainment of 'good lives' can be more effective than treatment focusing exclusively on managing risk for reoffending. Although there have been some tensions between the use of the R-N-R and GL models (see Andrews et al., 2011; Ward & Stewart, 2003a), the FMP incorporates elements of each.

Therapeutic alliance

Working collaboratively with residents is vital to ensure that the goals they are striving for are individual and relevant to them. The FMP develops the treatment alliance in order to enable discussion on some personal and intimate issues. Marshall et al. (2005) highlight the importance of the therapeutic alliance to develop self-efficacy, self-esteem and enhance hope. Akerman (2010) along with others (Marshall & Burton, 2010; Marshall, Marshall, Geris & O'Brien, 2011) describes how developing a treatment alliance with those who have committed sexual offences is not always easy due to the emotions evoked by the actions. Within the therapy, therapist style is very important (see Levenson & Willis, 2017; Marshall et al., 2003; Shingler & Mann, 2006). Recognising that the client is seeking alternatives to offending helps the therapist to reduce the tension they feel by viewing them as someone who has committed a serious offence and one who wants to change. Ackerman and Hilsenroth (2003) discuss a range of studies looking at therapist style and found that the therapist should demonstrate that they are working together with the client. The authors found that the therapeutic alliance was developed and enhanced through referring to common ground, something which may not be as straightforward in this particular area of work. The therapist may find it difficult to show this when it comes to understanding deviant sexual fantasy and arousal and so should work through these issues in supervision. The therapist should feel confident undertaking this work and have a thorough understanding of the role of fantasy so that they can feel able to be non-judgmental and empathic towards the client. Levenson and Willis (2017) emphasise the need to be aware of the trauma which the participants could have previously experienced and how this may affect the therapeutic alliance. Therefore, it is vital for supervision to be used to manage this. Rogers (1957) highlighted that the therapist needs to display warmth, empathy and genuineness, while later, Yalom (1980) described how the relationship between the resident and therapist could provide a healing power, and so this is an integral part of the programme. Therefore, this is considered throughout the FMP.

Positive Psychology

The position adopted by Positive Psychology (see for instance Seligman, 2002) is one which emanates from HMP Grendon and the FMP. In practice, it is evidenced by encouraging the premise that we should build on strengths: 'amplify client's strengths rather than repair weaknesses' (Seligman, 2002, p. 5). Therefore, consideration is given to what the participant has been good at and how this can be used in the future. Mahendren and Wilson (2015) found that those with increased protective strengths (as measured by the Inventory of Offender Risk, Needs, and Strengths) were found to be significantly associated with decreased levels of general, violent and sexual recidivism.

Developing self-management plans

Developing a sense of autonomy through having a range of alternative responses and behavioural techniques available (Serran, Firestone, Moulden & Marshall, 2007) is vital for self-actualisation. The plans are developed collaboratively with goals which are SMART (specific, measurable, achievable, realistic and time-bound) and include the views of others involved in treatment. The setting of goals helps overcome the previous chaotic lifestyle which may have been present leading up to offending and provides alternative areas for consideration other than sex.

Developing healthy relationship skills

Alongside those developed in therapy at HMP Grendon, the FMP provides the opportunity to practice expression of emotion and conflict handling, as difficulties in these areas can lead to an increase in the use of sexual thoughts as a means of coping. The difficulties integral to talking about intimate subjects is acknowledged throughout, and residents are encouraged to develop their relationship with treatment providers so they can do so in the future. Day-to-day difficulties encountered can be reframed through the use of role-play, consideration of alternative thinking, developing perspective-taking skills and challenging offence-related thoughts and beliefs. This is done alongside developing more acceptable alternatives. There is understanding that the participants may well continue to experience and miss the atypical sexual fantasies, but prefer the pleasure received from a satisfying intimate relationship. Much thought is given as to how such a relationship can be developed, while acknowledging the limitations in custody.

Using role-play and active challenging of offence-supportive thoughts can be effective to develop alternative viewpoints (Fernandez, Shingler & Marshall, 2005). The FMP uses a range of treatment methods (described in more detail later) to help develop the participants' ability to consider how others may view their actions, and by putting themselves in the shoes of the other person, can see their perspective. This helps to develop a wider range of options from which to choose and slow thinking down to enable more sound decision-making.

Programme design and content

The programme is cognitive-behavioural in basis and uses a range of techniques to convey learning points. These include:

- Motivational techniques such as summaries, reflections and affirmations (Levenson & Willis, 2017; Marshall et al., 2006; Prescott & Wilson, 2013). As Levenson and Willis highlight, many of those who have developed the use of sexual thoughts and actions as a means of coping have experienced previous trauma. This could be in their formative years, adolescence and from their own offending. Therefore, it is important to support the disclosure of material, which can be shameful and powerful for those participating, in a motivational manner.
- Socratic questioning is found to be effective to help participants make their own discovery.
- Group discussion leading to cognitive restructuring (practising the use of replacement thoughts and behaviours).
- Rehearsal (to consolidate learning), and this can be practised through role-play.

Motivational enhancement and group cohesion are central features of the initial sessions along with introduction of the GLM, with each participant applying it to current and future goals. There is discussion about what goods (in terms of Ward and Stewart, 2003b) are achieved through fantasy, e.g. physical satisfaction (health), intimacy (intimacy), emotion regulation (inner peace) and how else they could be achieved. Each participant identifies what they have gained from fantasy and how these needs could be met in pro-social ways. There is recognition that it is easier to manage this arousal in the context of a prison than in the real world, and plans were made to revisit this work with offender managers as they prepare for release.

Marshall, O'Brien and Marshall (2009) discuss some of the problems inherent in modifying sexual preferences but conclude that while it is not easy, it is possible. Drawing on Skinner's (1938) operant conditioning model, which suggests that extinction of a previously frequent behaviour is possible when the behaviour is replaced by another which produces greater rewards, a range of fantasy modification techniques are taught. Although the techniques can be described as behavioural, they also rely heavily on cognitive and emotional elements. The techniques include those which are aversive (pairing inappropriate sexual images with aversive experiences) or through associating appropriate sexual images with reward, such as masturbation.

Directed masturbation

This is described by Marshall, Marshall, Serran and Fernandez (2006) as pairing arousal with appropriate images, with masturbation thus reinforcing their excitement. The participant is encouraged to become aroused thinking of any image, but only reinforce appropriate arousal through masturbation.

A further technique is **covert association** (Marshall et al., 2009), which pairs personally aversive consequences (such as being in prison, creating more victims or being publicly humiliated) with each step of an offence-related fantasy. Marshall et al. (2006, p. 66) explain that pairing a stimulus and response will mean that when the stimulus is presented, the response will become automatic over time. Pocket-sized cards are used, each one depicting a step towards the behaviour being modified, for instance, approaching a child, with the other side of the card depicting a meaningful negative consequence for the individual. This may include getting caught in the act by a significant person, being exposed in the newspapers, appearing in court and so forth. The group members are instructed to look at these cards on a regular basis during each day, initially at the end point of the problematic behaviour and over time moving back to earlier in the sequence (for instance, when contemplating starting the cycle). McGrath, Cumming and Burchard (2003) found covert association the most effective procedure for modifying inappropriate sexual interests.

Another technique presented is **satiation**. That is, associating offence-related fantasies with boredom based on the principle that repeatedly evoking a currently attractive behaviour means it loses its valence. It must be undertaken during the refractory period, within a few minutes of orgasm, when it is not possible to become aroused again (Masters, Johnson & Kolodny, 1985). This period lasts for less than twenty minutes after orgasm, and it can prove difficult to continue to masturbate at this time, when arousal is unlikely, and so the participant can instead verbalise the behaviour they wish to extinguish aloud. This would not always be possible within a secure setting. Johnston, Hudson and Marshall (1992) recommend the use of directed masturbation followed by satiation, which demonstrated the most efficacy, which they assessed using pre- and post-phallometric assessments.

In addition, the principle of **urge surfing** or **distress tolerance** is considered. This involves remaining in a state of arousal without reinforcing it through masturbation, with the knowledge that the urge will pass in a few minutes. Distraction techniques can be used as a means of helping to tolerate the emotions. Finally, thought stoppers employed as means of managing arousal are also discussed and practised. These should be words or images, which are sufficient to interrupt the excitement of the fantasy and find an alternative thought and behaviour.

In addition to the specific techniques presented earlier, the following principles are discussed:

- The role of sexual preoccupation and using sex as a coping strategy and alternative strategies devised.
- Enhancing understanding of the victims' perspective through the use of discussion and role-play, with thought to how this would enhance relationships with others, knowledge and emotion regulation (inner peace).
- Role-play is used to explore the impact of current fantasy (sexual or violent) on a potential victim and to generate and practice alternative thinking and behaviour.
- Challenging offence-supportive thoughts and beliefs, such as '*I'm not hurting anyone*', by placing themselves in the position of a potential victim helped participants to develop perspective-taking skills.
- Developing intimacy and emotion regulation skills (Harris, 2000) (to enhance inner peace and healthy thoughts) and a rich emotional vocabulary. The participants had the opportunity to practise expressing emotions such as jealousy and anger and recognising the ability to manage their own emotions, thus increasing self-efficacy.
- There was discussion of potentially risky situations in the future, rating them as green (slight risk), amber (raised risk) and red (imminent risk) and how they could cope at each stage.
- In line with DTC principles, the on-going work can be integrated to individual treatment targets and progress monitored through therapy.

Marshall et al.1 (2009) explain that there is not a compelling evidence base for the efficacy of the techniques, and one of the factors of this is having a method through which to assess change. This will be discussed further next.

The FMP in practice

The programme was evaluated through feedback from the participants in the absence of a more objective measure. As the programme was undertaken as part of ongoing therapy, it was not possible to evaluate it as a stand-alone intervention, but this is the basis of further research. The feedback was that the intervention was useful in helping participants to understand and manage their offence-related arousal. At the end of each session, participants were given an evaluation sheet, which helped to ascertain the usefulness of the intervention. This feedback was collated at the end of each programme and considered when running the next one. One limitation of this method is that the feedback was given during the programme. It would be useful to collect further feedback following completion and when the techniques have had time to be used regularly. The participants may have a different perception of the programme some months after its completion. As stated previously, participants were drawn from throughout the establishment, and so they did not necessarily know each other. Those who were located on the wing for men who had committed sexual offences spoke of feeling more used to speaking in detail about their sexual interests and fantasies, whereas those on mixed wings were less so. Those more able to discuss their sexuality helped others to do so. With peers, it was easier to introduce the subjects, rather than just with a female facilitator.

Participants also used diaries to assess their progress in managing arousal. The diaries were useful for the participants to recognise times at which they were aroused (for instance, early in the morning) or in which mood (for instance, when bored or angry). The behaviour techniques were explained at the start of the programme and their use evaluated in each session. Each participant used the technique that worked best for them, and here is a brief qualitative summary of some of the findings; however, all of this will be on-going work, given the length of the programme.

Evaluation of the programme

While considering means of evaluating the programme, a literature review of the current measures of sexual interest was completed (Akerman & Beech, 2011) and the need for a psychometric measure was identified. The Current Sexual Interest Measure (CSIM, Akerman, 2015) was developed through discussion with residents in two prisons and a probation hostel with men serving their sentence in a community in Texas in the United States, using focus groups, and experienced practitioners and academics using the Delphi method. The data were collected and analysed using principal components analysis, with factors relating to sexual preoccupation, sexual interest in others, sexual arousal with hurting others and disinterest in deviant sex. The CSIM showed good concurrent validity in relation to comparison with My Private Interests (Williams, 2005) and The Multiphasic Sex Inventory (Nichols & Molinder, 2000) and was shown to have reliable findings through test/retest assessment (Akerman, 2012). Given the diversity within sexual interests, it is not possible to include items to cover the full range, but it is hoped that the measure will provide an opportunity to discuss this intimate subject. The measure was also administered via computer to a group of students to ascertain whether the sexual interests described were more diverse with people in the community as compared to those who had committed sexual offences. In order to make the measure more indicative of a range of sexual interests, items relating to more mainstream interests were added, and items pertaining to sexual activities available to those outside of custody were also added (such as use of internet pornography). For the student sample, an item relating to sexual thoughts about a previous victim was removed. The measure has proved useful to provide a platform for discussing sexual interests in a more open manner, but as it was designed to assess sexual interests in the past six months, it would need to be used for longer periods after the programme to assess change. Through analysis, a measure for use with those in custody and one for those in the community were developed.

To develop a more objective measure, the Sexual Offence Paralleling Behaviour Checklist (SOPBC, Akerman & Beech, 2013) was devised. This checklist is based on empirically developed risk factors (Mann, Hanson & Thornton, 2010), which could be evident to staff within a custodial setting. SOPB evident in the therapeutic community (TC) was linked to that known to be psychologically meaningful, as identified by Mann et al. (2010). This checklist can be used to help inform treatment and enable discussion of behaviour related to risk.

Case examples

Mr W was highly sexually preoccupied in the time leading up to his offending and held hostile, offence-supportive attitudes towards women, having been sexually abused by a female. Earlier in his time in the TC he spoke about sex frequently, using banter and telling sexual jokes. He possessed a great deal of pornography and produced drawings of a previous sexual partner in a sexual pose and having objects placed inside her. These images were discussed in his therapy as examples of current sexual interest. Following the FMP he reported how he had developed his understanding of what had led to offend in the way he did and the function of his sexual preoccupation as a means of defending against negative mood states. He used covert association and found it beneficial. He practised urge surfing too, rather than masturbating, whenever he felt the need to do so, first analysing his own emotional state. His understanding was that described by Kahr (2007): he had used sex as a means of managing feeling powerless when being sexually abused. He had placed himself in the position of power and incorporated what had been done to him into his fantasies, with himself in control. The staff commented on his SOPBC that there was a reduction in his bringing sex into conversations and his preoccupation with the adult magazine he purchased monthly.

Mr X described committing rape when he felt angry and belittled. He offended against his partner and on another occasion against a woman who was slightly known by him. In the TC, he had rubbed his genitals through his pocket in an education class when he felt belittled by the female tutor. Further, he became angry when challenged by a female member of the staff and purposefully rubbed against her. He was able to recognise many deficits in his relationship skills through the use of role-play, which he found particularly useful. Being in the position of the other person helped him to internalise the thoughts and feelings other people may have. He could understand the impact on the tutor having experienced how she may have felt through role reversal. Although he stated he practised the techniques, it was not clear how much he actually did so or how much had changed in his sexual life. Staff were not able to detect a difference in his behaviour over time.

Mr Y had committed rape against his partner, having previously committed other violent offences. He developed his understanding of how sex had become important to him and how he had used it within relationships as a form of control. This was the first opportunity he had to discuss sexual practices, such as masturbation, and recognise why he used them in the way he did. He had not previously understood the extent to which he had used it to relieve tension and for self-soothing. In therapy he had concentrated on his violent offending, finding it more socially acceptable to talk about that rather than his sexual offending. When the programme was fed back to his group and community, in line with TC principles, his group were more able to understand his motivation for using sex in his offence rather than violence. It also increased discussion within the groups as to the extent to which they had used sex as a way of controlling their partners. Mr. Y had found the reduction of his need to masturbate every time he had a sexual thought helpful and liberating and considered the amount of time he had wasted in that way. He was able to recognise the role sex had played in his life and practised urge surfing and distraction techniques.

Mr Z committed several sexual offences soon after release from another sentence. He describes feeling sexually preoccupied and using sexual fantasy as a way of coping. He had also exposed himself to female staff. Initially he denied having exposed himself or recognise how this impacted on his risk, but over time he was able to see why he had carried out this behaviour. In addition to covert association he found it useful to have an elastic band on his wrist, which he flicked if he found himself drifting into sexual fantasy. This brought him back to reality and allowed him to analyse his emotional state and current thoughts. His OPB had been evident prior to the programme (exposing himself and increased sexual preoccupation) but was less so six months after the programme when the SOPBC was repeated by staff.

Discussion

The programme was developed in line with research into group process and managing arousal that was deemed to be problematic to the resident concerned. The lack of space precludes a full description of its inception, but this can be found in Akerman (2008). One major drawback of the programme was the lack of an objective measure of arousal prior to and following the programme, and this is the subject of further research. The programme is planned so that it can be flexible to the needs of its participants and used to help them address an identified treatment need.

Generally, fantasy modification work relies on self-report to assess its effectiveness, but in order to confidently link this to a reduction in risk, a more objective measure would be required. Possible measures include phallometry or psychometric measures. However, research (e.g. Marshall et al., 2006) highlights that such arousal is thought to be trait based. For instance, fantasy and offending happening within the context of drugs and/or alcohol use and numerous other dispositional and situational issues, so 'it seems likely that measuring their sexual preferences when they are calm and sober will tell us little about their offence related sexual desires' (p. 88).

The participants in the programme reported an increased understanding of the role of sexual interests and fantasy and the ability to manage inappropriate fantasies and the desire to do so, but clearly on-going monitoring will be required. It is clear that some are practising the techniques more than others, and like any effort to change a long-held habit, it requires self-determination. Just as giving up smoking or increasing physical activity in order to get fit relies on a level of motivation to continue, this is also the case in changing sexual arousal patterns. They can be very entrenched, familiar and comforting, and so the motivation to change needs to be intrinsic and consistent. Each participant recognised the amount of time they had spent fantasising and how this enabled them to escape reality. They considered how that time could have been spent more productively and were beginning to do this. Having alternative strategies reportedly helped them to feel more in control of their own thoughts, feelings and fantasies as the programme progressed. As this programme is designed to run within the context of on-going treatment, evaluating it as a stand-alone intervention is problematic but will be subject to continual evaluation. One such measure could be the use of the Inventory of Offender Risk, Needs, and Strengths (Mahendren & Wilson, 2015) alongside the CSIM and SOPBC.

Limitations

The programme is evolving in line with research, and so future sessions on mindfulness will be included as a means of relieving anxiety and in consideration of the difficulty speaking about such issues for the first time and to female facilitators. Mindfulness is known to help counter the alarm system and develop the sense of safety, thus countering induction of trauma memories. Gilbert (2010) encourages the use of compassion-focussed therapy to soothe breathing and use the safe place technique to keep in mind a place where they feel safe and calm. In line with Levenson and Willis' (2017) recommendation of the importance of considering how previous trauma is evoked in sessions, to enhance their efficacy, every effort will be made to provide a safe and secure environment.

It is noted that the research on the CSIM and SOPBC is limited, although they are being used in a number of settings at present. With such limited research they cannot be used to inform risk assessment, but rather to enhance treatment. There would also need to be an objective evaluation of the programme. There is limited research into the efficacy of the behaviour modification techniques, and so this is also an area of future consideration.

References

Ackerman, S. J., & Hilsenroth, M. J. (2003). A review of therapist characteristics and techniques positively impacting on the therapeutic alliance. *Clinical Psychology Review*, *23*, 1–33.

Akerman, G. (2005). Applying fantasy modification techniques in line with the Good Lives model with learning disability as a confounding factor: A case study. *Nota News*, *49*, 12–14.

Akerman, G. (2008). The development of a fantasy modification programme for a prison based therapeutic community. *International Journal of Therapeutic Communities*, *29*, 180–188.

Akerman, G. (2010). Undertaking therapy at HMP Grendon with men who have committed sexual offences. In E. Sullivan & R. Shuker (Eds.), *Grendon and the emergence of forensic therapeutic communities: Developments in research and practice* (pp. 171–182). Wiley.

Akerman, G. (2012). *Sexual offence paralleling behaviour in secure conditions and how it relates to risk*. Paper presented at the 21st Annual DFP Conference, Cardiff Metropolitan University, 26–28th June 2012.

Akerman, G. (2015). *The development and validation of a psychometric measure of current sexual interest*. Thesis submitted to the University of Birmingham for a degree of Doctor of Philosophy. Retrieved from http://etheses.bham.ac.uk/5744

Akerman, G. (2019). Communal living as the agent of change. In D. Polaschek, A. Day, & C. Hollin (Eds.), *The Wiley international handbook of correctional psychology* (Chapter 37). Wiley Blackwell.

Akerman, G., & Beech A. R. (2011). A systematic review of measures of deviant sexual interest and arousal. *Psychiatry, Psychology and Law*, *19*, 118–143.

Akerman, G., & Beech, A. R. (2013). Exploring offence paralleling behaviours in incarcerated offenders. In J. Fuhrmann & S. Baier (Eds.), *Prisons and prison systems: Practices, types and challenges* (pp. 1–24). Nova Publishers. ISBN: 978-1-62417-850-4

Akerman, G., & Jamieson, S. (2020). Working in therapy with men who have committed a sexual offence and have learning difficulties. In *Sexual Crime and Intellectual Functioning* (pp. 113–130). Palgrave Macmillan, Cham.

Akerman, G., & Mandikate, P. (2018). Creating a therapeutic community from scratch: Where do we start? In R. Shuker & G. Akerman (Series Ed.), G. Akerman, A. Needs, & C. Bainbridge (Eds.), *Transforming environments, transforming lives: Understanding and harnessing contextual factors in the rehabilitation of offenders* (pp. 163–178). Taylor & Francis Group.

Akerman, G., Perkins, D., & Bartels, R. (Eds.). (2020). *Assessing and managing problematic sexual interests: A practitioner's guide*. Routledge.

Andrews, D., & Bonta, J. (1998). *The psychology of criminal conduct* (2nd ed.). Anderson Publishing.

Andrews, D., Bonta, J., & Wormith, S. (2011). The Risk-Need-Responsivity (RNR) model: Does adding the Good Lives model contribute to effective crime prevention? *Criminal Justice and Behavior, 38*, 735–755. doi:10.1177/0093854811406356

Bartels, R. M. (2020). Sexual fantasy use as a proxy for assessing deviant sexual interest. (115–129). In G. Akerman, D. Perkins, & R. Bartels (Eds.), *Assessing and managing problematic sexual interests: A practitioner's guide* (pp. 115–129). Routledge.

Carabellese, F., Maniglio, R., Greco, O., & Catanesi, R. (2010). The role of fantasy in a serial sexual offender: A brief review of the literature and a case report. *Journal of Forensic Sciences, 56*, 256–269. doi:10.1111/j.1556–4029.2010.01536.x

Fernandez, Y., Shingler, J., & Marshall, W. L. (2005). Putting "behaviour'" back into the cognitive behavioural treatment of sexual offenders. In W. L. Marshall, L. E. Marshall, & G. A. Serran (Eds.), *Sexual offender treatment: Controversial issues* (pp. 221–224). John Wiley & Sons.

Flak, V. E., Beech, A. R., & Fisher, D. (2007). Forensic assessment of sexual interest: The current position. *Issues in Forensic Psychology, 6*, 70–83.

Gannon, T. A., Olver, M. E., Mallion, J. S., & James, M. (2019). Does specialized psychological treatment for offending reduce recidivism? A meta-analysis examining staff and program variables as predictors of treatment effectiveness. *Clinical Psychology Review, 73*, 101752.

Gee, D. G., Devilly, G. J., & Ward, T. (2004). The content of sexual fantasies for sexual offenders. *Sexual Abuse: A Journal of Research and Treatment, 16*, 315–334.

Genders, E., & Player, E. (1995). *Grendon: A study of a therapeutic prison*. Oxford University Press. ISBN-13: 978–0198256779

Gilbert, P. (2010). *Compassion focussed therapy: Distinctive features*. Routledge.

Hanson, R. K., & Bussière, M. T. (1998). Predicting relapse: A meta-analysis of sexual offender recidivism studies. *Journal of Consulting and Clinical Psychology, 66*, 348–362. doi:10.1037/0022–006X.66.2.348

Hanson, R. K., & Morton-Bourgon, K. E. (2004). *Predictors of sexual recidivism: An updated meta-analysis* (Research Rep. No. 2004–02). Public Safety and Emergency Preparedness Canada.

Hanson, R. K., Morton-Bourgon, K. E., Helmus, L., & Hodgson, S. (2009). The principles of effective correctional treatment also apply to sexual offenders: A meta-analysis. *Criminal Justice and Behaviour, 36*, 865–891. doi:10.1177/0093854809338545

Harris, P. (2000). Understanding emotion. In M. Lewis & J. M. Haviland-Jones (Eds.), *Handbook of emotions* (2nd ed., pp. 281–292). Guildford Press.

Johnston, P., Hudson, S. M., & Marshall, W. L. (1992). The effects of masturbatory reconditioning with non-familial child molesters. *Behavior, Research and Therapy, 5*, 559–561.

Jones, L. F. (2004). Offence Paralleling Behaviour (OPB) as a framework for assessment and interventions with offenders. In A. Needs & G. Towl (Eds.), *Applying psychology to forensic practice* (pp. 34–63). Blackwell.

Kahr, B. (2007). *Sex and the psyche: The truth about our most secret fantasies*. Penguin. ISBN: 978-0-141-02484-4

Laws, D. R., & O'Neil, J. A. (1981). Variations on masturbatory conditioning. *Behavioural Psychotherapy, 9*, 111–136. doi:10.1017/S014134730000731X

Leitenberg, H., & Henning, K. (1995). Sexual fantasy. *Psychological Bulletin, 3*, 469–496. doi:10.1037/0033–2909.117.3.469

Levenson, J. S., & Willis, G. M. (2017). *Trauma informed care: Transforming treatment for people who have sexually abused*. Safer Society Press.

Mahendren, M., & Wilson, M. G. (2015). Rapid synthesis: Changing sexual offender behaviour and assessing risk for reoffending. McMaster Health Forum.

Mann, R. E., Hanson, R. K., & Thornton, D. (2010). Assessing risk for sexual recidivism: Some proposals on the nature of psychologically meaningful risk factors. *Sexual Abuse: A Journal of Research and Treatment, 22*, 191–217. doi:10.1177/1079063210366039

Marshall, W., & Burton, D. (2010). The importance of group processes in offender treatment. *Aggression and Violent Behavior, 15*, 141–149.

Marshall, W. L., Marshall, L. E., Geris, S., & O'Brien, M. (2011). *Rehabilitating sexual offenders: A strengths-based approach*. American Psychological Association.

Marshall, W. L., Marshall, L. E., Serran, G. A., & Fernandez, Y. M. (2006). *Treating sexual offenders: An integrated approach*. Routledge.

Marshall, W. L., O'Brien, M. D., & Marshall, L. (2009). Modifying sexual preferences. In A. R. Beech, L. A. Craig, & K. D. Browne (Eds.), *Assessment and treatment of sex offenders: A handbook*. Wiley.

Marshall, W. L., Serran, G. A., Fernandez, W. M., Mulloy, R., Mann, R. E., & Thornton, D. (2003). Therapist characteristics in the treatment of sexual offenders: Tentative data on their relationship with indices of behaviour change. *Journal of Sexual Aggression, 9*, 25–30.

Marshall, W., Ward, T., Mann, R. E., Moulden, H., Fernandez, Y. M., Serran, G., & Marshall, L. E. (2005). Working positively with sexual offenders: Maximizing the effectiveness of treatment. *Journal of Interpersonal Violence, 20*(9), 1096–1114.

Masters, W. H., Johnson, V. E., & Kolodny, R. C. (1985). *Human sexuality* (2nd ed.). Little, Brown.

McGrath, R. J., Cumming, G. F., & Burchard, B. L. (2003). *Current practices and trends in sexual abuser management: The Safer Society 2002 Nationwide Survey.* Safer Society Press.

McGuire, J., & Priestly, P. (2000). Reviewing what works: Past, present and future. In J. McGuire (Ed.), *What works: Reducing reoffending, guidelines from research and practice.* John Wiley & Sons.

Nichols, H. R., & Molinder, I. (2000). *Multiphasic sexual inventory II* (version 2). Available from Nichols and Molinder, 437 Bowes Drive, Tacoma, WA, 98466, USA.

Prescott, D. S., & Wilson, R. (2013). *Awakening motivation for difficult changes.* Neari Press.

Rogers, C. (1957). The necessary and sufficient conditions of therapeutic personality change. *Journal of Consulting Psychology, 21*, 95–113.

Ryan, K. M. (2004). Further evidence for a cognitive component of rape. *Aggression and Violent Behavior, 9*, 579–604.

Seligman, M. E. P. (2002). Positive psychology, positive prevention and positive therapy. In C. R. Snyder & S. L. Lopez (Eds.), *Handbook of positive psychology* (pp. 3–9). Oxford University Press.

Serran, G., Firestone, P., Moulden, H., & Marshall, W. (2007). Changes in coping following treatment for child molesters. *Journal of Interpersonal Violence, 22*, 1199–1210.

Shine, J., & Morris, M. (2000). Addressing criminogenic needs in a prison therapeutic community. *Therapeutic Communities, 21*, 197–218.

Shingler, J., & Mann, R. E. (2006). Collaboration in clinical work with sexual offenders: Treatment and risk assessment. In W. L. Marshall, W. M. Fernandez, L. E. Marshall, & G. A. Serran (Eds.), *Sexual offender treatment: Controversial issues* (pp. 225–239). Wiley.

Shuker, R., & Sullivan, E. (2010). *Grendon and the emergence of forensic therapeutic communities: Developments in research and practice.* Wiley-Blackwell. ISBN: 978-0-470-99055

Skinner, B. F. (1938). *The behaviour of organisms: An experimental analysis.* Appleton-Century.

Stinson, J. D., & Becker, J. V. (2008). Assessing sexual deviance: A comparison of physiological, historical, and self-report measures. *Journal of Psychiatric Practice, 14*, 379–388. doi:10.1097/01.pra.0000341892.51124.85

Ward, T., & Mann, R. E. (2004). Good lives and the rehabilitation of offenders: A positive approach to sex offender treatment. In P. A. Linley & S. Joseph (Eds.), *Positive psychology in practice* (pp. 598–616). John Wiley & Sons.

Ward, T., & Stewart, C. A. (2003a). The treatment of sex offenders: Risk management and Good Lives. *Professional Psychology Research and Practice, 34*, 353–360.

Ward, T., & Stewart, C. A. (2003b). Criminogenic needs and human needs: A theoretical model. *Psychology Crime and Law, 9*, 125–143.

Williams, F. (2005). *My private interest measure.* Unpublished manuscript. Available from Reducing Re-offending Policy Group, HM Prison Service, Room 128, Abell House, John Islip Street, London SW1P 2AW.

Williams, K. M., Cooper, B. S., Howell, T. M., Yuille, J. C., & Paulhaus, D. L. (2009). Inferring deviant behavior from corresponding fantasies: The role of personality and pornography consumption. *Criminal Justice and Behavior, 36*, 198–222. doi:10.1177/0093854808327277

Yalom, I. (1980). *Existential psychotherapy.* Basic Books.

Geraldine Akerman is the Therapy Manager of the Enhanced Assessment Unit at HMP Grendon.

4
Boundaries and boundary setting in clinical practice

Laura Hamilton and Lee Bacon

Introduction

Balancing the dialectic tension between care (treatment) and control (security) is the essence of forensic rehabilitation (Hamilton, 2010; Stowell-Smith, 2006). Security is focused on protection of the public, seeking to ensure that patients do not escape or abscond (Tilt et al., 2000). But security is not an end in itself; rather, "the most effective form of security and, indeed, safety lies in the treatment of the patient" (Reed Report, 1994 cited in Exworthy & Gunn, 2003, p. 469). Security in all its facets provides external controls, creating a safe space for treatment to happen, with therapy ultimately aiming to help the service user develop internal mechanisms which reduce their risk of re-offending and enhance mental well-being. Security and treatment are therefore compatible and inter-related interventions which form the bedrock for forensic rehabilitation. The ultimate goal should be for both security and treatment interventions to become redundant in the service user's life – they are ideally friends for a season, facilitating the transition of self-regulation from external sources to internal resources. However, for those with indeterminant sentences, like life sentences or indeterminant sentences for public protection, supervision/security will be in their life forever.

The concept of security in forensic services has been considered extensively, with the security triad a widely adopted boundary set (Tilt et al., 2000; Kennedy, 2002; Collins & Davies, 2005). The security triad is posited to involve physical (environmental), procedural and relational (dynamic) components, but these are not separate entities and instead an indivisible whole (Exworthy & Gunn, 2003). Typically, monetary resources and energy have been heavily invested in

DOI: 10.4324/9780429262074-4

developing tangible structures (physical/environmental security) and secure procedures to keep those deemed dangerous detained and separate from the public (Department of Health, 2010; Classified National Security Framework, no date). Relational security has, however, been largely ignored and often treated as an operational aside. For example, Tilt et al.'s (2000) supposedly comprehensive review of security in high-secure forensic hospitals made 48 recommendations and only one of these eluded to relational security. Failure to consider the relational component weakens security overall and runs the risk of falling into the trap by which "dangerous patients can be managed economically in extremis by confining them to their rooms, but no therapeutic progress will then be achieved" (Kennedy, 2002, p. 437).

More recently there have been attempts to redress this imbalance, with research and commentary confirming relational security is a complex, multi-faceted and dynamic phenomena (Allen, 2010; Chester, Alexander & Morgan, 2017; Skopje, 2018; Tighe & Gudjonsson, 2012). Hamilton (2010) indirectly addresses the relational security question by focusing on the common factors which connect security and treatment interventions, coining the term relational boundaries to denote processes involved in creating a safe space for forensic rehabilitation. Hamilton's (2010) work on relational boundaries in a forensic psychiatric hospital illuminated relational security and boundary management in action. The applied notion that relational security and boundary management is about "singing from the same hymn sheet" was denounced. Instead, a dynamic model of consistent boundary management is offered, where consistency refers to consistency of process, not outcome. Relational boundary management can neither be quantified accurately nor every event legislated for; rather, it is attachment and relational work occurring within a complex and dynamic systemic structure.

Regardless of theoretical or professional orientation, boundaries and their management play a crucial role in any forensic or non-forensic intervention (Gutheil & Gabbard, 1993). Given the importance of boundaries, it is surprising just how frequently even the most obvious professional standards are breached. For example, Halter, Brown and Stone's (2007) literature review of professional sexual misconduct found that 3% to 10% of healthcare professionals reported sexual contact with a current or former patient. These breaches of boundaries have far-reaching consequences for patients, staff and organisations and fundamentally society's trust in forensic services and interventions to protect the public. Despite the importance of boundaries in forensic interventions, surprisingly little attention has been given to the conceptual unit of a boundary. It remains poorly defined; is used interchangeably with the term limit; and is preceded by an array of terms, such as therapeutic, professional, ego, personal, physical, relational, treatment, intrapsychic, interpersonal, behavioural, spatial, verbal, somatic, logistical and energetic (Blundell, 2017; Goldberg, 2008). This chapter aims to stimulate a movement towards conceptual precision and offers a theoretical standpoint to underpin the boundary seesaw model which is widely used in training programmes, clinical supervision and reflective practice (Carradice, 2016; Institute of Mental Health, 2013). Firstly, an ontological position on boundaries will be offered, which draws upon philosophical, psychological and geographic boundary studies. Next the nature of human boundaries will be explored and an argument put forward for a systems-based approach. Finally, these ideas will be applied to a practice context with a view to offering a more parsimonious lexicon for boundaries and ideas about future applications of boundary theory and techniques.

Ontology of boundaries

Varzi (2013) identified four major areas of philosophical concern in boundary ontology:

1   Are boundaries real or mere mental abstractions?
2   How sharp or vague is the endpoint of a boundary?
3   Who owns the boundary, or are they continuous, constantly contracting and expanding between or within people?
4   How many dimensions does a boundary have, which Varzi (2013) calls bodiless vs. bulky boundaries?

Each of these ontological boundary concerns will be considered and a position offered.

Are boundaries real?

Whether boundaries are real or mere mental abstractions has not been explored extensively in psychological boundary studies, but there is a substantial corpus of geographic and philosophical work that may guide our thinking on this matter. Smith (1997) defines real (bona fide) boundaries as those which exist without human judgment confirming its existence, and it can be unambiguously separated from things around it. Smith's (1997) philosophical analysis of boundaries reveals there are no true bona fide boundaries, and those apparently *real*, naturally occurring boundaries dissolve into shades of grey, as human intervention is required to define their edges and shape. For example, how do we know where the sea meets the airspace, land and seabed, and at what point do we decide the material is sea as opposed to air or land (Robinson, 2012; Galton, 2007)? These questions require cognitive processes and evaluative judgments, and these may differ from person to person depending upon their unique perspective. Smith (1997) argues therefore that all boundaries are fiat, as they exist and are sustained in existence only because of certain cognitive acts, practices or institutions. Security and therapeutic boundaries are personified by Smith's definition of fiat boundaries. They are never absolute or real, as they cannot exist separately from us – they are part of us, inventions of our minds which we choose to take seriously. This does not mean we should give up on the boundary concept as it is unknowable; rather, it is argued later that maybe we need to adopt a more systemic approach to understanding boundaries. It also does not negate the fact that despite boundaries being fiat, they can still have very real effects on people's lives.

Do boundaries have an endpoint?

A common starting point for defining a person's boundaries is often where the body ends and what distinguishes between that which belongs to the body and that which belongs to others or the world (Abrahamsson & Simpson, 2011). The idea that the body and its skin is a definitive endpoint of a person presupposes that the body can fully enclose that which belongs to us and separate that which belongs to others. It also presupposes that the skin is the definitive edge of a person, an absolute dividing line separating inside and outside.

To focus solely on the physical attributes of an individual as the defining features of a person's boundaries denies the complexity of personhood and implies there are some absolute human boundaries. Complex system theory explicates this point, stating that humans do not have a clearly defined endpoint; rather, parts of them are embedded in others or within groups or wider society (Heylighen, Cilliers & Gershenson, 2007). The boundary of a person is not just their body and skin. Components of their matter, energy and information live within other humans creating a network of relations. For example, ideas, memories, stories and phrases provided by others can become stored within us and become part of our boundary processes and narrative. An individual's boundaries are so clearly interconnected with internal, relational and social forces that what is ours and what is others' is indecipherable. Human boundaries are abstractions of our mind(s), their origins may be indecipherable and what is inside or outside may be ambiguous. A human boundary is therefore never finished or fixed – its edge is always dynamic.

Parker's (2006) analysis of geographic borders offers the idea of a continuum of boundary dynamics. One pole is the spatially restrictive "linear dividing lines, fixed in a particular space . . . the weighting characteristic of borders is that they mark political, administrative, and in most cases also military, boundaries" (p. 79). The other pole is a "dynamic, fluid zone" where boundaries are porous and spatially expansive areas between or at the edge of cultural spheres and therefore embody the loci within which culture contact takes place (Parker, 2006, p. 77). Some human boundaries may therefore be more fixed, such as the body and its skin, and whilst they are a useful territorial marker of what is mine and yours, they are not the absolute endpoint of a person. Rather, where one stops and starts is blurry, dynamic and so inextricably intertwined with social processes that systemic theory is needed to explain them.

Who owns the boundary?

The ontological question of who owns the boundary is difficult to answer. Geographic and psychological boundary studies indicate that there are some aspects of a boundary which are solely owned, but the edge is often dynamic, meaning there is an area where ownership is uncertain (Agnew, 2000; Parker, 2006). Where boundaries are more visible and clearly defined, such as the skin and inside our physical bodies, attribution of ownership is easier. However, there are grey areas, a no man's land if you like where the boundaries are constantly being negotiated. Complex systems theory captures this ontological position by conceptualising humans as intrinsically open systems which reside on the dialectic between absolute order and chaos. Humans are constantly interacting and adapting to their environment, synthesising between the polarities of chaos and order to create a sense of a temporal stability, a structure to cope with environmental and cultural demands. As an open system, the need for boundaries is not negated; rather, it increases the requirement to avoid chaos. Boundaries provide a form of operational closure in an open system, they enclose a spatial area which is inextricably linked to human functioning and our understanding of reality, existence, history, knowledge, values, reason, mind, language and so on (Cilliers, 2001; Richardson & Lissack, 2001; Waldenfels, 2004). Boundaries give the system its own identity whilst also permitting a reciprocal exchange of matter, energy and information across that boundary, allowing the system to stay alive and adaptively integrate with other systems. In summary, it is posited that human boundaries can be solely owned and shared, but given that the edge of a boundary is always fluid, there is a grey area where ownership is uncertain and negotiated between parties.

Are boundaries more than a two-dimensional line?

Boundaries are often thought of as lines, but geographic boundary studies and proxemics research would suggest a person's boundaries are bulky. They incorporate horizontal and vertical planes and are likely three-dimensional spatial areas rather than a boundary line, enclosing a circle or surface (Robinson, 2012). These 3-D boundary areas are unlikely to be uniform in shape (Ogden, 2015), and each person is posited to have their own unique boundary signature. A unique spatial area reflecting a person's mental constructions about boundaries and this spatial need is likely underpinned by biotemperamental biases, personal history and internalisation of socio-cultural processes. A person's boundary signature is not permanently fixed; rather, the edge is dynamic, contracting and expanding relative to the context and the reciprocating person.

Applying the ontological perspective outlined earlier to Abrahamsson and Simpson's (2011) definition of a human boundary, a boundary is conceptualised in this chapter as a subjective three-dimensional area reflecting where we think our sphere of influence ends at a given moment in time and what we think distinguishes between that which belongs to us and that which belongs to others or the world.

Boundaries and boundary making

Boundaries and the bounding process serve to give shape to self, others and the world, and it will be argued that they incorporate social, interpersonal, intrapersonal and somatic aspects. **Interpersonal aspects** of boundaries reflect what happens between reciprocating or respective parties when they come into contact or collide. Proxemics theory and research reveal how people perceive, interpret and use distance, posture and orientation to mediate relations to other people and to the fixed (immobile) and semi-fixed (movable) features in their environment (Hall, 1966). However, proxemics research is underpinned by the positivist assumption that the body is a bona fide (real) boundary and there are some universal laws of interpersonal boundaries that can be observed outside the body. For instance, Hall's theory suggests that interpersonal boundaries are separated into four types of proxemic spaces: intimate (from 0 to about 0.5 m), personal (0.5 to 1.2 m), social (1.2 to 3 m) and public (greater than 3 m). Whilst these simple rules about personal space are appealing, they have not been verified. The notion of a three-dimensional spatial area surrounding people has been confirmed, but its size and shape are not fixed. Temporal positioning of one's interpersonal spatial area has been shown to be influenced by characteristics such as gender, age, nationality, the social environment, attitude of the other, current ego state and motivational state (Sorokowska et al., 2017). In therapy, Gutheil and Brodsky (2008) call these pragmatic factors, with the therapist's interpersonal boundary positioning influenced by prior training (Webb, 1997), therapeutic tradition and professional identity (Mearns & Thorne, 2013; Rønnestad & Skovholt, 2003), personal attitude and personality (Feltham, 2010; Hartmann, 2011), personal and cultural experiences (Gabriel, 2005) and nefarious motives (Gabbard, 2016; Garrett, 1998).

Intrapersonal aspects of boundaries are in the mind, our internal scaffolding used to organise our narrative about who we are, who others are and where self and others differentiate. The emphasis placed on intrapersonal aspects of boundaries varies across therapeutic traditions, with various terms used to describe them such as ego boundaries, self-boundaries, intrapsychic structures and so on. Regardless of terminology, it is commonly accepted that intrapersonal aspects of boundaries help separate internal experience from external reality and help differentiate self and other (Epstein, 1994). Hartmann (1991) extends this conceptualisation of intrapersonal boundaries, resting ultimately on a neurobiological basis that socialisation experiences then shape. Hartmann (1991) argues that individuals are neurobiologically predisposed to having thin (permeable) or thick (impermeable) inner and outer boundaries. Individuals with thin permeable boundaries are thought to have greater fluidity and openness in regard to the boundaries between self and others. At one level, this likely induces a greater connectedness to others and a receptiveness to their affect, but there is also a greater vulnerability to enmeshment, and there may be a lack of cohesion in self-identity. Individuals with thick or impermeable boundaries according to Hartmann (1991) have a much more fixed and solid idea of where they stop and another begins. This gives a greater sense of control over self, others and their world and a greater stability and coherence in self-identity. But excessive belief in the absolute correctness of one's intrapersonal boundaries and in turn the expression of this inner world in the form of fixed interpersonal boundaries likely increases disconnection and misattunement to the needs and affect of others (Landis, 1970; Hamilton, 2010).

As stated previously, we are not just bounded by the skin and our unique cognitive processes; we are influenced by our history, context, and time and are inextricably intertwined with social and cultural processes (Abrahamsson & Simpson, 2011; Jacobs & Van Assche, 2014; Waldenfels, 2004). A person's boundaries include people concepts, such as class, culture, sexuality, psychiatric diagnosis and offending groups, which help categorise and enable in-group and out-group distinctions (Jacobs & Van Assche, 2014). Gutheil and Gabbard (1998, p. 411) warn that "thinking about boundaries can lead one to an absurd end point, unless one understands the critical role of the context in which behaviour occurs". Boundaries mean something and are embodied differently across contexts, cultures and groups of people. This meaning is built selectively on earlier communications, becoming established, evolving and degrading with every new communication (Abrahamsson & Simpson, 2011, p. 187). Boundaries are therefore a dynamic relational interaction, contingent upon, maybe even created by, the context and social norms. Our personal history and experiences also play a part in our boundary processes and perhaps how our neurobiological boundary biases become expressed (Hartmann, 1991; Lynch, 2018). For example, Landis (1970) hypothesised that a secure attachment by 12 months of age is associated with healthy, flexible, relatively permeable interpersonal boundaries. Boundary solidification problems were associated with insecure attachment and adverse childhood experiences, which in some cases may manifest in pathological boundary permeability (e.g. borderline personality disorder) or pathological boundary impermeability (e.g. obsessive compulsive personality disorder). The endpoint and positioning of a person's boundaries are therefore not just a matter of personal choice and neurobiology; they include a myriad of formal and informal social norms, contextual factors and time. Environmental experiences shape our boundaries and how we manage these, and it is impossible to disentangle what is purely ours from what is others or social owned.

Somatic resources and possibly energy sources, which extend beyond the person's physical body, are thought to be involved in setting and managing boundaries. Different terminology and theoretical explanations of the somatic aspects of boundaries have been offered, such as transference-countertransference (Gutheil & Gabbard, 2011), responses to neuroceptive stimuli (Lynch, 2018; Ogden, Minton & Pain, 2006), social signalling (Lynch, 2018) and energetic boundaries in the form of an electromagnetic or electrostatic field around the body (Dale, 2011). Regardless of theoretical perspectives, there is consensus that our bodies are able to communicate with others about our preferred boundaries, without activating higher-order cognitive functioning and verbal acts. Ogden (2012) writes that the "body speaks in a variety of languages: visceral sensations, rhythm, prosody, movement, gesture, arousal states, scents, posture, facial expressions, breath, physical symptoms, and so forth" (p. 607). These somatic aspects of boundaries appear to communicate, mostly out of awareness and perhaps via mirror neuron processes, each other's preferred level of connection and disconnection (Hall, 1966; Lynch, 2018; Ogden & Fisher, 2015). Attuning to these somatic markers of discomfort and comfort in social interactions and therapy enables an intimate intra- and interpersonal dance of subtle spatial positioning as we search for a place of mutual coexistence. Somatic markers of discomfort might be awareness of increases and decreases in bodily tension, holding of the breath, noticing shallow breathing, avoidance of eye contact, body bracing, fidgeting and so on. Within therapy, Ogden (2012) reflected that once an optimal distance has been reached, it is not unusual for both therapist and client to indicate this by taking a breath. Somatic aspects of boundaries indicate that the body not only acts as a reference point for boundaries but also plays an active role in negotiating and setting boundaries using non-verbal processes. Bodily feedback about the uneasiness of the temporal boundary position may also prompt conscious boundary-type questions, which can make the boundaries visible.

In summary, the subjective three-dimensional area about where we think our sphere of influence ends and how we differentiate what is ours from others is thought to include intrapersonal, interpersonal, somatic and social components. A person's boundaries are opined to extend inside the skin as well as outside the skin, that is above, below, front, back, left and right of a person and then way beyond the physical body in some intangible complex social network. Boundaries are thought to be person, context and time dependent, and individuals are likely to have biotemperamental tendencies that influence the firmness and flexibility of their personal boundaries. Variability in boundary positioning along a continuum of boundary dynamics is expected, with context and verbal and non-verbal communication integral in creating, degrading, strengthening and re-creating our personal boundaries and temporal positioning.

Boundary making process and clinical practice

"The human being, characterised by its behaviour which is channelled neither by instinctive regulations nor by artificial programmes, is a creature that is not enclosed by fixed boundaries, but rather relates to its boundaries in a certain manner" (Waldenfels, 2004, p. 71).

The continuum of boundary dynamics identified in geographic and philosophical boundary studies (Cilliers, 2001; Parker, 2006) parallels the continuum of boundaries found by Hamilton (2010) when examining forensic workers' relational boundaries in action. This boundary continuum has a "fixed zone" where boundaries are so persistent, impermeable, fixed and visible that for most intents and purposes, people believe them to be real and absolute dividing lines. These more fixed boundaries act like a territorial mark or more solid enclosure. Smith (1997) reflects that humans can become bonded to these and will seek to defend these boundaries to prevent invasion by others or to exclude others, using some combination of advertisement, threat and attack. These more fixed boundaries are what Hamilton (2010) calls our non-negotiables, the limits of what we know to be me and mine, such as our body. Ultimately, these fixed boundaries are not real; they are fixed fiat boundaries and reflect humans' inherent need to mark territory and to categorise, herein simplifying the complexity of our worlds and making it more understandable and less chaotic.

Structural aspects of therapy and prison management are akin to these more visible and fixed fiat boundaries. They help provide a scaffolding, reference point or territorial shadow. These fixed fiat boundaries demarcate what is therapy and scaffold the therapeutic space, making it more predictable and safer, which in turn allows deep psychological exploration. Numerous terms have been used to define these fiat boundaries in the security and therapeutic literature, such as procedural security, structural boundaries, logistical boundaries, therapeutic boundaries, professional boundaries, treatment contracts, therapeutic frame, codes of conduct and so on (BACP, 2016; Bond, 2015; Simon, 1995). To simplify the lexicon, the term structural therapeutic boundaries is used in this chapter, referencing the more fixed fiat boundaries which create an internal structure for security and therapy, a territorial shadow which demarcates what belongs to the forensic intervention.

The character of structural therapeutic boundaries has been subject to considerable examination, and some consensus about the themes has been reached, although operationalisation varies greatly across therapeutic modalities.

- Structural aspects include boundaries linked to time, place, space, contract, fees, clothing and gifts (Bond & Mitchels, 2015; Johnston & Farber, 1996).
- Therapeutic aspects include boundaries linked to the underlying operating assumptions associated with a treatment orientation and professional ethics, such as neutrality, honesty, enhancing client's autonomy, fiduciary relationship and avoidance of dual relationships (Pope & Keith-Spiegel, 2008).
- Therapist–client interaction aspects include boundaries linked to language, self-disclosure, physical contact, use of somatic resources and social contact (Audet, 2011; Westland, 2011; Zur, 2004, 2010).

For the most part, structural therapeutic boundaries provide guidance on what may be appropriate within a particular forensic intervention, but definitive real (bona fide) structural therapeutic boundaries, a list of do's and don'ts, has been unsurprisingly elusive. What emerges from the literature are mental constructions in the form of fundamental underlying professional principles that should be acceptable fiat boundaries across similar contexts, patients, professions and treatment modalities. These fundamental principles can over time become more firm, explicit and owned by particular groups of therapists and forensic professionals, especially when they are incorporated into professional codes of conduct and published therapy models. This process of reification and naturalisation of the boundary reinforces identification with it as a "real" thing, e.g., a benchmark to judge what is "real" therapy from pseudo-therapy. However, "we cannot escape the moment of choice, and thus we are never free of normative considerations. Whatever we do has ethical implications, yet we cannot call on external principles to resolve our dilemmas in a final way" (Bogg & Geyer, 2007, p. 130).

The boundary continuum also includes a *dynamic, fluid zone* where boundaries can be permeable, flexible, often less obvious and typically jointly owned. Smith (1997) presents a case for a different kind of bounding process in this fluid zone, referring to these as "force dynamic boundaries". Force dynamic boundaries operate in areas where there is no crisp demarcation between people; instead, one works in perpetual grey areas not quite under either's control. Here the boundaries between people are constantly being negotiated and determined by the actual or potential dynamic actions and capacities of the reciprocating people (Smith, 1997; Abrahamsson & Simpson, 2011). Boundaries and boundary management in the grey areas therefore make a statement about power and ownership. Inevitably boundary disputes occur, and these reveal the underlying power dynamics and shifts in the balance of power between the reciprocating people (Jacobs & Van Assche, 2014).

In a therapy context, force dynamic boundaries reflect the concept of relational boundaries outlined in Hamilton (2010). Siegel's (2010) idea about *me* and *we* maps perhaps reflects this dynamic self-organising boundary process. For instance, relational boundary management decisions likely involve the elicitation and synthesis of multiple components of *me maps* and *we maps* linked to profession, therapeutic orientation, workplace, legal obligations, patient characteristic, informal social workplace norms and so on. Consequently, in making one boundary decision, a multitude of *me maps* and *we maps* may be elicited. Perhaps this is like a number of songs playing at once which somehow humans are able to organise into a semblance of order, or a jazz composition of *me* and *we* maps which are part of a shared activity, negotiating with each other to produce an emergent decision about whether the relational boundary should contract, solidify or extend to bring in or keep out a given experience. Therapist capacity to appropriately form these relational boundaries and attune to, navigate and/or repair boundary irritation or relational ruptures is pivotal for therapy effectiveness and could be central therapeutic moments in their own right (Mitchell, 1993; Lazarus, 1994; Reamer, 2012).

A case is outlined earlier for a continuum of boundaries in clinical practice. At one pole are the more static and firm boundaries, and the other a fluid zone. The term structural therapeutic boundaries (the fulcrum of the boundary seesaw) are used to refer to the more fixed fiat boundaries, which are likely written down in theories and professional codes of conduct and ethics. It is important to remember, however, that these boundaries are inventions of our minds which we choose to take seriously, and their edge is blurry and requires judgment in the grey area.

Distribution of boundary stabilities and therapy

Getting the right mix of what Richardson, Cilliers and Lissack (2001) call boundary stabilities is fundamental to the in-the-moment boundary making process and is essential for psychological well-being and ultimately survival. The quantities or distribution of common boundary stabilities, such as visibility, ownership, permeability and flexibility, are a matter of choice, and each decision will be located somewhere on the boundary continuum (Parker, 2006; Hamilton, 2010). Unsurprisingly, various conclusions about the right distribution of boundary stabilities to create the most effective structural therapeutic and relational boundaries is evident in psychological boundary studies.

In the psychoanalytic tradition, structural therapeutic boundaries and relational boundaries are closely aligned. Boundaries not only contain by protecting the transference and structuring the psyche; they also provide a holding-facilitating environment. Bridges (1999) states "the treatment boundary is a psychological containment field maintained by the therapist's mental capacity to encompass the patient's symptomatology and symbolic communications . . . the built-in structure to contain and process communications" (Bridges, 1999, p. 293). Langs (1982) described the therapeutic frame as the "ground rules of psychotherapy" and "the parameters to appropriate behaviour" in therapy, with management of boundaries "perhaps the single most important determinant of the therapeutic experience" (p. 282). Spruiell (1983) similarly conceptualises the therapeutic frame as the rules of the analytic game, the unchanging basic elements that define psychotherapy and distinguish it from other kinds of social events and other types of relationships.

In the psychoanalytic tradition, structural therapeutic boundaries are the responsibility of the therapist to set and maintain. Visibility of the boundary is paramount in this tradition, along with limited, possibly no, permeability or flexibility in the boundaries making up the psychoanalytic therapeutic frame. The analyst's constancy, reliability and capacity to contain affective communication creates the impression of a protective parental relationship and is the foundation for deep intrapsychic exploration (Modell, 1988). Clear boundaries are thought to set a standard for unambiguous communication between therapist and client, decreasing the possibility for misinterpretations of the therapist's messages, motives and behaviours (Langs, 1982; Simon, 1992). This strict approach to structural therapeutic boundaries and separation of therapist's personal self are thought to allow the social, intrapersonal, interpersonal and somatic aspects of relational boundaries to emerge and be worked on in therapy sessions.

Advocates of more permeable and flexible boundaries contend that the excessive formality, remoteness and strictness of the boundary management style posited by Langs and others is problematic. It is argued that overly rigid structural therapeutic and relational boundaries may be ineffective for a large percentage of patients (Mitchell, 1993), and may even prevent therapy from even beginning (Epstein, 1994). Beauchamp (1999) makes the point that structural therapeutic boundaries are not rules, as "an absolutist position concerning treatment boundary guidelines cannot be taken . . . effective treatment boundaries . . . define a fluctuating, reasonably neutral, safe space that enables the dynamic psychological interaction" (cited in Aravind, Krishnaram & Thasneem, 2012, p. 23). Whilst there is acknowledgement of the fundamental ethical principles of therapy and acceptance of a need for structural therapeutic boundaries, the emphasis is placed on the relational boundaries when applying more humanistic therapy-based modalities. The therapeutic space is jointly owned, and, where possible, boundaries are a collaborative construction based on specific character-istics of each unique therapist–patient dyad. Boundary setting and management therefore depends upon their psychological significance for both patient and therapist, "the same boundary enforcement experienced as rigid and unrespon-sive by one patient might be experienced as strong and comforting to another" (Mitchell, 1993, p. 125). For example, one therapist might extend beyond an established therapeutic boundary to maintain emotional connection or out of anxiety about damaging the therapeutic relationship, while another might hold firm to contain a patient's anxiety or show strength in response to patient manip-ulation (Hamilton, 2010; Mitchell, 1993). From this perspective each therapist–patient dyad brings their own territorial marks and 3-D spatial areas to any given interaction, and between them they create a mutual relating space specific to that dyadic interaction through negotiating explicitly and implicitly the relational boundaries. Humans' ability to engage in this explicit and implicit boundary negotiation process is likely impacted by what the body can do. Abrahamsson and Simpson (2011) call this the body's limits of capacity, "in other words what its affects are, how they can or cannot enter into composition with other affects and with the affects of another body" (p. 332). Limits of capacity include access to intrapersonal, interpersonal and somatic resources, and in the absence of these, the individual's ability to access social resources may also exert influence on the everyday life of the person, e.g., the child has limited capacity but the mother's ability to successfully mediate the relationship with others is likely to influence the child's experience. Limited cognitive and social resources, in addition to biotemperamental biases, socialisation experiences, cultural norms, context and timing, may also correlate with a human need for particular permutations of boundary stabilities. For example, someone who is acutely distressed may need more static boundaries for a time until they recover, whilst someone who is healthy and psychologically well-resourced may prefer to work with relational boundaries in the grey areas.

Where a boundary is located and the mix of boundary stabilities imbued in them is always a clinical and ethical decision. Getting the correct distribution of boundary stabilities or being flexible enough to correct misattunement is critical for self and relationships, including the therapeutic relationship and relational security. Too much stability can result in boundary rigidity, which can prevent proactive adaptive change and suppression of the person's actual thoughts, feel-ings and behaviours. Boundary violations, such as physical abuse of service users, bullying and unhelpful control, are more likely with too much stability (Blom-Cooper Inquiry, 1992; Zimbardo, 2008). Too loosely bounded, and humans adapt so much that they lose their personal reference points and may find it impossible to self-manage (Fallon et al., 1999; Richardson et al., 2001). Dual relationships, boundary violations associated with inappropriate sexual relationships and exploitation of services users become more likely with excessive flexibility (Gutheil & Gabbard, 2011; Hamilton, 2010). Inconsistent boundary management, a chronic flipping between excessive rigidity and excessive flexibility, is also problematic, causing confusion and disorganisation for all parties in the relating dyad (Gutheil & Gabbard, 2011).

Conclusion

The ontological perspective offered in this chapter is that psychological boundaries are fiat, three-dimensional mental abstractions with no definitive endpoint; their edge is blurred, restless and dynamic; and at least some part of the boundary is shared with others. This leads to a conclusion that we never know where we end and another person begins, and trying to identify definitive (real) psychological boundaries and sub-classifications of real boundaries is folly. Boundaries are ultimately indefinite. That being said, there is no escaping the boundary question; they are "so natural and pervasive it is hard to deny them a central place in our conceptual scheme to describe the spatiotemporal world" (Varzi, 1997, p. 27). Boundaries define existence; they give character to things; they determine human identity; and the enclosing nature of boundaries brings about familiar safety, with accepted boundaries creating respect, harmony and connection as well as separation. Boundaries aren't real things in their own right, but they have real effects upon all of us, especially when involved with the criminal justice system.

A continuum of boundary dynamics is posited. At one end is a fixed and impermeable pole, and at the other end a fluid and flexible pole, with temporal boundary positioning thought to occur somewhere along this continuum. In a security and therapy context, more static boundaries have been referred to as procedural security or structural therapeutic boundaries. These boundaries act as a scaffolding for security and therapy interventions, providing stable reference points for staff members and service users from which to position their therapeutic stance. Hamilton (2010) talks about these more static boundaries as being the fulcrum on the boundary seesaw, the contextual, theoretical and personal operating assumptions which act like a benchmark for in-the-moment boundary decisions. These more fixed boundaries are typically created by consensus and written down, such as the National Security Framework, Prison Service Orders, therapeutic frame, codes of conduct, ward rules and therapeutic models. Consensus may also come from inside the therapist, a type of boundary management heuristic developed through repeated experiences of working effectively with a particular clinical presentation or in a specific context (Hamilton, 2010). Acceptance of more fixed boundaries can result in the creation of a more permanent boundary style, but we must never forget that boundaries are our inventions and they must be open to reconsideration and review, both individually and at a societal level. Boundaries are always fiat.

Boundaries which are more fluid and flexible in security and treatment interventions have been named relational boundaries in this chapter. Relational boundary formation and management is considered a dynamic social interaction involving infinite combinations of boundary stabilities, that is flexible to inflexible, permeable to impermeable, explicit to implicit and almost solely owned to mostly shared. Even though boundaries and their management may have visible effects, it is rarely possible to describe objectively and identify where the boundary could be. The distribution of boundary stabilities and temporal positioning on the boundary continuum is constantly being constructed, deconstructed and reified through inner and outer communication. This boundary negotiation process is complicated, as boundaries are individualised to person, group or society and are so obviously intertwined with history and context that perhaps a more effective way to conceptualise them may be via systems theory, in particular complex systems theory (Cilliers, 2001; Jacobs & Van Assche, 2014).

Variability in relational boundary practices is therefore expected, and individuals likely move back and forth on the boundary continuum, eventually resting on a temporal position which fits a given interaction in the specific context. Relational boundary work in any setting cannot therefore be algorithmic; rather, it is a continuous emergent process that reflects the ongoing alignment of systemic processes with internal and external human activity. Boundaries involve a dynamic process of communication events, and looking at the narratives of how others separate and frame boundaries in a given context in a moment in time is likely more important than observing actual boundaries or trying to define bona fide (real) boundaries. Megoran (2012) provides an applied account of how the biography method which details the history of a boundary and the borders may be an effective methodology for understanding boundaries and how they materialise, rematerialise and dematerialise in different spatial and discursive sites over time.

Future applications

Given the importance of boundaries to human existence and the well-being of forensic institutions, staff training and formal psychological treatments should explicitly educate participants about the concept of boundaries. Discussing and sharing boundary biographies or stories may be a medium for bringing into consciousness the organisation's and individual's answers to the four ontological boundary questions posed at the start of this chapter. Understanding one's ontological boundary position will in turn illuminate how we position ourselves on the boundary continuum and help understand organisational and individual boundary making processes. Training exercises making explicit the non-negotiables and fixed boundaries in a given context, as well as the more flexible boundaries, would also help staff and service users negotiate the complex world of human boundary making. This would also challenge the naive assumption that boundary management can be based on algorithmic approaches and reinforce the idea that relational boundary management is a dynamic process with consistency in communication and relational processes at the heart of effective security and treatment interventions.

Use of "boundary biographies" or "boundary stories" as a way of understanding systemic, group and individual boundary management processes is reflected in Hamilton's (2010) attempt at addressing the clinical question of what consistent boundary management is. A grounded theorising approach was applied to forensic hospital staff's stories about real-life boundary management interventions, which resulted in a model of boundary management for this context, i.e., the boundary seesaw model. The boundary seesaw model has subsequently been revised and adapted to fit the boundary narratives of other clinical and forensic services (Carradice, 2016), and is a widely used training and supervision model (IoMH, 2013; Chapman-Gibbs, Mannix & Harvey, 2019; Doggett, 2017).

Boundary stories may also enlighten us about why some forensic environments become "toxic institutions" (Campling, Davies & Farquharson, 2004) and why cultures of silence occur even around the most extreme boundary violations. Examples of high-profile professional abuse include patient neglect and abuse (Francis Report, 2013), sexual abuse (Kerr Haslam Inquiry, 2006; Wolff & Shi, 2009), physical abuse (Ford, 2004; Wolff & Shi, 2009) and systemic safeguarding failures (Dearden, 2020; Senior, 2016). Research examining the boundary stories of staff members who violate professional boundaries could help understand how the processes involved in an individual's boundary making become too rigid or too fluid. This research is critical, especially given the prevalence of boundary violations in forensic institutions. For example, Ministry of Justice (MoJ) figures released between January 2008 and 2010 show that, on average, one prison worker per week has been investigated and found to have had an inappropriate relationship with a prisoner in an English or Welsh prison (*The Telegraph*, 8 June 2014). A similar frequency of serious boundary breaches (2013–2018) was noted in the freedom of information request reported in *The Guardian* (29 April 2019). The direct and indirect impact of boundary breaches on organisations, team members and service users has rarely been examined. Boundary stories could help us understand the widespread and long-lasting impact of boundary violations. Staff members are often sacked and sometimes imprisoned, but the consequences on service users when staff members violate professional standards is rarely spoken about, especially in forensic services. Richardson et al. (2008) provides one published account of the far-reaching impact of professional abuse; however, the impact of being labelled a "staff corrupter" in a prison context has not been examined. The term in itself is a misnomer. It negates the staff members' responsibility to uphold the boundaries and instead blames the victim for the offensive behaviour of another and indirectly gives staff members permission to behave badly, as the prisoner can be easily blamed. In my experience, the label "staff corrupter" is also something that follows a prisoner throughout their institutional career. This label also indirectly sanctions the prisoner to a life of suspicion about any connection they seek, as all too often "staff corruptor" becomes a lens through which their relating behaviour is judged. This labelling is likely to negatively affect the impact of any forensic intervention, as research suggests the quality of the therapeutic relationship accounts for much of the observed treatment effect.

Boundary stories may also be a useful forensic intervention technique in their own right, as fundamentally engaging in a criminal act is a temporal boundary position in which a decision is made that breaches someone's boundaries or a moment in time where there is a confusion about where one stops and another begins. Understanding what causes these moments in time in which the boundaries between people are blurred and what may be the antecedents for such behavioural acts is a central goal of forensic interventions. Boundary stories may be a less shaming and potentially transformative way of exploring boundary violations/offending behaviour.

Understanding our own and others' unique spatial boundary areas could also be achieved by using boundary experiment exercises outlined in Ogden (2015). Psychoeducation and skills training on how boundaries are verbally and non-verbally communicated may help staff and service users practice healthier boundary management and repair boundary irritations more quickly. This may in turn reduce the number of serious boundary issues and potentially life-threatening incidents, which often arise as a consequence of poor boundary management (Tighe & Gudjonsson, 2010). Such an understanding of self could assist individual staff and their teams to explore how their boundary style impacts upon the relationship with the patient. By utilising such an approach within team reflective practice sessions or clinical team meetings, it is posited that the psychological health of the team improves, alongside the quality of clinical formulation, interventions and therapeutic relationship with the patient. This approach would assist the move to proactive case management, as opposed to reactive responses following ruptures in the therapeutic relationship, or investigations and associated psychological damage from boundary violations.

Finally, boundaries are everywhere, and forensic interventions which ignore this critical component of human experience or treat it as an operational aside, e.g., group ground rules and procedural security, will be weakening security and treatment efforts overall. In turn, these forensic interventions will fail those relying on those services to improve their lives so they can be released, and society is failed, as it depends on these services to help make society safer for everyone.

References

Abrahamsson, S., & Simpson, P. (2011). The limits of the body: Boundaries, capacities, thresholds. *Social and Cultural Geography, 12*(4), 331–338.

Agnew, J. A. (2000). Global political geography beyond geopolitics. *International Studies Review, 2*(1), 91–99.

Allen, E. (2010). *See think act: Relational security in secure mental health services*. Department of Health.

Aravind, V. K., Krishnaram, V. D., & Thasneem, Z. (2012). Boundary crossings and violations in clinical settings. *Indian Journal of Psychological Medicine, 34*(1), 21–24. https://doi.org/10.4103/0253-7176.96151

Audet, C. T. (2011). Client perspectives of therapist self-disclosure: Violating boundaries or removing barriers? *Counselling Psychology Quarterly, 24*(2), 85–100.

Blom-Cooper Inquiry. (1992). *Report of the Committee of Inquiry into Complaints about Ashworth Hospital* (Vol. 1). HMSO, The Stationery Office Books.

Blundell, P. J. (2017). *The concept of "boundary" within the field of counselling*. Doctoral thesis (PhD). Manchester Metropolitan University.

Bogg, J., & Geyer, R. (Eds.). (2007). *Complexity, science and society*. Radcliffe.

Bond, T. (2015). *Standards and ethics for counselling in action* (4th ed.). SAGE Publications.

Bond, T., & Mitchels, B. (2015). *Confidentiality and record keeping in counselling and psychotherapy* (2nd ed.). SAGE Publications.

Bridges, N. A. (1999). Psychodynamic perspective on therapeutic boundaries: Creative clinical possibilities. *Journal of Psychotherapy Practice & Research, 8*(4), 292–300.

British Association for Counselling and Psychotherapy (BACP). (2016). *Ethical framework for the counselling professions*. Leicestershire: BACP House.

Campling, P., Davies, S., & Farquharson, G. (Eds.). (2004). *From toxic institutions to therapeutic environments: Residential settings in mental health services*. Gaskell.

Carradice, A. (2016). Supervising CAT consultancy in mental health teams. In D. Pickvance (Ed.), Cognitive analytic supervision: A relational approach (Chapter 16, pp. 209–221). Routledge.

Chapman-Gibbs, P., Mannix, K., & Harvey, D. (2019). Relational risk management in a Psychologically Informed Planned Environment (PIPE) approved premises. *Probation Journal, 66*(3), 356–369. https://doi.org/10.1177/0264550519856096

Chester, V., Alexander, R., & Morgan, W. (2017). Measuring relational security in forensic mental health services. *Psychiatric Bulletin, 41*. doi:10.1192/pb.bp.116.055509

Cilliers, P. (2001). Boundaries, hierarchies and networks in complex systems. *International Journal of Innovation Management, 5*(2), 135–147.

Collins, M., & Davies, S. (2005). The security needs assessment profile: A multidimensional approach to measuring security needs. *International Journal of Forensic Mental Health, 4*, 39–52.

Dale, C. (2011). *Energetic boundaries: How to stay protected and connected in work, love, and life.* Sounds True.

Dearden, L. (2020). *Grooming gang review kept secret as Home Office claims releasing findings not in public interest.* Retrieved July 12, 2020, from www.independent.co.uk/news/uk/homenews/grooming-gang-rotherham-review-home-office-findings-a9344896.html

Department of Health. (2010). *Classified national security framework.* no date.

Doggett, L. (2017). 'Staff-resident relationships in approved premises: What a difference a door makes': A practitioner response. *Probation Journal, 64*(4), 405–412. https://doi.org/10.1177/0264550517734927

Epstein, R. S. (1994). *Keeping boundaries: Maintaining safety and integrity in the psychotherapeutic process.* American Psychiatric Press.

Exworthy, T., & Gunn, J. (2003). Taking another tilt at high secure hospitals: The Tilt Report and its consequences for secure psychiatric services. *The British Journal of Psychiatry: The Journal of Mental Science, 182*, 469–471. doi:10.1192/bjp.182.6.469

Fallon, P., Bluglass, R., Edwards, B., et al. (1999). *Report of the Committee of Inquiry into the Personality Disorder Unit, Ashworth Special Hospital* (Vol. 1, Cm 4194, II). Stationery Office.

Feltham, C. (2010). *Critical thinking in counselling and psychotherapy.* Sage Publications.

Ford, R. (2004). Prisoners win £2 million for warders violent abuse. *The Times Newspaper.* Retrieved July 12, 2020, from www.thetimes.co.uk/article/prisoners-win-pound2-million-for-warders-violent-abuse-j5jxhn8xn3r

Francis, R. (2013). *Report of the Mid Staffordshire NHS Foundation Trust Public Inquiry.* Stationery Office.

Gabbard, G. O. (2016). *Boundaries and boundary violation in psychoanalysis*. American Psychiatric Association Publishing.

Gabriel, L. (2005). *Speaking the unspeakable: The ethics of dual relationships in counselling and psychotherapy*. Routledge.

Galton, A. (2007). On the paradoxical nature of surfaces: Ontology at the physics/geometry interface. *The Monist, 90*, 379–390.

Garrett, T. (1998, May). Sexual contact between patients and psychologists. *The Psychologist*, 227–229.

Goldberg, A. (2008). Some limits of the boundary concept. *Psychoanalytic Quarterly, 77*(3), 861–875.

Gutheil, T. G., & Brodsky, A. (2008). *Preventing boundary violations in clinical practice*. Guilford Press.

Gutheil, T. G., & Gabbard, G. O. (1993). The concept of boundaries in clinical practice: Theoretical and risk-management dimensions. *The American Journal of Psychiatry, 150*(2), 188–196. https://doi.org/10.1176/ajp.150.2.188

Gutheil, T. G., & Gabbard, G. O. (1998). Misuses and misunderstandings of boundary theory in clinical and regulatory settings. *The American Journal of Psychiatry, 155*(3), 409–414. https://doi.org/10.1176/ajp.155.3.409

Gutheil, T. G., & Gabbard, G. O. (2011). *Boundary violations in clinical practice*. Guilford Press.

Hall, E. T. (1966). *The hidden dimension*. Doubleday.

Halter, M., Brown, H., & Stone, J. (2007). *Sexual boundary violations by health professionals: An overview of the published empirical literature*. Council for Healthcare Regulatory Excellence.

Hamilton, L. (2010). The Boundary Seesaw model: Good fence make for good neighbours. In A. Tennett & K. Howells (Eds.), *Using time, not doing time: Practitioner perspectives on personality disorder and risk*. John Wiley & Sons Ltd.

Hartmann, E. (1991). *Boundaries in the mind: A new psychology of personality*. Basic Books.

Hartmann, E. (2011). *Boundaries: A new way to look at the world*. CIRCC EverPress.

Heylighen, F., Cilliers, P., & Gershenson, C. (2007). Complexity and philosophy. In J. Bogg & R. Geyer (Eds.), *Complexity, science and society*. Radcliffe Publishing.

Institute of Mental Health. (2013). *The national personality disorder knowledge and understanding framework: Prospectus*. People, Work and Pictures.

Jacobs, J., & Van Assche, K. (2014). Understanding empirical boundaries: A systems-theoretical avenue in border studies. *Geopolitics, 19*, 182–205. doi:10.1080/14650045.2013.830106

Johnston, S. H., & Farber, B. A. (1996). The maintenance of boundaries in psychotherapeutic practice. *Psychotherapy, 33*(3), 391–402.

Kennedy, H. G. (2002). Therapeutic uses of security: Mapping forensic mental health services by stratifying risk. *Advances in Psychiatric Treatment, 8*, 433–443. doi:10.1192/apt.8.6.433

The Kerr/Haslam Inquiry. (2006). *Clinical Risk, 12*(5), 180–183. https://doi.org/10.1258/135626206778494983

Landis, B. (1970). *Ego boundaries.* International University Press, Inc.

Langs, R. (1982). *Psychotherapy: A basic text.* Jason Aronson.

Lazarus, A. A. (1994). How certain boundaries and ethics diminish therapeutic effectiveness. *Ethics and Behavior, 4*(3), 255–261.

Lynch, T. R. (2018). *Radically open dialectical behavior therapy: Theory and practice for treating disorders of over-control.* New Harbinger Publications, Inc.

Mearns, D., & Thorne, B. (2013). *Person-centred counselling in action* (4th ed.). SAGE Publications.

Megoran, N. (2012). Rethinking the study of international boundaries: A biography of the Kyrgyzstan-Uzbekistan boundary. *Annals of the Association of American Geographers, 102*(2), 464–481. doi:10.1080/00045608.2011.595969

Mitchell, S. A. (1993). *Hope and dread in psychoanalysis.* Basic Books.

Modell, A. H. (1988). On the protection and safety of the therapeutic setting. In A. Rothstein (Ed.), *How does treatment help* (pp. 95–104). International Universities Press, Inc.

Ogden, P. (2012). Commentary on paper by Ellen F. Fries. *Psychoanalytic Dialogues, 22*(5), 606–615.

Ogden, P. (2015). Proximity, defence and boundaries with children and care-givers: A sensorimotor psychotherapy perspective. *Children Australia, 40*(2), 139–146. doi:10.1017/cha.2015.10

Ogden, P., & Fisher, J. (2015). *Sensorimotor psychotherapy: Interventions for trauma and attachment.* W. W. Norton and Co.

Ogden, P., Minton, K., & Pain, C. (2006). *Trauma and the body: A sensorimotor approach to psychotherapy.* W. W. Norton.

Parker, B. J. (2006). Toward an understanding of borderland processes. *American Antiquity, 71*(1), 77–100.

Pope, K. S., & Keith-Spiegel, P. (2008). A practical approach to boundaries in psychotherapy: Making decisions, bypassing blunders, and mending fences. *Journal of Clinical Psychology, 64*(5), 638–652.

Reamer, F. G. (2012). *Boundary issues and dual relationships in the human services* (2nd ed.). Columbia University Press.

Richardson, et al. (2008). *Broken boundaries: Stories of betrayal in relationships of care*. Witness.

Richardson, K. A., Cilliers, P., & Lissack, M. (2001). Complexity science: A "gray" science for the "stuff in between". *Emergence: Complexity and Organization, 3*(2).

Richardson, K. A., & Lissack, M. R. (2001). On the status of boundaries, both natural and organizational: A complex systems perspective. *Emergence, 3*(4), 32–34.

Robinson, E. H. (2012). Reexamining fiat, bona fide and force dynamic boundaries for geopolitical entities and their placement in DOLCE. *Applied Ontology, 7*(1), 93–108.

Rønnestad, M. H., & Skovholt, T. M. (2003). The journey of the counselor and therapist: Research findings and perspectives on professional development. *Journal of Career Development, 30*, 5–44.

Senior, J. (2016). *Broken and betrayed: The true story of the Rotherham Abuse Scandal by the woman who fought to expose it* (Main Market ed.). Pan.

Siegel, D. (2010). *Mindsight: The new science of personal transformation*. W. W. Norton.

Simon, R. I. (1992). Treatment boundary violations: Clinical, ethical, and legal considerations. *Bulletin of the American Academy of Psychiatry and the Law, 20*, 269–288.

Simon, R. I. (1995). The natural history of therapist sexual misconduct: Identification and prevention. *Psychiatric Annals, 25*, 90–94.

Skopje. (2018). *Trainers' manual on dynamic security*. Council of Europe.

Smith, B. (1997). The cognitive geometry of war. In P. Koller & K. Puhl (Eds.), *Current issues in political philosophy* (pp. 394–403). Holder-Pichler-Tempsky.

Sorokowska, A., Sorokowski, P., Hilpert, P., Cantarero, K., Frackowiak, T., Ahmadi, K., et al. (2017). Preferred interpersonal distances: A global comparison. *Journal of Cross Cultural Psychology, 48*, 577–592. doi:10.1177/0022022117698039

Spruiell, V. (1983). The rules and frames of the psychoanalytic situation. *Psychoanalytic Quarterly, 52*, 1–33.

Stowell-Smith, M. (2006). States and reciprocal roles in the wider understanding of forensic mental health. In P. H. Pollock, M. Stowell-Smith, & M. Gopfert (Eds.), *Cognitive analytic therapy for offenders: A new approach to forensic psychotherapy* (pp. 66–81). Taylor and Francis.

Tighe, J., & Gudjonsson, G. (2012). See, think, act scale: Preliminary development and validation of a measure of relational security in medium- and low-secure units. *Journal of Forensic Psychiatry & Psychology, 23*, 1–16.

Tilt, R., Perry, B., Martin, C., et al. (2000). *Report of the review of security at the high security hospitals*. Department of Health.

Varzi, A. C. (1997). Boundaries, continuity, and contact. *Noûs, 31*, 26–58.

Varzi, A. C. (2013). *Boundary: The Stanford encyclopedia of philosophy*. Retrieved October 4, 2014, from https://plato.stanford.edu/entries/boundary/

Waldenfels, B. (2004). The boundaries of orders. *Philosophica, 73*, 71–86.

Webb, S. B. (1997). Training for maintaining appropriate boundaries in counselling. *British Journal of Guidance & Counselling, 25*(2), 175–188.

Westland, G. (2011). Physical touch in psychotherapy: Why are we not touching more? *Body, Movement and Dance in Psychotherapy: An International Journal for Theory, Research and Practice, 6*(1), 7–29. doi:10.1080/17432979.2010.508597

Wolff, N., & Shi, J. (2009). Contextualization of physical and sexual assault in male prisons: Incidents and their aftermath. *Journal of Correctional Health Care: The Official Journal of the National Commission on Correctional Health Care, 15*(1), 58–82.

Zimbardo, P. (2008). *The Lucifer effect: How good people turn evil*. CPI Cox and Wyman.

Zur, O. (2004). To cross or not to cross: Do boundaries in therapy protect or harm? *Psychotherapy Bulletin, 39*(3), 27–32.

Zur, O. (2010). *Boundaries in psychotherapy: Ethical and clinical explorations*. American Psychological Association.

5
Radically Open-Dialectical Behaviour Therapy

A new treatment of people with maladaptive overcontrol who offend

*Laura Hamilton, Lee Bacon,
and Emma Longfellow*

Introduction

This chapter argues for a transdiagnostic approach to treating offending behaviour and offers an account of early adoption experiences of implementing a new transdiagnostic treatment, Radically Open Dialectical Behavioural Therapy (RO DBT). RO DBT is a specialist treatment for overcontrolled conditions, based on Lynch's (2018) novel conceptualisation of overcontrol which includes three components: bio-temperamental biases (nature), socio-developmental experiences (nurture) and compulsive self-control (coping). Implementation of RO DBT with forensic in-patients parallels changes occurring in the UK and United States, with movement away from categorical-based research and disorder-specific treatment pathways towards transdiagnostic approaches which target a small number of core latent constructs or spectra (Eaton, Rodriguez-Seijas, Carragher & Krueger, 2015; Insel et al., 2010; Mullins-Sweatt et al., 2020).

Mullins-Sweatt et al. (2020) argue the use of dimensional models of personality and psychopathology has the potential to transform approaches to psychological research and treatment. Acceptance of this hypothesis means rejection of the notion that we require treatments for specific psychological disorders or specific types of offending behaviour; rather, forensic interventions should be developed with a specific goal of treating transdiagnostic constructs. This rethinking of psychiatry and psychology from categorical disease models to dimensional

DOI: 10.4324/9780429262074-5

continuous structures is still in the early stages of development, and various hierarchical models and groups of constructs, spectra and domains have been proffered (Insel et al., 2010; Kotov et al., 2017; Widiger & McCabe, 2020). To date this suggested paradigm shift in psychiatric and psychological practices has not gained much attention in forensic practice, remaining a potentially fruitful area for further in-depth theoretical consideration and/or practical application. A simple analysis, all that is permitted within the scope of this chapter, is that many of the core latent constructs posited in transdiagnostic models reflect empirically identified risk factors associated with violent, sexual and general offending.

Clinically, the transdiagnostic approach emphasises the importance of a person-oriented application, with the focus on the organisation of different variables or dimensions within the person and how these configurations can be used to define different prototypes. A promising area showing consistent findings across numerous longitudinal studies employing different clinical and general-population samples are three major personality prototypes, i.e. Resilient, Overcontrolled and Undercontrolled (Asendorpf & van Aken, 1999; Bohane et al., 2017; Robins, John, Caspi, Moffitt & Stouthamer-Loeber, 1996).

Longitudinal studies and cross-sectional studies provide some information about the relationship between the three personality prototypes and propensity for involvement in criminal behaviour later in life (Moffitt et al., 2011, 2013). A systematic review (Hamilton, Winder, Norman & Baguley, submitted for publication) of forensic-specific research similarly provides support for the Overcontrolled and Undercontrolled prototypes, with a handful of studies also identifying a Resilient cluster (Widom, 1978; Low & Day, 2015; Herzberg & Hoyer, 2009; Herzberg & Roth, 2006). The Overcontrolled and Undercontrolled personality prototypes were consistently identified across different sample characteristics (age, nationality, sex, offence groups), different instruments (questionnaire, observational measures, Q-sort), different methods of deriving types (cluster analysis, factor analysis) and different judgements involving self- and other-ratings (Hamilton et al., submitted for publication).

Meaningful differences between Overcontrolled and Undercontrolled individuals' tendencies to behave, think and feel were noted from the review. Hamilton et al. (submitted for publication) concluded the Resilient people were characterised by a generally well-adjusted personality profile, normal levels of anger and weak-to-moderate crime supportive attitudes and beliefs. The Overcontrolled people with convictions were also characterised by normal personality profiles with concomitant high levels of defensiveness, low impulsivity and elevated inhibitory control. Mixed results were reported regarding levels of affective distress and interpersonal difficulties, and forensic cross-sectional studies point to the idea that these apparent inconsistencies may reflect two Overcontrolled subtypes (Black-burn, Logan, Donnelly & Renwick, 2008). Hamilton et al. (submitted for pub-lication) called these two Overcontrolled groups the "Controlled Repressor" and "Inhibited Suppressor". The Controlled Repressor group was characterised by high defensiveness, high inhibitory control and apparently low levels of psycho-pathology, emotional tension/distress and interpersonal difficulties. The Inhibited Suppressor Overcontrolled group were also characterised by high defensiveness and high inhibitory control, but reported moderate-high anxiety, high depression, lower dominance and a tendency to turn hostility onto self. Interpersonally the Inhibited Suppressor group were extremely shy, social anxious, introverted and struggled in managing relationships. Lynch (2018) similarly identifies two Over-controlled subtypes in clinical populations. The "Overly Disagreeable" subtype was characterised by a motivation to be perceived as competent but not compli-ant, willing to be disagreeable to achieve an objective, and they valued correctness over interpersonal relations. The "Overly Agreeable" subtype was character-ised by a motivation to be perceived as competent and socially acceptable. They avoided conflict and social disapproval, preferring to blend into the group, but their social signalling can be disingenuous and incongruent, which may result in others finding them inauthentic and insincere. Whether these are true distinct subtypes or reflect an overcontrol spectrum is an empirical question requiring further examination. The current hypothesis based upon the findings from the systematic review is that the Inhibited Suppressor group are in the more extreme ranges of maladaptive overcontrol progressing to Controlled Repressors and then into the healthy flexible control (resilient–overcontrolled) range.

Developing a rationale for specialist overcontrolled treatment

Criminal behaviour is fundamentally seen as a problem of poor self-control (Gottfredson & Hirschi, 1990), and forensic interventions typically aim to improve a person's capacity to cognitive, emotionally and behaviourally regulate in order to reduce risk and restore prosocial tendencies. In contrast, longitu-dinal studies, cross-sectional studies and modelling research consistently iden-tified that a substantial proportion of people with convictions have too much self-control, suggesting the relationship between self control and offending is unlikely to be linear (Mears, Cochran & Beaver, 2013). Maybe a quadratic (inverted U) model better describes the relationship between self-control and criminal behaviour, whereby extremes of self-control – either *undercontrolled or overcontrolled* – increase the risk of offending.

The original conceptualisation of overcontrol in forensic psychology linked it specifically to one-off, often lethal, violent offences (Megargee, 1966). Subse-quent research, however, has confirmed that Overcontrol prototypes have been identified in samples examining intimate partner violence (Redondo, Cantos, Graña, Muñoz-Rivas & O'Leary, 2019), sexual offending (Worling, 2001) and general offending (Henderson, 1983). Bacon, Longfellow and Hamilton (2020) also postulated that mass killings and school shootings could be linked with over-controlled individuals, and Hamilton, Bacon, Longfellow and Tennant (2018) speculated about a relationship between overcontrol and radicalisation/violent extremism. In summary, overcontrol appears to be a latent construct across all major offending behaviour groups with a remarkably consistent prevalence rate identified in forensic samples. For instance, Hamilton et al. (submitted for publication) concluded that one in every three prisoners and as many as one in two forensic psychiatric in-patients exhibit characteristics associated with the Overcontrolled prototype.

Despite mounting evidence of an association between overcontrol and serious offending, criminal acts associated with high moral certitude, excessive inhibitory control, forward planning and desires for revenge remain poorly understood and understudied. In contrast, there has been an enormous amount of theory, research and forensic interventions addressing the needs of undercontrolled individuals with convictions (Day, Howells, Mohr, Schall & Gerace, 2008; Gottfredson & Hirschi, 1990; Pratt & Cullen, 2000). Traditional offending behaviour treatment programmes still ubiquitously teach skills aimed at increasing inhibitory control (Lee & DiGiuseppe, 2018), despite commentary and empirical studies confirming a relationship between high self-control and offending. For instance, Davey, Day and Howells (2005) commented that "teaching specific [anger inhibition] strategies to those who already overuse these strategies is likely to be at best ineffective and at worst counter-productive in that they are likely to reinforce and entrench the problem" (p. 631). A seminal paper by Low and Day (2015) tested this hypothesis and confirmed the only prototype that derived benefit from a standard medium-intensity violent offending treatment programme (VOTP) was predicated on the notion that those with criminal convictions have low self-control and were those classified as "Under-regulated" (Undercontrolled)."Over-regulated" men with violent convictions in this sample derived minimal to no benefit from VOTP, and some overcontrolled individuals evidenced an iatrogenic effect with emotional inhibition increasing. Redondo et al. (2019) found similar results and reaffirmed Megargee's (1966) assertion made some 50 years ago: overcontrolled and undercontrolled individuals with convictions need different treatment interventions. "Undercontrolled offenders need to learn anger and self-control skills, such as relaxation and distraction techniques, while overcontrolled individuals will likely benefit from training in communication and assertiveness skills" (Redondo et al., 2019, p. 1714). Empirically derived criminogenic and clinical needs for undercontrolled individuals with convictions broadly concur with Redondo et al.'s conclusion (Bonta & Andrews,

2017; Douglas et al., 2013; Wong & Gordon, 2006). Our clinical experience, theoretical leanings (Lynch, 2018) and Hamilton et al.'s systematic review does not, however, affirm Redondo et al.'s conclusion about treatment needs for over-controlled individuals, even though we endorse the sentiment for specialised treatment. A proof-of-concept study examining Lynch's new neurobiosocial theory of overcontrol (Hamilton et al., submitted for publication) confirmed previous prevalence rates, with 44% of admissions to the UK maximum-secure personality disordered service in a forensic psychiatric hospital classified as over-controlled. Overcontrolled individuals typically reported a non-violent lifestyle, negative attitudes about the use of violence and often had fewer convictions and lower rates of supervision failures. Clinically the overcontrolled group were found to be highly inhibited, rigid and they often had interpersonal problems with little social support. Staff members often experienced the overcontrolled patients as withdrawn, lacking in spontaneity and overly serious.

At this time there is an ethical, clinical and empirical imperative to implement a forensic intervention for individuals with too much self-control, as up until now their specific treatment needs have been unaddressed by traditional offending behaviour treatment programmes predicated on the assumption that offending is underpinned by undercontrolled coping. Additionally, there is an economic push, with overcontrolled individuals more commonly found in expensive hospital beds costing around £250,000 per year, and as we will see, many of these individuals are chronic long-stay in-patients (Pickersgill, 2013).

Radically Open Dialectical Behavioural Therapy

Hamilton et al. (2018) outlines the rationale for this personality-based treatment approach using the therapy modality of dialectical behavioural therapy (Linehan, 2015; Lynch, 2018). Briefly, it was proposed that undercontrolled personality disordered individuals with convictions should be referred to dialectical behaviour therapy (Linehan, 2015), as it addresses the difficulties associated with poor inhibitory control and emotion regulation. RO DBT was recommended for overcontrolled individuals, as it aims to improve:

- Receptivity and openness, such as a tendency to avoid feedback and novel situations.
- Flexible responding, such as a compulsive need for structure and rigid responding.
- Emotional expression and awareness, in particular inhibited or disingenuous expressions.
- Social connectedness and intimacy, specifically a tendency to be aloof and distant in relationships.

In 2015, the first RO DBT forensic service in the world was initiated, and next is a summary of the early adoption experiences. RO DBT was selected, as it is the only evidence-based treatment specifically treating overcontrolled conditions and it had a sound theoretical basis (Lynch, 2018). Pragmatically the RO DBT treatment goals aligned with the clinical needs identified in the systematic review and anecdotal information based on observations of overcontrolled forensic service users.

Step 1: implementation of forensic RO DBT

Hempel et al. (2018) outlines the steps to consider in setting up an RO DBT service, and this chapter includes some of the early thinking and experiences about setting up an RO DBT forensic intervention in a high-secure hospital. Building upon our earlier thinking outlined in (Hempel et al., 2018), a conservative implementation strategy was employed in 2015 with a small sample (Group 1, $N = 4$) of very protracted overcontrolled individuals who had a primary diagnosis of personality disorder and had never successfully completed treatment even after an average length of stay of 15 years in high-secure forensic hospitals. Positive experiences of this initial pilot resulted in the RO DBT skills class and individual treatment being extended to three other cohorts of patients. RO DBT treatment Group 2 (2016, $N = 6$) had a primary diagnosis of personality disorder, and in 2017 a decision was made to more fully embrace the transdiagnostic premise outlined earlier. Group 3 (2018, $N = 7$) and Group 4 (2019, $N = 8$) were diagnostically mixed – all patients were identified as overcontrolled but had primary diagnoses of autistic spectrum disorder, personality disorder or major mental illness, such as schizophrenia. As treatment progressed, it became apparent that many in-patients had previously unidentified eating-related issues, which included planned binge eating episodes and restrictive eating. These eating issues were not treated separately; rather, they were considered a side effect of maladaptive overcontrol. Consequently, it was hypothesised that treating the maladaptive overcontrol would ameliorate the eating-related issues (Lynch, 2018).

Step 2: training and therapist selection

All practitioners delivering the RO DBT intervention completed the two-week intensive training programme and received regular team consultation and some expert supervision. More detailed information about the initial treatment team and training strategy are outlined in Hempel et al. (2018), with other less experienced clinicians joining the team over time. Lynch (2018) recommends that at least one facilitator should lean to undercontrol (UC); however, we found out that undercontrolled therapists in our service were rare. This finding was consistent with Lynch (2018, p. 161), noting that many therapists lean towards an overcontrolled (OC) personality style. Due to operational constraints, we had to facilitate with various facilitator permutations and reflected on the facilitator combinations in team consultation, concluding a mixed OC and UC facilitator team was optimum. Having a UC facilitator helped prevent inadvertent collusion between the OC therapist and OC patient; the UC also provided an alternative perspective based on different biotemperamental tendencies which supported flexibility. The OC therapist modelling the mindfulness skill "outing yourself" by sharing with the skills class their leaning to overcontrol was helpful in signalling sameness, connectedness and reduced shame associated with feeling different. Therapists "outing oneself" early in skills class also reflects the emphasis placed on therapists to be "Tribal Ambassadors" who model living a "radically open" life, as well as "smuggling" the idea that mindfulness is key to having a "life worth sharing" (Lynch, 2018). Key to the delivery of these therapeutic messages and the treatment overall is the capacity to share in an easy manner. This easy manner is signalled through physical positioning; lyrical tone of voice; use of inadvertent gaze; and an ability to communicate that the therapist likes, trusts and believes in the person they are working with and enable face saving when fault occurs (Lynch, 2018, p. 161).

Matching therapist style to individual patients was something we considered in team consultation, with a major factor being whether the individual therapist genuinely liked the patient. This was important, as the therapist's authenticity or inauthenticity would be easily identified by the hyper-sensitive, threat-oriented and detail-focused overcontrolled in-patient, i.e., they will notice the mismatch between what is said and what is socially signalled. A lack of genuineness or perceived inauthentic behaviour goes against the RO DBT treatment principles and goal of "radical genuineness" and would likely result in alliance ruptures and potential premature disengagement. As we developed as a team through consultation and specialist supervision, therapists also explored their own edges to improve matches and understand how their own social signalling impacted therapy and their relationships.

Step 3: preparing the physical environment before commencing treatment

As per RO DBT treatment guidelines (Lynch, 2018), all RO DBT skills classes occurred in a large room that facilitated a table being placed in the middle with chairs placed around it (see Hempel et al., 2018, p. 164). The facilitators positioned themselves at each end, with one person acting as lead facilitator and the other co-facilitating. There was some initial anxiety that this room setup would feel like school, triggering trauma scars associated with negative schooling experiences. This hypothesis was disconfirmed, despite many of the participants having school adjustment problems. Patients said they preferred the RO DBT setup to the standard DBT group room, which was set up in traditional open, semi-circular format. As hypothesised by Lynch (2018), patients shared that the tables helped regulate physiological arousal associated with fear of closeness and intimacy. Lynch (2018) also suggests that the room needs to be cool and well aerated; hence the suggestion of a fan and windows in the room to minimise conditioned stimulus such as sweating linked to anxiety and avoidance (p. 99).

Similarly, all individual therapy rooms were set up as per RO DBT guidelines (see Hempel et al., 2018, p. 164), which was a shift for some therapists, as it varied from traditional models and modes of therapy. Lynch (2018) explained that the angle of seating was specified to avoid direct facing of each other, which can be associated with aggressive or highly intimate exchanges (p. 98). The distance between seating was noted as important to ensure enough personal space within the room, as many OC clients prefer greater personal space, experiencing close contact as an indication of risk, aggression or unwanted intimacy.

Step 4: assess clients for suitability of RO DBT

The process of screening RO DBT treatment referrals and case identification was initially time consuming, requiring a considerable amount of clinician expertise and discussion in team consultation. A specific overcontrol measure which has demonstrated sensitivity and specificity would advance the field considerably, and this remains an ongoing research endeavour. Initially the process of assigning patients to RO DBT vs. DBT was threefold and heavily influenced by the presenting difficulties of the population:

1 **Personality disorder diagnosis**: If the patient had predominantly Cluster A and C diagnoses, they were identified as leaning to overcontrol and referred to the RO DBT for assessment. Predominant Cluster B diagnoses suggested leanings to undercontrol, and a referral to DBT was indicated. Over 90% of the in-patients had an antisocial personality disorder diagnosis, and this was excluded when making these initial screening decisions. Over time, screening focused less on diagnostic labels and more on the clinical descriptors for OC and UC.
2 **Screening process:**
   • **Assessment styles of coping word-pairs** (Lynch, 2018) was administered during the initial in-take assessment and contributed to the initial treatment planning decision to refer to RO DBT or DBT. In later cohorts the OUT'M (Over- and Under-control Trait Measure; Lynch, 2015) was utilised, which was then replaced with the BOS (Brief Overcontrol Scale; Lynch, 2018).

- **Staff observations**: Qualitative markers were identified from a study examining staff perceptions of OC patients. In brief, Gardner and Hamilton (2017) found that staff felt OC patients had a reputation, "they put the frighteners on people" . . . "had been in every single institution in probably the country, usually in the highest secure institutions" and "they were stuck" as "no one knows how to work with them effectively" or "they were disliked". These qualitative markers were contextualised as being present despite OC patients "not displaying extreme problem behaviours but just because of the uncertainty about them". If these observations were noted, a referral for an RO DBT assessment was recommended.

3   **RO DBT treatment assessment:**

- **Clinical interview** completed by an RO DBT facilitator; this was modelled on the initial sessions of RO DBT and key aspects of the Overcontrolled Global Prototype Rating Scale and Clinician Rated OC Trait Form (Lynch, 2018, p. 385).
- The OC trait rating scale and the Overcontrolled Global Prototype Rating scale (Lynch, 2018, p. 381) were fully completed after the clinical interview.

4   Various pre- and post-treatment measures have been used. Initially the STAXI-2 was used based on Megargee's (1966) hypothesis that overcontrol is a problem of excessive anger regulation; however, this hypothesis is now debunked (D'Silva & Duggan, 2010). Hamilton et al.'s proof-of-concept study also did not identify excessive anger regulation as a clinical problem for overcontrolled people with convictions but did confirm that lack of social support, emotional inhibition more generally, hypervigilance and relational distancing were areas of clinical need. The following measures are currently being used:

- Chart of Interpersonal Reactions in Closed Living Environments (CIRCLE, Blackburn & Renwick, 1996).
- UPPS Impulsive Behaviour Scale (UPPS, Whiteside & Lynam, 2001).
- Core-OM (Evans et al., 2002).
- Social Safeness and Pleasure Scale (Gilbert et al., 2009).

Step 5: implementation of individual treatment, skills groups and staff training

RO-DBT intervention: RO DBT treatment involves a minimum of two pre-commitment sessions and 30 skills class sessions of 2.5 hours each. Our experience has been that total delivery time varied between groups. Operational restrictions meant our initial skills class was often limited to 2 hours, which made it challenging to fit in all the session material outlined in the manual; consequently, some sessions run over two weeks. We made minor amendments to the RO DBT manual, mostly around tweaking examples to apply to individuals with convictions, and as discussed in Hempel et al. (2018), we added extra emotion sessions based on Linehan (2015), as in-patients often had profound deficits in emotion labelling and in-the-moment emotional identification. In later cohorts this additional material was not utilised and instead focused upon clients exploring their responses to situations utilising the neuroregulatory model of emotions, the awareness continuum and self-enquiry (Lynch, 2018).

The majority of forensic in-patients who completed the RO DBT treatment had significant lengths of stay within high-secure hospital provision. The average length of stay in hospital was 20.8 years (Group 1), 12.3 years (Group 2), 11.8 years (Group 3) and 7.4 years (Group 4). Common across all groups were in-patients expressing a sense of "being stuck" and they shared thoughts such as "don't label me", "I am not like other people", "nobody appreciates how hard I'm working", "no one is capable of understanding me" and "always have an answer, even if it's a question". Most RO DBT patients shared a similar frustration, that they had "done what was asked" and "did not understand" or "it wasn't fair why they were not progressing" to less restrictive conditions outside a high-secure hospital. They often made social comparisons between their progress and undercontrolled patients who had been acting out but still got a medium-secure placement. Clinical teams often experienced a sense of being stuck, uncertainty about whether a patient had made any genuine change and confusion about what to do to help in-patients whose behaviour in hospital did not explicitly look risky yet it seemed that core risk work was incomplete. This mismatch of expectations and perceptions would often result in alliance ruptures between a patient and their clinical team, with both seeing the other as intransigent, and over time these perceptions could become deeply entrenched. These alliance ruptures were posited to be a consequence of the patients' maladaptive overcontrolled deficits combined with a lack of team knowledge about overcontrol. It was posited that a lack of team knowledge about overcontrol was a consequence of the emphasis on undercontrol in mental health and forensic training along with the societal assumption that you can never have too much self-control (Lynch, 2018). Improving self-control in order to restore 'normal functioning' is therefore a key treatment assumption amongst forensic mental health practitioners, but this clearly does not fit the overcontrolled patient who probably has higher levels of self-control than most people – yet they have committed criminal acts.

Staff training: Gardner and Hamilton (2017) found that in the initial stages of implementation, the RO DBT team experienced a lot of resistance and catastrophising about what radically open could mean to security and patient well-being. A participant in the study commented:

> Bringing in any new treatments you're going to get resistance, especially when you start talking about radically open to some people in this setting that strikes the fear of God into them . . . . are you going to turn our patients into, erm you know we don't want under controlled messes thank you very much.
>
> (Morgan)

A lack of meaningful engagement from 'the system' and staff was likely to hinder the implementation of RO DBT, the patient's progress and generalisation of RO DBT skills into everyday life on the ward. RO DBT awareness sessions were included in the staff induction, and a series of one-day staff training events were scheduled based on Lynch's original RO DBT 101 training (Lynch, 2015). The aim of this intervention was to address the shortfall in mental health training and to challenge assumptions about the linear relationship between self-control and offending. Staff training on treatments has also been found to increase positive patient and staff outcomes (Ewers, Bradshaw, McGovern & Ewers, 2002). Having credible staff of a sufficiently high grade and good professional relationships leading the treatment and training was pivotal in tackling this resistance and creating a momentum for systemic change. "I think that comes down to not only the treatment but I think the integrity of the people . . . team to start with that people will listen and treat seriously and because you know how embedded they are" (Morgan, in Gardner & Hamilton, 2017).

Step 6: RO DBT consult and expert supervision

The RO DBT consult is a place for therapists to practice being radically open and learn from the wisdom of the tribe, as it can be difficult to know when one is open and when one is closed. More details can be found in Lynch (2018, pp. 198–207). Consult sessions were considered key to the successfulness of RO DBT treatment, and participants in Gardner and Hamilton (2017) described consult sessions positively using words like "invaluable" (Lucy) and "brilliant" (Sparkle) and a supportive space to consider RO DBT, practice skills and receive an extra source of training, particularly when accessing micro-supervision from an RO DBT expert. A participant in Gardner and Hamilton (2017) shared how RO DBT consolidates learning from training, commenting, "(Training) gives you a good idea of how the manual works but I think you do need some . . . additional supervision from Tom [Lynch] and that has been really important because it's just some of the nuances and subtleties that you can read in the manual but it's a bit two-dimensional". This finding was in line with prior research, which found that the most significant factor in increasing therapist adherence and skill was not the training modality, but the number of consultation hours after training (Beidas, Edmunds, Marcus & Kendall, 2012). Areas for improvement in the RO DBT consult were identified in the Gardner and Hamilton (2017) study, such as making sure the time was protected to allow team consult to occur consistently and use of the consult agenda outline in the RO DBT treatment manual to keep it focused. Having a mix of personalities in consult was also identified as important, as this avoided OC-centric thinking, provided multiple perspectives on a particular behaviour and broadened the types of practice activities brought to consult (Gardner & Hamilton, 2017).

Step 7: monitoring progress and client satisfaction

Evaluation of delivering treatment

The formal evaluation of the RO DBT intervention is ongoing and is focused upon collating outcome measures and qualitative case reviews. The drop-out rate throughout the cohorts has been low, with only one patient leaving the treatment and not engaging further. Three other patients disengaged from their original group; however, they subsequently requested to re-engage in another RO-DBT group and have completed ($N = 25$). Insufficient pre-commitment work and failure to gain explicit confirmation from the in-patient that they identified as being overcontrolled in the initial sessions was noted as a potential reason by therapists. Overall, the majority of patients in the cohorts who completed treatment reported feeling connected to the theoretical premises in RO DBT and reported enjoying learning the science behind the treatment, as well as the new skills. Qualitative analysis of participant experience highlighted themes of finally being "understood", "improved social signalling" and "improved connection". Example quotes included "I have done every treatment in every Special Hospital, and it is only RO DBT that relates to how I see the world" (In-patient A) and "every page of that manual appears to have been written with me in mind, it is how I have lived my life" (in-patient B). The focus upon being open and social signalling within RO DBT allowed our patients to shift, to consider repairing the relationship/alliance ruptures and engaging more effectively with their clinical teams. This was usually one of the first indicators that treatment was being effective, as clinical teams and nursing staff would begin to comment on how the patient was more engaged, conversational and less abrupt and aloof. A named nurse commented in a training evaluation form, "when I first met him (Patient C) he was cold, he was dead behind the eyes, and now I can't believe how happy and talkative he is, he even approached me and said hello!" One responsible clinician remarked that the multi-disciplinary team meeting was now prolonged and questioned "what have you done to him?" as the historical engagement was "how are you", "fine", "do you need anything", "no, thanks, goodbye". This had subsequently been replaced with an exploration of current concerns and treatment needs and a willingness to openly express and discuss these.

Whilst it is difficult to attribute all the changes in participants' social functioning to RO DBT, some other positive effects were noted post-treatment. These included no observations of significant life-threatening behaviour to others, two very long-term high-secure patients were progressed to medium-secure services, some patients opened up sufficiently to share in more detail their vulnerabilities which resulted in charges being brought against others who abused them and some provided more detail about their offending history. There was an observed increase in engagement particularly in trauma-focussed interventions post–RO DBT treatment, which may indicate greater awareness and comfortableness with emotional vulnerability. Although there was qualitative evidence of personal progress for individuals, some returned to prison and a number of patients remain stuck in high-secure services, having exhausted all treatment options yet not deemed suitable for conditions of less security.

This early adopter work provides a starting point to evaluate RO DBT, but in line with the ideas outlined in Chapter 2 of this book (Andrews & Justice, 2021), much more sophisticated treatment evaluation designs are required to determine the efficacy of RO DBT in a forensic context. Evaluations of RO DBT in community mental health services may provide useful insights into appropriate designs that could underpin future evaluation efforts (Lynch et al., 2020).

Staff training

In a two-year period, 16 one-day awareness sessions were facilitated as part of staff induction and ongoing training programmes in the hospital, with evaluation indicating better outcomes if the training facilitators were actively engaged in delivering RO DBT and were able to model the principles of RO DBT in their training delivery. These RO DBT training events were initially run only for the personality disorder service, but the shift to running a transdiagnostic group meant that the training intervention was extended to run across the diagnostically labelled directorates in the hospital.

Gardner and Hamilton (2017) found that training had increased understanding and buy-in from the staff about RO DBT. Staff started using the terms overcontrol and undercontrol to differentiate between patients and used Lynch's theoretical ideas to hypothesise about the everyday thinking, feeling and behaving of their OC service users. Staff also got better at identifying their own OC/UC leanings and being open enough to share their biases with patients, which in turn created a dialogue enhancing connectedness and mutual understanding. All the participants in Gardner and Hamilton (2017) felt more work was needed on developing staff understanding of overcontrol, commenting the RO DBT therapist team could "probably do a bit more work" on education because the OC patients are so different from others and require a radically different way of working with them. It was noted by the RO DBT therapist who conducted the initial pilots that OC patients' tendency to have high distress on the inside and low distress on the outside meant their distress often got missed, particularly when they were sharing a ward with undercontrolled patients who are highly skilled at drawing attention to their distress. Even after staff training and RO DBT skills training, OC patients found it difficult to get the same attention from staff as UC patients. This meant that OC patients often still struggle in silence, fearing that their requests for help, vulnerabilities and openness about rumination will not be consistently met with supportive intervention.

Further thoughts

These preliminary applications of RO DBT to forensic cases are a new development, and it appears this specialist treatment is helping previously hard-to-reach in-patients feel safer and more connected to people. In turn, a positive shift in patients' views about connectedness may encourage greater willingness to build and maintain therapeutic relationships, especially between patients and their clinical teams. The positive experience of these cohorts has also prompted the National High Secure Service for Women to deliver RO DBT (spring 2020), and the National High Secure Service for Learning Disability has commenced an adapted model of RO DBT in 2019. Since this pioneering work at Rampton High Secure Hospital, other forensic RO DBT or RO DBT informed forensic services have been popping up in prison (HMP Whatton, ACORN service) and lower-security forensic hospital services (Stockton Hall, Roseberry Park). There is also the National Forensic RO group (fROg), which is open to forensic services in the UK practicing RO DBT and is focused upon improving practice through supporting therapists and promoting a wider understanding, through research and formulation, of overcontrol and criminal behaviour.

Speculatively, applying a transdiagnostic approach to clinical practice and treatment intervention could help generate more valid practical decisions when identifying treatment needs and referring for psychological interventions to address personality difficulties and associated dynamic risk factors (Hamilton et al., 2018). Personality-based treatment may raise the internal validity and reduce variance in evaluation studies, and it could possibly lead to more consistent and clear results from evaluations of offending behaviour treatment programmes. A lack of adequate assessment procedures to screen and specifically assess for maladaptive overcontrol is hampering progress, however, and this area needs urgent attention. The overfocus in teaching curricula within mental health and forensic training programmes is something that also requires consideration, with greater attention given to those less eye-catching but often chronically debilitating conditions linked with having too much self-control (overcontrol) as opposed to too little self-control (undercontrol).

References

Asendorpf, J. B., & van Aken, M. A. G. (1999). Resilient, overcontrolled, and undercontrolled personality prototypes in childhood: Replicability, predictive power, and the trait-type issue. *Journal of Personality and Social Psychology*, 77, 815–832.

Bacon, L., Longfellow, E., & Hamilton, L. J. (2020). Don't get mad, get even!: Overcontrol and multiple victim violence. In G. A. Crews (Ed.), *Handbook of research on mass shootings and multiple victim violence* (pp. 193–200). IGI Global.

Blackburn, R., Logan, C., Donnelly, J. P., & Renwick, S. J. D. (2008). Identifying psychopathic subtypes: Combining an empirical personality classification of offenders with the psychopathy checklist-revised. *Journal of Personality Disorders*, 22(6), 604.

Blackburn, R., & Renwick, S. (1996). Rating scales for measuring the interpersonal circle in forensic psychiatric patients. *Psychological Assessment*, 8(1), 76.

Bohane, L., Maguire, N., & Richardson, T. (2017). Resilients, overcontrollers and undercontrollers: A systematic review of the utility of personality types in understanding adult mental health problems. *Clinical Psychology Review*, 57, 75–92.

Bonta, J., & Andrews, D. (2017). *The psychology of criminal conduct*. Routledge. https://doi.org/10.4324/9781315677187

Davey, L., Day, A., & Howells, K. (2005). Anger, overcontrol and serious violent offending. *Aggression and Violent Behavior*, 10(5), 624–635. doi:10.1016/j.avb.2004.12.002

Day, A., Howells, K., Mohr, P., Schall, E., & Gerace, A. (2008). The development of CBT programmes for anger: The role of interventions to promote perspective-taking skills. *Behavioural and Cognitive Psychotherapy*, 36(3), 299–312.

Douglas, K. S., Hart, S. D., Webster, C. D., & Belfrage, H. (2013). *HCR-20V3: Assessing risk of violence: User guide*. Mental Health, Law, and Policy Institute, Simon Fraser University.

D'Silva, K., & Duggan, C. (2010). Revisiting the overcontrolled: Undercontrolled typology of violent offenders. *Personality and Mental Health*, 4(3), 193–205.

Eaton, N. R., Rodriguez-Seijas, C., Carragher, N., & Krueger, R. F. (2015). Transdiagnostic factors of psychopathology and substance use disorders: A review. *Social Psychiatry and Psychiatric Epidemiology*, 50(2), 171–182. https://doi.org/10.1007/s00127-014-1001-2

Evans, C., Connell, J., Barkham, M., Margison, F., McGrath, G., Mellor-Clark, J., & Audin, J. (2002). Towards a standardised brief outcome measure: Psychometric properties and utility of the CORE-OM. *British Journal of Psychiatry*, 180, 51–60.

Ewers, P., Bradshaw, T., McGovern, J., & Ewers, B. (2002). Does training in psychosocial interventions reduce burnout rates in forensic nurses? *Journal of Advanced Nursing, 37,* 470–476. https://doi.org/10.1046/j.1365-2648.2002.02115.x

Gardner, N., & Hamilton, L. (2017). IPA analysis of RO-DBT therapists experiences of implementing a new programme in a high secure hospital. Msc dissertation. NTU.

Gilbert, P., McEwan, K., Mitra, R., Richter, A., Franks, L., Mills, A., Bellew, R., & Gale, C. (2009). An exploration of different types of positive affect in students and in patients with bipolar disorder. *Clinical Neuropsychiatry, 6,* 135–143.

Gottfredson, M. R., & Hirschi, T. (1990). *A general theory of crime.* Stanford University Press.

Hamilton, L., Bacon, L., Longfellow, E., & Tennant, A. (2018). Not everything is as it seems: RO DBT and overcontrolled disorders in forensic settings. *The Behavior Therapist, 41*(3), 157–160. ISSN: 0278–8403.

Hamilton, L., Winder, B., Norman, C., & Baguley, T. (submitted for publication). *The perils of high self control: A systematic review of maladaptive overcontrol and offending.*

Hempel, R., Booth, R., Giblin, A., Hamilton, L., Hoch, A., Portner, J., . . . & Wolf-Arehult, M. (2018). The implementation of RO DBT in clinical practice. *The Behavior Therapist, 41,* 161–173.

Henderson, M. (1983b). An empirical classification of non-violent offenders using the MMPI. *Personality and Individual Differences, 4*(6), 671–677.

Herzberg, P. Y., & Hoyer, J. (2009). Personality prototypes in adult offenders. *Criminal Justice and Behavior, 36*(3), 259–274. https://doi.org/10.1177/0093854808328331

Herzberg, P. Y., & Roth, M. (2006). Beyond resilients, undercontrollers, and overcontrollers? An extension of personality prototype research. *European Journal of Personality, 20*(1), 5–28. https://doi.org/10.1002/per.557

Insel, T., Cuthbert, B., Garvey, M., Heinssen, R., Pine, D. S., Quinn, K., . . . & Wang, P. (2010). Research domain criteria (RDoC): Toward a new classification framework for research on mental disorders. *The American Journal of Psychiatry, 167*(7), 748–751. https://doi.org/10.1176

Kotov, R., Krueger, R. F., Watson, D., Achenbach, T. M., Althoff, R. R., Bagby, R. M., . . . & Zimmerman, M. (2017). The Hierarchical Taxonomy of Psychopathology (HiTOP): A dimensional alternative to traditional nosologies. *Journal of Abnormal Psychology, 126,* 454–477. doi:10.1037/abn0000258

Lee, A. H., & DiGiuseppe, R. (2018). Anger and aggression treatments: A review of meta-analyses. *Current Opinion in Psychology, 19,* 65–74.

Linehan, M. M. (2015). *DBT skills training manual* (2nd ed.). Guilford Press.

Low, K., & Day, A. (2015). Toward a clinically meaningful taxonomy of violent offenders: The role of anger and thinking styles. *Journal of Interpersonal Violence, 32*(4), 489–514. https://doi.org/10.1177/0886260515586365

Lynch, T. R. (2015). *Training radically Open: Dialectical behavioral therapy manual*. Unpublished manuscript.

Lynch, T. R. (2018). *Radically open dialectical behavior therapy: Theory and practice for treating disorder of overcontrol*. New Harbinger Publications.

Lynch, T., Hempel, R., Whalley, B., Byford, S., Chamba, R., Clarke, P., ... & Russell, I. (2020). Refractory depression: Mechanisms and efficacy of radically open dialectical behaviour therapy (RefraMED): Findings of a randomised trial on benefits and harms. *The British Journal of Psychiatry, 216*(4), 204–212. doi:10.1192/bjp.2019.53

Mears, D., Cochran, J., & Beaver, K. (2013). Self-control theory and nonlinear effects on offending. *Journal of Quantitative Criminology, 29*(3), 447–476.

Megargee, E. I. (1966). Undercontrolled and overcontrolled personality types in extreme antisocial aggression. *Psychological Monographs: General and Applied, 80*(3), 1–29.

Moffitt, T. E., Arseneault, L., Belsky, D., Dickson, N., Hancox, R. J., Harrington, H., . . . & Caspi, A. (2011). A gradient of childhood self-control predicts health, wealth, and public safety. *Proceedings of the National Academy of Sciences, 108*(7), 2693–2698.

Moffitt, T. E., Poulton, R., & Caspi, A. (2013). Lifelong impact of early self-control. *American Scientist, 100*(5), 352–359.

Mullins-Sweatt, S. N., Hopwood, C. J., Chmielewski, M., Meyer, N. A., Min, J., Helle, A. C., & Walgren, M. D. (2020). Treatment of personality pathology through the lens of the hierarchical taxonomy of psychopathology: Developing a research agenda. *Personality and Mental Health, 14*(1), 123–141. https://doi.org/10.1002/pmh.1464

Pickersgill, M. (2013). How personality became treatable: The mutual constitution of clinical knowledge and mental health law. *Social Studies of Science, 43*(1), 30–53. https://doi.org/10.1177/0306312712457722

Pratt, T. C., & Cullen, F. T. (2000). The empirical status of Gottfredson and Hirschi's general theory of crime: A meta-analysis. *Criminology, 38*, 931–964. https://doi.org/10.1111

Redondo, N., Cantos, A. L., Graña, J. L., Muñoz-Rivas, M. J., & O'Leary, K. D. (2019). Treatment-induced changes in undercontrolled and overcontrolled anger subtypes of perpetrators of intimate partner violence and 5-year recidivism. *Criminal Justice and Behavior, 46*(12), 1700–1718. https://doi.org/10.1177/0093854819879201

Robins, R. W., John, R. W., Caspi, A., Moffitt, T. E., & Stouthamer-Loeber, M. (1996). Resilient, overcontrolled, and undercontrolled boys: Three replicable personality types. *Journal of Personality and Social Psychology, 70*, 157–171.

Spielberger, C. D. (1999). *State-Trait Anger Expression Inventory-2: Professional manual*. Psychological Assessment Resources.

Whiteside, S. P., & Lynam, D. R. (2001). The five factor model and impulsivity: Using a structural model of personality to understand impulsivity. *Personality and Individual Differences, 30*(4), 669–689.

Widiger, T. A., & McCabe, G. A. (2020). The Alternative Model of Personality Disorders (AMPD) from the perspective of the Five-Factor Model. *Psychopathology, 53*(3–4), 149–156. https://doi.org/10.1159/000507378

Widom, C. S. (1978). An empirical classification of female offenders. *Criminal Justice and Behavior, 5*(1), 35–52.

Wong, S. C. P., & Gordon, A. (2006). The validity and reliability of the violence risk scale: A treatment-friendly violence risk assessment tool. *Psychology, Public Policy, and Law, 12*(3), 279–309.

Worling, J. R. (2001). Personality-based typology of adolescent male sexual offenders: Differences in recidivism rates, victim-selection characteristics, and personal victimization histories. *Sexual Abuse: A Journal of Research and Treatment, 13*(3), 149–166.

6

A healthy sex programme for individuals with paraphilic interests convicted of sexual offending

Biopsychosocial processes and intervention procedures

Jamie S. Walton

Introduction

In the modern time of intervention science, a new question is upon us: "What core biopsychosocial processes should be targeted with this client given this goal in this situation, and how can they most efficiently and effectively be changed?" (Hayes & Hofmann, 2018a, p. 428). Answering it involves targeting established processes that promote change. The change sought by interventions is to the prosperity of the individual and their ability to live skilfully and non-harmfully, rather than in the mere absence of their risks. The question is undoubtedly more complex than a binary question, such as "does intervention work?" In the field of programmes for sexual offending, differences between interventions and weak standards of scientific rigor have made this question difficult to answer (Schmucker & Lösel, 2017; Walton, 2018). However, this new question requires clinicians to search from a wider spectrum of biological, behavioural, cognitive and emotion science and to specify core processes of change and their links to the intervention procedures used. In doing so, an emphasis on the mediators of change is likely to increase and, with it, an account of what, when, why and how programmes yield particular effects may begin to emerge.

In this chapter, I will describe the Healthy Sex Programme (HSP). The HSP is designed for adult men with convictions for sexual offending who experience

DOI: 10.4324/9780429262074-6

offence-related paraphilic interests. The HSP is delivered in prisons within Her Majesty's Prison and Probation Service (HMPPS) and is open to those with and without mild learning disability and challenges (LDC). The programme was revised in 2019 and has received accreditation from the Correctional Services Advice and Accreditation Panel (CSAAP). In the first section of this chapter, I will describe the biopsychosocial processes that shape the manifestation of paraphilia. In the second section, I will describe the intervention procedures that are used to achieve intervention goals with HSP participants. These procedures span different competencies from cognitive behavioural therapy (CBT). They include behaviour modification and self-management, modification of beliefs, mindfulness, values clarification, compassion work, urge management and intimacy/ interpersonal skills practice. Across mental healthcare, these procedures have been shown to lead to change and manipulate processes that mediate it. As such, they are considered to be evidence-informed (Hayes & Hofmann, 2018b). The change processes include behavioural learning processes, changes in cognition, increased metacognition, psychological acceptance, decentring, reduced rumination, values clarification, physiological soothing, increased compassion and improved interpersonal skills. I will discuss how the procedures are used in the HSP, but firstly and for the benefit of readers less familiar with this area, I provide a brief introduction to paraphilia.

Paraphilia

The term 'paraphilia' can be defined as "any intense and persistent sexual interest other than a sexual interest in genital stimulation or preparatory fondling with phenotypically normal, physically mature, consenting human partners" (American Psychiatric Association [APA], 2013, p. 685). 'Phenotypically normal' in this case refers to the typical characteristics of adults. There are currently eight classifiable paraphilic conditions according to the American Psychological Association (APA) (see Table 6.1, see also Beech, Miner & Thornton, 2016; First, 2014). Four of them, namely voyeurism, exhibitionism, frotteurism and paedophilia, if acted on, result in a criminal act. The others may be legally fulfilled with consenting partners. Some surveys suggest that voyeuristic, masochistic, and fetishistic experiences and fantasies are not unusual (Joyal & Carpentier, 2016). However, for other paraphilia they are much rarer. For example, the rates of fantasising about sexual acts with a pre-pubescent child has been reported to be about 4% in a male German sample (Dombert et al., 2016), about 1.8% in a male Canadian sample (Joyal, Cossette & Lapierre, 2015) and less than 1% in a sample of male Finnish twins (Santtila et al., 2015). Based on a range of available surveys, an informed guestimate for the prevalence of an actual paedophilic preference in the general male

Table 6.1 Clinically Recognised Paraphilia

Paraphilia	*Ability to derive sexual pleasure, excitement or arousal from:*
Voyeurism	Watching an unsuspecting nonconsenting person(s) nude, disrobing or engaging in sex
Fetishism	Non-living objects or specific body parts
Exhibitionism	Exposing one's own genitals to an unsuspecting non-consenting person(s)
Frotteurism	Touching or rubbing against a non-unsuspecting, non-consenting person(s)
Masochism	Being humiliated, hit, bound or otherwise suffering
Sexual Sadism	Physical or emotional suffering of others
Transvestitism	Cross-dressing that is sexually arousing
Paedophilia	Sexual activity with a child that is prepubescent (<13 years)

population is approximately 1%, and for women this is likely to be lower (see Seto, 2017, 2018 for reviews). The DSM-V (APA, 2013) uses the term 'paraphilic disorder' to classify paraphilia that lead to distress, impairment or harmful non-consenting sexual acts. This makes it possible for paraphilia to occur without a person receiving a mental health diagnosis. This is important because although paraphilia are associated with sexual recidivism (Mann, Hanson & Thornton, 2010), many people who experience them function without offending (Cantor & McPhail, 2016) or experiencing distress or impairment (Wismeijer & Assen, 2013). Therefore, it is 'paraphilic disorder' that distinguishes the dysfunctional manifestations of paraphilia. Paraphilia per se are not necessarily pathological.

There is debate about whether paraphilia are changeable, and some of this is related to a question of whether some are best defined as a sexual orientation. In terms of the first issue, all but one paraphilic disorder can be classified as 'in remission' according to the DSM-V. This is defined as a period of five years or more, where in an uncontrolled environment distress, impairment or harm has been absent. This does not necessarily mean that the paraphilia has disappeared. The specifier relates to the dysfunction, not the sexual interest. The exemption is 'paedophilic disorder', for which there is no remission specifier at all (APA, 2013). This omission would appear deliberate, but there is little evidence to suggest that the features of distress, impairment or risk of perpetrating harmful behaviour are more intractable for paedophilic disorder than they are for other paraphilia disorders. As such, this exemption is quite contentious (Briken, Fedoroff & Bradford, 2014).

Paedophilia itself, however, seems fairly stable. Large-scale surveys suggest that the onset occurs during puberty and then persists (Bailey, Hsu & Bernhard, 2016b; Grundmann, Krupp, Scherner, Amelung & Beier, 2016). Where change has been reported using phallometric testing (Müller et al., 2014), it has been the subject of criticism (Cantor, 2015; Bailey, 2015; Lalumière, 2015). Furthermore, the view that paedophilia and other paraphilia are stable now pervades some clinics, where goals toward self-management are favoured (Berlin Institute of Sexology and Sexual Medicine, 2013). Other clinicians claim that paraphilia are changeable (Marshall, 2008). Fedoroff (2016, 2018a) in particular suggests that clinicians should advise their clients that there is no evidence that paraphilia cannot be changed and that their prognosis is 'excellent'. This type of messaging is divisive (see Cantor, 2018). Clinicians should certainly try to evoke their client's motivation for change, but they should be careful not to engender false hope.

The second issue is whether certain paraphilia should be defined as a sexual orientation (e.g., paedophilia, Seto, 2012). Seto (2017) has argued that sexual orientation is a broad concept, defined as a tendency to orient people preferentially in terms of their attention, interest, attraction and arousal to classes of stimuli along different dimensions. These dimensions are not limited to gender, but could also include age and species. Seto (2017) suggests that sexual interests in different stages of maturation can be defined along a dimension of sexual orientation for age. Some have welcomed this idea and applied it to other paraphilia (e.g., zoophilia; Miletski, 2017) and others have rejected it entirely (Fedoroff, 2018b).

These issues are beyond the scope of this chapter. In short, the majority consensus is that paraphilia are stable. However, this should not be conflated with a view that people do not or cannot change. Some paraphilia are related to other presentations, for example, an emotional identification with children (Hermann, McPhail, Helmus & Hanson, 2017) and hypersexuality (Kafka, 2010). Paraphilic exclusivity also varies, with few people reporting exclusive sexual interests, particularly in children (McPhail, Olver, Brouillette-Alarie & Looman, 2018). This is important because an exclusive interest is associated with higher sexual recidivism and sexual compulsivity (McPhail et al., 2018; McPhail, 2018), as well as self-reported offending in non-forensic samples (Bailey, Bernhard & Hsu, 2016a). In the HSP, the agenda is orientated toward expanding functional repertoires for the thriving of the *whole person* toward a constructive crime-free life. Within this it is expected that change will look, feel and function differently for different people. This will depend on the biopsychosocial processes underlying how their paraphilia manifests and their capacities for change in other domains. The next section discusses several biopsychosocial processes that influence paraphilia.

Part 1: biopsychosocial processes underlying paraphilia

Biopsychosocial models of sexual offending and characteristics associated with recidivism have been proposed before (Marshall & Barbaree, 1990; Carter & Mann, 2016). However, in this chapter, I provide more of a focus on paraphilia. Typically, in a biopsychosocial model, 'biological processes' refers to genetics, hormones, physiology and neurobiology; 'psychological processes' refers to motivational and cognitive systems (e.g., perception, beliefs, memory) and learning processes, including observation and classical and operant conditioning; whereas 'social processes' are concerned with peer and societal influences, as well as the wider cultural context. Although these processes are presented separately, they should be thought of as bidirectional and reciprocally influential.

Biological processes

Starting broadly, sexual offending clusters in families (Långström, Babchishin, Fazel, Lichtenstein & Frisell, 2015). This is mostly explained by genetic and non-shared environmental factors. Some paraphilia, particularly paedophilia, may be heritable (Alanko, Gunst, Mokros & Santtila, 2016; Alanko, Salo, Mokros & Santtilla, 2013), but this does not mean that they are genetically predetermined. Genetic variations may play a role, but as with all complex behaviour, this will likely be about potential, not certainty. Genetic influences will be contextually dependent on other biological factors, learning and the social environment.

A neurohormonal model of paraphilia has been proposed by Kafka (2003). Paraphilias often co-occur with hypersexual behaviour, as well as mood disorders (Kafka, 2010). Kafka (2010) has suggested that these co-occurrences indicate a general biological vulnerability. He proposes disturbances in the processes of neurotransmitters such as dopamine and serotonin as the cause. These interact with the male sex hormone testosterone, providing a biological substrate for sexual drive. Sexual drive is certainly relevant. For example, in a survey of paraphilia, Dawson, Bannerman and Lalumière (2016) found that measures of sex drive and hypersexuality were related to paraphilia and accounted for the gender difference found in prevalence rates. These authors suggest a high sex drive motivates interests in rare sex acts and contributes to their development. However, in terms of Kafka's model, it remains unclear why disrupted neurotransmitter levels would affect the specificity of sexual interests.

Neuroscientific studies have so far offered the most extensive evidence of a biological mechanism for paraphilia. There have been two main lines of enquiry.

The first is the measurement of neurodevelopmental correlates. The second is neuroimaging of structural brain differences. The neurodevelopmental studies have revealed that men with paedophilia often have mild features associated with abnormal neurodevelopment. Examples include lower intellectual quotient (IQ) (Cantor et al., 2004), elevated rates of left-handedness (Fazio, Lykins & Cantor, 2014), shorter height and leg length (Fazio, Dyshniku, Lykins & Cantor, 2015; McPhail & Cantor, 2015) and minor physical abnormalities (Dyshniku, Murray, Fazio, Lykins & Cantor, 2015). These features are thought to be neurodevelopmental markers because they begin in utero, are affected by prenatal stress (e.g., maternal malnutrition, drug use) and solidify during childhood (Fazio, 2018). The neuroimaging studies have shown neural white and grey matter differences between individuals with and without paedophilia. Some authors suggest a pattern of *dys*connectivity in white matter circuitry associated with the sexual response processing in the brain (Cantor et al., 2015; Cantor et al., 2016).

One problem with the neuroscience so far is the reliance on forensic samples. This risks conflating factors associated with offence status (criminality) with sexual interest (paraphilia). For example, a lower IQ has since been found to relate to offence status, not paedophilia (Gerwinna et al., 2018). Some grey matter differences have also been attributed to offence status, rather than paedophilia (Schiffer et al., 2017). Therefore, it is possible that sexual offending rather than sexual preference better explains many of the differences observed in neuroscientific studies (Joyal et al., 2019). At present, although the possibility remains that neurodevelopmental anomalies are involved, the science suggests some caution should be applied. Most likely is that some paraphilia start prenatally, but that the course and manifestation are also shaped by learning processes and specific social niches.

Psychological processes

The learning processes set out by behaviourists such as Ivan Pavlov and B.F. Skinner were heralded as a cause of paraphilia for decades (e.g., McGuire, Carlisle & Young, 1965). The basic model suggests that when the natural response of arousal (unconditioned response) elicited by genital stimulation (unconditional stimulus) is paired with a neutral stimulus, for example, an inanimate object such as long leather boots, the neutral stimulus obtains the function of eliciting arousal (Figure 6.1a). It in turn serves as an antecedent for the contingency of positive reinforcement; that is, where the rewarding consequence of sexual pleasure increases the intensity and frequency of sexual response in its presence (Figure 6.1b). Generalisation can then allow the learning contingency to include other stimuli (e.g., other leatherwear). Long leather boots are a normalised and accepted fetishism, but other neutral stimuli could include children or violence.

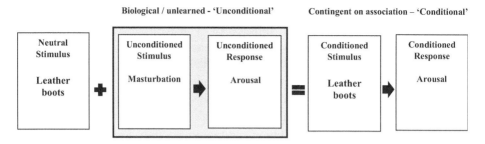

Figure 6.1a Stimulus-Response contingency: transfer of stimulus function of leather boots

Source: Images drawn by author.

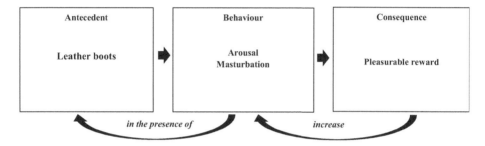

Figure 6.1b Positive reinforcement contingency: increase frequency and intensity of sexual response

Source: Images drawn by author.

Behaviour learning processes are unequivocal. However, as an explanation for paraphilia, researchers have reported parsimonious support because the evidence that paraphilia develop through contingency learning is weak (Camilleri & Quinsey, 2008; Seto, 2018). Contemporary behavioural learning accounts have been provided (Roche & Quayle, 2007). However, it remains the case that learning processes alone are insufficient as a causal explanation and that they probably influence paraphilia to the extent that an individual is already predisposed. This might include a biological predisposition as discussed earlier. Another potential predisposition is childhood adversity and the associated early learning experiences which affect life-course development.

Broadly, there is emergent evidence of significantly high (but by no means universal) levels of adverse childhood experiences (ACEs) in people convicted of sexual offending (Jespersen, Lalumière & Seto, 2009; Levenson, Willis & Prescott, 2016; Seto & Lalumière, 2010). Furthermore, individuals convicted of sexual offending report more ACEs consisting of sexual abuse than do individuals convicted of non-sexual offending (Jespersen et al., 2009; Reavis, Looman, Franco & Rojas, 2013; Seto & Lalumière, 2010). This is also found at the offence-type level, with those convicted of sexual offending against children reporting higher rates of childhood sexual abuse than those convicted of sexual offending against adults (Jespersen et al., 2009; Seto & Lalumière, 2010). High ACEs are also associated with higher sexual deviancy scores (Levenson et al., 2016; Levenson & Grady, 2016).

How could ACEs increase vulnerability for sexual offending and paraphilia? The first point to note is that childhood adversity impacts the attachment system. Attachment is a biological process as much as anything else, but it also encapsulates learning, memory and emotion responding, as well as the development of cognitive representations of self, others and the world. Growing up in a stressful, unpredictable, unsafe or otherwise emotionally impoverished environment can have drastic effects in these domains. Humans are born built to form a secure attachment bond, inclusive of validating biofeedback. When it is not provided, a cascade of neurodevelopmental changes can occur that impede abilities for self-regulation, intimacy, cognitive flexibility and social affiliation. It is of no surprise that the changes can manifest characteristics associated with recidivism in later life such as impulsivity, emotional dysregulation, hostility, intimacy difficulties, poor coping and an emotional identification with children. In many cases, a confused and frightened child has become a fragmented and insecure adult whose attempts to alleviate their own emotional pain increase injury to themselves and others. The absence of a childrearing environment that is in every sense of the word 'growth-facilitating', providing safe experiences for cooperation and prosocial learning, changes a person from how genes are expressed and brains grow to the internal psychological models that form and how social life unfolds. Quite literally, "the body keeps the score" (see van der Kolk, 2014 for a book-length review).

As for the way childhood adversity and abuse could increase a person's vulnerability for developing paraphilia, the causal processes are less clear. MacCulloch, Gray and Watt (2000), for example, suggest a process of 'sensory preconditioning' for sadism that results from sexual abuse. MacCulloch et al. outline how sexual abuse can evoke anger and aggression in a child and sometimes abuse-related arousal. If there are sufficient pairings of these experiences, it is proposed that anger and aggression could become antecedents for eliciting arousal. Observational learning is another process that has been considered (Burton, 2003). Individuals could simply copy abusive acts that were once perpetrated against them. Whilst these processes are plausible, they rely on little more than copying and associative learning. Because ACEs can have such disruptive effects on global neurodevelopment, it is more likely that other vulnerabilities develop which influence how paraphilia manifest. Examples might include an emotional identification with children, problems with sexual self-regulation and beliefs that endorse sexual abuse. These can co-vary with some paraphilia, for example, paedophilia (Hermann et al., 2017; McPhail, Hermann & Fernandez, 2014), and those who report a history of childhood sexual abuse as compared to those who do not can exhibit higher rates of them (Blank, Nunes, Maimone, Hermann & McPhail, 2018).

Social processes

Society and culture matter. From peer groups, to social norms, to cultural attitudes and media-technology, all are influential. Two social processes that are studied for their influence on paraphilia are internet pornography (Fisher, Kohut, Di Gioacchino & Fedoroff, 2013) and social stigmatisation (Jahnke, 2018a). These processes cannot be said to cause paraphilia, though they are researched for how they influence sexual behaviour and personal distress.

In terms of internet pornography, one issue is clear. Rapid technological growth has created seismic shifts in pornography accessibility and culture. Pornography has changed unrecognisably from the 1990s, when watching sexually explicit material often involved the acquisition of a VHS cassette or DVD. In recent years free-access licensed platforms such as 'RedTube' and 'PornHub' offer viewing of clips that people have upload to share with an online community. Clips are listed by category (e.g., 'Anal', 'Bondage', 'Gangbang'), and some are headed toward paraphilic themes (e.g., 'Teen'). PornHub publishes its annual usership data. Global use is colossal. In 2019 PornHub hosted 42 billion visits, averaging 115 million visits per day. PornHub's amateurs, models and content partners uploaded 6.83 million new videos.[1] To put this in perspective, PornHub.com in their 2019 Year in Review, state that if you merged all the content uploaded to PornHub in 2019 and started watching it way back in 1850, you would still be watching it in 2020. This level of unlimited novelty is what can be called a 'supernormal stimulus'. It is an artificially exaggerated imitation of sex. It recruits the reward system, but activates it on a level never faced by our ancestors. Some scientists have implicated the inexhaustible novelty and chronic dopamine activation in the conditioning of arousal, as well as increases in sexual dysfunction (Park et al., 2016). Others suggest we should not under- or over-credit it as a clinical issue (Fisher & Kohut, 2017).

Even authors with such differing views would surely agree that intervention is desirable when an individual is harmed by pornography. They will disagree on the extent to which evidence is sufficiently robust to draw causal inferences about general social harms. Pornography use is not a sufficient cause of paraphilia or sexual offending (Fisher et al., 2013). It does seem reasonable, though, that a person would seek pornography that reflects their sexual interests, paraphilic or not. This means that some people who search for child sexual exploitation material (CSEM), teen or sadomasochistic content on mainstream sites could already be engaged in harmful behaviour. For example, in a sample of 110 men, McCarthy (2010) found that 84% had engaged in child abuse before they possessed CSEM. Individuals such as these convicted of both contact sexual offending and downloading CSEM are most likely to have a sexual interest in children (Babchishin, Hanson & Van Zuylen, 2015). At the very least it seems that pornography in the context of previous contact sexual offending could influence paraphilia or otherwise obstruct offence-free living.

The stigmatisation of paraphilia is not universal. For some paraphilia, however, it is particularly harsh. Typecasts about paedophilia, for example, are that individuals are dangerous, amoral and in control of what they are attracted to (Imhoff, 2015; Imhoff & Jahnke, 2018; Jahnke, Imhoff & Hoyer, 2015; Jahnke, 2018b). Hate for individuals with paedophilia is found at all levels of Western society, including the young, educated and liberal-minded (Imhoff, 2015; Imhoff & Jahnke, 2018). The effects are bleak. They include marginalisation, stress (of disguise), anger, fear and shame, all of which are threatened states toxic to health. Recently, researchers have turned their attention to the harmful effects of stigmatisation on characteristics associated with sexual recidivism (Jahnke & Hoyer, 2013; Jahnke, Schmidt, Geradt & Hoyer, 2015) and how responses to such an internalising and suppressing stigma impact the wellbeing of people with paedophilia and their ability to seek help (Grady, Levenson, Mesias, Kavanagh & Charles, 2019; Lievesley, Harper & Elliott, 2020).

Biopsychosocial summary

Susceptibility to paraphilia likely emerges early, sometimes prenatally, but the manifestation is also shaped by the environmental niche provided. ACEs feature in the history of many people with paraphilia, and something corrosive has often happened. Many paraphilia are a puzzle (Seto, 2017). However, one thing is clear: no one chooses them. No one chooses their genetics or prenatal influences, the childhood experiences and learning processes that shape their beliefs or the cultural context in which they are born and whether society accepts or marginalises them. That said, everyone is responsible for safe sexual expression, and no one has the right to sexually abuse others. A programme can support a person to build capacities to realise this responsibility but not by merely removing their risks. It must promote a non-harmful life trajectory in which prosocial behaviour is appealing. To do this the programme needs to be responsive to the neurodevelopmental consequences of adversity and trauma. It would also benefit from attending to shame and teaching techniques that regulate threatened states of social rejection. Beyond this, the procedures would need to target emotion regulation, intimacy and cognition, as well as behavioural and arousal management. The HSP was recently revised with these aims in mind.

Part 2: the Healthy Sex Programme

The HSP is accessed via one of four programme pathways in HMPPS. People assessed as high risk without LDC who present with strong criminogenic needs across attitudinal, relationship and self-regulation domains access *Kaizen*, whilst those with LDC access *Becoming New Me Plus* (BNM+). Individuals who have less need and more pro-social skills access less intensive intervention, called *Horizon*, and those with LDC access *New Me Strengths* (NMS). Walton, Ramsay, Cunningham and Henfrey (2017), Ramsay, Carter and Walton (2020), and Ramsay (2020) have provided an overview of these programmes. The HSP is delivered in prisons to graduates of these programmes who exhibit paraphilia **and** are either experiencing distress **and/or** are assessed as requiring support to build skills for a leading law-abiding life.

The HSP offers 12 to 30 hours of one-to-one intervention divided across five modules which focus on engagement, formulation and planning, building skills for safe sexual self-regulation, sex and intimacy psychoeducation and relapse prevention. Each module contains a number of exercises, which are structured around different intervention procedures that make up the bulk of evidence-based CBT procedures. It is not possible to review all the exercises here, but the procedures will be described. Most exercises are optional, and they can be flexibly sequenced. This offers a tailorable programme that provides therapists with the scope to craft a bespoke intervention plan, which can be adjusted according to the emerging needs, strengths and responsivity requirements of their participants. Therapists are mostly psychologists, though some qualified probation officers are also trained. All therapists must be experienced in working with the people convicted of sexual offending. They must meet standards of competency on HSP training and receive supervision for each case from the HSP treatment manager or an HSP supervisor. Before discussing the intervention procedures, it is important to talk about how the programme aims to be responsive.

Responsivity to the neurodevelopmental effects of adverse childhood experiences

As already mentioned, childhood adversity can lead to corrosive neurodevelopmental injuries with implications for adult life. These can manifest in many domains, including verbal, attention and memory functions, as well as emotional dysregulation and cognitive inflexibility. To work with this, the HSP uses a brain-friendly approach that appeals more widely to neurodiversity, as described by Williams and Carter (2018). It is essentially a multimodal approach, whereby methods for sensory learning such as visual, auditory and kinaesthetic are used as much as possible. The aim is to minimise an excessive focus on traditional sedentary routines that are literacy-centred: sitting, verbalising, reading, writing and so forth. Alternative learning methods might include in-action 'body-movement' techniques, symbolising, drawing, gesturing, skills practice and brain-breaks. The idea is to blend such methods to achieve a rich variety of ways for learning.

Beyond the impact on neurocognitive functioning and learning, ACEs can also make it difficult for people to regulate threat. Without a predictable, reciprocal, caring and safe environment, the attachment system becomes specialised in processing threat. This can present differently for different individuals, depending on other risk vulnerabilities that may manifest such as emotional dysregulation or seeking emotional closeness and intimacy with children. For some individuals, resistance to perceived authority may present in observable ways, with aggression and antagonism, whilst a fear of adults could be observed in others. Much of this is understandable in the context of brains that have specialised in abandonment, threat and fear with little experience of a safe haven. Pressuring individuals who experience these challenges to engage in the HSP is unlikely to foster alliance and a basis for change. As such, like Kaizen, BNM+, Horizon and NMS, as a basis for engagement, HSP merely asks that a participant invests in learning new pro-social skills – building on personal strengths, trying new tactics and exploring what works. A lot of what risk management professionals view as 'needing' to change (e.g., hostility, rigidity, impulsivity, sexualised coping, etc.), although restrictive and/or harmful, often developed out of conditions that fall short of what is required for humans to pro-socially flourish. They frequently function for self-protection, and change or merely exploring different ways of doing things can be daunting.

To work with this the HSP therapist is encouraged to act as a supportive coach. What this means in practice is that they aim to inspire, motivate and affirm internal strength and evoke curiosity in the change process. It also means they compassionately support coping with the suffering linked to childhood adversity or stigmatisation as it surfaces, perhaps as anger, anxiety, fear or shame. In short, there is a sensitivity in the HSP toward the fact that even in the simple request to learn skills for change, participants will encounter uncomfortable territory and necessarily work with it in the service of increasing their behavioural repertoire for leading a crime-free life. This is partly the basis of developing a compassionate mind (Gilbert, 2010), and compassion training is an optional intervention procedure featured in the programme.

Building compassion

Compassion can be defined as a sensitivity to suffering in self and others, with a commitment to try to prevent and alleviate it (Gilbert & Choden, 2013). This is courageous because it requires a turn towards painful states that are often displaced, for example, anger, fear or disgust. It is also a strengthening act because it involves stimulating emotions and competencies that foster helpful rather than harmful living. Compassion is felt precisely when emotional pain shows up. It draws on a care-based motivational system that evolved first in mammals and a set of evolutionary newer competencies that are cognitive and unique to humans (Gilbert, 2019). Compassion training was designed for dealing with the exact type of painful state that is often experienced in people with certain paraphilia; namely, *shame*. There is evidence of positive outcomes for compassion intervention in healthcare (Kirby, Tellegen & Steindl, 2017). Compassion training is also adaptable for participants with LDC (Clapton, Williams, Griffiths & Jones, 2018; Cowles, Randle-Phillips & Medley, 2020). The HSP aims to develop two qualities of compassion, namely (1) to empathically engage with the suffering of self and others and (2) to build skills for taking helpful action in dealing with it. The work toward building these qualities is simply called 'Compassionate Me'.

Rather than convincing a participant that they should be compassionate, the idea is to introduce a model that helps them realise the inherent difficulties of being human such that compassion makes sense. The model is called 'Three Circles' (Figure 6.2), and it is developed from the work of Professor Paul Gilbert (Gilbert, 2010). It is grounded in the neuroscience of evolved emotion regulation systems that we share with our mammalian ancestors. In short, as mammals, humans have a threat system (red system). This system governs us, exhibiting emotions like anger, fear, disgust and anxiety. We also have states that activate us, for example, excitement and lust. These ensure we pursue resources and are reward driven (blue system). We also have abilities for bonding and feeling safe and soothed (green system). These safeness functions are central to our attachment system – a vital adaptation in all mammals. Unlike many mammals, though, and at the core of why being human is *so* difficult, we have new competencies such as language, reasoning, imagination and self-awareness. They are both our defining advantage and our greatest challenge. They produce unmatched intelligence, but also arbitrarily activate ancient motivations and emotions that for hundreds of millions of years have organised species to pursue, avoid and attack. This leads to profound sources of pain for us, for example, humiliation, vengeance and shame.

The HSP therapist works with the model to depathologise negative affect. Simply put, human emotion is not a human's fault. Our brains evolved through natural selection. We arbitrarily inherit them, and they are choreographed by the environment we coincidently inhabit. Little is chosen. Where ACEs have occurred, a therapist can sensitively suggest how it makes sense for *any* human to develop a robust threat system when threat has featured in life. However, in the case of paraphilia and sexual offending, because of how socially despised they are, the source of threat is often to the most crucial biological need for humans – the ability to belong (Walton, 2019). In turn, the threat system activates as it is meant to, but because of our cognitive competencies, the experience is imaginary and it is constructed cognitively and verbally. It may be oneself as 'bad', 'sick' and valueless to others. This experience is 'internal shame', and it can be agonising. Escaping the agony can include projecting one's shameful features onto others and attacking them (Gilbert, 2018) or constantly self-monitoring for one's inevitable faults (Gilbert, 2010). Both are survival strategies in response to threat, and this threat-based state can prioritise many such strategies,

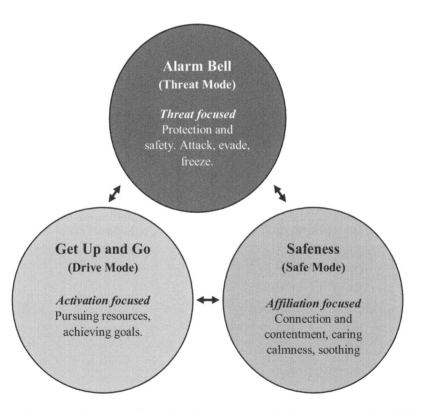

Figure 6.2 Three functionally evolved emotion regulation systems adapted from work by Paul Gilbert.

Source: Image drawn by author

including denial, blaming and hostility. In short, internal shame is unlikely to contribute toward a crime-free life because it shuts people off to caring for others, including the harms they have caused them. For a person to take responsibility for leading a crime-free life, they must experience a sensitivity to the suffering that they can cause to others. To do this, they need also to be able to engage with their own suffering and have the capacities to take helpful action in dealing with it.

Re-balancing the three systems is important. However, this is not a cognitive task, at least not initially. These systems are ancient, and much of their phenomena exist biophysically in the body's viscera. "The body keeps the score" (Van de Kolk, 2014), and so the work often needs to begin with the body to initiate the physiological functions of the safeness system, specifically those of the parasympathetic nervous system (PSNS), which acts as a counteracting force to the body's stress response. Similar to most compassion and emotion regulation work (Gilbert, 2010; McKay, 2018), the HSP uses a breathing technique that focuses on a slow rhythmic breath, deep from the diaphragm, extending the exhale to activate parasympathetic arousal. This technique can improve emotion regulation and self-control, and the main neurobiological process mediating these benefits appears to be respiratory stimulation of the vagus nerve (Gerritsen & Band, 2018). The vagus nerve is part of the PSNS and has connections to the voice, heart, lungs and visceral organs (Figure 6.3).

Slow rhythmic breathing can increase vagal activity, lowering heart rate and blood pressure and inhibiting stress response activity. As this happens, the body's slowing and soothing sensations can also influence cognitive perception of stressors through biofeedback channels facilitating further self-regulation (Gerritsen & Band, 2018). The aim with the technique in the HSP is to soften threat physiologically and shift to sensations of soothing facilitated by the PSNS. Of course, brains that have specialised in detecting threat can be triggered by these sensations. Therefore, it is vital that this work occurs slowly, anchored in Gilbert's three circles and explored from the secure base that the HSP therapist tries to provide.

With the soothing breathwork continuing on, the therapist and participant can begin to strengthen Compassionate Me – a wise, courageous and skilful version of self that is invested in being helpful, not harmful. Qualities and skills for compassion are developed by practising a set of self-regulation skills that feature across programmes, called the 'Great Eight' (Williams & Carter, 2018). Relevant skills include, *Here and Now* (mindful awareness), *Praise and Reward* (self-kindness), *Sticking at It* (resilience), *Their Shoes* (sensitivity to others), *Asking for Help* (supporting and receiving support) and *Better Life* (imagery of a healthier, more fulfilling life). Beyond this, the work focuses on compassionate imagery, thinking and behaviour. The emphasis is on developing courage and wisdom to work *with* the aspects of oneself that suffer and to deal helpfully with suffering.

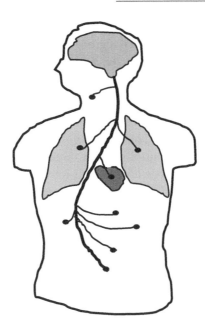

Figure 6.3 Vagus connects to voice chords, lungs, heart and organs below the diaphragm.

Source: Image traced and drawn by author

Anchored in the breathwork, a participant will imagine, try out or draw caring tones, expressions, postures and actions. These qualities, when strengthened, are then used to bravely contact the self that suffers – the critical, fearful, angry or shamed self. Again, this is not about rationalising self-talk. It is compassionate self-correction, designed to evoke the safeness system to work soothingly with distress. This means that by practising embodying a compassionate version of self, the participant practises wisely, appreciating that their shame, anger or fear is self-protective and understandably human, but in the way the threat system is narrowly focused and oversensitive, the efforts are not always actually helpful to leading a non-harmful, law-abiding life.

Mindfulness: *Here and Now*

Here and Now is used in all programmes. It is a mindfulness skill. The positive effects of mindfulness in forensic mental health have been reported (Yoon, Slade & Fazel, 2017). The processes that mediate the effects of mindfulness have been reviewed by Baer (2018) and include reduced cognitive and emotional reactivity and rumination, increased self-compassion and changes in metacognition – a process of being consciously aware of one's thinking. Neurobiological changes are also noted to occur in prefrontal regions of the brain associated with attention and regulating emotion (Hölzel et al., 2011; Siegle & Coan, 2018).

Here and Now as used in the HSP focuses on the interrelating processes of present-moment awareness, acceptance and defusion. Together these aim to change the way a participant relates to their experiences. Defusion techniques aim to reduce the automatic control of thoughts on emotions and behaviour. Thoughts have automatic control because humans often experience thoughts as literal truths. This is called *cognitive fusion*. It refers to the way the literal meaning of a thought and the process of thinking are experienced as one and the same, as if they are 'fused' together. Defusion reveals that the process of thinking is separate from the literal meaning of a thought. Experiencing thoughts less literally has been shown to have positive effects on the believability of difficult thoughts and related distress (Levin, Hildebrandt, Lillis & Hayes, 2012). A range of defusion techniques are used in the HSP from labelling 'the mind' or feelings and noticing thoughts to meditation practices.

Acceptance is the process of willingly opening up to present-moment experiences. A precursor to this is helping a participant recognise the internal experiences that they cannot eliminate and will intensify if they try. Avoidance of painful experiences through the use of sex and CSEM to cope are common in people who sexually offend, and acceptance techniques have recently been discussed as a means to support change (Quayle, Vaughan & Taylor, 2006; Walton & Hocken, 2020). Try as people might to get rid of unwanted experiences, there is no unlearning of what went before. Our nervous system is additive, not subtractive, and memories, thoughts and feelings cannot be selectively removed. Similar to putting too much salt in a soup, once incorporated, the excess salt cannot be extracted. The solution is to change the impact of the salt. To do this, you need to add more soup. Likewise, acceptance is about letting go of the struggle to remove discomforting internal experiences as if unlearning was possible. Defined in this way, acceptance is not about accepting thoughts about sexual abuse, and it should not be mistaken for this. Similar to defusion, it is about a person practising a functional change in how they relate to their thoughts and feelings, such that the unhelpful influences on their behaviour diminish. Said another way, it is about expanding their repertoire of functional responses (i.e., adding more soup). In the HSP, acceptance is taught using well-known metaphors and techniques (see Harris, 2019).

Values clarification

Clarifying personal values has been important in programmes for many years, but it has been secondary to an emphasis on goals. Values, unlike goals, are ongoing.

They represent what truly matters and gives life meaning, for example, love, security, connection and peace. Values work is now of increasing interest in this field (Quayle et al., 2006; Walton & Hocken, 2020). It deeply links skills for change to meaning and purpose. This is important because the reality of change for an HSP participant is a challenging one. It may entail forgoing the dependable gratification of arousal to thoughts about abusive sex and/or opening up to painful experiences associated with adversity and stigma. Why would they do these things? They may do them if it is in service of taking action that is consistent with what they deeply care about – perhaps their safety, health, wellbeing, family or autonomy. In short, the HSP focuses participants to clarify their values. This is because when skills for change are linked to values, the personal energy required to learn and use them is well spent. It is spent in the service of what truly matters in life.

Modifying beliefs

Beliefs that support sexual abuse are associated with sexual recidivism (Mann et al., 2010; Helmus, Hanson, Babchishin & Mann, 2013). Reappraising them is a goal of programmes such as Kaizen and BNM+. Those beliefs important to identify are the ones that a participant holds resolutely and which are rigid and narrow their behavioural repertoire. They can be identified using a self-guided formulation such as a life map and using Socratic questions which evoke reflection on learning from life events. The HSP provides an opportunity to continue with this work, but with a focus on beliefs about intimacy and sex and male and female roles. Identifying the relevant beliefs often shows how people's minds are shaped by the environments they inhabit. For HSP participants, with regular harsh, hurtful and abusive experiences in their life map, it is usually clear to see that many restrictive beliefs fulfil a safety function. Their short, rigid, antisocial and overgeneralised nature (e.g., "all women are liars") offers protection because it can be applied in a blanket fashion, making the world seem predictable with easy-to-follow rules to avoid feeling vulnerable or exposed (e.g., "don't trust women", "don't show weakness"). The goal is to work with the participant to distance them from these unhelpful beliefs enough to consider alternative ways of seeing things that are more flexible, pro-social and balanced. To do this safely and compassionately, therapists must appreciate their developmental origin and their function as contextualised working models.

HSP therapists may use cognitive reappraisal techniques such as evidence testing, self-talk and constructing alternative beliefs. These techniques may exert their effects through changing cognition, for example, altering beliefs and their meaning. However, ultimately the work aims to encourage participants to recognise their thought processes and change their relationship with them, seeing them not as absolute truths but as mere mental events. In this way, it is possible that changes in meta-cognition are also involved, and this has been reported in the general cognitive therapy literature (Hayes–Skelton & Graham, 2013). For this reason, cognitive reappraisal and Here and Now techniques are sometimes used together in the HSP in an integrated way towards a similar intervention goal.

Self-management

Self-management is a form of behaviour therapy. Behaviour therapy is based on behavioural learning processes, such as stimulus control and positive reinforcement. These are often used to understand and change behaviour using the well-known three-term behaviourist learning contingency, called *Antecedent-Behaviour-Consequence* (ABC). In the HSP, self-management involves functionally analysing and managing the antecedent stimuli that trigger paraphilic arousal and associated behaviour and increasing the antecedent stimuli that trigger thoughts about healthy sex. It also includes practising alternative behaviours that achieve the consequences of paraphilic arousal. To clarify some of these terms:

- An antecedent stimulus is a cue that comes before a behaviour. It is a trigger.
- Reinforcement is a process whereby the consequence of the behaviour increases the likelihood of the response recurring in the presence of the antecedent stimulus.
- A stimulus exerts control when the behaviour is more likely to occur in its presence.

Antecedent stimuli that tend to exert control over paraphilic arousal and behaviour can include uncomfortable (and so aversive) feelings like shame or loneliness, certain visual stimuli such as children, fetish items or violence, situational opportunities and specific states, for example, boredom. Behaviours such as accessing CSEM or fantasising and masturbating to abusive sex typically follow and are reinforced precisely because their consequence is the removal of the aversive stimulus and/or gaining of pleasurable reward. Self-management in the HSP focuses on shaping new contingencies that deal with the antecedent stimuli that exert control. In short, this procedure amounts to devising a self-management schedule using a functional analysis. In the HSP, the ABC contingency is simply called *What Happens, What I Do, What I Get* (Figure 6.4).

In an HSP exercise called *Getting the Good Things from Not OK Sexy Thoughts*, a participant can identify how fantasising about abusive sex provides reinforcing consequences, for example, feelings of mastery or intimate connection, or the

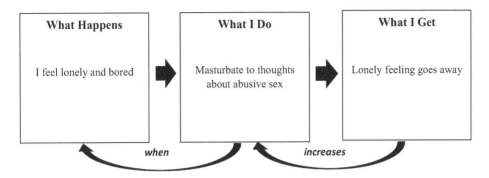

Figure 6.4 Accessible format: functional analysis of negatively reinforced stimulus control.

Source: Images drawn by author

removal of feelings of boredom or loneliness. The therapist and participant can then focus on equipping safer behaviours that can be similarly reinforced to obtain these consequences, for example, practising skills to develop self-efficacy, intimacy with adults or coping with discomforting feelings. Similarly, in an exercise called *Skills for Managing Triggers*, the participant can focus on practising skills to manage the antecedent stimuli that have gained control over paraphilic arousal (i.e., strong triggers). In both cases, for skills to be integrated into the participant's behavioural repertoire, the experience of using them must be reinforcing. The therapist must therefore help create rich schedules of reinforcement. One way to do this is to link the use of skills to values as outlined earlier. When this occurs, self-management skills are reinforced by virtue of them being linked to what the participant genuinely cares about.

Behaviour modification

Behavioural modification (BM) is also a form of behaviour therapy. BM uses behaviour learning processes such as reinforcement, punishment and extinction to shape sexual arousal (Marshall, O'Brien & Marshall, 2009). BM is associated with the contingency learning account of paraphilia described earlier (see Figure 6.1a and 6.1b), and has been a dominant intervention procedure for over 60 years. A recent meta-analysis found that BM reduced paraphilic arousal ('paedohebephilia' specifically), especially for those who show high levels of such arousal (McPhail & Olver, 2020). Whether these effects lead to decreases in long-term sexual recidivism or not is still unclear. Lösel and Schmucker (2005) found a significant effect on sexual recidivism for interventions that included BM. Gannon, Olver, Mallion and James (2019) have more recently reported that interventions that included BM produced larger reductions in recidivism than those that did not. However, both these sets of findings should be interpreted carefully. This is because the evaluations of interventions incorporating BM originally included by Lösel and Schmucker (2005) were heavily confounded. In an update of their meta-analysis using far stricter scientific rigor, Schmucker and Lösel (2017) excluded most of these evaluations because they were too methodologically weak. However, Gannon et al. (2019) included many evaluations that fall below the rigorous standards Schmucker and Lösel set. As such, it is perhaps expectable that Gannon et al. would report a similar optimistic effect to Lösel and Schmucker in their original meta-analysis.

Regardless of its empirical support, BM is unlikely to lead to permanent change. This is because it relies on creating new contingencies that govern changed arousal. An example is applying covert punishment such as aversive personal consequences to fantasise about abusive sex, the function being to reduce arousal to the fantasies. This is a BM technique called *modified covert sensitisation*. If the punishment is removed, (i.e., if a participant stops rehearsing the costs of abusive sex), the conditioned response of reduced arousal will diminish and a return of previous arousal levels may follow. Therefore, the use of BM on the HSP is introduced as a procedure that moderates arousal, with the conditioned effects being reliant on continuing practice. The HSP also uses a technique that capitalises on a person's natural desire to satisfy sexual appetite called *directed masturbation*. It works by rewarding progressively healthier fantasies with masturbatory-induced pleasure, thereby steadily shaping arousal to pro-social themes. Its use is important. Intervention cannot merely concern itself with removing risks as if a life of aversion and restriction could ever be fulfilling. Intervention has to offer viable new alternatives that can serve a pro-social life.

Urge management

HSP offers *Surfing the Urge* training to help with sexual urge management. Urge surfing is a Here and Now skill that aims to change one's functional relationship with an urge in order to increase behavioural control. It is supported as a coping skill for substance addiction and appears to work by moderating autonomic responses such as urges and cravings (Ostafin & Marlatt, 2008). However, there are currently no robust trials that test urge surfing with sexual urges.

Another urge management procedure is the use of certain drug therapies. These target serotonin and dopamine systems and testosterone production, all of which are important to sexual functioning. Such drugs are not able to change sexual interest. However, the features of sexual interest that are to do with sexual libido, impulsivity, emotion and urges are certainly amenable to manipulation using pharmacological treatments (Grubin, 2018). HSP participants can voluntarily undergo assessment for medication to manage sexual arousal at a number of funded prison clinics. Where a participant is dominated by an insatiable sex drive and strong sexual urges, the rapid decrease in arousability can serve as an adjunct therapy to the HSP in helping participants develop sexual self-regulation skills.

Interpersonal skills intimacy and relationships

Poor social skills are not related to sexual recidivism, but the lack of emotionally intimate relationships is (Mann et al., 2010). In short, negotiating general social situations is not usually a difficulty for people with convictions for sexual offending, but close intimacy tends to be, and for many reasons, they can find themselves emotionally out of sync with adults, fearful and struggling to connect. The HSP builds on intimacy skills work from Kaizen, BNM+, Horizon and NMS. The relationship exercises explore compatibility with partners, the concept of a healthy relationship, how to be sexual safely without a relationship and practising skills for intimacy. Commonly introduced interpersonal skills include negotiating, listening and expressing feelings appropriately. People are taught using a systematic method which involves introducing skill steps, modelling, coaching and giving reinforcing feedback. The focal process is improving skills for intimacy.

In an exercise called *Avoiding Relationships: Using My Values to Guide My Actions*, the therapist and participant can explore how as humans we desire connection with others, but by opening our hearts and being vulnerable to form this connection, we also inevitably expose ourselves to the risk of being hurt. When a loved one leaves us or betrays us, or if our childhood has told us that everything about an adult relationship will harm us, the threat system will do its job, and the mind can summon up many reasons as to why intimacy is unsafe or unfeasible. Unfortunately, people suffer by doing the 'safe thing' and avoiding relationships, because without intimacy, they rarely experience connection, acceptance and love – many of our primitive human needs and the things that usually matter most. The therapist carefully creates space for the participant to find this human irony – that what matters to us the most is often found inside what deeply pains us. This is explored safely with prepared fictional cards, with a worry statement on one side and a value on the other. The example of 'James' is presented in Figure 6.5.

Looking at the hurt and worry, the therapist can ask: "What does James really care about?", "What is on the other side of his worry?" and "What was it he

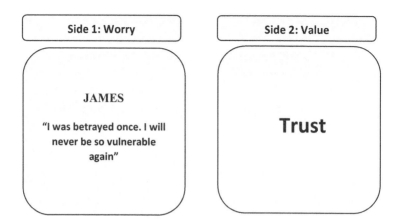

Figure 6.5 Accessible format: fear and value card.

Source: Image drawn by author

had that was so valuable?" In James's case, he can protect himself from being betrayed. By not letting people in, he will never be 'so vulnerable' again. But whilst he is not vulnerable, he is unable to (re)experience what he values – *trust*. The participant would then explore how James's response is a human response. By protecting ourselves so heavily to avoid being hurt, we risk limiting ourselves and experiencing what makes life meaningful. This can hurt in a different way, for example, in our loneliness or the harm we cause. The therapist might then explore with a participant if they are willing to make room for their worries if this is what it would take to live a fulfilling life. From here, skills for intimacy can be practised in the service of taking values-based action towards achieving an intimate relationship.

Conclusion

The HSP is a tailorable programme for individuals convicted of sexual offending whose paraphilic interests pose a risk to the public. It is grounded in a biopsychosocial model of paraphilia, offering a range of intervention procedures that are well known to clinical science. The HSP is part of the wider rehabilitative offering in HMPPS. It is a recently revised programme and will be subject to implementation monitoring and evaluation. Participants who access the HSP are graduates of other programmes that aim to build strengths in criminogenic areas more generally. Invariably, for those assessed as suitable for the HSP, they require more support than those without paraphilic interests. The HSP offers the chance for them to learn skills intended to change their functional relationship with their paraphilia and their associated distress and risks to others. The best evidence suggests that people do not consciously choose to be sexually interested in abusive behaviour. Despite this, such interests often endure for life. If people are to lead crime-free lives, many public protection efforts will be needed. Effective intervention is just one.

Note

1 www.pornhub.com/insights/2019-year-in-review

References

Alanko, K., Gunst, A., Mokros, A., & Santtila, P. (2016). Genetic variants associated with male pedophilic sexual interest. *Journal of Sexual Medicine*, *13*, 835–842.

Alanko, K., Salo, B., Mokros, A., & Santtila, P. (2013). Evidence for heritability of adult men's sexual interest in youth under age 16 from a population-based extended twin design. *Journal of Sexual Medicine*, *10*, 1090–1099.

American Psychiatric Association. (2013). *Diagnostic and statistical manual of mental disorders* (5th ed.). American Psychiatric Publishing.

Babchishin, K. M., Hanson, R. K., & Van Zuylen, H. (2015). Online child pornography offenders are different: A meta-analysis of the characteristics of online and offline sex offenders against children. *Archives of Sexual Behaviour*, *44*, 45–66.

Baer, R. (2018). Mindfulness practice. In S. C. Hayes & S. G. Hofmann (Eds.), *Process-based CBT: The science and core clinical competencies of cognitive behavioural therapy* (pp. 389–413). New Harbinger.

Bailey, J. M. (2015). A failure to demonstrate changes in sexual interest in pedophilic men: Comment on Müller et al. (2014) [Commentary]. *Archives of Sexual Behaviour*, 44, 249–252.

Bailey, J. M., Bernhard, P. A., & Hsu, K. J. (2016a). An internet study of men sexually attracted to children: Correlates of sexual offending against children. *Journal of Abnormal Psychology*, *125*(7), 989–1000.

Bailey, J. M., Hsu, K. J., & Bernhard, P. A. (2016b). An internet study of men sexually attracted to children: Sexual attraction patterns. *Journal of Abnormal Psychology*, *125*(7), 976–988.

Beech, A. R., Miner, M. H., & Thornton, D. (2016). Paraphilias in the DSM-5. *Annual Review of Clinical Psychology*, *12*(1), 383–406.

Berlin Institute of Sexology and Sexual Medicine. (2013). *The Berlin Dissexuality Therapy Program*. Gutenberg Druckerei GmbH.

Blank, C., Nunes, K. L., Maimone, S., Hermann, C. A., & McPhail, I. V. (2018). Is child-hood sexual victimization associated with cognitive distortions, self-esteem and emo-tional congruence with children? *Journal of Sexual Aggression*. Advance online publication.

Briken, P., Fedoroff, J. P., & Bradford, J. W. (2014). Why can't pedophilic disorder remit? *Archives of Sexual Behaviour*, *43*, 1237–1239.

Burton, D. (2003). Male adolescents: Sexual victimization and subsequent sexual abuse. *Child and Adolescent Social Work Journal*, *20*, 277–296.

Camilleri, J. A., & Quinsey, V. L. (2008). Pedophilia: Assessment and treatment. In D. R. Laws & W. T. O'Donohue (Eds.), *Sexual deviance: Theory, assessment and treatment* (Section ed., pp. 183–212). Guilford.

Cantor, J. M. (2015). Purported changes in pedophilia as statistical artefacts: Comment on Müller et al. (2014) [Commentary]. *Archives of Sexual Behaviour*, *44*, 253–254.

Cantor, J. M. (2018). Can pedophiles change? *Current Sexual Health Reports*, *10*, 203–206.

Cantor, J. M., Blanchard, R., Christensen, B. K., Dickey, R., Klassen, P. E., Beckstead, A. L., . . . & Kuban, M. E. (2004). Intelligence, memory, and handedness in pedo-philia. *Neuropsychology*, *18*, 3–14.

Cantor, J. M., Lafaille, S. J., Hannah, J., Kucyi, A., Soh, D. W., Girard, T. A., & Mikulis, D. J. (2016). Independent component analysis of resting-state functional magnetic resonance imaging in pedophiles. *Journal of Sexual Medicine*, *13*(10), 1546–1554.

Cantor, J. M., Lafaille, S. J., Soh, D. W., Moayedi, M., Mikulis, D. J., & Girard T. A. (2015). Diffusion tensor imaging of pedophilia. *Archives of Sexual Behaviour*, *44*, 2161–2172.

Cantor, J. M., & McPhail, I. V. (2016). Non-offending pedophiles. *Current Sexual Health Reports*, *8*(3), 121–128.

Carter, A. J., & Mann, R. E. (2016). Organising principles for an integrated model of change for the treatment of sexual offending. In A. R. Beech & T. Ward (Eds.), *The Wiley Blackwell handbook on assessment, treatment and theories of sexual offending* (Vol. 1, pp. 359–382). Wiley.

Clapton, N. E., Williams, J., Griffiths, G. M., & Jones, R. S. (2018). "Finding the person you really are . . . on the inside": Compassion focused therapy for adults with intel-lectual disabilities. *Journal of Intellectual Disabilities*, *22*(2), 135–153.

Cowles, M., Randle-Phillips, C., & Medley, A. (2020). Compassion focused therapy for trauma in people with intellectual disabilities: A conceptual review, *Journal of Intellec-tual Disabilities*, *24*(2), 212–232.

Dawson, S. J., Bannerman, B. A., & Lalumière, M. (2016). Paraphilic interests: An exam-ination of sex differences in a nonclinical sample. *Sex Abuse: A Journal of Treatment and Research*, *28*(1), 20–45.

Dombert, B., Schmidt, A. F., Banse, R., Briken, P., Hoyer, J., Neutze, J., & Osterheider, M. (2016). How common is males' self-reported sexual interest in prepubescent children? *Journal of Sex Research, 53*, 214–223.

Dyshniku, F., Murray, M. E., Fazio, R. L., Lykins, A. D., & Cantor, J. M. (2015). Minor physical anomalies as a window into the prenatal origins of pedophilia. *Archives of Sexual Behaviour, 44*(8), 2151–2159.

Fazio, R. L. (2018). Toward a neurodevelopmental understanding of pedophilia. *Journal of Sexual Medicine, 15*(9), 1205–1207.

Fazio, R. L., Dyshniku, F., Lykins, A. D., & Cantor, J. M. (2015). Leg length versus torso length in pedophilia: Further evidence of atypical physical development early in life. *Sexual Abuse, 29*(5), 500–514.

Fazio, R. L., Lykins, A. D., & Cantor, J. M. (2014). Elevated rates of atypical handedness in paedophilia: Theory and implications. *Laterality, 19*, 690–704.

Fedoroff, J. P. (2016). Managing versus successfully treating paraphilic disorders. In S. B. Levine, C. B. Risen, & S. E. Althof (Eds.), *Handbook of clinical sexuality for mental health professionals* (pp. 345–361). Routledge.

Fedoroff, J. P. (2018a). Can people with pedophilia change? Yes they can! *Current Sexual Health Reports, 10*, 207–212.

Fedoroff, J. P. (2018b). More puzzles: A response to Seto's (2017) "The Puzzle of Male Chronophilias". *Archives of Sexual Behaviour, 47*, 2171–2173.

First, M. B. (2014). DSM-5 and paraphilic disorders. *Journal of the American Academy of Psychiatry and the Law, 42*(2), 191–201.

Fisher, W. A., & Kohut, T. (2017). Pornography viewing: Keep calm and carry on. *Journal of Sexual Medicine, 14*(3), 320–322.

Fisher, W. A., Kohut, T., Gioacchino, L. A., & Fedoroff, P. (2013). Pornography, sex crime, and paraphilia. *Current Psychiatry Reports, 15*(6), 362.

Gannon, T. A., Olver, M. E., Mallion, J. S., & James, M. (2019). Does specialized psychological treatment for offending reduce recidivism? A meta-analysis examining staff and program variables as predictors of treatment effectiveness. *Clinical Psychology Review, 73*. ISSN: 0272–7358.

Gerritsen, R. J. S., & Band, G. P. H. (2018). Breath of life: The respiratory vagal stimulation model of contemplative activity. *Frontiers of Human of Neuroscience, 12*, 397. https://doi.org/10.3389/fnhum.2018.00397

Gerwinna, H., Weiß, S., Tenbergene, G., Amelungg, T., Födisch, C., Pohla, A., & Massauc, C., et al. (2018). Clinical characteristics associated with paedophilia and child sex offending: Differentiating sexual preference from offence status, *European Psychiatry, 51*, 74–85.

Gilbert, P. (2010). *Compassion focused therapy: Distinctive features*. Routledge.

Gilbert, P. (2018). *Living like crazy*. Annywn House.

Gilbert, P. (2019). Explorations into the nature and function of compassion. *Current Opinion in Psychology*, *28*, 108–114.

Gilbert, P., & Choden. (2013). *Mindful compassion*. Robinson.

Grady, M. D., Levenson, J. S., Mesias, G., Kavanagh, S., & Charles, J. (2019). "I can't talk about that": Stigma and fear as barriers to preventive services for minor-attracted persons. *Stigma and Health*, *4*, 400–410.

Grubin, D. (2018). The pharmacological treatment of sex offenders. *The Wiley Blackwell handbook of forensic neuroscience*, *1*, 703–723.

Grundmann, D., Krupp, J., Scherner, G., Amelung, T., & Beier, K. M. (2016). Stability of self-reported arousal to sexual fantasies involving children in a clinical sample of pedophiles and hebephiles. *Archives of Sexual Behaviour*, *45*, 1153–1162.

Harris, R. (2019). *ACT made simple: An easy-to-read primer on acceptance and commitment therapy* (2nd ed.). New Harbinger Publications, Inc.

Hayes, S. C., & Hofmann, S. G. (2018a). Future directions in CBT and evidence-based therapy. In S. C. Hayes & S. G. Hofmann (Eds.), *Process-based CBT: The science and core clinical competencies of cognitive behavioural therapy* (pp. 415–426). New Harbinger.

Hayes, S. C., & Hofmann, S. G. (2018b). *Process-based CBT: The science and core clinical competencies of cognitive behavioural therapy*. New Harbinger.

Hayes-Skelton, S., & Graham, J. (2013). Decentering as a common link among mindfulness, cognitive reappraisal, and social anxiety. *Behavioural and Cognitive Psychotherapy*, *41*, 317–328.

Helmus, L., Hanson, R. K., Babchishin, K. M., & Mann, R. E. (2013). Attitudes supportive of sex offending predict recidivism: A meta-analysis. *Trauma Violence and Abuse*, *14*(1), 34–53.

Hermann, C. A., McPhail, I. V., Helmus, L. M., & Hanson, R. K. (2017). Emotional congruence with children is associated with sexual deviancy in sexual offenders against children. *International Journal of Offender Therapy and Comparative Criminology*, *61*(12), 1311–1334.

Hölzel, B. K., Lazar, S. W., Gard, T., Schuman-Olivier, Z., Vago, D. R., & Ott, U. (2011). How does mindfulness meditation work? Proposing mechanisms of action from a conceptual and neural perspective. *Perspectives on Psychological Science*, *6*(6), 537–559.

Imhoff, R. (2015). Punitive attitudes against pedophiles or persons with sexual interest in children: Does the label matter? *Archives of Sexual Behaviour*, *44*, 35–44.

Imhoff, R., & Jahnke, S. (2018). Determinants of punitive attitudes towards people with pedophilia: Dissecting effects of the label and intentionality ascriptions. *Archives of Sexual Behaviour*, *47*, 353–361.

Jahnke, S. (2018a). The stigma of pedophilia clinical and forensic implications. *European Psychologist, 23*, 144–153.

Jahnke, S. (2018b). Emotions and cognitions associated with the stigma of non-offending pedophilia: A vignette experiment. *Archives of Sexual Behaviour, 47*, 363–373.

Jahnke, S., & Hoyer, J. (2013). Stigmatization of people with pedophilia: A blind spot in stigma research. *International Journal of Sexual Health, 25*, 169–184.

Jahnke, S., Imhoff, R., & Hoyer, J. (2015). Stigmatization of people with pedophilia: Two comparative surveys. *Archives of Sexual Behaviour, 44*, 21–34.

Jahnke, S., Schmidt, A. F., Geradt, M., & Hoyer, J. (2015). Stigma related stress and its correlates among men with pedophilic sexual interests. *Archives of Sexual Behaviour, 44*, 2173–2187.

Jespersen, A. F., Lalumière, M. L., & Seto, M. C. (2009). Sexual abuse history among adult sex offenders and non-sex offenders: A meta-analysis. *Child Abuse Neglect, 33*(3), 179–192.

Joyal, C. C., & Carpentier, J. (2016). The prevalence of paraphilic interests and behaviours in the general population: A provincial survey. *The Journal of Sex Research, 54*(2), 161–171.

Joyal, C. C., Cossette, A., & Lapierre, V. (2015). What exactly is an unusual sexual fantasy? *Journal of Sexual Medicine, 12*, 328–340.

Joyal, C. C., Kärgel, C., Kneer, J., Amelung, T., Mohnke, S., Tenbergen, G., . . . & Walter, H. (2019). The neurobiological origins of pedophilia: Not that simple. *Journal of Sexual Medicine, 16*(1), 153–154.

Kafka, M. P. (2003). The monoamine hypothesis for the pathophysiology of paraphilic disorders: An update. *Annals of the New York Academy of Sciences, 989*, 86–94.

Kafka, M. P. (2010). Hypersexual disorder: A proposed diagnosis for DSM-V. *Archives of Sexual Behaviour, 39*, 377–400.

Kirby, J. N., Tellegen, C. L., & Steindl, S. R. (2017). A meta-analysis of compassion-based interventions: Current state of knowledge and future directions. *Behaviour Therapy, 48*, 778–792.

Lalumière, M. L. (2015). The lability of pedophilic interests as measured by phallometry [Commentary]. *Archives of Sexual Behaviour, 44*, 255–258.

Långström, N., Babchishin, K., Fazel, S., Lichtenstein, P., & Frisell, T. (2015). Sexual offending runs in families: A 37-year nationwide study. *International Journal of Epidemiology, 44*, 713–720.

Levenson, J. S., & Grady, M. D. (2016). The influence of childhood trauma on sexual violence and sexual deviance in adulthood. *Traumatology, 22*, 94–103.

Levenson, J. S., Willis, G. M., & Prescott, D. S. (2016). Adverse childhood experiences in the lives of male sex offenders: Implications for trauma-informed care. *Sexual Abuse: A Journal of Research and Treatment, 28*, 340–359.

Levin, M. E., Hildebrandt, M. J., Lillis, J., & Hayes, S. C. (2012). The impact of treatment components suggested by the psychological flexibility model: A meta-analysis of laboratory-based component studies. *Behaviour Therapy, 43*, 741–756.

Lievesley, R., Harper, C., & Elliott, H. (2020). The internalization of social stigma among minor-attracted persons: Implications for treatment. *Archives of Sexual Behavior, 49*, 1291–1304.

Lösel, F., & Schmucker, M. (2005). The effectiveness of treatment for sexual offenders: A comprehensive meta-analysis. *Journal of Experimental Criminology, 1*(1), 117–146.

Mann, R. E., Hanson, R. K., & Thornton, D. (2010). Assessing risk for sexual recidivism: Some proposals on the nature of psychologically meaningful risk factors. *Sexual Abuse: A Journal of Research and Treatment, 22*(2), 191–217.

Marshall, W. L. (2008). Are pedophiles treatable? Evidence from North American studies. *Polish Sexology, 6*(1), 39–43.

Marshall, W. L., & Barbaree, H. E. (1990). An integrated theory of the etiology of sexual offending. In W. L. Marshall, D. R. Laws, & H. E. Barbaree (Eds.), *Handbook of sexual assault: Issues, theories and treatment of the offender* (pp. 257–275). NY: Plenum.

Marshall, W. L., O'Brien, M. D., & Marshall, L. E. (2009). Modifying sexual preferences. In A. R. Beech, L. A. Craig, & K. D. Browne (Eds.), *Assessment and treatment of sexual offenders: A handbook* (pp. 311–327). John Wiley & Sons.

MacCulloch, M., Gray, N., & Watt, A. (2000). Brittain's Sadistic Murderer Syndrome reconsidered: An associative account of the aetiology of sadistic sexual fantasy. *Journal of Forensic Psychiatry, 11*(2), 401–418.

McCarthy, J. A. (2010). Internet sexual activity: A comparison between contact and non-contact child pornography offenders. *Journal of Sexual Aggression, 16*(2), 181–195.

McGuire, R. J., Carlisle, J. M., & Young, B. G. (1965). Sexual deviation as conditional behaviour: A hypothesis. *Behaviour Research and Therapy, 2*, 185–190.

McKay, M. (2018). Arousal reduction. In S. C. Hayes & S. G. Hofmann (Eds.), *Process-based CBT: The science and core clinical competencies of cognitive behavioural therapy*, (pp. 245–260). New Harbinger.

McPhail, I. V. (2018, December 1). *Examining pedophilic interest as a risk factor for sexual re-offending* [Weblog post]. Retrieved from https://nextgenforensic.wordpress.com/2018/12/01/examining-pedophilic-interest-as-a-risk-factor-for-sexual-re-offending/

McPhail, I. V., & Cantor, J. M. (2015). Pedophilia, height, and the magnitude of the association: A research note. *Deviant Behaviour, 36*, 288–292.

McPhail, I. V., Hermann, C. A., & Fernandez, Y. M. (2014). Correlates of emotional congruence with children in sexual offenders against children: A test of theoretical models in an incarcerated sample. *Child Abuse and Neglect, 38*, 336–346.

McPhail, I. V., & Olver, M. E. (2020). Interventions for pedohebephilic arousal in men convicted for sexual offenses against children: A meta-analytic review. *Criminal Justice and Behavior*. Early View.

McPhail, I. V., Olver, M. E., Brouillette-Alarie, S., & Looman, J. (2018). Taxometric analysis of the latent structure of pedophilic interest. *Archives of Sexual Behaviour*, *47*(8), 2223–2240.

Miletski, H. (2017). Zoophilia: Another sexual orientation? *Archives of Sexual Behaviour*, *46*(1), 39–42.

Müller, K., Curry, S., Ranger, R., Briken, P., Bradford, J., & Fedoroff, J. P. (2014). Changes in sexual arousal as measured by penile plethysmography in men with pedophilic sexual interest. *Journal of Sexual Medicine*, *11*(5), 1221–1229.

Ostafin, B. D., & Marlatt, G. A. (2008). Surfing the urge: Experiential acceptance moderates the relation between automatic alcohol motivation and hazardous drinking. *Journal of Social and Clinical Psychology*, *27*, 404–418.

Park, B. Y., Wilson, G., Berger, J., Christman, M., Reina, B., et al. (2016). Is internet pornography causing sexual dysfunctions? A review with clinical reports. *Behavioural Sciences*, *6*(3), 17.

Quayle, E., Vaughan, M., & Taylor, M. (2006). Sex offenders, internet child abuse images and emotional avoidance: The importance of values. *Aggression and Violent Behaviour*, *11*(1), 1–11.

Ramsay, L. (2020). Strengths-based programmes for men with sexual convictions, who have learning disability and learning challenges. In K. Hocken., B. Winder, N. Blagden, R. Lievesley, H. Elliott, & P. Banyard (Eds.), *Sexual crime and intellectual functioning* (pp. 59–88). Palgrave Macmillan.

Ramsay, L., Carter, A. J., & Walton, J. S. (2020). Contemporary programs designed for the tertiary prevention of recidivism by people convicted of a sexual offense: A review, and the U.K. perspective. In J. Proulx, F. Cortoni, L. A. Craig & E. J. Letourneau (Eds.), *The Wiley handbook of what works with sexual offenders: Contemporary perspectives in theory, assessment, treatment, and prevention* (pp. 185–199). John Wiley & Sons, Ltd.

Reavis, J., Looman, J., Franco, K., & Rojas, B. (2013). Adverse childhood experiences and adult criminality: How long must we live before we possess our own lives? *The Permanente Journal*, *17*, 44–48.

Roche, B., & Quayle, E. (2007). *Sexual disorders*. In J. Wood & J. Kanter (Eds.), *Understanding behaviour disorders: A contemporary behavioural perspective* (pp. 341–368). Context Press.

Santtila, P., Antfolk, J., Räfså, A., Hartwig, M., Sariola, H., Sandnabba, N. K., & Mokros, A. (2015). Men's sexual interest in children: One-year incidence and correlates in a population-based sample of Finnish male twins. *Journal of Child Sexual Abuse*, *24*, 115–134.

Schiffer, B., Amelung, T., Pohl, A., Kärgel, C., Tenbergen, G., Gerwinn, H., et al. (2017). Gray matter abnormalities in pedophiles with and without a history of child sexual offending. *Translational Psychiatry, 7*(5), e1129.

Schmucker, M., & Lösel, F. (2017). Sexual offender treatment for reducing recidivism among convicted sex offenders: A systematic review and meta-analysis. *Campbell Systematic Reviews, 13*(1), 1–75.

Seto, M. C. (2012). Is pedophilia a sexual orientation? *Archives of Sexual Behaviour, 41*(1), 231–236.

Seto, M. C. (2017). The puzzle of male chronophilias. *Archives of Sexual Behaviour, 46*(1), 3–22.

Seto, M. C. (2018). *Paedophilia and sexual offending against children: Theory, assessment and intervention* (2nd ed.). Washington, DC: American Psychological Association.

Seto, M. C. (2019). The motivation-facilitation model of sexual offending. *Sexual Abuse, 31*(1), 3–24.

Seto, M. C., Hermann, C. A., Kjellgren, C., Priebe, G., Svedin, C. G., & Langström, N. (2015). Viewing child pornography: Prevalence and correlates in a representative community sample of young Swedish men. *Archives of Sexual Behaviour, 44*, 67–79.

Seto, M. C., & Lalumière, M. L. (2010). What is so special about male adolescent sexual offending? A review and test of explanations through meta-analysis. *Psychological Bulletin, 136*, 526–575.

Siegle, G. J., & Coan, J. (2018). Neuroscience relevant to core processes in psychotherapy. In S. C. Hayes & S. G. Hofmann (Eds.), *Process-based CBT: The science and core clinical competencies of cognitive behavioural therapy* (pp. 154–178). New Harbinger.

Van der Kolk, B. (2014). *The body keeps the score: Brain, mind and body in the healing of trauma*. NY: Viking.

Walton, J. S. (2018). Random assignment in sexual offending programme evaluation: The missing method. *Journal of Forensic Practice, 20*(1), 1–9.

Walton, J. S. (2019). The evolutionary basis of belonging: Its relevance to denial of offending and labelling those who offend. *Journal of Forensic Practice, 21*(4), 202–211.

Walton, J. S., & Hocken, K. (2020). Compassion and acceptance as interventions for paraphilic disorders and sexual offending behaviour. In G. Akerman, D. Perkins, & R. Bartels (Eds.), *Assessing and managing deviant sexual interest and arousal: A practitioner's guide* (pp. 149–170). Routledge.

Walton, J. S., Ramsay, L., Cunningham, C., & Henfrey, S. (2017). New directions: Integrating a biopsychosocial approach in the design and delivery of programs for high risk services users in Her Majesty's prison and probation service. *Advancing Corrections: Journal of the International Corrections and Prison Association, 3*, 21–47.

Williams, F., & Carter, A. J. (2018). Engaging with offenders: A biologically informed approach. In A. Beech, A. J. Carter, R. E. Mann, & P. Rotshtein (Eds.), *Handbook of forensic neuroscience* (pp. 577–599). Wiley-Blackwell.

Wismeijer, A. A., & Assen, M. A. (2013). Psychological characteristics of BDSM practitioners. *Journal of Sexual Medicine, 10*(8), 1943–1952.

Yoon, I. A., Slade, K., & Fazel, S. (2017). Outcomes of psychological therapies for prisoners with mental health problems: A systematic review and meta-analysis. *Journal of Consulting Clinical Psychology, 85*(8), 783–802.

7
The importance of being earnest

Rethinking the "problem" of categorical denial in men with sexual convictions

*Nicholas Blagden, Ruth E. Mann,
and Jamie S. Walton*

Introduction

Many clinicians working with men with sexual convictions, and in many jurisdictions, are uncertain about what to do with individuals who categorically deny they committed the offences of which they are convicted. The "problem" of denial lies in the fact that the dominant model of rehabilitation – the risk–needs–responsivity model (Andrews & Bonta, 2010) – requires that intervention focus heavily on criminogenic needs – which can otherwise be understood as those dynamic risk factors that seem likely to have a statistically significant association with reoffending (Mann, Hanson & Thornton, 2010). In the cognitive behavioural model of programmes, the causes of a behaviour are uncovered by a functional analysis of the behaviour – what preceded it and what reinforced it. The cognitive

A note from the authors

This was an emotional chapter to finish. Ruth and I started this chapter nearly 10 years ago, and despite working on numerous projects, revisiting it on many occasions and keeping in regular contact, we never got to finish it. We'd often refer to Project Tiobe (the importance of being earnest), joke that we'd be retired before it was completed, but how we needed to finish it. The creation and writing of this chapter was very much a critical dialogue of our thinking of 'denial', and I really enjoyed our process of revisiting it over the years. I regret not being able to finish it with Ruth. All of the good stuff in this chapter is hers. I'm grateful to Jamie for the fresh perspective and additions which got us over the line. This is for you Ruth, we got there in the end with Tiobe!

DOI: 10.4324/9780429262074-7

behavioural model and the identification of criminogenic needs for any individual may feel rather unworkable if an individual denies that the behaviour occurred at all. The clinician is left in a dilemma: should they proceed with a functional analysis without the client's cooperation, or should they focus on trying to overcome the denial? If the former approach is taken, the clinician is often left feeling uncomfortably limited by the problem that many risk factors for sexual offending are internal to the person – for instance, sexual arousal to children, beliefs that support sexual abuse, a sense of personal inadequacy – and therefore not easily identified without the person's willingness to report them. As a consequence, perhaps, 'offender responsibility' has been a core target for most cognitive behavioural programmes designed for people convicted of sexual offences (McGrath et al., 2010; Ware & Mann, 2012; Wright & Schneider, 2004). Frequently, therefore, denial is viewed as a factor that impedes progress by reducing a person's responsibility-taking for their offending (Wright & Schneider, 2004).

Clarifying denial in terms of definition, conceptualisation, context and implications for practice is important because categorical denial has been and continues to be used to exclude people from programmes in many jurisdictions. People in denial of the sexual offences they were convicted of are not simply a minority group. Research indicates that the incidence of categorical denial is around 30% to 35% (see Hood et al., 2002; Kennedy & Grubin, 1992). Indeed, most prison-based programmes in North America focus on admission and responsibility-taking. McGrath, Cumming, Burchard, Zeoli and Ellerby (2010) find that 91% of programmes in the United States included "offender responsibility" as a treatment target. Furthermore, 33.4% of adult programmes in the United States required full disclosure for successful programme completion. Denial and accepting responsibility are therefore key terms in rehabilitation efforts, and while there have been critical reviews of responsibility-taking in people convicted of sexual offences (see Ware & Mann, 2012), there have been very few critical reviews focusing on denial in men with sexual convictions (Cooper, 2005; Ware, Marshall & Marshall, 2015).

In this chapter, we will challenge the dominant notion that denial inherently matters to the change process. We will propose that the drive to overcome categorical denial as an organising principle for programmes has needed rethinking for some time. We will re-examine the extant definitions and conceptualisations of denial, especially the currently popular notion that denial should be understood as a continuum or typology of distorted representations of offending. We will focus on the "problem" of categorical denial by reviewing empirical studies of denial in people convicted of sexual offences. We will consider the nature, function and context of denial in people convicted of sexual offences and its implications for intervention and policy. We also aim, driven by a concern about the lack of experimental work on this matter, to identify research questions for future empirical study of categorical denial.

Defining and conceptualising denial

Defining and conceptualising denial is important for forensic practice, as it will guide interactions and interventions with those in denial. It is also necessary so that different researchers can complement and extend each other's work. The literature on denial in men with sexual convictions is rife with definitions, many of which place categorical denial at the end of a continuum of denial rather than making a simple distinction between categorical denial and any form of admission. Hence, many definitions of denial are designed to encompass both categorical and non-categorical denial (see e.g. Carich & Calder, 2003). For example, on a practical level, in England and Wales a person is considered 'in denial' if they satisfy the Offender Assessment System (OASys) criteria of not accepting responsibility, which is defined as:

> a person is not considered to accept responsibility if they excuse their offense
> or shift blame to others, insist on minimizing the seriousness of the offense or
> their involvement in it, claim the offense was out of character for them or if
> they partially or completely deny committing the offense(s).

Clearly this variable cannot be used as an indicator of categorical denial, as it includes minimisations, excuse making and external blame attribution. Indeed, given the high likelihood that individuals in this group minimise/excuse, it is difficult to imagine many not fitting such an over-inclusive definition. Research has been hampered by small sample sizes and a lack of a consistent definition of denial (Ware et al., 2015).

Janoff-Bulman and Timko (1987) have argued that denial can be seen as a transitory phenomenon which allows the self-concept to be protected and shielded from deleterious information. They argue that denial is like a form of scaffolding, which is taken down when it is perceived to be safe to do so. However, in forensic practice, most people who deny do not get the opportunity to take down the 'scaffolding' because no constructive work is undertaken with them. This conceptualisation of denial would warn against the typical notions of confronting and breaking down denial (Northey, 1999), particularly as the client may not be ready to let go of denial. As Yalom said, "Never take away anything [from the client] unless you have something better to offer. Beware of stripping a patient who can't bear the chill of reality" (Yalom, 1991, p. 154). We find Janoff-Bulman and Timko's (1987) conceptualisation of denial, now over 30 years old, particularly useful in modern-day practice. It should be noted at this point that those in categorical denial (also termed total and outright denial) were, until recently, excluded from programmes in the UK. In England and Wales the landscape for programmes has changed, and denial is no longer an organising principle of treatment, and programmes are no longer confession orientated (Blagden, 2011; Ramsay, Carter & Walton, 2020). However, in many other countries, denial remains an important variable in intervention.

Denial as a continuum

The Penguin Dictionary of Psychology (Reber, 1985) defines a continuum as a variable capable of being represented as a continuous series. That is, the notion of continuum requires that the variable has a number of levels, progressing from low in intensity to high in intensity, with regular spaces between the levels. Recently, denial has typically been understood not as a binary construct or categorical variable, but instead as a continuum (see Barbaree, 1991; Gibbons, de Volder & Casey, 2003; Levenson, 2011; Marshall, Anderson & Fernandez, 1999; Schneider & Wright, 2004). For instance, Levenson (2011) argued that denial exists on a "continuum of distorted cognitions" (p. 361) which includes minimising impact of sexual assault on victims, externalising blame or low acknowledgment of their sexual behaviour problem and its impact. Carich and Calder (2003) also criticise the dichotomised conceptualisation of denial and argue that denial is best thought of as spectrum or continuum of behaviours and not a single state. Between the two extremes (full denial and full admission) individuals may vary considerably on the level of responsibility they take for their behaviour. The notion that denial is a continuum has become a popular position; however, such a conceptualisation has led to ambiguities about what denial actually is and what it means in practice. It can be argued that instead of the continuum approach offering a more sophisticated view, it actually increases conceptual ambiguity and makes it more difficult to operationalise for research. We will consider this conceptualisation in more detail in the coming paragraphs.

Continuum or typology?

Many authors have put forward different 'types' of denial based either upon research outcome or direct clinical experience (see Schneider & Wright, 2004; Marshall, Anderson & Fernandez, 1999; Brake & Shannon, 1997; Winn, 1996; Prins, 1995; Pollock & Hashmall, 1991; Stevenson, Castillo and Sefarbi (1990). For example Happle and Auffrey (1995) propose 12 types of denial, including denial of the crime itself, denial of responsibility, denial of intent and premeditation and denial of injury to victims. It is striking that there is considerable overlap between these dimensions/types, with the differences appearing largely semantic.

A typology should differ from a continuum in that it identifies distinct types or categories of denial, without implying a graduated change in intensity between levels. The literature has outlined numerous typologies of denial, though such typologies have also been considered as forming a continuum by others (see e.g. Carich & Calder, 2003; Schlank & Shaw, 1997). Indeed, the literature often treats denial 'typologies' and 'continuum' as synonyms, and this has led to confusion in the literature (see Cooper, 2005; Schlank & Shaw, 1997). What appears clear is that many types of denial are successfully supported in the early stages of intervention (Schlank & Shaw, 1997) and so are probably best construed as something akin to 'workable' denials (see Blagden, Winder, Gregson & Thorne, 2013). If types of denial are simply part of the 'process' of early intervention, the clinical utility of identifying types of denial should be questioned, particularly if they do not correspond to psychologically meaningful risk factors in any logical way.

As noted, numerous researchers have proposed typologies of denial, and Table 7.1 presents some examples that have been put forward by various authors. In this table, we have organised the various typologies in light of Schneider and Wright's (2004) proposal that there are three categories of denial: refutation (which we have adapted to mean only complete refutation i.e. categorical denial), minimisation (this category is seen as progress from refutation, but includes denials that get in the way of full disclosure) and depersonalisation (which is a more deeply entrenched denial and rejects the possibility that the individual is the sort of person vulnerable to committing sexual offences).

We would argue that while such typologies allow for descriptive labels of various forms of minimisation, they are qualitatively different from categorical denial. Indeed, the 'minimisation' and 'depersonalisation' categories are to do with responsibility-taking rather than refutation. Conceptualising these 'types' of denial as 'denial' in empirical research has led to, and will continue to lead to, findings that are difficult to interpret. Indeed, research has been limited by small samples of categorical deniers in empirical investigations of denial (see e.g. Harkins, Beech & Goodwill, 2010; Ware et al., 2015). While there may be a relationship between minimisation and denial (see e.g. Nunes & Jung, 2013; Schneider & Wright, 2004), we suggest that categorical denial be distinct. Given that many types of denial (aside from categorical denial) are akin to minimisation, rationalisation and justification, it is unsurprising that types of denial are associated with beliefs that support sexual abuse (Nunes & Jung, 2013). We would argue that there has been a distinct lack of empirical research that has investigated and tried to make sense of categorical 'denial' in people convicted of sexual offending.

While many authors have advocated a continuum approach, none have set out the various steps along the continuum or indicated what kinds of denial would be seen as more or less progressive (see Levenson, 2011; Carich & Calder, 2003; Happle & Auffrey, 1995). This is similarly the case for the different types of denial. Gibbons, de Volder and Casey (2003) found no difference between offence type and denial type, i.e. there was no type of denial which was characteristic of either people convicted of rape or child sexual abuse, and instead found the spread of denial to be variable. This finding calls into question the clinical utility of a

Table 7.1 Typologies of Denial in People Convicted of Sexual Offences

Author(s)	Refutation	Minimisation	Depersonalisation
Happle and Auffrey (1995)	Denial of crime	Denial of frequency of deviant acts Denial of injury and victim impact	Denial of paraphilic interests
Kennedy and Grubin (1992)	Denial of offence	Denial of internal attribution Denial of responsibility	Denial of paraphilic interests
Marshall et al. (1999)	Complete denial	Denying/minimising harm Minimising responsibility Minimising the offence	Denying/minimising fantasy
Stevenson, Castillo and Sefarbi (1990)	Denial of offence	Denial of responsibility Denial of frequency and duration Denial of victim	Denial of sexual enjoyment and gratification
Winn (1996)	Denial of facts	Denial of awareness Denial of responsibility Denial of impact	Denial of sexual arousal and inappropriate arousal of non-sexual problems Denial of grooming oneself and the environment

typology approach. That is, labelling a person's denial according to a typology does not assist the clinician in understanding the function of the denial, nor does it suggest how to respond to the denial. If denial is on a continuum, then the continuum needs to have clinical utility and needs to distinguish denial from other phenomena such as beliefs that endorse sexual abuse. In our view, labelling offence-supportive beliefs as forms of denial only adds to the confusion surrounding an already confusing phenomenon (Maruna & Mann, 2006; Ware & Mann, 2012).

We have one other serious concern about most of the denial typologies. This is that many of the statements categorised as one or another form of denial could be quite legitimate statements for a person to make. For instance, several typologies contain a category of denial that relates to "denial of 'deviant' or atypical sexual interest". However, it is now quite clearly established that many people who have been convicted of sexual offences are not driven by deviant sexual interest (Seto, 2019). Indeed, it may actually be a healthy adaptive response to reject such a stigmatising label (Blagden, Winder, Gregson & Thorne, 2014; Walton, 2019). Therefore, to automatically categorise every person who denies a paraphilic interest as a denier seriously over-pathologises their stance. This kind of over-labelling can place people into no-win situations in assessment and intervention. For example, Waldram (2007) described people convicted of sexual offences in programmes as learning to put on a "performance", where they give up their own reality and adopt the therapist's preferred narrative in order to survive the "rehabilitative" correctional experience. Similarly, Lacombe (2008) has warned of the dangers of turning people convicted of sexual offences into confession-machines, a process at odds with normal social interaction. The rehabilitative process should not be something that people convicted of sexual offences have to "survive" by accepting stigmatising labels and pathology that are not warranted.

We suggest therefore that viewing denial as a continuum or a typology is unhelpful for at least five reasons: 1) Most forms or types of denial that the typologies articulate are addressed in intervention, e.g. as offence-supportive beliefs. 2) There is no evidence for a continuum of denial that has progressive steps from more to less denial or that distinguishes between different types of denial/'deniers' (see Gibbons et al., 2003). 3) Some of the types of "denial" that have been articulated could, in fact, be legitimate descriptions of people's motivation or modus operandi. 4) Neither the continuum nor typology approach are informative about the function of denial and therefore do not provide ideas about how to respond to denial. 5) The preoccupation with denial may blind practitioners to understanding the person's reality, and hence may obscure identification of their treatment needs and any progress they make (see Blagden, Winder, Thorne & Gregson, 2011). As pointed out, labelling denials as minimisations and rationalisations is problematic and runs counter to recent advice, which recommends much greater tolerance of excuses and minimisation than was previously the case (e.g. Maruna & Mann, 2006; Ware & Mann, 2012).

Categorical denial, however, is still frequently seen as the main barrier to entry for intervention for men with sexual convictions. In order to understand this form of denial and how to respond to it in intervention, we must first consider its function, cause and context. From this point onward when we discuss denial, we mean categorical denial.

The functions and causes of categorical denial

We have presented some concerns about how denial is defined and conceptu-alised and now will focus on a more contextual understanding of categorical denial. This is often neglected when thinking about denial in men with sexual convictions, but can help us understand and make sense of their denial. Indeed, a good starting point is to pose the question: Why do so many people convicted of sexual offences categorically deny their offending? In order to answer this ques-tion, it is interesting to examine the nature, prevalence and function of denial in everyday life. In forensic contexts, denial is generally construed as maladaptive; however, outside forensic settings, denial performs many adaptive functions, and it is a vital resource in many social interactions (Gosling, Denizeau & Oberle, 2006; Goleman, 1989; Livingstone-Smith, 2004; Russell, 1993). For example, Russell (1993) has found that denial can maintain self-esteem and can increase a person's capacity to cope. Similarly, Taylor and Brown (1988) argue that positive illusion, which is conceptually linked to denial, fosters better life functioning as well as positive psychological adjustment. Snyder and Higgins (1988) also con-tend that positive illusions and excuses have beneficial affective, performance and health benefits. They further argue that the conventional view that it is adaptive to have an accurate appraisal of reality and maladaptive to self-deceive or use positive illusions is something of a misnomer. Denial can allow face-saving manoeuvres to be performed, can work pre-emptively to present the self in a positive light and is something that everyone does to some extent (van Dijk, 1992; Snyder & Higgins, 1988). Indeed, it could be argued that it is taking responsibility for one's offending behaviour, and not denial, which causes psy-chological distress (Xuereb, Ireland & Davies, 2009).

More recently there has been evidence to suggest that denial may actually work as a protective factor for some men with sexual convictions, i.e. a factor that seems to assist desistance from sexual offending. Marshall, Marshall and Kingston (2011) reported denial to be negatively related to items on three risk instruments (STATIC-99, VRS-SO, STABLE 2000), suggesting that denial may actually sig-nal a lower chance of reoffending. Harkins et al. (2010) found that people with sexual convictions classed as high risk/high denial were less likely to recidivate than people classed as low denial/low risk. Such findings bolster Maruna's (2004) assertion that the "constructive use of cognitive distortions, such as externalising blame, might actually promote desistance [from crime]. . . . Personal reform or rehabilitation may itself be a cognitive distortion of sorts" (pp. 189–190). Indeed, psychological well-being research suggests that honest self-appraisals are more likely to be linked to depressive disorders (Seligman, 1975). As Cohen (2001, p. 56) noted, "Mental health, it turns out, depends not on being in touch with reality, but on illusion, self-deception and denial". In short, research suggests that failure to ascribe responsibility of bad acts to oneself (particularly as part of one's core identity) is a common aspect of human cognition and not pathological or a sign of deviancy (Friestad, 2012). People with convictions making internal stable dispositions for their offending are more likely to find desisting from crime a challenge (see e.g. Maruna, 2001).

Denial in men with sexual convictions is most likely caused by the same phenomena that motivates denial in people without convictions. Research has found that denial can avoid feelings of shame and stigma and maintain a coherent self-identity in men with sexual convictions (Blagden et al., 2011; Marshall, Marshall & Ware, 2009). Denial of sexual offences can help men survive prison (Schwaebe, 2005), maintain family and friendship ties (see e.g. Blagden et al., 2011; Schlank & Shaw, 1997; Sefarbi, 1990) and avoid feelings of shame and worthlessness (Tangney & Dearing, 2002). Rogers and Dickey's (1991) adaptational model of denial in men with sexual convictions accounts for this influence of context. Their model rests on three assumptions: 1) The individual sees that they are in an adversarial setting; 2) they believe that if they disclose their offence they have something to lose and that there is something to be gained from denial; and 3) the individual considers what the best approach is for them to achieve their goals. Essentially the individual enters a cost–benefits analysis, and where personal disclosure is perceived as high risk, denial is utilised to avoid negative consequences and achieve consonance (Rogers & Dickey, 1991).

The context of categorical denial

The perception of denial as functional and adaptive rather than dysfunctional and maladaptive appears to rest on the context in which the denial is observed and the perspective and assumptions of the observer. For example, Zimmermann (2004, 2007) found that terminally ill patients and their families were often labelled as being 'in denial' if they did not accept their diagnosis, treatment or make provisions for palliative care. Zimmermann pointed to a power dynamic where the clinician has the power to label a patient as 'in denial' and so enabling the clinician to blame the individual for their denial. That is, the implication that the denial is maladaptive stems from the physician's wish for the patient to adopt a certain view, rather than resting on evidence that denial is harmful to patients. There are some striking parallels between forensic and certain medical contexts. For instance, in both contexts denial can affect levels of service and care, because the dominant model of care requires the patient to accept the diagnosis. When this requirement is in force and a patient is considered to be "in denial", the focus of the service becomes the need to overcome the denial. Zimmermann and Rodin (2004) strongly contested this, arguing that the focus should be on reducing suffering rather than combating denial in medical contexts. A similar dynamic can be noted in forensic settings where the labelling as 'in denial' generally means the individual is excluded from treatment. Denial is seen as something that unquestionably interferes with treatment and that therefore needs to be broken down before treatment can be offered. It is interesting to note that in both these settings there is a clear power dynamic between the two individuals: patient/client and doctor/treatment professional. Furthermore, it needs to be remembered that denial is an interpersonal and relational interaction and not necessarily a reflection of internal pathological state. That is, denial occurs in a context of particular relationships. As Weisman (1972, p. 61) put it, "no one can deny by himself, in utter solitude".

There is therefore a need to consider the context in which men with sexual convictions find themselves, as through understanding this context we can begin to better understand concepts such as denial and treatment resistance/refusal. It is not surprising that such individuals often perceive their environment as adversarial and threatening and fear the loss of family, friends and status. The physically unsafe and sometimes unfamiliar prison environment (where people with convictions for sexual offences are positioned at the bottom of informal but powerful hierarchies), coupled with punitive societal responses and other external fears, mean that denial could be accurately understood as an adaptive rather than maladaptive reaction. Denial is thus based on an evaluation about the best course of action for that individual (Sewell & Salekin, 1997).

The specific environment of prison, where many men with sexual convictions are expected to undertake rehabilitative interventions, may encourage rather than discourage denial. Mann et al. (2010) concluded that the adaptational model of denial was the best fit to the data collected on those not opting to undertake treatment in HM Prison and Probation Service. That is, there was strong evidence that context influenced the decision to deny and that making this decision was a rational choice. How an individual explains, interprets and perceives events in prison may not be consistent with his worldview on the outside (Friestad, 2012). Indeed, perhaps we should worry more about those who admit their convictions in such circumstances.

Managing identity and reducing shame and associated stigma

Blagden et al. (2011) have argued that identity and stigma are two crucial concepts in understanding denial in men with sexual convictions. According to Crocker and Quinn (2001), having a stigmatised social identity raises doubts about one's humanity, because such individuals are subjected to negative stereotypes and are devalued and dehumanised by others. Men with sexual convictions are stigmatised like almost no other group and face vociferous public indignation. Furthermore, such individuals do not live in hermetically sealed vacuums and are fully aware of the public's views of them (Hudson, 2013). Thus, when a non-stigmatised individual (like a person before conviction) becomes stigmatised (like when convicted of a sexual offence), the individual may want to manage and present a desirable identity. It is not uncommon when people become a member of a group they previously felt anger or fear towards that they turn those feelings inward to themself. It is therefore unsurprising that individuals who go through a transition into a stigmatised group want to retain their old identities and reject the labels assigned to them (Hebl & Kleck, 2002). Indeed, it has been argued that a sense of personal identity is derived from a perception of temporal consistency (e.g. "I am a good and moral person, always have been, so incapable of being a sexual offender") (Ross, 1989). People who deny their convictions often express complete revulsion towards people who admit sexual offences and actively distance themselves from them, thereby highlighting the disparity between the prototypical 'sex offender' and 'them' (Hudson, 2013). However, this position may have adaptive benefits.

Recent studies have suggested that denial may be a way of doing identity management (Blagden et al., 2014). Denial and identity transformation are shaped by and through social interactions (Presser & Kurth, 2009); therefore, it is necessary to consider the relational properties of denial in forensic contexts and the latitude denial allows for identity management and deviance disavowal. In Blagden et al's (2014) study, all people denying their offence rejected the label "sex offender" and actively distanced themselves from such a label. However, this is likely an adaptive strategy, as it allows the individual to resist internalising a problem category that may impair one's ability to achieve self-respect and affiliation with mainstream society. Similarly, Hulley (2016) found neutralisations appeared to assist desistance narratives from sexual offending by allowing for the negotiation of stigma and rejection of the "sex offender" label, thus providing for the development of a non-offending, pro-social identity. In Farmer, McAlinden and Maruna's (2016) study of men with sexual convictions who had desisted for a long period of time, they found that when participants accounted for their offending behaviour, they were more likely to externalise situational rather than dispositional factors. This enabled the participants to manage shame attached to their offences and gave them a means of accounting for the harm they had caused to others. Thus a 'denier's' presentation of someone not capable of committing such offences or of someone with 'moral character' (See Blagden et al., 2014), may enable enactment of such identities. Such narratives may allow the individual to create good and moral selves by rejecting and distancing themselves from the label of 'sexual offenders', thus highlighting that their crime does not reflect the real them, presenting a desirable identity, and thus denying is not surprising. Walton's (2019) recent exploration of denial as an evolutionary response reminds us that responses like denial are archetypal forms – ancient biological motives that are manifesting in our cognition. Taking such positions does the important evolutionary work of allowing us to belong to desirable in-groups, a core human desire. This also allows individuals the ability to distance themselves from groups that are a 'social curse', i.e. those groups which are a burden, that impact on your ability cope and which stigmatise your identity (Wakefield et al., 2019).

Resistance to being labelled a 'sexual offender' is likely to have positive implications for an individual, in that adopting and internalising such a label leaves them with an impaired ability to achieve self-respect and achieve affiliation with mainstream society (Maruna, LeBel, Naples & Mitchell, 2009). This 'golem effect' (low expectation of people, leads to poor outcome) has been linked to recidivism (for non-sexual offenders). For instance, it has been found that those who were formally labelled are significantly more likely to recidivate within two years than those who were not (Maruna et al., 2009; see also Chiricos, Barrick, Bales & Bontrager, 2007). Identity transformation has also been linked to redemption, which can be construed as a negative past being reconstrued as a positive (McAdams, 2006). It may be that an individual's disavowal of stigmatised labels and their failure to ascribe bad things to themself allow them the latitude to construct moral and adaptive selves which provide a blueprint to live up to. Presenting a positive or desirable identity is then a normal and adaptive process, which happens on a regular basis in social interaction. External explanations, reasons and justifications for behaviour are well documented in the traditional actor–observer asymmetry where 'actors' attribute their behaviour to the situation but the observer attributes the behaviour to 'stable dispositions'. One psychological process key in this asymmetry is impression management, which has been found to be crucial in an individual's reason explanations in social interactions, particularly when motivated by their own goals (e.g. distancing self from perceived negative groups) (Malle, 2007). Many men with sexual convictions are concerned that labels such as 'paedophile' and 'sexual offender' will become their 'master status' (the key referential trait that overshadows all other characteristics) (Blagden et al., 2011).

Is denial important?

As we have seen, denial is a ubiquitous feature of being human – we have evolved to be good deceivers, and there's good reason for this. Denial can be an adaptation to context or a way to avoid shame and stigma. From this understanding, we contend that denial is important in intervention and for men with sexual convictions, but not for the reasons that treatment providers generally consider. Instead of viewing accounts as false, they should be construed as a form of meaning making. From this standpoint denial becomes an interaction, something to be understood and worked with rather than something that is in need of challenge (Blagden et al., 2014). It is important to understand the relevance and utility of denial and the social and evolutionary mechanisms.

Consider what happens when you sense others disapprove of your actions. The chances are you feel a level of discomfort with associated thoughts such as "what must they of think me" and "what will happen if other people find out". The sense of disapproval would not even need to be from those most important to you for this state to arise. For most of us, it is quite enough that vaguely familiar people might disapprove of what we have done, and this would also be the case even if their disapproval was relatively mild. You would not need to sense that they were utterly horrified or appalled at your actions for you to experience anxiety about being besmirched and rejected. *Why*? Why do you and all other humans experience this state when sensing others' disapproval? It is because you, we, *all of us*, are *adapted* to. Evolution has programmed this emotional pain to occur when our minds and bodies are faced with the prospect of social rejection, and this is essentially because humans, like other social mammals, are biologically built end-to-end to belong (Walton, 2019). From our first breath we are entirely dependent on connectedness with others for our survival. We must be soothed, regulated and cared for, and we must have the capacity to arouse this level of emotional investment from others for our entire lives. It is profoundly important to our well-being. Being alone and isolated or feeling lonely kills us, either literally or slowly by hastening our death. In real terms, the effects of loneliness are comparable to major risk factors for early mortality like smoking or obesity (Holt-Lunstad, Smith, Baker, Harris & Stephenson, 2015). Our nervous system is socially orientated. It longs for connection, and when we sense the risk of being devalued by others, threat-based, high-alert states organise our minds and bodies. From this position denial in those with sexual convictions should not be seen as a maladaptive – it should be expected.

The prevention of being devalued by others is a prehistoric concern. It has always been an adaptive problem for species which depend on group cooperation and well-functioning alliances for survival. As a result, evolution has left an ancient signature on our nervous system in the form of "self-conscious emotions" that are designed to maintain our fitness to belong. Examples include shame, guilt, humiliation and pride. The emotions have a self-evaluative social function to them, operating like a "sociometer" (De Hooge et al., 2014), ensuring that we are sensitive to how we exist for others. Even the most primitive awareness of this kind was of benefit for early ancestral species. Those attentive to the social cooperative standards of their group benefited from mutual altruism and high survival and reproductive success, whilst their kinsfolk who were exiled for non-cooperative behaviour perished, typically at the hands of starvation, pack hunters or apex predators. These selective pressures have ensured that being of value to others and being strategically skilled in recovering one's value when it is under threat is one of the strongest primeval preoccupations in life (Sznycer et al., 2016, 2018; Sznycer, 2019). As a result, we can do almost anything to maintain our social value and regain it when it is risked by our incongruous actions. Minimising, refuting, excusing and blaming others for our dishonest, offensive or harmful behaviours (vis-à-vis 'denial') are among the basic strategies we use. '*We*' can also apologise, repair and seek to heal, but we can also do much worse, and we do, all in pursuit of maintaining our ability to belong.

Now place this in the context of sexual offending. In today's society, for those convicted of sexual offences, and in particular those labelled as "paedophiles", the threat of devaluation is formidable. Hatred towards these individuals is found at all levels of society, including the young, educated and liberal-minded (Jahnke, 2018; Jahnke, Schmidt, Geradt & Hoyer, 2015). Facing this public revulsion, it is unsurprising that people convicted of sexual offences deny such acts or appeal to external causes. Compared to those who admit their convictions, those who deny tend to report higher rates of shame (Ware et al., 2020). If they do at some point acknowledge their harmful acts, they often report that their denial was due to stigma, to uphold a credible identity, and because of the disgrace of being called a "sex offender" (Blagden et al., 2011, 2014). This is precisely what would be expected of an evolutionarily adaptive system that deals with the fitness costs of being socially devalued and ousted from the social group.

Oddly, if the threat of being rejected was lowered or if sanctions for and condemnation of the *behaviour* could be distinguished from organisational cues that support the (*re*)acceptance of the *person*, their need for safety strategies might be reduced. In other words, denial would be less required, and this would be because one could continue to belong despite their damaging actions. Calling people 'sex offenders', 'rapists' and 'child molesters' which clinicians, scientists and researchers of professional institutions continue to do, probably does not help with that. If nothing else, these labels convey a stigmatised identity which attracts the fierce hatred of society. These labels fuse people to the worst version of themselves and the most socially reviled and harmful behaviour they have ever exhibited. Whilst occupying this rejected label, it is difficult for people to actually acknowledge and turn towards the harm they have caused to their victims and society, '*seeing it*' and building skills for doing things differently, namely living a non-harmful, law-abiding life in the future.

Is overcoming denial and accepting responsibility related to successful rehabilitation and lower recidivism?

There is little evidence that overcoming denial is necessary, as it has been found to be unrelated to sexual offence recidivism (Hanson & Bussière, 1998; Hanson & Morton-Bourgon, 2005; Marshall et al., 2009). Hanson et al. (2009) label denial a non-criminogenic need, and while some studies have found an interaction with risk, research has found no overall effect for denial on recidivism.

Recent research has reported interactions with risk. For example, Harkins et al. (2010) found that low-risk deniers were more likely to recidivate, while high-risk deniers recidivated at lower levels. Nunes et al. (2007) found also found that low-risk (incest) deniers were more likely to recidivate than admitters; however, they also found that categorical denial was associated with decreased recidivism in high-risk offenders.

'Being in denial' has been found to be over-emphasised in terms of a risk factor for future recidivism (see e.g. Vaughan, 2007). It could even be argued that the reverse may be true and that denial in men with convictions could be (in some cases) protective (Harkins et al., 2010; Mann et al., 2010). This could be for reasons outlined in the last section, e.g. it could be that for some people their offence is so repugnant to their own self-image that they reject it and thus refuse to accept their sexual offending as a reflection of their true self (Vaughan, 2007). This view of denial fits with the crime desistance literature, which emphasises multiple internal factors in the change process, the importance of personal identity in personal reform and the building of daily pro-social habits (Serin & Lloyd, 2009). It has been argued that crime desisters seldom make internal stable and intentional attributions for their criminal behaviour (Maruna & Mann, 2006). Perhaps instead of putting so much energy into getting people out of denial, we should be trying to get people in denial. This is, of course, tongue in cheek, but there is very little evidence for the position that individuals in denial need to be admitting.

Implications for practice

Denial has been described as a 'potentially misleading risk factor' by Hanson and Morton-Bourgon (2005) due to its lack of relationship with recidivism risk. Given that denial is not an empirically grounded risk factor, why do we give it so much credence in treatment? It appears that denial continues its importance due to widely held, but largely false, entrenched beliefs by clinicians that those who deny their offence are "risky", make poor progress in treatment and lack insight. Despite a lack of evidence regarding denial as a risk factor, these widely held beliefs prevail, and denial remains a key organising principle for treatment in many jurisdictions (Blagden, 2011).

There is no doubt that responding effectively with denial can be challenging and complex. We agree with Schneider and Wright (2004) that denial is a source of rich clinical information, but we disagree that focusing on categorical denial can only be done through attempts at eliminating denial. We also disagree and challenge the conventional wisdom in forensic settings that breaking down denial is necessary for successful rehabilitation. We are also critical of the traditional "battle of wills" exemplified in the following quote; "[T]he breakdown of denial is an extended process involving intense conflict, many reverses and only tentative victories" (Levin in Laflen & Sturm, 1994, p. 21). We argue that such a position is the very 'problem' with denial in that the therapeutic relationship is orientated around the idea that denial needs to be broken down and that change in individuals comes with personal "victories" (see also Blagden et al., 2013). Focusing on the denial itself is not the best approach and actually may be counterproductive. Instead, it is better to understand the context of the person's denial, the possible motives for denial and what the denial means for that individual (Vanhoeck & Van Daele, 2011). Denial needs to be construed as a form of sense making. From this perspective, whether an account is true or false is largely irrelevant – we are always dealing with an illusion of introspective awareness from participants/clients in this setting (or any setting). Verbalisations are not truths, nor do they reveal underlying cognitive processes; instead, they tell us about the 'meaning' or intentionality of human experience (Churchill, 2000). Instead, we need to understand what the narrative says about the individual, what does it achieve, how does it position them, what are they telling are us, how is the person standing themselves in the narrative? Such a construal views denial as a responsivity factor and one we need to be much more responsive to. If then we begin to construe denial as something to work with rather than against, where do we go from here? How should we engage with people who deny convictions? Next we consider several possible positions.

Do nothing?

This is currently the approach that is taken by many jurisdictions or programmes with men with sexual convictions who are currently in categorical denial. The "do nothing" option places responsibility for "coming out of denial" with the person denying. Until they are prepared to admit their offence, they may be effectively unable to connect with any rehabilitative services.

There are several disadvantages to this "no-action" option. First – and perhaps most persuasively at this time of global financial strain – it is expensive to do nothing with people who deny their conviction. Despite the evidence, the lay belief persists strongly that denial means a higher risk of recidivism than acceptance, and hence many people denying convictions serve longer in prison because of a reluctance by parole boards to release them (O'Donohue & Letourneau, 1993; Hood et al., 2002). There is a financial cost to society of these longer prison sentences. Secondly, there is no solid evidence that denial prevents successful treatment completion once accepted into the intervention. Indeed, when we consider empirically guided risk factors, e.g. the "central eight" (see Andrews, Bonta & Wormith, 2006), all can be addressed without explicit admittance on the part of the offender. By doing nothing, we are excluding individuals from addressing needs in their lives, which may help them lead positive offence-free lives.

Group intervention with those denying their offences

It has been nearly 25 years since Schlank and Shaw (1997) reviewed the approaches to treating people in denial. Since then there has been slow progress in developing interventions and working constructively with this population. Two approaches to denial have been reported in the literature. In the first approach, programmes have been reported which aimed to move clients from denial to admission; these can typically be classed as 'early approaches' (see Schlank & Shaw, 1996; O'Donohue & Letourneau, 1993; Brake & Shannon, 1997). These programmes had commonality, in that they all were brief, structured interventions for men denying their guilt, with most commenting on progress made (in terms of observable markers, e.g. reductions in denial).

The exceptions to the explicit aim of reducing denial are more 'progressive approaches' to working with denial, and these include Roberts and Baim (1999), Marshall et al. (2001) and Ware and Marshall (2008). Roberts and Baim's (1999) programme began as confession-orientated but shifted its ethos to more educational in origin due to unsuccessful modifying and engagement of denial. As Roberts and Baim (1999, p. 227) explain, "it would be an understatement to say that [denial] led to a degree of worker frustration and despair". Their approach was non-confrontational, and once participants realised that they were not being tricked or being led into confession, they became more engaged and made good progress through treatment. Marshall's (2001) programme was an adaptation of traditional sex offender treatment programmes (SOTPs) in that it targeted all known criminogenic needs, but did so without attempting to elicit admission. Marshall et al. (2010) evaluated the programme and found it to be successful, with the programme significantly reducing recidivism in men in denial.

Individual and motivational strategies

In addition to group-based intervention for people denying (be that exclusively for those in denial or into existing programmes), there has been the development of individual-based strategies. In this approach, people denying are understood as individuals with rational, adaptive reasons for their denial. Understanding a client's worldview should be at the heart of doing constructive work with them. Through understanding their position and how they are making sense of their world, their denial becomes therapeutically relevant, not in the sense that it should be broken down, but rather it represents something personally meaningful for the client (Northey, 1999). Denial is something that is reconstrued as something to work with rather than against.

Motivational interviewing (MI) is an evidence-based approach for working with clients in denial that has strong empirical support with other client groups such as substance misusers. Motivational interviewing has frequently and passionately been mooted as an appropriate strategy for working with people denying (see e.g. Mann & Rollnick, 1996). The following table outlines how some of the core MI strategies could be applied to working with men in categorical denial. However, it must be emphasised that MI is not a set of strategies to use to "get someone out of denial". Rather, MI rests on a set of principles that are fundamentally respectful of the client's internal world and complex cost–benefit calculations. Denial is instead viewed as a client's ambivalence to change (Mann & Rollnick, 1996; Mann, Ginsburg & Weekes, 2002).

The disadvantages of the individualised/motivational approach are 1) it is an expensive approach, requiring one-on-one meetings between therapist and client, which may not be possible in financially hard-pressed jurisdictions and

Strategy	Description	Examples
Simple reflection	Respond to the denial with non-resistance rather than trying to argue it. Acknowledge the client's disagreement, emotion or perception. Avoid the confrontation–denial trap. Use reflection to shift emphasis.	You don't feel that you have any problems, and you feel angry that other people keep telling you that you have. You just want to be left alone. However, you realise that that's not going to happen.
Amplified reflection	Exaggerate what the client has said. Attempt by doing so to elicit the other side of the client's ambivalence (assumed always to exist).	You don't feel that you have any problems at all, and you are not interested in anything we have to offer you.

Strategy	Description	Examples
Double-sided reflection	Acknowledge what the client has said and then add to it the unspoken other side of their ambivalence.	You don't feel that you have any problems . . . but it worries you that other people think you have.
Shifting focus	Go round the problem rather than tackle it head on.	I really agree that labels are destructive and unhelpful. Let's get away from them and talk about you as a unique individual.
Agreement with a twist	Offer apparent agreement with what the client is saying, but with a slight twist or change of direction.	I can understand that you feel this is your own business; it's rare to find someone brave enough to be fully honest about these things.
Emphasise personal choice	Persons in denial can often be freed up by a reminder that it is them who will determine what happens.	I don't want to put any pressure on you about what you should do. That is completely up to you. All I'm here for today is to let you know what is on offer should you want it.

2) the therapist must be carefully trained in MI, which again carries a cost. On the other hand, studies with other client groups have indicated that MI can be effective in even very small doses, so it does not appear that the therapeutic relationship needs much time to be developed (McMurran, 2009). Blagden et al. (2013) have stressed the importance of developing trusting and meaningful relationships with the therapeutic alliance crucial to positive outcome with this group. Mann and Marshall (2009) commented that in their research study, people in denial became observably more interested in treatment programmes simply as a result of a research interview, presumably because the style of interview was non-directive and based on listening and understanding rather than trying to persuade.

This type of strategy or intervention may help people 'get ready' for treatment and prepare them for it, but it should be pointed out that its purpose would not be to explicitly 'move' people from denial to admittance. We have argued that it is necessary to abandon the position that denial is a marker for progress, as it causes a great deal of frustration, and this frustration is counterproductive to effective therapeutic work.

Deniers into regular treatment

In order to allow those that are denying into intervention with those who are not, there would need to be a shift in one of the core organising principles of treatment (Carter & Mann, 2016; Blagden, 2011). Overcoming denial, accepting responsibility and offence disclosure would have to no longer be key aspects of intervention. Instead, programmes would focus on empirically derived, psychologically meaningful risk factors which can be addressed without admission (Mann et al., 2010; Marshall, Thornton, Marshall, Fernandez & Mann, 2001). There is empirical support for allowing people in denial into groups with those who are not (see e.g. Ware & Marshall, 2008; Marshall et al., 2001). Indeed, Marshall et al. (2011) have argued that in their programme clients' denials and distortions become less pronounced as treatment progresses without any challenge to them. This fits with the definition earlier of denial as a form of 'social scaffolding', and so naturally through the treatment process denial would begin to rescind. It may be that the best way to effectively deal with denial is by not dealing with denial. While allowing people in denial into conventional treatment may mean a shift in programme focus, it does appear that programmes which make no attempt to address denial but do target empirically derived criminogenic needs can be effective.

The most current approach to interventions with men with sexual convictions which does not require explicit disclosure are the Kaizen and Horizon programmes for men with sexual convictions in England and Wales. These programmes support participants to develop the optimism and skills to strengthen their pro-social identity and plan for a life free of offending (MoJ, 2021). The model of change is underpinned by Mann and Carter's (2012) biopsychosocial framework for intervention and Carter and Mann's (2016) organising principles of intervention with men with sexual convictions. Carter and Mann's (2016) position, partly influenced by Blagden's (2011) argument that much treatment activity is driven by informal 'organizing principles', was that intervention needed clear organising principles which will greatly benefit those who deliver and receive the programme. Offence disclosure and responsibility are not to be explicit treatment targets (Carter & Mann, 2016). The shift towards focusing on skills, values, identity and good lives (as well as risk–need–responsivity [RNR] principles) has taken place alongside the development of a biopsychosocial model of change that has led to better targeting of needs and the strengthening of responsivity factors (Ramsay et al., 2020).

Environmental change

As Mann (2009) pointed out, the first response to those who refused to engage in interventions or deny their guilt should be to listen to their perceptions about their context and strive to understand their anxieties about being identified, being labelled and being punished. Through this process of being heard, individuals may start to overcome their fears of opening up to others about their offending and its causes. Ware (2017) has argued that taking account of the context can improve the effectiveness of treatment programmes. If denial is an adaptive response to a context, then arguably the first appropriate response is to change the context so that it encourages and reinforces admission rather than denial. While it is a considerable challenge to overcome public and political attitudes about men with sexual convictions, it may be possible to effect some smaller-scale reductions in stigmatisation within criminal justice contexts such as individual prisons. The move towards considering the rehabilitative climate of prisons, and notably in the work of Blagden et al. (2016) and Blagden and Wilson (2020), highlights the importance of a rehabilitative prison culture in the rehabilitation of men with sexual convictions. The work demonstrates the experience of prisons for men with sexual convictions and the importance of prisoner–staff relationships, opportunities to change (e.g. interventions), active citizenship, peer support and experienced safety for the change process.

Future directions

As highlighted in this chapter, research has been severely hampered by conceptual and definitional ambiguities. We have suggested that categorical denial be seen as a distinct category to other types of minimisations, justifications and rationalisations that are routinely dealt with in early intervention. Complete denial needs more constructive approaches to intervention. However, our knowledge of categorical denial is surprisingly weak. There have been very few empirical studies of categorical denial, and those that have been done are hampered by small sample sizes and inconsistent definitions (Ware et al., 2015). Aside from a handful of empirical studies, we know very little about their characteristics (IQ, personality, background) and even less about their mind-set (how they construe the world, how they construe themselves and others) (Blagden et al., 2014; Baldwin & Roys, 1998). Ware, Blagden and Harper (2020) found those denying their offences were significantly more shame-prone and likely to use externalisation as a method of impression management. The link between shame and denial is important, particularly for clinical practice. For example, Gilbert and Procter (2006) argue that denial is a safety strategy associated with shame and contend that working with shamed individuals needs to focus on building compassionate abilities, which allows one to process distress rather than deny it.

The exploration of shame and denial needs further empirical study. Xuereb et al. (2009) found a link between shame, avoidance and denial in people convicted of non-sexual offences. Avoidant coping has been found to correlate with psychological distress; thus, just because someone is denying their offence does not necessarily mean they are untroubled by it (Xuereb et al., 2009). There is some limited empirical support for this. Blagden et al. (2011), in a study interviewing people who had previously denied their offence, found that they articulated that denial was a burden or "heavy weight" that affected the participants psychologically. This appears to demonstrate the ambivalence of denial; denying can have positive effects, but prolonged use of denial can lead to dissonance.

The key to effective working with denial appears to be understanding denial and understanding its function for that person. Stripping away that denial or challenging it before the individual is ready may have deleterious consequences (Yalom, 1991). Categorical denial is still an underexplored research area, and future research needs to seek both to clarify categorical denial's role and its relevance for recidivism and needs to explore the psychological importance for individuals.

Conclusions

We have debated several key issues pertaining to denial in people convicted of sexual offences. The chapter critiqued traditional definitions and typologies regarding denial in people in this group. We advanced the argument that giving so-called different types of 'denial' labels and placing them on a continuum is unhelpful. Labelling cognitive distortions, minimisations, excuses and rationalisations as denials only leads to confusion and conceptual ambiguity. This is because it becomes intrinsically difficult to tease apart what is an actual denial. This ambiguity has caused inconsistencies in operationalising research and has led to conflicting and contradictory results. We argue that categorical denial is the only form of denial that should be labelled as such. This is important for at least two reasons: 1) categorical denial is the only form of denial which excludes participation from treatment and 2) it allows for clear research comparisons between categorical denial and conceptually linked phenomena (e.g. minimisations and justifications). This will allow research to say something meaningful about denial's relationship with recidivism, which is currently limited.

We have been critical of construing denial purely as pathology and have highlighted that denial has adaptive functions outside of deliberate dissimulation. Denial is an everyday occurrence, is something that can help maintain self-identity and is a human resource. It is important to be mindful of the context of denial and be mindful that challenge to denial is likely to be counterproductive. We have suggested that not attending to denial could be the most effective way of dealing with it. Finally we have argued that treatment need not focus on reducing denial and promoting offender disclosure. As Ware and Mann (2012) have argued, the task for treatment providers is to provide clients with the skills necessary to reduce the likelihood that they will commit further crimes. This can be done without admittance of sexual offending (Marshall et al., 2001; Ware & Marshall, 2008).

Excluding participation in sexual offender treatment programmes based on categorical denial is no longer a tenable position. It also enables a situation whereby a potentially high-risk and/or high-need individual is declined the very treatment that they need and may even be seeking (even while still denying) due to their denial (see Ware & Marshall, 2008). This situation is unacceptable and echoes Maletzky's sentiments that "to deny a crime is natural; to deny treatment to those who deny is a crime itself" (Maletzky, 1996, p. 4). While admittance/disclosure is one way of doing intervention with men with sexual convictions, it is not the only way, and denial does not need to be the last word in intervention.

References

Andrews, D. A., & Bonta, J. (2010). *The psychology of criminal conduct*. Routledge.

Andrews, D. A., Bonta, J., & Wormith, J. S. (2006). The recent past and near future of risk and/or need assessment. *Crime & Delinquency*, *52*(1), 7–27.

Baldwin, K., & Roys, D. T. (1998). Factors associated with denial in a sample of alleged adult sexual offenders. *Sexual Abuse: A Journal of Research and Treatment*, *10*(3), 211–226.

Barbaree, H. (1991). Denial and minimization among sex offenders: Assessment and treatment outcome. *Forum on Corrections Research*, *3*, 30–33.

Blagden, N. J. (2011). *Understanding denial in sexual offenders: The implications for policy and practice*. Doctoral dissertation, Nottingham Trent University, UK.

Blagden, N. J., & Wilson, K. (2020). "We're all the same here": Investigating the rehabilitative climate of a re-rolled sexual offender prison: A qualitative longitudinal study. *Sexual Abuse*, *32*(6), 727–750.

Blagden, N. J., Winder, B., Gregson, M., & Thorne, K. (2013). Working with denial in convicted sexual offenders: A qualitative analysis of treatment professionals' views and experiences and their implications for practice. *International Journal of Offender Therapy and Comparative Criminology*, *57*(3), 332–356.

Blagden, N. J., Winder, B., Gregson, M., & Thorne, K. (2014). Making sense of denial in sexual offenders: A qualitative phenomenological and repertory grid analysis. *Journal of Interpersonal Violence*, *29*(9), 1698–1731.

Blagden, N. J., Winder, B., & Hames, C. (2016). "They treat us like human beings": Experiencing a therapeutic sex offenders prison: Impact on prisoners and staff and implications for treatment. *International Journal of Offender Therapy and Comparative Criminology*, *60*(4), 371–396.

Blagden, N. J., Winder, B., Thorne, K., & Gregson, M. (2011). "No-one in the world would ever wanna speak to me again": An interpretative phenomenological analysis into convicted sexual offenders' accounts and experiences of maintaining and leaving denial. *Psychology, Crime & Law*, *17*(7), 563–585.

Brake, S. C., & Shannon, D. (1997). Using pretreatment to increase admission in sex offenders. In B. K. Schwartz & H. R. Cellini (Eds.), *Sex offender: New insights, treatment innovations and legal developments*. Civic Press.

Carich, M. S., & Calder, M. C. (2003). *Contemporary treatment of adult male sexual offenders*. Russell House Publishing.

Carter, A. J., & Mann, R. E. (2016). Organizing principles for an integrated model of change for the treatment of sexual offending. In *The Wiley handbook on the theories, assessment and treatment of sexual offending* (pp. 359–381). Wiley.

Chiricos, T., Barrick, K., Bales, W., & Bontrager, S. (2007). The labeling of convicted felons and its consequences for recidivism. *Criminology*, *45*(3), 547–581.

Churchill, S. (2000). "Seeing through" self-deception in narrative reports: Finding psychological truth in problematic data. *Journal of Phenomenological Psychology*, *31*(1), 44–62.

Cohen, S. (2001). *The states of denial*. Routledge.

Cooper, S. (2005). Understanding, treating, and managing sex offenders who deny their offence *Journal of Sexual Aggression*, *11*(1), 85–94.

De Hooge, I. E., Verlegh, P. W., & Tzioti, S. C. (2014). Emotions in advice taking: The roles of agency and valence. *Journal of Behavioral Decision Making*, *27*(3), 246–258.

Farmer, M., McAlinden, A. M., & Maruna, S. (2016). Sex offending and situational motivation: Findings from a qualitative analysis of desistance from sexual offending. *International Journal of Offender Therapy and Comparative Criminology*, *60*(15), 1756–1775.

Friestad, C. (2012). Making sense, making good, or making meaning? Cognitive distortions as targets of change in offender treatment. *International Journal of Offender Therapy and Comparative Criminology*, *56*(3), 465–482.

Gibbons, P., de Volder, J., & Casey, P. (2003). Patterns of denial in sexual offenders. *American Academy of Psychiatry and Law*, *31*(3), 332–344.

Gilbert, P., & Procter, S. (2006). Compassionate mind training for people with high shame and self-criticism: Overview and pilot study of a group therapy approach. *Clinical Psychology & Psychotherapy: An International Journal of Theory & Practice*, *13*(6), 353–379.

Goleman, D. J. (1989). What is negative about positive illusions? When benefits for the individual harm the collective. *Journal of Social and Clinical Psychology*, *8*(2), 190–197.

Gosling, P., Denizeau, M., & Oberle, D. (2006). Denial of responsibility: A new mode in dissonance reduction. *Journal of Personality and Social Psychology*, *90*(5), 722–733.

Hanson, R. K., Bourgon, G., Helmus, L., & Hodgson, S. (2009). The principles of effective correctional treatment also apply to sexual offenders: A meta-analysis. *Criminal Justice Behaviour*, *36*(9), 865–891.

Hanson, R. K., & Bussière, M. T. (1998). Predicting relapse: A meta-analysis of sexual offender recidivism studies. *Journal of Consulting and Clinical Psychology*, *66*, 348–362.

Hanson, R. K., & Morton-Bourgon, K. (2005). The characteristics of persistent sexual offenders: A meta-analysis of recidivism studies. *Journal of Consulting and Clinical Psychology*, *73*, 1154–1163.

Happle, R. M., & Auffrey, J. J. (1995). Sex offender assessment: Interrupting the dance of denial. *American Journal of Forensic Psychology*, *13*(2), 5–22.

Harkins, L., Beech, A. R., & Goodwill, A. M. (2010). Examining the influence of denial, motivation, and risk on sexual recidivism. *Sexual Abuse*, *22*(1), 78–94.

Hebl, M. R., & Kleck, R. E. (2002). Acknowledging one's stigma in the interview setting: Effective strategy or liability? *Journal of Applied Social Psychology*, *32*(2), 223–249.

Holt-Lunstad, J., Smith, T. B., Baker, M., Harris, T., & Stephenson, D. (2015). Loneliness and social isolation as risk factors for mortality: A meta-analytic review. *Perspectives on Psychological Science*, *10*(2), 227–237.

Hood, R., Shute, S., Feilzer, M., & Wilcox, A. (2002). Sex offenders emerging from long term imprisonment: A study of their long term reconviction rates and parole board members' judgements of their risk *British Journal of Criminology*, *42*(2), 371–394.

Hudson, K. (2013). *Offending identities: Sex offender's perspectives on their treatment and management*. Willan Publishing.

Hulley, J. L. (2016). "While this does not in any way excuse my conduct . . . ": The role of treatment and neutralizations in desistance from sexual offending. *International Journal of Offender Therapy and Comparative Criminology*, *60*(15), 1776–1790.

Jahnke, S. (2018). The stigma of pedophilia: Clinical and forensic implications. *European Psychologist*, *23*(2), 144.

Jahnke, S., Schmidt, A. F., Geradt, M., & Hoyer, J. (2015). Stigma-related stress and its correlates among men with pedophilic sexual interests. *Archives of Sexual Behavior*, *44*(8), 2173–2187.

Janoff-Bulman, R., & Timko, C. (1987). Coping with traumatic life events: The role of denial in light of people's assumptive worlds. In C. R. Snyder & C. Ford (Eds.), *Coping with negative life events: Clinical and social psychological perspectives*. Plenum.

Kennedy, H. G., & Grubin, D. H. (1992). Patterns of denial in sex offenders. *Psychological Medicine*, *22*(1), 191–196.

Lacombe, D. (2008). Consumed with sex: The treatment of sex offenders in risk society. *British Journal of Criminology, 48,* 55–74.

Laflen, B., & Sturm, W. (1994). Understanding and working with denial in sexual offenders. *Journal of Child Sexual Abuse, 3*(4), 19–36.

Levenson, J. S. (2011). "But I didn't do it!": Ethical treatment of men with sexual convictions in denial. *Sexual Abuse: A Journal of Research and Treatment, 23,* 346–364.

Levenson, J. S., & McGowan, M. (2004). Engagement, denial, and treatment progress among sex offenders in group therapy. *Sexual Abuse: A Journal of Research and Treatment, 16,* 49–63.

Livingstone-Smith, D. (2004). *Why we lie: The evolutionary roots of deception and the unconscious mind.* St. Martin's Press.

Maletzky, B. (1996). Denial of treatment or treatment of denial? *Sexual Abuse: A Journal of Research and Treatment, 8*(1), 1–5.

Malle, B. F., Knobe, J. M., & Nelson, S. E. (2007). Actor-observer asymmetries in explanations of behavior: New answers to an old question. *Journal of Personality and Social Psychology, 93*(4), 491.

Mann, R. E. (2009). Getting the context right for sex offender treatment. In *Building motivation for change in sexual offenders* (pp. 55–73). Safer Society Press.

Mann, R. E., & Carter, A. J. (2012). Organising principles for the treatment of sexual offending. *Behandlung von Straftätern: Sozialtherapie, Maßregelvollzug, Sicherungsverwahrung* (pp. 398–420). Centaurus Verlag & Media.

Mann, R. E., Ginsburg, J. I., & Weekes, J. R. (2002). Motivational interviewing with offenders. In *Motivating offenders to change: A guide to enhancing engagement in therapy* (pp. 87–102). Wiley–Blackwell.

Mann, R. E., Hanson, K. R., & Thornton, D. (2010). Assessing risk for sexual recidivism: Some proposals on the nature of psychologically meaningful risk factors. *Sexual Abuse: A Journal of Research and Treatment, 22*(2), 191–217.

Mann, R. E., & Rollnick, S. (1996). Motivational interviewing with a sex offender who believed he was innocent. *Behavioural and Cognitive Psychotherapy, 24,* 127–134.

Marshall, L. E., Serran, G., O'Brien, M., & Marshall, W. (2010). *Denial in sexual offenders.* Paper presented at Rampton Hospital Seminar Series.

Marshall, W. L., Anderson, A., & Fernandez, Y. (1999). *Cognitive behavioural treatment of sex offenders.* Wiley.

Marshall, W. L., Marshall, L. E., & Kingston, D. A. (2011). Are the cognitive distortions of child molesters in need of treatment? *Journal of Sexual Aggression, 17*(2), 118–129.

Marshall, W. L., Marshall, L. E., & Ware, J. (2009). Cognitive distortions in sexual offenders: Should they all be treatment targets? *Sexual Abuse in Australia and New Zealand, 2*(1), 21.

Marshall, W. L., Thornton, D., Marshall, L., Fernandez, Y., & Mann, R. (2001). Treatment of sexual offenders who are in categorical denial: A pilot project. *Sexual Abuse: A Journal of Research and Treatment, 13*(3), 205–215.

Maruna, S. (2001). *Making good: How ex-convicts reform and rebuild their lives.* American Psychological Association.

Maruna, S. (2004). Desistance and explanatory style: A new direction in the psychology of reform. *Journal of Contemporary Criminal Justice, 20,* 184–200.

Maruna, S., LeBel, T., Naples, M., & Mitchell, N. (2009). Looking-glass identity transformation: Pygmalion and Golem in the rehabilitation process. In *How offenders transform their lives* (pp. 30–55). Willan.

Maruna, S., & Mann, R. (2006). A fundamental attribution error? Rethinking cognitive distortions. *Legal and Criminological Psychology, 11*(2), 155–177.

McAdams, D. P. (2006). The redemptive self: Generativity and the stories Americans live by. *Research in Human Development, 3*(2&3), 81–100.

McGrath, R. J., Cumming, G., Burchard, B., Zeoli, S., & Ellerby, L. (2010). *Current practices and emerging trends in sexual abuser management: The Safer Society 2009 North American Survey.* Safer Society Press.

McMurran, M. (2009). Motivational interviewing with offenders: A systematic review. *Legal and Criminological Psychology, 14,* 83–100.

Northey, W. (1999). The politics of denial: A post-modern critique. In B. Schwartz (Ed.), *The sex offender: Theoretical advances, treating special populations and legal developments.* Civic Research Institute.

Nunes, K. L., Hanson, K., Firestone, P., Moulden, H., Greenberg, D., & Bradford, J. (2007). Denial predicts recidivism for some sexual offenders. *Sexual Abuse: A Journal of Research and Treatment, 19,* 91–105.

Nunes, K. L., & Jung, S. (2013). Are cognitive distortions associated with denial and minimization among sex offenders? *Sexual Abuse, 25*(2), 166–188.

O'Donohue, W., & Letourneau, E. (1993). A brief group treatment for the modification of denial in child sexual abusers: Outcome and follow-up. *Child Abuse & Neglect, 17*(2), 299–304.

Pollock, N. L., & Hashmall, J. M. (1991). The excuses of child molesters. *Behavioral Sciences & the Law, 9*(1), 53–59.

Presser, L., & Kurth, S. (2009). "I got a quick tongue": Negotiating ex-convict identity in mixed company. In B. M. Veysey, J. Christian, & D. J. Martinez (Eds.), *How offenders transform their lives.* Willian Publishing.

Prins, H. (1995). *Offenders deviants or patients.* Routledge.

Ramsay, L., Carter, A. J., & Walton, J. S. (2020). Contemporary programs designed for the tertiary prevention of recidivism by people convicted of a sexual offense: A review, and the UK perspective. In *The Wiley handbook of what works with sexual offenders*. Wiley.

Reber, E. S. (1985). *The Penguin dictionary of psychology*. Penguin.

Roberts, B., & Baim, C. (1999). A community-based programme for sex offenders who deny their offending behaviour. *Probation Journal, 46*, 225–233.

Rogers, R., & Dickey, R. (1991). Denial and minimization among sex offenders: A review of competing models of deception. *Annals of Sex Research, 4*, 49–63.

Ross, M. (1989). Relation of implicit theories to the construction of personal histories. *Psychological Review, 96*, 341–357.

Russell, G. (1993). The role of denial in clinical practice. *Journal of Advanced Nursing, 18*, 938–940.

Schlank, A. M., & Shaw, T. (1996). Treating sexual offenders who deny their guilt: A pilot study. *Sexual Abuse: A Journal of Research and Treatment, 8*(1), 17–23.

Schlank, A. M., & Shaw, T. (1997). Treating sexual offenders who deny: A review. *The Sex Offender: New Insights, Treatment, Innovations and Legal Developments, 2*, 61–67.

Schneider, S., & Wright, R. (2004). Understanding denial in sexual offenders: A review of cognitive and motivational processes to avoid responsibility. *Trauma, Violence & Abuse, 1*, 3–20.

Schwaebe, C. (2005). Learning to pass: Sex offenders' strategies for establishing a viable identity in the prison general population. *International Journal of Offender Therapy and Comparative Criminology, 49*(6), 614–625.

Sefarbi, R. (1990). Admitters and deniers among adolescent sex offenders and their families: A preliminary study. *American Journal of Orthopsychiatry, 60*(3), 460–465.

Seligman, M. E. P. (1975). *Helplessness: On depression, development & death*. Freeman.

Serin, R. C., & Lloyd, C. D. (2009). Examining the process of offender change: The transition to crime desistance. *Psychology, Crime & Law, 15*(4), 347–364.

Seto, M. C. (2019). *The motivation-facilitation model of sexual offending*. Sexual Abuse, 31(1), 3–24.

Sewell, K. W., & Salekin, R. T. (1997). Understanding and detecting dissimulation in sex offenders. In R. Rogers (Ed.), *Clinical assessment of malingering and deception* (2nd ed., pp. 328–350). New York, NY: Guilford.

Snyder, C. R., & Higgins, R. L. (1988). Excuses: Their effective role in the negotiation of reality. *Psychological Bulletin, 104*(1), 23.

Stevenson, H. C., Castillo, E., & Sefarbi, R. (1990). Treatment of denial in adolescent sex offenders and their families. *Journal of Offender Counseling, Services & Rehabilitation, 14*(1), 37–50.

Sznycer, D. (2019). Forms and functions of the self-conscious emotions. *Trends in Cognitive Sciences*, *23*(2), 143–157.

Sznycer, D., Tooby, J., Cosmides, L., Porat, R., Shalvi, S., & Halperin, E. (2016). Shame closely tracks the threat of devaluation by others, even across cultures. *Proceedings of the National Academy of Sciences*, *113*(10), 2625–2630.

Sznycer, D., Xygalatas, D., Agey, E., Alami, S., An, X. F., Ananyeva, K. I., . . . & Tooby, J. (2018). Cross-cultural invariances in the architecture of shame. *Proceedings of the National Academy of Sciences*, *115*(39), 9702–9707.

Tangney, J. P., & Dearing, R. L. (2002). *Shame and guilt*. Guilford Publications.

Taylor, S. E., & Brown, J. D. (1988). Illusion and well-being: A social psychological perspective on mental health. *Psychological Bulletin*, *103*(2), 193.

Van Dijk, T. A. (1992). Discourse and the denial of racism. *Discourse & Society*, *3*(1), 87–118.

Vanhoeck, K., & Van Daele, E. (2011). Denial of sexual crimes: A therapeutic exploration. Wiley Online Library. https://doi.org/10.1002/9781119990420.ch18

Vaughan, B. (2007). The internal narrative of desistance. *British Journal of Criminology*, *47*, 390–404.

Wakefield, J. R., Bowe, M., Kellezi, B., McNamara, N., & Stevenson, C. (2019). When groups help and when groups harm: Origins, developments, and future directions of the "Social Cure" perspective of group dynamics. *Social and Personality Psychology Compass*, *13*(3).

Waldram, J. B. (2007). Everybody has a story to tell: Listening to imprisoned sexual offenders. *Qualitative Health Research*, *17*(7), 963–970.

Walton, J. S. (2019). The evolutionary basis of belonging: Its relevance to denial of offending and labelling those who offend. *Journal of Forensic Practice*, *21*(4), 202–211.

Ware, J. M. (2017). Understanding and treating convicted sexual offenders who are in categorical denial. Unpublished doctoral dissertation. University of New South Wales, Australia.

Ware, J. M., Blagden, N., & Harper, C. (2020). Are categorical deniers different? Understanding demographic, personality, and psychological differences between denying and admitting individuals with sexual convictions. *Deviant Behavior*, *41*(4), 399–412.

Ware, J. M., & Mann, R. E. (2012). How should "acceptance of responsibility" be addressed in sexual offending treatment programs? *Aggression and Violent Behavior*, *17*(4), 279–288.

Ware, J. M., & Marshall, W. L. (2008). Treatment engagement with a sexual offender who denies committing the offence. *Clinical Case Studies*, *7*(6), 592–603.

Ware, J. M., Marshall, W. L., & Marshall, L. E. (2015). Categorical denial in convicted sex offenders: The concept, its meaning, and its implication for risk and treatment. *Aggression and Violent Behavior, 25*, 215–226.

Weisman, A. D. (1972). On dying and denying: A psychiatric study of terminality. Behavioral Publications.

Winn, M. (1996). The strategic and systematic management of denial in cognitive/behavioural treatment of sexual offenders. *Sexual Abuse: A Journal of Research and Treatment, 8*, 25–36.

Wright, R. C., & Schneider, S. L. (2004). Mapping child molester treatment progress with the FoSOD: Denial and explanations of accountability. *Sexual Abuse: A Journal of Research and Treatment, 16*(2), 85–105.

Xuereb, S., Ireland, J. L., & Davies, M. (2009). Chronic and offence-related factors and coping styles in offenders. *Personality and Individual Difference, 46*, 465–471.

Yalom, I. D. (1991). *Love's executioner and other tales of psychotherapy.* Penguin.

Zimmermann, C. (2004). Denial of impending death: A discourse analysis of the palliative care literature. *Social Science & Medicine, 59*(8), 1769–1780.

Zimmermann, C. (2007). Death denial: Obstacle or instrument for palliative care? An analysis of clinical literature. *Sociology of Health and Illness, 29*(2), 297–314.

Zimmermann, C., & Rodin, G. (2004). The denial of death thesis: Sociological critique and implications for palliative care. *Palliative Medicine, 18*(2), 121–128.

8
Deaf treatment programmes

Nicola Payne, Helen O'Connor,
and Rebecca Lievesley

Introduction

The treatment of hearing men who have committed sexual offences is a well-researched topic, and treatment pathways are well established within the prison service. The same can be said for treating individuals with complex needs, such as those with learning difficulties. But what are the options for treatment if the individual has committed a sexual offence and is profoundly deaf? Understanding the specific and unique needs of this client group is important for both treatment planning and risk management. This chapter will summarise previous research which has explored the topic of sexual offending in the deaf population and will discuss the varying opinions on best practice for treating and managing this client group. It will also discuss pioneering treatment that is being completed within a Category C sex offender estate in the UK for men who are deaf and have been convicted of sexual offences. It will conclude with thinking about how treatment for deaf sexual offenders can continue to develop and expand within the prison service.

Developing an understanding

Understanding deafness

Deafness is the second most common disability in the United Kingdom (Austen & Jeffery, 2007), affecting more than 11 million people, which equates to one in six people (Action on Hearing Loss, 2011) and of these, 900,000 people in the UK are estimated to be profoundly or severely deaf. Action on Hearing Loss estimate that at least 24,000 people across the UK use British Sign Language (BSL) as their main language. The term deafness covers various conditions, including

DOI: 10.4324/9780429262074-8

those that are born deaf or acquire deafness, those whose deafness presents in both ears (bilateral) or in one ear (unilateral), and deafness that can be profound or partial. The impact that deafness has on individuals depends on a number of factors, including the severity of deafness and the age of onset of deafness.

Deafness is defined by the extent of hearing loss, which can be caused by a multitude of reasons such as illness, birth complications/prematurity, injury, or age-related hearing decline. Profound deafness results in individuals having little or no hearing, partial deafness results in individuals hearing speech with the use of hearing aids or cochlea implants, and hard-of-hearing individuals have mild hearing loss (Smith, 2010). However, when considering a definition of deafness, it is important to distinguish between those who are culturally Deaf and those who are deaf but view themselves as culturally hearing. Those that are part of the hearing culture adopt the previous medical definition of deafness and may use equipment such as hearing aids to aid communication where possible. In contrast, those that are part of the Deaf culture reject the medical perspective for viewing an individual only in terms of the functioning of their ears. Instead, deafness is viewed and defined in terms of cultural affiliation, worldview, upbringing, and methods of communication, and they are more likely to refuse hearing equipment and adopt BSL or similar.

Communication in a deaf population

No two deaf individuals communicate in the same way. Some may use oral communication and audiological equipment such as hearing aids or cochlear implants to aid their hearing, whereas others may adopt BSL, Sign Supported English (SSE), lip-reading, or a mixture of these. Communication methods vary according to numerous factors, for example, the type and degree of deafness, age of onset, cognitive abilities, type of schooling, family views, personal preference, culture, or the situation. A common misconception about the deaf population is that although they cannot hear, they can probably still communicate through reading and writing. However, this is not the case. For those that use BSL, English is an entirely different language, so relying on the written word could be akin to an English person being expected to read something written in French or Russian. Even if a deaf individual is familiar with English, literacy levels are much lower in the deaf population than in the hearing population, with the majority of deaf individuals finding the written word restrictive (Brennan & Brown, 1997). As a consequence, Brennan and Brown identified that deaf individuals can often be incorrectly assumed to be lower in intelligence (discussed later within the chapter).

Many individuals who are born deaf develop severely delayed and impoverished language skills even if they can sign, read, write, or speak. This is known as 'language dysfluency' (Mayberry, 2002). Research has shown that those born to deaf parents develop stronger communication skills than those born to hearing parents because they are exposed to a language-rich environment (Hindley, Hill, McGuigan & Kitson, 1994) and do not suffer the same level of language deprivation. However, 90% of deaf individuals are born to hearing parents (The British Psychology Society, 2008).

Characteristics of deaf individuals

It is difficult to generalise about deaf people since the differences amongst them are as great as those found in hearing people (Glickman, 2013). However, in most cases of hearing loss at birth or during early life, there is trauma to the brain resulting in other medical, neurological, and cognitive problems.

> *Brain function*: There is evidence of increased prevalence of disabilities which can impact on brain function, such as impulse control or executive functioning, within the Deaf population (Vernon & Greenberg, 1999; Vernon, Steinberg & Montoya, 1999; Young, Monteiro & Ridgeway, 2000). Of the Deaf population, 40% have additional disabilities with varying degrees of brain damage associated with the cause of their deafness such as meningitis, rubella, and prematurity (Crocker & Edwards, 2004). Deaf people also often experience environmental stressors such as abuse, limited education, antisocial peers, and high crime residence which can exacerbate these issues (Crocker & Edwards, 2004).

> *Mental health*: Little is known about the prevalence of mental disorders in deaf people (Gahir, 2007). Previously it was thought that deaf people were more likely to develop personality and/or adjustment disorders compared to hearing people (Gentile & McCarthy, 1973; Graham & Rutter, 1968; Meadow, 1981). However, research suggests that deaf people have the same level of mental health problems as hearing people (Kitson & Thacker, 2000). There is controversy regarding deaf people and biological mental illness such as schizophrenia. Early research suggested deaf people are no more or less likely to develop schizophrenia than hearing people (Vernon, 1980). However, more recently it has been suggested they are likely to have a higher prevalence of schizophrenia than hearing people (Gray & Du Feu, 2004). A diagnosis of a mental disorder with deaf people is harder than with hearing people because the DSM-V and ICD-10 are culturally based and do not take into account differences in presentation in deaf people (O'Rourke & Grewer, 2005). Similarly, the diagnosis of personality disorder is culturally biased. Many deaf characteristics could be viewed as personality disorder, such as blunt language being perceived as negative attitudes.

IQ: Research suggests that deaf people have the same range of intelligence as hearing people. However, currently there are no valid and reliable IQ tests designed for deaf people. There is controversy in the literature surrounding whether to use standardised IQ tests with this population. Clinical psychologists have used the non-verbal subtests of the Wechsler Adult Intelligence Scale (WAIS) to produce estimates of intellectual capacity in deaf people (Braden, 1994; O'Rourke & Reed, 2007). Braden (1994) states that performance-only subtests can be used to obtain a valid global IQ; their research demonstrated that the mean non-verbal IQ in deaf children with no additional disabilities was within the normal range (Braden, 1994). However, additional disabilities bring IQ scores down significantly (Schildroth, 1976). This is significant because as many as 40% of deaf children have additional disabilities. However, others argue that standard IQ tests are biased because they are based on knowledge of the English language (Pollard, 1998). There is a lack of standardisation of questions once they are interpreted, and there are no norms from the Deaf community. Clients still need some linguistic competence to follow the task instructions for the performance subtests. If the person has minimal language skills, this could underestimate their IQ score because they did not understand the task, rather than as a result of their intellectual abilities (Cromwell, 2005). While IQ tests also measure academic achievement, deaf people may have had difficulty at school for many reasons besides intellectual disabilities (IDs): communication at school (even with an interpreter, deaf people tend to learn less than hearing people in hearing schools), access to education, type of schooling, and the socio-political climate of the time. Shifts in government policy have altered whether deaf children were taught using oralism or manualism. Manualism refers to the use of sign language, whereas oralism prohibits the use of sign language and believes that deaf people should assimilate with the hearing world and communicate using lip reading, reading and writing in English, speech, and mimicking the mouth shapes and breathing patterns of speech (Greenwald, 2009). It was recognised that deaf children taught using an oralism approach preferred using sign language (manualism) and struggled to gain oral language. Manualism proponents felt oralism restricted deaf children from being able to communicate in their native language; limited their learning; and stripped them of their identity, community, and culture (Winefield, 1987). Therefore, the laws forbidding the use of sign language in the classroom were retracted in 2010 (World Federation of the Deaf, 2016).

Childhood abuse: Research has shown that there are higher rates of maltreatment and physical and sexual abuse of deaf children than hearing children (Glickman, 2013). Some suggested reasons for this are that Deaf children are more vulnerable and less able to report abuse and because they often attend residential schools, where there are more opportunities to offend (Obinna, Kruegard, Osterbaan, Sadusky & DeVore, 2006; Sullivan, Brookhouser & Scanlan, 2000; Sullivan, Vernon & Scanlan, 1987). Abuse is often not prosecuted due to difficulties obtaining a clear and reliable account, so there may not be any official record of this.

Social learning and isolation: Hearing children learn rules of behaviour incidentally (for example, overhearing conversations, watching television), whereas deaf children are not privy to incidental learning. Hearing parents of deaf children tend to use physical punishment more often or just tell their child no (Knutson, Johnson & Sullivan, 2004). This means the deaf child does not have the opportunity to learn why they should not do something, which makes it more difficult to transfer learning of implicit rules to different contexts. Alternatively, some hearing parents express sympathy and leniency towards their deaf child. For example, "Don't tell him off. He can't help it, he's deaf", thereby rewarding bad behaviour, modelling poor problem-solving, and demonstrating or tolerating aggressive behaviour (Knutson et al., 2004). Due to social and educational policies, many deaf children grow up isolated. For example, political climates changed, resulting in the closure of schools for Deaf children. This lead to Deaf children having to travel long distances to attend a specialist school, leaving them isolated within their home area. Ten percent of Deaf children are born to Deaf parents/families and tend to have better social and linguistic role models which helps them socialise more and have higher self-esteem (Woolfe, 2001). In the past Deaf children went to residential schools and so had a Deaf peer group. However, currently attendance at hearing schools with support is encouraged, and so 90% of deaf children born to hearing families grow up rarely meeting another deaf person. This isolation contributes to them lacking access to crucial information about the world (Pollard, 1998).

Substance misuse: Alcohol abuse in the deaf population is at least equal to or greater than the hearing population (Boros, 1981; Guthmann & Graham, 2004; Guthmann & Sandberg, 1995, 1998). Davidson (2002) estimated the prevalence of alcohol use disorder in deaf psychiatric patients as 24% as opposed to 8% to 15% in hearing mental health service users. Those at greatest risk are those socially isolated, less connected with the Deaf or hearing communities, and less fluent in BSL (Guthmann & Blozis, 2001). Research has shown that deaf people may have similar levels of addictive behaviour to hearing people but much less access to information and services to address substance misuse (Austen & Checinski, 2000).

Offending behaviour in the deaf population

Due to a lack of systematic recording, the exact number of deaf individuals convicted of crimes and/or incarcerated within the Prison Service is unknown, with estimates suggesting there are approximately 135 deaf or hard-of-hearing individuals in the prison system within the UK (Williamson & Grubb, 2015; Berry & Brown, 2006; Gahir, O'Rourke, Monteiro & Reed, 2011). However, it is accepted that deaf individuals are over-represented within the criminal justice system (Gahir et al., 2011), and particularly among those convicted of sexual offences (Williamson & Grubb, 2015; Young et al., 2000; Miller & Vernon, 2003).

While very little is known about the characteristics or prevalence of offending in the deaf population (Andrews & Conley, 1977; O'Rourke & Grewer, 2005; Young, Monteiro & Ridgeway, 2001, 2000), research has demonstrated that the deaf forensic population form a distinct group whose offences are primarily of a violent or sexual nature (Miller et al., 2005; Miller, 2004). Various studies have highlighted the prevalence of and a trend in sexual crimes in the deaf forensic population (Young et al., 2000; Denmark, 1985). Miller and Vernon (2003) reported that the rate of sexual offending by deaf prisoners was four times the rate of hearing offenders, with more than half of the deaf offenders having sexual convictions against children. However, it is difficult to generalise these findings to the deaf forensic population or accurately compare these to the hearing forensic population, as existing studies use small samples from mental health units.

Understanding sexual offending in the deaf prison population

As very little is known about the deaf forensic population, information is often extrapolated from hearing research and assumed to apply to deaf individuals (O'Rourke & Grewer, 2005; Dennis & Baker, 1998). For example, research with hearing individuals who sexually offend offers a number of risk factors for sexual offending, such as a lack of social confidence, loneliness, and lack of intimacy (Mann, Hanson & Thornton, 2010). It is thought that deafness can increase the likelihood of developing these feelings and deficits (Becker, 1994; Bramley, 2007; Burgess, Hartman, Ressler, Douglas & McCormack, 1986), which may contribute to sexual offending.

One potential explanation for sexual offending in this population relates to a lack of sex education (Vernon & Rich, 1997). Case reviews of deaf men who sexually offended against children found that very few had received accessible sex education or showed an awareness of sexual health issues. In line with this, deaf individuals convicted for sexual offences have been described as lacking knowledge regarding sex (Griffiths, Hingsburger & Christian, 1985) and being sexually naive (Allam, Middleton & Browne, 1997).

In addition, characteristics associated with the deaf population generally (as discussed previously) are often linked to understanding offending in this population. For example, language deprivation and dysfluency are linked to challenging behaviour (Woolfe, 2001), as it is difficult to learn socially appropriate behaviour (Kentish, 2007), and this impedes the development of theory of mind (Woolfe, 2001). Having a limited language means that deaf individuals may not experience discussions about feelings or explorations of reasons behind decisions and rules, meaning they do not develop psychosocial life skills such as distress tolerance, problem-solving, and conflict management (Glickman, 2013). Furthermore, childhood trauma, victimisation, and isolation, which are prevalent within the deaf population, can contribute to a lack of self-esteem, distorted thinking, and the development of violent fantasies (Burgess et al., 1986; Harry, 1984; Sullivan et al., 1987).

Treatment services for deaf sexual offenders

As outlined previously, the characteristics of offending behaviour in the deaf forensic population is unknown, and it is widely acknowledged that further research is required to better understand this population (O'Rourke & Grewer, 2005; Young et al., 2001, 2000). In the absence of this understanding, the treatment of deaf individuals who have been convicted of sexual offences has been restricted (Young et al., 2000).

Treatment of deaf individuals who have committed sexual offences has focused solely (prior to 2012) on the treatment of the small distinct group in deaf forensic clinical settings (Izycky, Gibbon, Baker & Gahir, 2007; O'Rourke & Grewer, 2005; Young et al., 2000; Bramley, 2007; Hindley, 2000; Vernon & Rich, 1997; Vernon et al., 1999; Young et al., 2001). In the UK, this is limited to four NHS units:

1   The Connaught ward at Rampton Hospital, Nottingham: This provides the specialist National High Secure deaf service for men. The service uses the principles of a therapeutic community in its practice.
2   The John Denmark Unit, Manchester: This is an 18-bed inpatient service specialising in mental health and deafness. The service is for deaf adults who use BSL but can also support other deaf, deafened, and deaf/blind individuals.
3   The National Deaf Mental Health Service, Birmingham: This provides a culturally appropriate service to deaf and deaf-blind individuals with a range of complex needs.
4   The National Deaf Mental Health Service, London: This service offers a 16-bed inpatient unit and includes psychological therapies and assessment.

As a result of this, deaf individuals convicted of sexual offences who did not require mental health services, for example, all those within prison establishments instead of healthcare settings, were unable to access treatment. This was hugely problematic, resulting in deaf individuals being incarcerated for sexual offences but unable to progress through their sentence due to a lack of treatment provision, often resulting in them being detained for longer (Denmark, 1994; O'Rourke & Reed, 2007). As a response to this identified need for treatment, a group-based deaf sexual offender treatment programme (deaf SOTP) was developed and piloted in 2012, which is explored within the remainder of this chapter.

Becoming New Me for Deaf People (BNMD)

In 2012, HMP Whatton piloted a group-based treatment programme for deaf men who had been convicted of a sexual offence. To date, four programmes have been delivered (2012, 2014, 2016, and 2018) with 12 individuals having completed the group. Further individual work is offered where there are outstanding treatment needs following group.

Development of the programme

In developing treatment methods for working with deaf individuals convicted of sexual offences, the majority of techniques are adapted versions of those used with hearing populations or with individuals with ID (Iqbal, Dolan & Monteiro, 2004; Bramley, 2007). However, any interventions that rely on oral communication are not suitable for deaf individuals and visual learning is required (Bramley, 2007), along with the use of repetition and rehearsal (Marschark, 2003). As such, the use of role plays, mime, and skills practice is advocated as a means of enhancing learning, increasing social interactions, and developing improved self-esteem (O'Rourke & Grewer, 2005; Izycky et al., 2007). In addition, research has shown that visual aids such as drawings and diagrams are advocated for overcoming language barriers (Berry & Brown, 2006), with a combination of these approaches found to promote a positive and empowering group experience (Marshall, Fernandez, Hudson & Ward, 1998).

Based on this knowledge from previous research of what might work in treatment with deaf individuals, the core concepts of the deaf programme were based on the Becoming New Me (BNM) programme, which is a prison-based intervention delivered to hearing sexual offenders with IDs. The intervention was not developed with the assumption that the individuals were lower functioning; rather, the BNM intervention model does not rely on written English and uses limited vocabulary.

Although deaf offenders may not have ID, they may be considered language-deprived because BSL has a limited vocabulary in comparison to the English language. The BNM model uses a variety of methods of communication, such as imagery, pictorial prompts displayed around the room, and skills practice. The BNM programme also relies on more concrete concepts compared with other interventions which often use abstract concepts, which can be difficult for individuals who have a limited language base to process. As such, this style of intervention was considered to best meet the needs of deaf individuals who communicate using BSL. In addition, the pace of the BNM programme is much slower compared with other interventions, and it was expected that this would work well with deaf offenders, as the interpretation process creates a slower pace throughout treatment.

The use of interpreters

There is controversy within the literature about whether therapeutic work with deaf individuals should be undertaken with the assistance of interpreters or whether it should be delivered by professionals who are fluent in BSL or ideally Deaf professionals. Many researchers advocate the use of interpreters to ensure that treatment is accessible for deaf individuals (Schneider & Sales, 2004; Harper & Connell cited in Austen & Jeffrey, 2007; Bramley, 2007; Berry & Brown, 2006). Interpreters are considered to be an important advocate for deaf individuals, enabling them to communicate in a hearing world and to communicate their specific cultural needs. However, working with interpreters can bring difficulties through the addition of a third person into the interpersonal dynamics. The Deaf world is small, but the interpreter world is smaller. There are only around 800 qualified BSL interpreters nationally (Murray, 2013). This means that the deaf client and the interpreter may have met elsewhere such as socially or in court or may know friends or family members. This can impact on the client's ability to trust the interpreter, as they have concerns about whether the interpreter will maintain confidentiality when working elsewhere in the deaf world (Marshall et al., 1998). Furthermore, simply having another person present can impact on the therapeutic relationship which is essential to treatment progress (Bachelor & Horvath, 1999).

HMP Whatton decided to use interpreters, as they recognised a number of deaf prisoners were stuck in the system and needed to access treatment. However, there are no facilitators fluent in BSL within the service to deliver this treatment. Although a pool of facilitators were trained to varying levels of BSL with a view to deliver treatment directly, the length of time and breadth of experience needed to achieve BSL fluency meant this was not possible. Therefore interpreters were employed to ensure accuracy of translation, although facilitators did use their BSL skills to communicate with group members outside of the treatment setting. The training in BSL also provided deaf awareness knowledge to allow them to provide a culturally affirmative approach.

It was considered important that the interpreters had a similar style of delivering to the facilitators in order to support and promote a therapeutic environment. As such, the interpreter selection involved an interview process and completion of psychometric measures[1] to identify factors such as levels of warmth, empathic concern, coping, and resilience.

Programme inclusion and exclusion criteria

Inclusion criteria for attendance in the treatment programme was that the individuals should have a current or previous conviction for sexual offending. Selection considered whether the individual needed the deaf programme or whether they could engage in a hearing group with additional support. As such, the adaptive functioning of potential group members was taken into consideration, along with how they coped generally in a hearing world. From the groups that have run to date, two men have been deselected (removed after initial selection) from the intervention due to displaying violent behaviour. One was able to recommence following individual work to help manage emotions prior to starting another programme.

Example of individual deemed not suitable

A hard-of-hearing individual who had lost their hearing through aging but could speak and read English was not eligible, as the programme was designed to be culturally responsive for men whose first language was BSL or SSE.

Example of individual deemed suitable

An individual with a cochlear implant who was more hearing cultured and didn't use BSL but tended to socialise with the deaf men on the wing and struggled to 'get by' in a hearing world. It was determined that he would have struggled with a hearing group because of background noise and so he was offered a place, as it meant we could explore how his hearing affected his development of relationships.

Delivering the programme

The programme is delivered over a five-month period, three days per week, to reduce the risk of cognitive overload due to a group setting being a new experience for the men, and with the absence of any incidental learning about programmes from on the wing. The group includes no more than four group members. This smaller number helps with group management and communication dynamics, given the need for a slower pace and the different communication styles amongst the group members. The group includes up to four interpreters and three facilitators. Facilitators and interpreters would work on a rotational basis, with no more than two of each in the group at any one time. As such, consideration should be given to all of these factors before appointing interpreters to work in a clinical setting, with regular preparation meetings in advance (The British Psychological Society, 2008).

Programme content

The programme has gone through various iterations in line with the evidence base for hearing men who have been convicted of sexual offences. Each programme varies in intensity and content according to the risk and needs of the group members. However, generally each programme involves:

- Group bonding exercises
- Managing shame
- Personal history review
- Diarying of skills application
- Developing a support network
- Appropriate sex and urge management
- Problem-solving skills
- Emotional regulation
- Relationship skills
- Development of protective factors
- Relapse prevention

Evaluation

In order to understand the effectiveness of the programme, a scheme of research was undertaken which involved:

1   Post-programme interviews with group members and facilitators.
2   Pre- and post-programme offence accounts.

3   Pre- and post-programme treatment needs analysis (TNA) and protective
    factor grids.

For the purpose of this chapter, the combined results are summarised next, but
for a more detailed analysis of the results, please see Payne et al. (in prep).

Insight into offending

Through attendance in the programme, group members were able to develop
an understanding and awareness of their offending. This is important, as previous research has proposed that deaf sexual offenders blame their deafness for their
offending (Dennis & Baker, 1998); however, the current research did not support
this. Instead, group members were able to generally acknowledge and describe factors related to their offending and risk areas, although they demonstrated difficulty
in recalling or labelling specific risk areas. This was not considered a concern, as
it is recognised that those with language difficulties may face challenges with this,
and it is suggested that by relying on recall, this could result in a measurement
of memory and communication rather than understanding (Hocken, Winder &
Grayson, 2013). However, this does not mean that the group members took full
responsibility for their offending, and instead there was some evidence of victim
blaming. This demonstrates that levels of minimisation and denial identified in
individuals accessing hearing SOTPs (e.g. Schneider & Wright, 2004) are also
present within deaf individuals convicted of sexual offences. These findings were
supported within facilitator and pre-/post-offence accounts.

Addressing and managing risk

The pre-/post-TNA grids suggest that key risk areas have largely been identified
and addressed through the programme, although for some group members, areas
such as sexual interest were not addressed and remained untreated. This may be
due to the time constraints of the programme, particularly as when working with
interpreters the pace is much slower (Steinberg, 1991), and as group members each
had numerous dynamic risk factors and varying sexual interests, it was difficult to
explore each of these within the one programme. For individuals accessing hearing
programmes, such specific risk areas would be addressed within additional modules
or one-to-one work. With the deaf men, this is completed if the post-treatment
risk assessment makes these recommendations. Furthermore, following the programme, group members were able to identify basic risk management strategies,
which largely fell into three categories: 1) avoidance of risky situations, 2) applying
the new skills they have developed, or 3) reliance on others. This was endorsed by

facilitators who considered the avoidance strategies to be the most strongly adopted approach by group members, with recognition of the difficulties in the group members' abilities to be able to reflect and challenge their thinking.

Developing protective factors

Findings from both the group member interviews and TNA grids suggest that all group members had developed protective factors through treatment. All group members discussed a direct contrast between how they felt both pre- and post-treatment, with the most notable changes from the interviews related to their level of confidence and self-esteem, as well as reports of starting to develop a more active life while in prison. From the TNA grids, areas of particular development related to their ability to get on with others and being a responsible member of society, both of which showed improvements. This was all supported within facilitator accounts, with the suggestion that this was partly due to being given the opportunity to develop positive relationships with professionals (the facilitators and interpreters) and the development of a sense of self through the ability to communicate with both professionals and peers in a group setting, which has not previously been possible while in prison.

Conclusion

In summary, the process of planning, developing, and delivering an intervention for deaf men who have been convicted of sexual offending requires a multi-disciplinary approach and an understanding of deaf culture and language. The current prison-based intervention has strived to develop a programme that is both responsive to the needs of the men and adequate in addressing their offending behaviour risk areas. The programme remains relatively early in its development and is continually being updated, but nevertheless it offers a viable treatment option to this population in prison when previously nothing existed and appears to show promising results.

Note

1 Coping Styles Questionnaire – Revised (CSQ-R, Roger, Jarvis & Najarian, 1993)
Emotional Control Questionnaire – Revised (ECQ-R 3, Roger & Nesshoever, 1987; Roger & Najarian, 1989)
Interpersonal Reactivity Index (IRI, Davis, 1980)
Compassion Satisfaction/Fatigue Self-Test for Helpers (CFST, Figley, 1999)
Assessment for Dynamic Adaptation (ADA, Clarke & Roger, 2004)

References

Action on Hearing Loss. (2011). *Facts and figures on hearing loss, deafness and tinnitus.* Retrieved April 16, 2016, from www.actiononhearingloss.org.uk/

Allam, J., Middleton, D., & Browne, K. (1997). Different clients, different needs? Practice issues in community-based treatment for sex offenders. *Criminal Behaviour and Mental Health, 7*(1), 69–84.

Andrews, J., & Conley, J. (1977). Beer, pot, and shoplifting: teenage abuses. *American Annals of the Deaf*, 557–562.

Austen, S., & Checinski, K. (2000). Addictive behaviour and deafness. In P. Hindley, & N. Kitson (Eds.), *Mental health and deafness* (pp. 232–252). Whurr.

Austen, S., & Jeffrey, D. (2007). *Deafness and challenging behaviour.* Wiley & Sons.

Bachelor, A., & Horvath, A. (1999). The therapeutic relationship. In M. A. Hubble, B. L. Duncan, & S. D. Miller (Eds.), *The heart and soul of change: What works in therapy* (pp. 133–178). American Psychological Association.

Becker, J. V. (1994). Offenders: Characteristics and treatment. *The Future of Children: Sexual Abuse of Children, 4*, 176–197.

Berry, M., & Brown, J. (2006). Some aspects of possible vulnerability of deaf people in the forensic world. *Forensic Update, 85*, 27–33.

Boros, A. (1981). Activating solutions to alcoholism among the hearing impaired. In A. J. Schecter (Ed.), *Drug dependence and alcoholism: Social and behavioural issues* (pp. 1007–1014). Plenum Press.

Braden, J. P. (1994). *Deafness, deprivation and IQ.* Plenum Press.

Bramley, S. (2007). Working with deaf people who have committed sexual offences against children: The need for an increased awareness. *Journal of Sexual Aggression, 13*(1), 59–69.

Brennan, M., & Brown, R. (1997). *Equality before the law: Deaf people's access to justice.* Deaf Studies Research Unit, University of Durham.

The British Psychology Society (2008). *Working with interpreters in health settings: Guidelines for psychologists.* University of East London.

Burgess, A. W., Hartman, C., Ressler, R. K., Douglas, J. E., & McCormack, A. (1986). Sexual homicide motivational model. *Journal of Interpersonal Violence, 1*, 251–272.

Clarke, J., & Roger, D. (2007). The construction and validation of a scale to assess psychological risk and well-being in sex offender treatment providers. *Legal and Criminological Psychology, 12*(1), 83–100.

Crocker, S., & Edwards, L. (2004). Deafness and additional difficulties. In S. Austen & S. Crocker (Eds.), *Deafness in mind: Working psychologically with deaf people across the lifespan* (pp. 252–269). Whurr.

Cromwell, J. (2005). Deafness and the art of psychometric testing. *The Psychologist, 18*(12), 738.

Davidson, B. (2002). *Prevalence of alcohol use disorders among deaf psychiatric patients.* Unpublished MSc dissertation. University of London, London.

Davis, M. H. (1980). Interpersonal reactivity index. Edwin Mellen Press.

Denmark, J. C. (1985). A study of 250 patients referred to a department of psychiatry for the deaf. *British Journal of Psychiatry, 146*(March), 282–286.

Denmark, J. C. (1994). *Deafness and mental health.* Jessica Kingsley Publishers.

Dennis, M. J., & Baker, K. A. (1998). *Evaluation and treatment of deaf sexual offenders.* In Sourcebook of Treatment Programs for Sexual Offenders (pp. 287–302). Springer.

Deuchar, M. (2013). *British Sign Language.* Routledge.

Figley, C. R. (1999). Compassion fatigue: Toward a new understanding of the costs of caring. In B. H. Stamm (Ed.), *Secondary traumatic stress: Self-care issues for clinicians, researchers, and educators* (2nd ed., pp. 3–28). Lutherville, MD: Sidran.

Gahir, M. (2007). High secure care for deaf people in England and Wales. In S. Austen & D. Jeffery (Eds.), *Deafness and challenging behaviour* (pp. 275–291). Wiley & Sons.

Gahir, M., O'Rourke, S., Monteiro, B., & Reed, R. (2011). The unmet needs of deaf prisoners: A survey of prisons in England and Wales. *International Journal on Mental Health and Deafness, 1*(1).

Gentile, A., & McCarthy, B. (1973). *Additional handicapping conditions among hearing impaired students.* Office of demographic studies, Gallaudet University.

Glickman, N. (Ed.). (2013). *Deaf mental health care.* Routledge.

Graham, P., & Rutter, M. (1968). Organic brain dysfunction and child psychiatric disorder. *British Medical Journal, 3*(5620), 695–700.

Gray, A., & Du Feu, M. (2004). The causes of schizophrenia and its implications for deaf people. In S. Austen & S. Crocker (Eds.), *Deafness in mind: Working psychologically across the lifespan* (pp. 206–221). Whurr.

Greenwald, B. H. (2009, Spring). The real "toll" of A.G. Bell: Lessons about eugenics. *Sign Language Studies, 9*, 262.

Griffiths, D., Hingsburger, D., & Christian, D. (1985). Treating developmentally handicapped sexual offenders: The York behaviour management treatment programme. *Psychiatric Aspects of Mental Retardation Reviews, 4*, 45–52.

Guthmann, D., & Blozis, S. A. (2001). Unique issues faced by deaf individuals entering substance abuse treatment and following discharge. *American Annals of the Deaf, 146*(3), 294–304.

Guthmann, D., & Graham, V. (2004). Substance abuse: A hidden problem within the deaf and hard of hearing communities. *Journal of Teaching in the Addictions, 3*(1), 49–64.

Guthmann, D., & Sandberg, K. A. (1995). Clinical approaches in substance abuse treatment for use with deaf and hard of hearing adolescents. *Journal of Child & Adolescent Substance Abuse, 4*(3), 69–79.

Guthmann, D., & Sandberg, K. (1998). Assessing substance abuse problems in deaf and hard of hearing individuals. *American Annals of the Deaf, 143*(1), 14–21.

Harry, B. (1984). A deaf sex offender. *Journal of Forensic Science, 29*(4), 1140–1143.

Hindley, P. (2000). Child and adolescent psychiatry. In P. Hindley & N. Kitson (Eds.), *Mental Health and Deafness* (chapter 3). London: Whurr Publishers.

Hindley, P. A., Hill, P. D., McGuigan, S., & Kitson, N. (1994). Psychiatric disorder in deaf and hearing impaired children and young people: A prevalence study. *Journal of Child Psychology and Psychiatry, 35*(5), 917–934.

Hocken, L., Winder, B., & Grayson, A. (2013). *Putting responsivity into risk assessment: The use of the Structured Assessment of Risk and Need (SARN) with intellectually disabled sexual offenders.* Unpublished thesis.

Iqbal, S., Dolan, M., & Monteiro, B. (2004). Characteristics of DSO's referred to a specialist mental health unit in the UK. *Journal of Forensic Psychiatry & Psychology, 15*(3), 494–510.

Izycky, A., Gibbon, S., Baker, K., & Gahir, M. (2007). Application of therapeutic community principles to a high secure deaf service. *Therapeutic Communities, 28*, 4.

Kentish, R. (2007). Challenging behaviour in the young deaf child. In S. Austen & D. Jeffery (Eds.), *Deafness and challenging behaviour* (pp. 75–88). Wiley & Sons.

Kitson, N., & Thacker, A. (2000). Adult psychiatry. In P. Hindley & N. Kitson (Eds.), *Mental health and deafness* (pp. 25–98). Whurr.

Knutson, J. F., Johnson, C. R., & Sullivan, P. M. (2004). Disciplinary choices of mothers of deaf children and mothers of normally hearing children. *Child Abuse and Neglect, 28*(9), 925–937.

Mann, R. E., Hanson, R. K., & Thornton, D. (2010). Assessing risk for sexual recidivism: Some proposals on the nature of psychologically meaningful risk factors. *Sexual Abuse: A Journal of Research and Treatment, 22*(2), 191–217.

Marschark, M. (2003). Cognitive functioning in Deaf. *Oxford Handbook of Deaf Studies, Language, and Education*, 464.

Marshall, W. L., Fernandez, Y. M., Hudson, S. M., & Ward, T. (1998). *Sourcebook of treatment programs for sexual offenders.* Plenum Press.

Mayberry, R. I. (2002). Cognitive development in deaf children: The interface of language and perception in neuropsychology. *Handbook of Neuropsychology, 8*, 71–107.

Meadow, K. P. (1981). Burnout in professionals working with deaf children. *American Annals of the Deaf, 156*(1), 13–22.

Miller, K. R. (2004). Linguistic diversity in a Deaf prison population: Implications for due process. *Journal of Deaf Studies and Deaf Education, 9*(1), 112–119.

Miller, K., & Vernon, M. (2003). Deaf sex offenders in a prison population. *Journal of Deaf Studies and Deaf Education, 8*(3), 357–362.

Miller, K. R., Vernon, M., & Capella, M. E. (2005). Violent offenders in a deaf prison population. *Journal of Deaf Studies and Deaf Education, 10*(4), 417–425.

Murray, K. (2013, May 7). Lack of British Sign Language interpreters putting deaf people at risk. *The Guardian*. Retrieved from www.theguardian.com/society/2013/may/07/lack-interpreters-deaf-people-risk

Obinna, J., Kruegard, S., Osterbaan, C., Sadusky, J. M., & DeVore, W. (2006). *Understanding the need the victims of sexual assault in the Deaf Community*. Council on Crime and Justice.

O'Rourke, S., & Grewer, G. (2005). Assessment of deaf people in forensic mental health settings: A risky business! *Journal of Forensic Psychiatry & Psychology*, *16*(4), 671–684.

O'Rourke, S. and Reed, R. (2007), "*Deaf people and the criminal justice system*", in Austen, S. and Jeffrey, D. (Eds), Deafness and Challenging Behaviour: The 360° Perspective, Wiley, Chichester.

Pollard, R. (1998). Psychopathology. In M. Marschark & M. D. Clark (Eds.), *Psychological Perspectives on Deafness* (pp. 171–197). Lawrence Erlbaum Associates.

Roger, D., Jarvis, G., & Najarian, B. (1993). Detachment and coping: The construction and validation of a new scale for measuring coping strategies. *Personality and Individual Differences, 15*(6), 619–626.

Roger, D., & Najarian, B. (1989). The construction and validation of a new scale for measuring emotion control. *Personality and Individual Differences, 10*(8), 845–853.

Roger, D., & Nesshoever, W. (1987). The construction and preliminary validation of a scale for measuring emotional control. *Personality and Individual Differences, 8*(4), 527–534.

Schildroth, A. (1976). The relationship of nonverbal intelligence test scores to selected characteristics of hearing impaired students. Gallaudet College: *Office of Demographic Studies*.

Schneider, N. R., & Sales, B. D. (2004). Deaf or hard of hearing inmates in prison. *Disability & Society*, *19*(1), 77–89.

Schneider, S., & Wright, R. (2004). Understanding denial in sexual offenders. *Trauma, Violence and Abuse*, *5*(1), 3–20.

Smith, C. (2010). *An analysis of the assessment and treatment of problematic and offending behaviours in the deaf population*. Unpublished thesis.

Steinberg, A. (1991). Issues in providing mental health services to hearing impaired persons. *Hospital and Community Psychiatry*, *42*, 380–389.

Sullivan, P. M., Brookhouser, P., & Scanlan, M. (2000). Maltreatment of deaf and hard of hearing child. In P. Hindley & N. Kitson (Eds.), *Mental health and deafness* (pp. 149–184). Whurr.

Sullivan, P. M., Vernon, M., & Scanlan, J. M. (1987). Sexual abuse of deaf youth. *American Annals of the Deaf, 132*(4), 256–262.

Vernon, M. (1980). Perspectives of deafness and mental health. *Journal of Rehabilitation of the Deaf, 13*, 9–14.

Vernon, M., & Greenberg, S. F. (1999). Violence in deaf and hard of hearing people: A review of the literature. *Aggression and Violent Behaviour, 4*(3), 259–272.

Vernon, M., & Rich, S. (1997). Pedophilia and deafness. *American Annals of the Deaf, 142*(4), 300–310.

Vernon, M., Steinberg, A. G., & Montoya, L. A. (1999). Deaf murderers: Clinical and forensic issues. *Behavioural Sciences and the Law, 17*(4), 495–516.

Williamson, L., & Grubb, A. (2015). An analysis of the relationship between being deaf, and sexual offending. *Journal of Sexual Aggression, 21*(2), 224–243.

Winefield, R. (1987). *Never the twain shall meet.* Gallaudet University Press.

Woolfe, T. (2001). The self-esteem and cohesion to family members of deaf children in relation to the hearing status of their parents and siblings. *Deafness and Education International, 3*, 80–95.

World Federation of the Deaf. (2016). *21st International Congress on the Education of the Deaf (ICED) in July 2010 in Vancouver, Canada.* Retrieved from https://wfdeaf.org

Young, A., Howarth, P., Ridgeway, S., & Monteiro, B. (2001). Forensic referrals to the three specialist psychiatric units for deaf people in the UK. *Journal of Forensic Psychiatry, 12*, 19–35.

Young, A., Monteiro, B., & Ridgeway, S. (2000). Deaf people with mental health needs in the criminal justice system: A review of the UK literature. *Journal of Forensic Psychiatry, 11*(3), 556–570.

Glossary

British Sign Language (BSL)   is the first or preferred language of approximately 70,000 Deaf people in the UK. It is not a communication system that simply replaces English words with signs. It is a recognised language in its own right. It is a visual form of communication with its own grammatical structure and syntax. It makes use of gesture, lip patterns, and facial expressions as well as spatial positioning. It is not dependant on nor closely related to English (Deuchar, 2013). English is translated into BSL (and vice versa) in units of meaning rather than word for word, so some concepts take longer to explain. English is a linear language, whereas BSL is spatial. This means you can say two words at the same time in BSL, which you cannot do in English.

A cochlear implant   is an electronic medical device that replaces the function of the damaged inner ear. Unlike hearing aids, which make sounds louder, cochlear implants do the work of damaged parts of the inner ear (cochlea) to provide sound signals to the brain.

Lip reading is a technique of understanding speech through visually interpreting the speaker's lip, face, and tongue movements. Lip-reading skills depend on educational experience and degree and onset of deafness.

A protective factors grid is a grid which identifies key protective factors, or success factors, which may help an individual convicted of sexual offences to manage their risks. Protective factors can include external factors, such as hobbies or employment, or internal, such as having a positive attitude towards authority.

Sign Supported English (SSE) is another form of sign language but is not recognised as a language in itself. It uses the same signs as BSL, but they are used in the same order as spoken English. SSE is used to support spoken English, especially in schools where deaf children are learning English grammar alongside their signing, or by people who mix mainly with hearing people.

A therapeutic community is a structured, psychologically informed environment where social activities, structure, and activities are designed to help an individual's rehabilitation.

A treatment needs analysis grid is a grid which identifies key treatment areas for men who have been convicted of sexual offences. The grid is separated into domains, including 'sexual interests', 'relationships', 'self-management', and attitudes'.

9
Compassion-focused therapy as an intervention for sexual offending

Kerensa Hocken and Jon Taylor

A brief history of sexual offending treatment

Before exploring the benefits of a new approach to working with sexually harmful behaviour, it is necessary to briefly review the history and development of intervention initiatives for sexual offending. Although science has been trying to understand and treat sexual offending for centuries, e.g. Krafft-Ebing (1886), modern treatment for sexual offending has its roots in behaviourism. Largely based on the work of Pavlov (1928), Thorndike (1905) and Skinner (1953), behaviourism understands human behaviour to be a series of responses to the environment via respondent and operant conditioning. These theories were applied to understanding sexual interest and saw atypical sexual interests as resulting from contingency learning, where sexual arousal was paired with another stimuli such as children and then reinforced via masturbation (McGuire, Carlisle & Young, 1965). Laws and Marshall (1990) provide a detailed account of the acquisition and maintenance processes for what they refer to as a conditioning theory for sexual offending. Treatment approaches were broadly split into those that aimed at reducing arousal to offence-related interest (e.g. Laws, Meyer & Holmen, 1978) and those that aimed to increase arousal to healthy sexual interest (e.g. Marquis, 1970). Evaluation shows some short-term positive gains from these techniques (Bancroft, 1974); however, behaviourism has been beset by weak research methodologies, using single case designs, with little use of controlled experimental designs (Akins, 2004). A meta-analysis by Furby, Weinrott and Blackshaw (1989) examined 42 studies completed in this era and concluded that there was little or no difference in re-offending among treated and untreated samples.

DOI: 10.4324/9780429262074-9

As cognitive behavioural therapy (CBT) became increasingly dominant in mainstream psychotherapy, interventions for people who commit sexual offences followed suit, and CBT remains the primary approach (Schmucker & Lösel, 2017). This led to an explosion in research and treatment approaches which placed the focus of treatment on changing faulty thinking. An early influential model of sexual offending against children was the Four Preconditions Model (Finkelhor & Araji, 1986) in which one of the four preconditions essential for sexual abuse was disinhibition, facilitated by cognitive distortions. Cognitive distortions are considered, in this context, to be faults or distortions in beliefs that facilitate offending because they justify or permit the behaviours, for example, via child abuse–supportive beliefs and rape-supportive beliefs (Ó Ciardha & Ward, 2013). A prominent criticism of this model is the assumption that each precondition is essential (Ward & Hudson, 2001). In a more nuanced theory of sexual offending, Ward and Siegert (2002) propose that cognitive distortions are one possible route into sexual offending. Nevertheless, theories placing emphasis on thinking, attitudes and beliefs gathered pace because they represented something that was more easily targeted than sexual interests. Cognitive restructuring became one of the most common components of sexual offending interventions (McGrath, Cumming, Burchard, Zeoli & Ellerby, 2009). It had a focus on offence denial or minimisation of offending, leading to the popular treatment goal of working on offence responsibility (Salter, 1988). This era of treatment also saw the use of schema therapy for people with sexual convictions, drawing on research suggesting that schema-driven cognitions interacting with negative life events are causally relevant to sexual offending for some individuals (Mann, 2004). Schemas observed to be relevant to offending were labelled 'dysfunctional', understood to be acquired via developmental experiences. The therapeutic goal was to reconstruct schemas into functional equivalents.

The concept of relapse prevention was often central to CBT programmes for sexual offending. This focused clients on recognising their relapse cycles, spotting high-risk situations and faulty thinking and deploying strategies to manage these. Avoidance was a common strategy encouraged in the early versions of these interventions (Laws, 1989). Interventions in previous eras have actively avoided acknowledgment of trauma in the developmental history of clients or as being a contextual feature of the pathway to offending. In the clinical experience of the chapter authors, discussion of past trauma in interventions for sexual offending was considered to offer an opportunity to minimise or excuse their offending or distract the focus of treatment from their own behaviour, and so this was discouraged. Indeed, a feature of these interventions was an absence of formulation that identifies the evolution of the factors considered to be casually related to offending. For example, the evolution of harm denial (as a defence against trauma) and the biological basis of sexual interests were rarely considered.

The early 2000s saw the introduction of a model of correctional programming that was directed according to risk level and criminogenic need and could respond to individual factors (risk, need, responsivity [RNR]: Andrews & Bonta, 2003). The criminogenic need aspect of the model set out the expectation that intervention would target for reduction or elimination those factors that were relevant to recidivism. In a review of the contents and implementation of US programmes, McGrath et al. (2009) found that the top three most reported intervention targets for residential and community programmes were offence responsibility, social skills training and victim empathy. A year later Mann, Hanson and Thornton (2010) demonstrated that none of these factors, at least as they have been defined and measured, were supported as risk factors for sexual offending, highlighting poor adherence to the need principle for many interventions. This discrepancy between evidence and intervention goal is not surprising when considered against the inconsistent outcomes for sexual offending intervention. One of the first significant meta-analyses of the CBT-era interventions was Hanson et al. (2002). This study was cautiously optimistic, as the sexual re-offence rate was lower for intervention groups (12.3%) than comparison groups (16.8%), with the newer modalities (e.g. CBT) doing better than older ones (such as behavioural only). The picture became more complex with the publication of the Marques, Wiederanders, Day, Nelson and van Ommeren (2005) study. Although they examined only one intervention with a heavy focus on offence responsibility and denial, it garnered a lot of attention due to there being no difference between intervention and comparison groups for recidivism. At the same time Lösel and Schmucker (2005) published a large-scale meta-analysis, looking at several different modalities of intervention. They concluded that CBT interventions designed specifically for sexual offending did reduce recidivism (11.1% versus 17.5% for the comparison group), but some non-CBT interventions had a negative effect. Ten years later a more rigorous and updated meta-analysis by Schmucker and Lösel (2015) showed CBT interventions had a positive impact on recidivism (10.1%) against comparison groups (13.7%), Gannon, Olver, Mallion and James (2019) report a reduction in recidivism of 4.6% for intervention versus comparison groups.

Despite meta-analyses indicating gains in reducing recidivism, the outcomes for interventions are not universally positive; some interventions show iatrogenic effects (e.g. higher recidivism rates for the intervention than the comparison group) (Mews, Di Bella & Purver, 2017). Clearly some interventions work for some individuals; however, the question about what works for whom and when remains elusive. An important question in sexual offending interventions is *how* they are delivered. For example, some interventions may be delivered in a manner that stimulates shame (Levenson, 2014); however, shame has been implicated as an inhibitor to engagement in therapy and behaviour change (Tangney, Stuewig & Hafez, 2011; Walton, 2019). A further consideration is that outcomes in the prevailing research have focused on recidivism, and very few studies measure or report client wellbeing as an outcome worthy of note. This is a feature of sexual offending intervention that sets it apart from its mainstream psychotherapy counterparts, where client wellbeing is considered to be a primary reason for intervention.

The focus on risk and risk reduction as the primary ethos for the intervention of people who offend was questioned by Ward (2002) in his Good Lives Model (GLM) of rehabilitation. The GLM's inherent assumption is that people are not inherently pathological and that all human behaviour has an evolutionary function. Understood in this context, offending is considered to be motivated by the pursuit of unmet human needs. For example, a person may commit a sexual offence against a child in the pursuit of the need for emotional connection and sexual reward (Laws & Ward, 2011). Intervention therefore should aim to equip individuals with the skills to achieve these needs in pro-social ways. The GLM emphasises the importance of addition, not elimination, which is the need to work towards developing strengths and capabilities rather than eradicating problematic factors, a mainstay of many interventions for sexual offending. Laws and Ward (2011) argue for an ecological model of rehabilitation to reflect the realities of human interdependence on others and the environment and emphasising the importance of context-aware interventions. The GLM represents a significant evolution in thinking about sexual offending and the response to it, depathologising in favour of emphasising individuals' strengths. The GLM is a framework for intervention that can be incorporated into psychotherapeutic intervention models and can work alongside RNR (Willis, Ward & Levenson, 2014). Its refreshing and humanistic stance has been received well by practitioners and clients (Harkins, Flak & Beech, 2012), and some, but by no means all, therapeutic interventions for sexual offending have adopted a GLM approach, including those for juveniles (Chu, Koh, Zeng & Teoh, 2015). Outcomes are not currently well evidenced, partly because it is a relatively new approach and it takes time to research intervention effectiveness. Additionally, many interventions use GLM alongside more dominant models of intervention, and untangling the influence of GLM is almost impossible without fine-grained, process-based analysis. Early outcomes for interventions which have incorporated GLM suggest that it is as good as an established relapse prevention intervention in bringing about change (Harkins et al., 2012) and seems to reduce attrition (Ward & Willis, 2013). A review by Barnao and Ward (2015) suggests that GLM offers a promising overarching rehabilitation framework and points towards a more humanistic and person-centred approach as a useful focus for contemporary offence work. It is worth noting, however, that much of the research that supports the GLM has been inspired and motivated by many of the key architects of the theory. Whilst this does not undermine the value of the findings, it is perhaps important to recognise the vulnerability to bias that can be levelled against such research.

After decades of research on the effectiveness of interventions for sexual offending, the inconsistent outcomes suggest that, like psychotherapy generally, current approaches are only helpful for some people, some of the time (Gloster et al., 2019). This points to need for a range of interventions to cater for varying need and a move away from a 'one size fits all' approach.

Trauma, adversity and the evolution of criminogenic need

As we have seen in the previous section, there have been various incarnations of interventions for sexual offending. In each one, the emphasis has changed, from changing sexual preferences to challenging denial (and promoting remorse), to developing absent skills. These various incarnations have a recurring theme – that the individual is perceived as intrinsically faulty, whether that be due to deviant arousal pathways, distorted patterns of thinking or skill deficits. In essence, the assumption is that the people who receive treatment are different, not just as determined by their actions but by something that renders them fundamentally different from others. Essentially, therefore, they are split away and cast into an out group, stimulating shame and therefore reducing the capacity to engage openly with intervention efforts. Perhaps this is an expectable response, given the harm caused by these offences and the imperative to eliminate or reduce anything that could lead to a recurrence of harm. However, the focus on risk ignores the circumstances that contributed to the evolution of criminogenic capacities and the function that was apparent as these capacities emerged. Rather, as we have said, the emphasis has been on individual pathology, an approach that is likely to stimulate shame (and a sense of maladaptation), enhance a pathological identity (self as deviant, distorted, etc.) and lower self-esteem. We argue that a formulation of the origins of criminogenic need is critical to effective intervention and that an absence of such a consideration may not only neglect predisposing factors but may reinforce the circumstances that evolved these factors. Consider, for example, the conditions that might encourage a youngster to develop a callousness or indifference to the feelings (and suffering) of others. For some children who experience sexual abuse, the indifference to their distress can feel intolerable, particularly when that indifference is communicated by a parent. If a child remains connected to this distress, then he or she may begin to act out the distress (however that is manifest) and thus place themselves at risk from reprisals. If, on the other hand, they are able to disconnect from feelings and remain loyal or obedient to the parent, then they may limit the possibility of angry/ reprisal/dominance reactions from their parent. In this sense disconnecting from distress, albeit their own, is highly functional, adds survival value and thus is likely to be a resilient strategy. As a learned survival strategy, of course, this readiness to disconnect from distress is likely to continue into later life and may begin to become generalised and/or projected onto the distress that other people experience. Alternatively, consider a teenager who is beginning to experience sexual pleasure and notices that sexual arousal is paired with children – they haven't set out to create this pairing; rather, they notice its presence as they discover sexual activity. As with other sexual preferences, a young person cannot choose what they find arousing – they simply discover their sexuality as their development unfolds. Clearly a sexual interest in children is highly problematic and potentially harmful, but we are not to blame for our sexual interests, regardless of the direction they take. This is not to say that a person should pursue such interests, but recognises what we can control and what we can't control.

These examples illustrate the differing ways that criminogenic needs can emerge and offer some insight into the various factors that can influence their development. In our opinion, and indeed in our experience, developing an awareness of the function of criminogenic factors is essential to effective therapeutic practice and supports people who have these capacities to develop effective management strategies without the burden of shame.

An exploration of the impact of trauma and early adversity offers some insight into why this may be the case. The relationship between early trauma and later life difficulties has been widely documented thanks in part to the Adverse Childhood Events (ACE) research programme (Felitti et al., 1998). Bowlby's early work on attachments speculated about the link between early experiences and the capacity to form secure relationships in adults. Bowlby suggested that disrupted attachments, particularly those caused by neglectful or harmful parenting, interfere with our innate need for connections and can contribute to poor mental health and anti-social behaviour. Since Bowlby's seminal work (1958, 1959, 1960), numerous studies have pointed towards an association between childhood adversity and later difficulties, including psychosis (Waxman et al., 2014), a diagnosis of personality disorder (Wu et al., 2010) or drug and alcohol dependency (Strine et al., 2012).

An exploration of the impact of trauma and early adversity may offer some insight into the links between life experiences, learning and harmfulness. More than 50 years have passed since Bowlby began to speculate about the links between attachment disruptions and challenges emerging later in life. In his lecture to the Eugenics Society (1967), Bowlby suggested that both mental health difficulties and anti-social behaviour stem from a disruption to the early *affectional* bond. Indeed, Bowlby went on to propose that such a disruption was a feature of an atypical and adverse family environment (p. 87). In the same lecture, Bowlby called for more longitudinal research into these types of adversities and their consequences across the lifespan. Bowlby's hopes were perhaps realised when the CDC-Kaiser

Permanente Adverse Childhood Experiences (ACE) Study (Centers for Disease Control and Prevention, 2013) investigated childhood abuse, neglect and other household challenges and later-life health and wellbeing. The original ACE Study was conducted between 1995 and 1997 with two waves of data collection and over 17,000 participants. The first paper to emerge from the ACE research identified a clear association between seven categories of adverse early experiences and a broad range of later-life difficulties, including alcoholism; suicide; drug use; depression; and physical health difficulties such as heart disease, cancer, lung and liver disease (Felitti et al., 1998). Since the publication of Felitti's initial paper, there has been a plethora of studies further examining the links between childhood adversity and difficulties later in life. ACEs have been linked to increased experiences of anxiety and depression (Merrick et al., 2017), to dissociative strategies such as psychosis (Varese et al., 2012), increased likelihood of drug and alcohol dependency (Strine et al., 2012) and disruptions to personality development (DeLisi et al., 2019).

It is perhaps unsurprising that studies have also revealed an association between these *harmful* experiences and offending (*harmful*) behaviour. In terms of general offending rather than specific offence types, numerous studies have pointed towards an association between early adversity and offending in later life (Reavis, Looman, Franco & Rojas, 2013; Topitzes Mersky & Reynolds, 2011). Furthermore, the impact of these experiences on offending is found to emerge during the developmental period, with harmful and offending behaviour emerging by adolescence (Abram et al., 2004; Tyler et al., 2008; Becker & Kerig, 2011; Ford, Chapman, Connor & Cruise, 2012). A similar picture emerges when we focus more exclusively on those people who commit sexual offences, with high rates of sexual abuse evident during childhood (Jespersen, Lalumière & Seto, 2009; Reavis et al., 2013), as well as generally high rates of adverse early experiences (Levensen, Willis & Prescott, 2016). These findings have led some authors to suggest that there needs to be "targeted interventions" that focus on trauma (Wolff & Shi, 2012, p. 1923).

Of particular note in the context of early trauma and chronic adversity is the significance of shame. Shame has been cited extensively as a repercussion of trauma, abuse and maltreatment (Shahar, Doron & Szepsenwol, 2015). Although different clinicians use differing definitions of shame, there seems to be a general consensus that shame is a self-conscious emotion that leaves us feeling judged as a consequence of a transgression or wrongdoing (Tangney & Fischer, 1995). In the context of early maltreatment, this sense of wrongdoing is likely to emerge as a youngster is encouraged to feel responsible or complicit in acts of abuse, neglect or recurring adversity, either directly or as a result of a sense that they invite mistreatment due to some inherent problem with their character or behaviour. As we will see later, from a compassion-focused perspective, shame, like other emotions, is understood in terms of its evolutionary function whereby it motivates us to manage ourselves in order to avoid such judgments and social rejection. When proactive, shame can guide our social interactions (as we seek to avoid the feeling). However, when we feel shame as a consequence of our actions and in response to judgements, then shame motivates us to engage in a range of behaviours that will retain our social group, rank and status. The fear of social rejection and exclusion from our group will organise us to seek approval and inclusion. We will look for opportunities to deny the behaviour that could cause exclusion. If this is not available to us, then we may try to justify our behaviour, offer a rationale for what we did, blame others, suggest various different sources of responsibility and draw attention to mitigating conditions. All of these strategies could be driven by shame and a need to feel connected to others. However, while shame may help us to achieve a sense of belonging, it also organises us to turn away from the consequences of our actions for others and focuses us on consequences for ourselves in order to preserve our social rank. We argue that where shame has been prompted by early trauma, it stimulates adaptive responses and builds our capacity to use these responses throughout life.

The information that has emerged from the various ACE studies cited earlier points towards the role of trauma and adversity in the genesis of criminogenic need and the interruption of various developmental trajectories, including relational abilities, empathy, social responsibility and psychological wellbeing. These abilities to regulate emotions, sustain affiliative relationships, mentalise and empathise, acknowledge responsibility and feel guilt are all areas of human functioning that have, at various incarnations of intervention for sexual offending, been primary targets. Although the salience of these areas has changed over time, a trauma-informed understanding may facilitate greater insight into how the interruption of these capacities may increase criminogenic vulnerability. In turn, an understanding of this vulnerability can orientate forensic practitioners to consider interventions that are explicitly sensitive to the trauma that may have impacted on the development of compassion and the sensitivity towards suffering of others that can appear to be absent in the actions of those who commit offences.

Trauma-informed interventions

ACEs in the lives of those who commit sexual offences speak to a dose–response relationship in that a higher number of ACEs is associated with several indictors of anti-sociality in sexual offending populations. These indictors include higher risk scores, lower victim age and greater use of force in the offence (Levenson et al., 2014), persistence and versatility of offending (Levenson & Socia, 2015), sexual deviance score, sexual violence score and mixed (sexual and non-sexual) offending (Levenson & Grady, 2016). There is tentative evidence to suggest that childhood sexual victimisation is associated with the development of psycho-logical characteristics related to sexual offending, such as beliefs about children and sex, and emotional congruence with children (Blank, Nunes, Maimone, Hermann & McPhail, 2018). The exact mechanisms that connect ACEs with later-life sexual offending have been the subject of much speculation, and possi-ble hypotheses include the disruption caused to attachment and inhibitory con-trol systems via trauma experiences (Hamilton, 2020; Marshall & Barbaree, 1990) and early sexualisation leading to the development of early sexualised behaviour, paraphilias and sexual compulsivity (Cale, Leclerc & Smallbone, 2014; Lussier, Leclerc, Cale & Proulx, 2007).

In light of the growing evidence for trauma prevalence in the histories of people who sexually offend, Levenson and Grady (2016) suggest that CBT inter-ventions for sexual offending should take account of the research on trauma, attachment and developmental psychopathology in the approach and response to individuals. They highlight the need to explore and recognise the underlying origins of dynamic risk for individuals to understand how trauma experiences have shaped their lives and linked to offending. A means of achieving this is to move towards trauma-informed intervention models (Levenson, Willis & Pres-cott, 2017). Viewed in this way, psychological characteristics related to sexual offending (dynamic risk factors) can be understood as adaptive and understand-able responses to threatening life situations. Trauma-informed care therefore is not an intervention in itself, but a framework for delivering intervention that takes account of the traumatic underpinnings of criminogenic need and pro-motes safety, trust, choice, collaboration and empowerment at the core of the interaction (Levenson, 2017).

Levenson (2014) argues that trauma-informed care can be incorporated into current models or theories for sexual offending intervention such as RNR and GLM. Trauma-informed care requires that interventions for sexual offending be trauma responsive in both process and content. Process takes account of the interaction between clients and therapists, ensuring that actions are not inadvert-ently reinforcing of previous trauma experiences, as confrontational approaches are likely to do. This is particularly important for interventions that take place in secure settings (Jones, 2017). Therapists should use the relational process to model healthy attachment and coach skills for healthy relationships. Levenson suggests that the content of the intervention should help individuals understand their responses to trauma as contextually adaptive and recognise the impact of these responses across the lifespan and within domains of psychological function-ing. Together the intervention should help individuals to develop new and more functional ways of relating (to self and other) and behaving. Few authors have offered specific recommendations for the therapeutic approaches that could be utilised in trauma-informed care. Grady, Levenson and Bolder (2017) propose attachment as a mediator variable for ACEs and sexual offending and suggest that attachment-based therapies, which aim to improve emotional and behaviour regulation and relational capacity, offer promise. Prison-based democratic therapeutic communities (DTCs) are one model of trauma-informed work in forensic services. DTCs are residential communities based on trauma-informed principles which offer intensive therapeutic input for residents to address their trauma histories and understand the links to their offending (Akerman & Andrews, 2020).

Building on this foundational work by Levenson and colleagues, we have previously proposed that approaches that embrace a change focus (such as CBT) alongside a process sensitivity and a trauma-informed methodology are essential for trauma-informed care (Taylor, Akerman & Hocken, 2020). We argue that compassion-focused therapy (CFT) (Gilbert, 2010), a motivation-based form of psychotherapy that combines techniques from CBT with evolutionary and neuroscience influences, may offer this potential. We suggest a combination of a trauma-informed approach with CFT to create trauma-informed and compassion-focused practice can offer a model of intervention for those who commit serious harm.

Compassion-focused therapy

CFT was initially developed for people whose high levels of shame rendered them unable to benefit from traditional CBT (Gilbert, 2014). CFT is a motivation-focused therapy that helps people to access and stimulate the affiliative emotions, motives and competencies underpinning compassion. The combination of these capacities plays an important role in threat regulation, wellbeing and pro-social behaviour (Gilbert, 2014; Clapton, 2016). In CFT, compassion is conceptualised as a motivation (not an emotion) of two psychologies: a sensitivity to suffering and a commitment to alleviating suffering. Where capacities for this are stimulated, an individual's motivation is fundamentally shifted towards a caring mentally, directed both at others and oneself. The ability for CFT to stimulate the motivational caring system has obvious benefits for people who harm.

As with many therapeutic approaches, CFT incorporates a number of core components:

1   Psychoeducation provides an overview of the core components of CFT, which outline that the human brain evolved in a way that resulted in certain inbuilt problems, including biases and inherent conflicts, many of which make us vulnerable to anti-social behaviour and mental health problems. Furthermore, much of what happens in our brains is neither our design nor our intention and as such is not our fault. This is not to invalidate our

responsibility for our own actions, but simply to recognise that the archi-tecture of our brain is not something that we choose. For example, a child who experiences abuse from a parent may learn to deny their experience of abuse in order to retain the important aspects of that relationship (the need for food, shelter, etc.). In so doing, they may train their mind to deny harmful acts and inadvertently lay a foundation from which their own anti-social behaviour can easily emerge. CFT suggests that the more individuals identify with the problems of common humanity and the troubles of the evolved (and tricky) brain, the less personalised and the easier it is to work with shame and take responsibility for change. Part of psycho-education also involves helping individuals begin to understand the nature of their different emotion systems and how they can learn to be more physically and mind-fully aware, thus enabling people to be more attentive to what is going on in their own minds and bodies as they arise. In addition, CFT teaches specific breathing exercises (called soothing rhythm breathing) that are designed to stimulate the parasympathetic system, which in turn has an impact on the frontal cortex and capacities for reflective thinking (Lin, Tai & Fan, 2014). Within forensic CFT, we propose a number of key concepts that should occur early in the therapeutic process:

- The nature of our evolved brain
- Evolved emotions and emotion regulation systems
- Compassion
- Fears, blocks and resistance to compassion
- The way our motives organise our attention, thinking, feeling and behaviour, known as 'multiple selves'
- Reconceptualising criminogenic need

2   Formulation is based on the evolutionary model of human nature and aims to help people understand that many of their life strategies for dealing with threats and trying to advance oneself are the consequence of genes interact-ing with social contexts. Helping individuals to understand the unintended and often unhelpful consequences of their safety or acquisition strategies is therefore important and facilitates a de-shaming process. Formulation is also a co-production that aims to capture an autobiographical narrative. The formulation is explicitly based on certain key assumptions – that we have an evolved brain and that the way the person presents to us has been shaped by lifetime experiences and therefore represents a functional and survival-based response to their lifetime. Furthermore, there is an explicit recognition that effective survival responses are inevitably resilient to change (rather than treatment resistant). Formulation is also based on a phenomenological rather than categorical understanding and is written in a style that ensures that it is accessible and available and can be held in mind by the author.

3   In CFT, the development of compassionate motivation is seen as a core transforming process that arises from insight. There are a range of interventions for building compassion motivation, including the use of compassion imagery, compassionate reflection, compassion-focused empathy, developing a compassionate self-identity, regular practice of compassion and behaviour and keeping compassion diaries (Gilbert, 2010). It is helpful to recognise that sometimes individuals can practice behaving and thinking in compassionate ways long before they start 'feeling' compassion.

4   As compassionate motivation is developed, this capacity can be used to support individuals to grieve for their own distress, and as the ability to experience sadness and vulnerability is developed, they can be supported to develop compassion and remorse for their own harmful actions. Within CFT, it is acknowledged that the capacity for genuine remorse (i.e. a sadness for the harm caused and a feeling of guilt) is unlikely to develop without a capacity for sadness for one's own distress. Attending to personal trauma is therefore central to the therapeutic process and is woven throughout the process of therapy.

5   Within forensic settings, CFT also supports people to understand the origins of criminogenic need. By adopting a developmental and phenomenological approach, people can be supported to understand how they acquired or nurtured capacities that may contribute to risk or harmfulness. By tracking the development of criminogenic factors over time, we can support people to recognise the function of criminogenic factors in their original context (typically safety related). Supporting people to understand the original function can offer a rationale and therefore reduces the potential for shame. Enabling people to see that they needed to disconnect from other people's feelings (callousness) or that they needed to be ready to react (impulsivity) allows people to begin to address these factors without feeling they were at fault for having them in the first place.

CFT, then, is a motivation-focused form of psychotherapy and sees the motivational states of mind – whether we want to cause suffering or whether we want to alleviate suffering – as central to working with people who cause harm to others. CFT encourages an understanding that early life experiences may have compromised people's capacity for caring by over-stimulating the threat system and under-stimulating the soothing system. The effect on self-relating that emerges from early trauma is seen to be a driving feature behind the experience of shame in men and women who cause harm and, similarly, an inhibitor of guilt.

As a psychotherapeutic intervention, forensic CFT adopts a trauma-sensitive approach and recognises that much of what we learn is beyond our control. CFT empowers individuals to take notice of the consequences of their learning and develop their skills and competencies in order to manage themselves in a harm-free manner. CFT encourages compassion-based guilt rather than disempowering shame. Application of CFT as an intervention for offending is novel and has most readily been used an approach for working with those who experience anger (Kolts, 2012), violence (Taylor, 2017) and, more recently, youth in custody (Da Silva et al., 2019). However, in our view, the ability of CFT to address trauma and shame and to stimulate caring motivations towards others positions it as a promising intervention for those who commit sexual harm (Walton & Hocken, 2020).

Intervention case examples

In this section, we set out two different interventions that utilise CFT as their primary therapeutic approach. We provide a brief overview of each intervention, drawing together a number of specific considerations for forensic CFT. We conclude the chapter with a brief summary of early outcome data from the two interventions.

The Aurora Project for sexual offence prevention

The Aurora Project (TAP) is a community-based group intervention. Beginning in 2018, it aims to help people who experience sexual thoughts and feelings that, if acted upon, would cause harm. TAP is part of a range of interventions offered by the Safer Living Foundation (SLF) charity (www.saferlivingfoundation.org/) to prevent harm caused by sexual offending. The intended client group is those who have not committed a sexual offence, the principle being that first-time offending could be prevented. Only an outline of TAP is provided here, but for a more detailed description see Hocken (2018).

The development of TAP drew heavily on the emerging literature around people attracted to children but not having offended (self-identified as non-offending paedophiles). The psychological needs of this group are varied and diverse, but common needs identified are coming to terms with their sexual interests (Dombert et al., 2016); managing self-hatred, shame and stigma related to their interest (Jahnke & Hoyer, 2013); and loneliness, isolation and mental ill health (Grady, Levenson & Bolder, 2017). These needs set alongside the research indicating that, for some, a sexual interest in children is immutable (Cantor & McPhail, 2016) point to an intervention that builds capacities for self-compassion and acceptance. The presence of inflated ACEs in this group (Grady, Levenson & Bolder, 2017; Levenson & Bolder, Levenson, Willis & Vicencio, 2017) suggests a trauma-informed approach is necessary.

TAP utilises two therapeutic modalities: CFT and acceptance and commit-ment therapy (ACT), these being indicated by Walton and Hocken (2020) as being promising for intervention for paraphilias. CFT and ACT work as com-plementary approaches, and both share the evolutionary model at their core. ACT offers an explicit focus on developing psychological flexibility mediated by mindful awareness, acceptance and values-based living. TAP takes a rolling group format, although clients will have a number of individual sessions in preparation for the group phase and at any subsequent point as needed. The structure revolves around ten modules which are based on the three flows of compassion (from self to others, from others to self and from self to self), psy-choeducation, the core processes of psychological flexibility from ACT and a problem-specific module on healthy sex. The modules and components of Aurora are shown in Table 9.1.

The modules are not distinct phases, and they are not completed chronologi-cally or exclusively. The concepts from each module are continually referred to

Table 9.1 Components of the Aurora project intervention

Component	Content
1 Understanding the brain	Psychoeducation of model – tricky brain, emotional regulation model
2 Values	Identifying what matters (values) and developing skills and motivation for value-based living
3 Self-compassion	Fears, blocks and resistances; stimulating a caring motivation towards the self; multiple selves; shame; self-criticism; guilt
4 Compassion for others	Stimulating a caring motivation towards others, skills for caring behaviours, guilt
5 Compassion from others	Stimulating a capacity to receive care from others
6 Defusion	Decentring and skills for meta-cognition (noticing, naming and standing back from internal experiences)
7 Acceptance	Motivation and skills for acceptance of internal and external experiences
8 Present moment	Attentional training, grounding, mindfulness, soothing breathing
9 Identity	Multiple selves, compassionate self
10 Healthy sex	Skills from the previous areas applied to sexual, thinking feeling and behaviour

and linked to the other modules. For example, where a session is focusing on self-compassion, it will draw on the other areas as relevant. Each client starts with psychoeducation in pre-group individual sessions to lay the foundation for the intervention, and they join the group knowing the basic concepts of tricky brain and emotional regulation systems. However, psychoeducation is a concurrent thread, referred to regularly, as it underpins every other module.

The client journey begins with individual assessment with a therapist to explore their needs and undertake assessments that map on to the module areas. Based on this, a regularly reviewed collaborative formulation is developed, which is used to guide the priority need areas the client will focus on. The formulation is conceptualised as a compass, depicted as a circle with ten segments containing each module (see Figure 9.1), and the relative need is noted on the compass in some way by the client, typically by drawing a line to show how 'full' the segment is. The compass signifies direction, and meeting the needs in each area helps clients move in the life direction they want to go. Sessions are loosely planned around each module, taking into account individual need areas. Participants are also set between session assignments to develop learning and help them generalise this to their daily life.

Aurora is subject to both process and outcomes evaluation using a mixed-methods approach. A waiting-list controlled study evaluates intervention outcome by assessing change on multiple psychometric measures pre-, during and six-weeks post-intervention. Aurora is still in its infancy, and only five people have completed

Figure 9.1 Aurora life compass formulation.

the intervention; therefore, results are preliminary. Assessments show that most individuals entering Aurora are experiencing high levels of internalised shame, depression, anxiety, little-to-some hope for the future, low mental wellbeing, reduced levels of perceived social safety and moderate-to-low psychological flexibility. Preliminary results show positive changes at 24 weeks into Aurora. Mental wellbeing is in the clinically normal range, closer to the average of the general population. There is a steep reduction in internalised shame, while depression and stress are also reduced to normal levels. In addition to this, there was a statistically significant reduction in anxiety. Participants also display a greater hope for the future and increased levels of social safety. Psychological flexibility is largely unchanged. These are promising results and suggest that, at the least, Aurora is improving the quality of life for participants. Whether this leads to prevention of offending will be unknown until long-term follow-up can be done.

Compassion-focused forensic psychotherapy programme

CFT has been used in HMP Whatton (as a collaboration between healthcare and the Psychology Department) as an overarching framework to organise work with men in prison for sexual offences who have not been able to respond to the cognitive behavioural interventions. Drawing on the theoretical foundations we have described earlier, the therapeutic work strives to support the men to develop their capacity to feel guilt (and therefore guide their actions away from harmfulness) by supporting them to process their own experiences of adversity and understanding how they have been shaped by experience. Taking into account our evolved architecture, including our innate readiness to cause harm, and adopting a perspective that 'we learn what we live', men are supported to provide and experience their own autobiographical formulation as a foundation for subsequent work. A fundamental aspect of the work is based on the notion that experiences happen in a sequence and therefore need to be processed in a sequence; childhood trauma needs to be processed effectively before we are able to process experiences that occur later in life – including offences. Attempting to promote remorse or empathic concern, for example, is unlikely to happen if men have been abused and were left feeling responsible for that abuse, while encouraging emotional regulation is similarly unlikely to be successful if emotional dysregulation was learned as a survival strategy. In other words, we need to establish a foundation before we try to build skills or competencies that support resilience and desistence. Although the work is very much process driven and ebbs and flows with the dynamics in the room, we have conceptualised the work within a sequence (see Table 9.2). The conceptualisation is based on practice over the last ten years or so and has been shaped and informed by feedback from men detained in both hospital and prison settings.

As we can see, the framework has much in common with TAP and builds on key components of the CFT model. However, there are also some key differences between the two models. Clearly, the men at Whatton are serving prison sentences and have therefore been convicted of causing harm. The programme therefore explicitly addresses criminogenic capacities and aspires to operate as a risk-reducing intervention. As such, there is a module that addresses harmful capacities, including directly criminogenic areas such as sexual interests, sexual preoccupation and values that promote harmful behaviour. In addition, less direct characteristics that can contribute to harm, such as difficulties in accepting responsibility, externalising blame and accountability and an indifference to suffering, are also included in order to ensure a broad context for intervention. Men are encouraged to lead on the development of a formulation of their harmful behaviour by contextualising the origins of their criminogenic needs within their personal life story. Much of the work is based on processing experiences and developing meaning around these experiences. Indeed, the bulk of the intervention is trauma focused, and this then forms a basis that allows men to develop insight into the origins of their criminogenic need and the function or purpose

Table 9.2 Trauma-sensitive forensic CFT

Module/phase	Components
Psychoeducation	Evolved minds and tricky brains; evolved emotional regulation system; compassion; multiple selves; fears, blocks and resistances.
	Therapeutic objectives.
Mindful compassion	Soothing rhythm breathing; attention training; mindfulness; visualisation; self-compassion.
	Concurrent module that runs across the programme.
Formulation	Autobiographical narratives; formulating a good life.
Trauma sensitivity	Psychoeducation (how we respond to trauma); creating a trauma-informed understanding; facing trauma (compassion for our life story, emotional mirroring, offence trauma).
Understanding criminogenic need	Origins of criminogenic need; criminogenic need in current context; witnessing consequences.
Facilitating guilt	Understanding harm caused; mentalising the people we harm; practicing guilt, restorative commitments.

of these as they emerged. For example, beliefs that promote an anti-social life-style may have been the dominant in a person's childhood home, and they may have needed to absorb the same values to feel connected to others – the crimino-genic nature of these beliefs initially promoting connection and inclusion. Alter-natively, an individual may have grown up in a setting where they were harmed and were repeatedly told that this was legitimate and justified. Their emotional experience of life – knowing that they felt that they were being hurt – was incongruent with the expressed views of those in authority, and they therefore developed an anti-authority value system as a defence.

Having developed a compassionate understanding of the initial function of crim-inogenic factors, the therapeutic work moves to develop insight into the harmful repercussions of these factors. Critically here it is important to contrast the initial function with the unintended consequences and highlight the initial function com-pared with the harmful repercussions once operating outside of the original con-text. So, using the example earlier, anti-social values that defended a person against harmful authority now organise a person to reject a more nurturing authority. Men are supported to develop this insight into all areas of criminogenic need.

With an understanding of the initial function of criminogenic capacities, the focus can then shift into a more offence-focused arena. It is considered impor-tant that this does not start until individuals have developed the capacity for self-compassion and a clear understanding of how their learning experiences have influenced their ways of relating to others. Fundamentally, the capacity for remorse (i.e. the motivation to avoid causing harm) rests on the ability to express sadness and grief, and these competencies are typically blocked in people who have not been able to process their own traumatic experiences. When this has been established, individuals are encouraged to begin to explore how their ways of behaving will have impacted on other people's lives. Within CFT, the aspi-ration here is that people can now visit this work, having developed both the competencies and the motivations for compassionate and pro-social behaviours.

Considerations in forensic CFT

As we can see from Figure 9.1, like many psychotherapies, CFT starts by social-ising the client to the model. We have added to the content of this module over time (on the basis of client feedback) and alongside the psychoeducational work we aim to set the tone for the work. In other words, we teach the core compo-nents of CFT with compassion, with a willingness and a sensitivity to noticing distress and a genuine intention to alleviate suffering. There is also a constant balance between delivering content and responding to processes in the room. As we have said, the bulk of the therapeutic work is trauma (in its broadest sense) and adversity focused, and we draw heavily on trauma-focused CFT, which is described in elegant detail elsewhere (Lee & James, 2012). As we have developed our practice, we have been eager to learn from the men (primarily) who have endeavoured to work in this way, and we have become aware of some particularly nuanced aspects of forensic CFT that are worth attention.

Process issues

First, despite the vast array of psychotherapies, almost all are united in the assumption that the therapist wants the client to improve for himself or herself. Carl Rogers' (1957) notion of the core conditions for therapy offers a scaffold for the development of a containing relationship that allows people to disclose information about themselves. Without this relationship, shame can inhibit disclosure (Black, Curran & Dyer, 2013). Whilst the core conditions form a foundation for psychotherapy generally, they may not have been a felt experience for people who have undertaken offence-related psychological programmes. Certainly, some interventions have focused on the 'other' (victim) rather than 'self', and as a consequence may have been experienced as being somewhat dismissive of personal experience(s). For people with histories of trauma and adversity, this is likely to inhibit a productive therapeutic alliance and may even cause further harm (Puszkiewicz & Stinson 2019). Creating a psychotherapeutic culture (acceptance, validation, compassion and curiosity) is therefore the first step when we commence this work in forensic settings. Working towards this culture supports us (as clinicians) to guide our intentions and therefore direct our behaviour in sessions.

Second, by drawing attention to the nature of the relationships in the therapy room, we create opportunities to explore social processes and dynamics. In turn, this allows us to consider the role of social mentalities and the social contexts that organise us to adopt different mentalities. In the context of forensic practice understanding the algorithms (stimulus–response rules) that orchestrate our different motivational systems seems particularly pertinent. For example, developing awareness of the conditions that trigger someone to turn off their caring mentality may be a central aspect of risk management. Similarly, knowing why and how someone recruits the various behavioural repertoires of a rank-based mentality may shed light on a need for dominance and thus may also be central to understanding and managing the risk of further harmful behaviour.

Third, by introducing social processes into the scrutiny of therapeutic work, we can begin to explore these as they emerge, particularly within the therapeutic relationship (see Figure 9.2). In other words, we can explore the transferences – the feelings and attitudes held about and between different members and facilitators of the group – and what this may reveal about earlier relationships and their

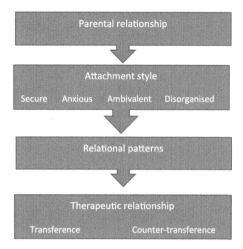

Figure 9.2 The dynamic of a therapeutic alliance.

influence on current relating styles. Exploring this in the context of CFT, where we understand the influence of evolution and learning, allows us to depersonalise and de-shame the therapeutic relationship. As we will see later (early outcomes), this is an important area for exploration in order to identify and work around barriers to therapeutic progress.

Brain architecture (tricky brain)

The concept of a *tricky brain* is a central aspect of CFT. In essence, the idea is that the basic architecture of the human brain leaves us vulnerable to a range of difficulties – including those that are often described as psychiatric or criminogenic. From the experience that we have gained from working with CFT in forensic settings, three aspects of the evolved and tricky mind concept stand out. First, evolved brains allow us to recognise that much of what happens in our minds is not a result of our own design and therefore not our fault. We have found that a critical issue here is understanding a shift from a stance that advocates blame and shame into one that encourages guilt and responsibility. In the former, an individual may be made to feel that they are to blame for everything about themselves – their ability to manage emotions, the fear that they experience in relationships and their sexual interests. Internally, they may recognise that they have not chosen to have these challenges in their lives, but a lived experience of blame may stimulate shame and reduce agency and capacity for change. In the latter position, on the other hand, we encourage people to notice what they are and what they are not responsible for and therefore what they can begin to develop more control over.

If we consider the issue of sexual interests, the blame/shame stance suggests that sexual interests are wilfully and inevitably pursued, while the guilt/responsibility position recognises that we do not choose our sexual preferences (these are most likely determined in a epigenetic fashion), but we can consider the consequences of our interests if we choose to pursue them or not.

The second area of difficulty here concerns life experiences and learning. In the example provided earlier, a sexual interest in children may be understood in terms of genetic influences, and this level of understanding often allows people to separate blame and responsibility. To illustrate, I am not to blame for my poor colour vision, but I am responsible for the way I manage a car when I arrive at a set of traffic lights. However, where our presentation is based on learning and experience, this can be trickier, and we have often been greeted with statements like "so it's not my fault I raped that child" or " I'm not to blame for the way she reacted". Clearly, we would not endorse this perspective, but would again encourage people to notice what is, and what is not, their responsibility. So, returning to our earlier example where someone has a sexual interest in children and feels inhibited from developing relationships with adults, we would encourage them to understand that neither of these challenges are of their design or could be considered to be their fault. We would, however, engage in a reflective consideration of what experiences nurtured their sense of anxiety with adults and similarly want to encourage clients to notice the consequences if they pursued their sexual interests.

Finally, a third area that may need some attention can arise when our clients have experienced abuse or hurt in their earlier lives and they mistake the idea of a *tricky brain* to mean that the person who caused them harm is also not responsible for their actions. As discussed earlier, this can quickly prompt questions directed towards the therapist along the lines of "so you're saying it is not his fault he used to batter me every time he got drunk" or "so I guess it was my fault I got raped". As we have already indicated, this is absolutely not what we are suggesting, and these understandable reactions allow us to emphasise the distinction between fault and responsibility. However, this sort of interaction also allows the compassion-focused therapist to invite their client to explore the therapeutic alliance, including the therapist's thoughts and feelings towards the client and vice versa.

Formulation

While formulation is a common aspect of all psychotherapies, many forensic formulations have become organised around risk factors and, in some formats, have gradually become a *risk diagnosis* – a tick box of criminogenic symptoms. As with all aspects of this work, an awareness of risk is clearly important, but the evolutionary understanding of human development that sits at the heart of CFT recognises both the phylogenetic (evolution over time) and ontogenetic (evolution over a life span) influences on human behaviour. To enhance phenomenological experiences and embody trauma sensitivity, we invite clients to begin a formulation with the phrase "when I was little . . ." and find that this helps us to orientate this process towards their own autobiographical experience of life. For many people who have spent time living within forensic settings, this can prove challenging. For example, it is not unusual for people to be accused of deflecting or justifying if they speak about their own experience of adversity. Similarly, comments that reduce or minimise harm may have been met with accusations of denial without an understanding of the role of shame and the function of denial. Issues concerning trust and anxiety that material disclosed may be used as evidence of risk can also emerge. Similarly, we have found that many practitioners are anxious to use an autobiographical approach, believing that a first-person narrative may be seen as unprofessional and unacceptable to parole boards or tribunals. However, we argue that the aim of a formulation process is to enhance understanding and support someone to develop insight into their own *human* nature. Furthermore, the ownership of a formulation should rest with the person who it describes, and ownership is clarified with a first-person narrative account.

Criminogenic need in an autobiographical context

Criminogenic need has been an important construct that has enhanced our understanding of the types of factors, characteristics and lifestyle choices that may increase the likelihood of harmful behaviour. However, interventions that seek to address these various factors rarely support clients to understand the biological and genetic origins of our behaviours, nor how these behaviours come to be cultivated over the course of our life. Understanding criminogenic need in these ways can therefore stimulate shame and encourage a range of shame management strategies that we have referred to previously.

The CFT approach to formulation that we have outlined earlier provides a different understanding of criminogenic challenges because it allows us to witness the evolution of these factors across the developmental period. As indicated in Table 9.2, the formulation is followed by trauma-focused work where we are able to understand the childhood survival strategies that were necessary. As we move into this phase of the work, we begin to turn attention to the manifestation of these strategies in adulthood and support a person to notice the unintended consequences that may have arisen from trauma responses. "What are your risks and where did they come from?" is a phrase developed by one of the groups that worked to this model and allowed them to understand their lack of agency as these various factors came into being, whilst encouraging their responsibility to develop strategies to manage, contain or inhibit harmful capacities. Conversely, however, embedded within this understanding is the notion that we cannot un-learn and therefore we are not able to leave behind those aspects of ourselves that can be harmful. Understanding the significance of trauma, adversity and the need to develop ways to survive these conditions helps to illustrate the challenge in this. Language acquisition can be a useful metaphor at this stage. Children learn to speak at pretty well the same age, but what they learn to speak depends on their context. Children growing up in an Italian context learn Italian, while children growing up in Kenya learn to use a different language. What is learned is adaptive for the context. If these children swap contexts, though, then they will need to learn a new language to fit in and understand their social environment. This does not mean that their early learning was maladaptive or distorted. Nor does it mean that we expect the initial language to be forgotten. But we do need to learn a new way to communicate and relate to others. In terms of harmfulness, therefore, we have to learn ways to manage these aspects of ourselves and new adaptive ways of meeting the needs these old harmful behaviours once met.

This can challenge previous interventions where the concept of old me/new me was used as a metaphor for risk management. We have found that a person who has invested in the *old me* concept can be reluctant to acknowledge that they still possess the capacity to be harmful and can experience some distress (or anger) as we encourage them to turn towards this aspect(s) of themselves.

Facilitating guilt (compassion for others and compassion for my victims)

Although we have argued that psychological welfare is a legitimate outcome target from our work in forensic services, we recognise that forensic services are also designed to promote the potential for successful community reintegration and that this rests fundamentally on the likelihood of further harm. Much of the work that we have described so far is concerned with preparing those we work alongside to develop the resilience to sustain compassionate motivations. As mentioned earlier, in CFT we see compassion as the key motivation that will enable our clients to turn towards the distress that they can cause and strive to alleviate suffering. In other words, we are facilitating the experience of guilt. As with other components of this particular way of supporting people, the details of this work are described elsewhere (Gilbert, 2014), and our focus here is on those aspects of this work that can be particularly challenging. After reflecting on the work with the people who have been willing to undertake it, two areas have been experienced as particularly challenging at this stage of the work. The first refers to balancing feelings of guilt with shame, while the second is linked to the grief that arises when guilt is experienced and the barriers to restoration in relation to victims.

In terms of the balance between these two emotions, we have been helped to understand that many people who cause serious harm to others experience shame and are therefore motivated (by shame) to seek to regain status and social acceptance. In turn, various behaviours (denial, rationalising, seeking forgiveness, etc.) facilitate this process and protect the individual from having a deep understanding of the harm that they have caused. For many of the men we have worked with, shame has become a practiced emotion and one that can readily be used. Our balance to this is to invite responsibility by encouraging these individuals to recall times when they have caused minor harm or distress to others. Drawing on their new ability to generate self-compassion and the courage and strength that accompany compassionate motives, men (in terms of our current practice) can allow themselves to experience compassion flowing outwards and bring to mind increasing levels of harm that they have caused. Having processed their own experience of being harmed and having grieved for their own losses associated with this, men can turn towards the distress that they have caused and experience the grief that they have caused. Inevitably, this is a challenging area of work and rests both on the capacity for the men to cultivate compassion and on the quality of the therapeutic relationships.

The second area that causes challenges for the men involved in our work concerns the experience of repair. Compassion involves both noticing and wanting to relieve distress, and the evolution of guilt has rooted behavioural change into the process of harm reduction. When our own actions have caused such considerable harm as to prevent us from talking to our victim(s), the opportunity for direct reparation is blocked. We have learned that this can create a fracture in the experience of compassion (including guilt), as men may be left feeling exposed to the harm that they have caused and motivated to alleviate suffering but unable to do so. As guilt involves a behavioural component that is designed to reduce suffering, we have drawn on the concept of redemption scripts (Maruna, 2001) as a framework to support men to identify compassionate lifestyles that evidence a commitment to be "helpful not harmful" (Gilbert, 2020).

Conclusion

The development of trauma-aware practice demonstrates the prevalence of adverse child experiences in the histories of people with sexual offences and points to functional links between trauma and sexual offending. However, a common feature of the predominant intervention models is a focus on criminogenic needs without attention to the (often traumatic) genesis for these. We have argued here that survival responses to trauma and adversity give rise to the development of criminogenic needs, and it is necessary to address the origins of criminogenic factors in order to prevent further harm. We propose that CFT offers a therapeutic model for doing this, providing a means to formulate criminogenic needs in the context of trauma and a means of developing a motivation that moves people away from harmful behaviour. The two case examples of interventions that use CFT as their main component show promising outcomes for psychological wellbeing and acknowledgment risk.

References

Abram, K. M., Teplin, L. A., Charles, D. R., Longworth, S. L., McClelland, G. M., & Dulcan, M. K. (2004). Posttraumatic stress disorder and trauma in youth in juvenile detention. *Archives of General Psychiatry, 61*(4), 403–410.

Akerman, G., & Andrews, T. (2020). Abuse, offending and addressing this in therapy: A staff and service user's perspective on the journey to self-acceptance and a crime-free life. In H. Swaby, B. Winder, R. Lievesley, K. Hocken, N. Blagden, & P. Banyard (Eds.), *Sexual crime and trauma.* Palgrave Macmillan.

Akins, C. (2004). The role of Pavlovian conditioning in sexual behavior: A comparative analysis of human and nonhuman animals. *International Journal of Comparative Psychology, 17*(2).

Andrews, D. A., & Bonta, J. (2003). *The psychology of criminal conduct* (3rd ed.). Anderson.

Bancroft, J. (1974). *Deviant sexual behaviour.* Oxford University Press.

Barnao, M., & Ward, T. (2015). Sailing uncharted seas without a compass: A review of interventions in forensic mental health. *Aggression and Violent Behavior, 22,* 77–86. https://doi.org/10.1016/j.avb.2015.04.009

Becker, S. P., & Kerig, P. K. (2011). Posttraumatic stress symptoms are associated with the frequency and severity of delinquency among detained boys. *Journal of Clinical Child & Adolescent Psychology, 40*(5), 765–771.

Black, R. S., Curran, D., & Dyer, K. F. (2013). The impact of shame on the therapeutic alliance and intimate relationships. *Journal of Clinical Psychology, 69*(6), 646–654.

Blank, C., Nunes, K. L., Maimone, S., Hermann, C. A., & McPhail, I. V. (2018). Is childhood sexual victimization associated with cognitive distortions, self-esteem, and emotional congruence with children? *Journal of Sexual Aggression. 24*(3), 259–273. doi:10.1080/13552600.2018.1509574

Bowlby, J. (1958). The nature of the child's tie to his mother. *International Journal of Psychoanalysis, 39,* 1–23.

Bowlby, J. (1959). Separation anxiety. *International Journal of Psychoanalysis,* 41, 1–25.

Bowlby, J. (1960). Grief and mourning in infancy and early childhood. *The Psychoanalytic Study of the Child, 15,* 3–39.

Cale, J., Leclerc, B., & Smallbone, S. (2014). The sexual lives of sexual offenders: The link between childhood sexual victimization and non-criminal sexual lifestyles between types of offenders. *Psychology, Crime & Law, 20*(1), 37–60.

Cantor, J. M., & McPhail, I. V. (2016). Non-offending pedophiles. *Current Sexual Health Reports, 8*(3), 121–128.

Centers for Disease Control and Prevention. (2013). *Adverse childhood experience study: Major findings.* Retrieved from www.cdc.gov/ace/findings.htm

Chu, C. M., Koh, L. L., Zeng, G., & Teoh, J. (2015). Youth who sexually offended: Primary human goods and offense pathways. *Sexual Abuse: A Journal of Research and Treatment, 27*, 151–172. doi: 10.1177/1079063212499188

Clapton, N. (2016). *Growing kind minds: Adapted group Compassion Focused Therapy for Adults with Intellectual Disabilities (CFT-ID).* Bangor University (United Kingdom).

da Silva, D., Rijo, D., Salekin, R. T., Paulo, M., Miguel, M., & Gilbert, P. (2021). Clinical change in psychopathic traits after the PSYCHOPATHY.COMP program: Preliminary findings of a controlled trial with male detained youth. *Journal of Consulting and Clinical Psychology, 89*(6), 1–42.

da Silva, D. R., Salekin, R. T., & Rijo, D. (2019). Psychopathic severity profiles: A latent profile analysis in youth samples with implications for the diagnosis of conduct disorder. *Journal of Criminal Justice, 60*, 74–83

DeLisi, M., Drury, A. J., & Elbert, M. J. (2019). The etiology of antisocial personality disorder: The differential roles of adverse childhood experiences and childhood psychopathology. *Comprehensive Psychiatry, 92*, 1–6.

Dombert, B., Schmidt, A. F., Banse, R., Briken, P., Hoyer, J., Neutze, J., & Osterheider, M. (2016). How common is men's self-reported sexual interest in prepubescent children? *The Journal of Sex Research, 53*(2), 214–223.

Felitti, V. J., Anda, R. F., Nordenberg, D., Williamson, D. F., Spitz, A. M., Edwards, V., Koss, M. P., PhD, & Marks, J. S. (1998). Relationship of childhood abuse and household dysfunction to many of the leading causes of death in adults: The Adverse Childhood Experiences (ACE) study. *American Journal of Preventive Medicine, 14*(4), 245–258. doi: 10.1016/S0749-3797(98)00017-8

Finkelhor, D., & Araji, S. (1986). *A sourcebook on child sexual abuse.* Sage.

Ford, J. D., Chapman, J., Connor, D. F., & Cruise, K. R. (2012). Complex trauma and aggression in secure juvenile justice settings. *Criminal Justice and Behavior, 39*(6), 694–724.

Furby, L., Weinrott, M. R., & Blackshaw, L. (1989). Sex offender recidivism: A review. *Psychological Bulletin, 105*, 3–30.

Gannon, T. A., Olver, M. E., Mallion, J. S., & James, M. (2019). Does specialized psychological treatment for offending reduce recidivism? A meta-analysis examining staff and program variables as predictors of treatment effectiveness. *Clinical Psychology Review, 73*, 101752.

Gilbert, P. (2010). *Compassion focused therapy: Distinctive features*. Routledge.

Gilbert, P. (2014). The origins and nature of compassion focused therapy. *British Journal of Clinical Psychology*, *53*, 6–41.

Gilbert, P. (2020). Creating a compassionate world: Addressing the conflicts between sharing and caring versus controlling and holding evolved strategies. *Frontiers in Psychology*, *11*, 1–36.

Gloster, A. T., Rinner, M. T. B., Ioannou, M., Villanueva, J., Block, V. J., Ferrari, G., Benoy, C., Bader, K., & Karekla, M. (2019). Treating treatment non-responders: A meta-analysis of randomized controlled psychotherapy trials. *Clinical Psychology Review*, *75*, 101810. doi:10.1016/j.cpr.2019.101810

Grady, M., Levenson, J. S., & Bolder, T. (2017). Linking adverse childhood effects and attachment: A theory of etiology for sexual offending. *Trauma, Violence, & Abuse*, *18*(4), 433–444.

Hamilton, J. A. (2020). *Exploring the relationships between personality disorder, sexual preoccupation, and adverse childhood experiences among individuals who have previously sexually offended*. Nottingham Trent University (United Kingdom).

Hanson, R. K., Gordon, A., Harris, A. J. R., Marques, J. K., Murphy, W., Quinsey, V. L., & Seto, M. C. (2002). First report on the collaborative outcome data project on the effectiveness of psychological treatment for sex offenders. *Sexual Abuse: A Journal of Research and Treatment*, *14*, 169–194.

Harkins, L., Flak, V. E., & Beech, A. R. (2012). Evaluation of a community-based sex offender treatment program using a Good Lives Model approach. *Sexual Abuse: A Journal of Research and Treatment*, *24*(6), 519–543.

Hocken, K. (2018). Safer Living Foundation: The Aurora Project. In *Sexual Crime and Prevention* (pp. 83–109). Palgrave Macmillan, Cham.

Jahnke, S., & Hoyer, J. (2013). Stigmatization of people with pedophilia: A blind spot in stigma research. *International Journal of Sexual Health*, *25*, 169–184. doi:10.1080/193 17611.2013.795921

Jespersen, A. F., Lalumière, M. L., & Seto, M. C. (2009). Sexual abuse history among adult sex offenders and non-sex offenders: A meta-analysis. *Child Abuse & Neglect*, *33*(3), 179–192.

Jones, L. (2017). Trauma-informed care and "good lives" in confinement: Acknowledging and offsetting adverse impacts of chronic trauma and loss of liberty. In Akerman, G., Needs, A., & Bainbridge, C. (Eds.), *Transforming environments and rehabilitation: A guide for practitioners in forensic settings and criminal justice*. London: Routledge.

Kolts, R. (2012). *The compassionate-mind guide to managing your anger: Using compassion-focused therapy to calm your rage and heal your relationships*. New Harbinger.

Krafft-Ebing, R. (1884 [1934]) *Psychopathia sexualis: With especial reference to the antipathic sexual instinct: A medico-forensic study*. F. J. Rebman (trans.). Eugenics Publishing Company, 134.

Laws, D. R. (Ed.). (1989). *Relapse prevention with sex offenders*. The Guilford Press.

Laws, D. R., & Marshall, W. L. (1990). A conditioning theory of the etiology and maintenance of deviant sexual preference and behavior. In W. L. Marshall, D. R. Laws, & H. E. Barbaree (Eds.), *Handbook of sexual assault*. Applied Clinical Psychology. Springer.

Laws, D. R., Meyer, J., & Holmen, M. L. (1978). Reduction of sadistic arousal by olfactory aversion: A case study. *Behaviour Research and Therapy*, *16*, 281–285.

Laws, D. R., & Ward, T. (2011). *Desistance from sex offending: Alternatives to throwing away the keys*. Guilford Press.

Lee, D., & James, S. (2012). *The compassionate mind approach to recovering from trauma: Using compassion focused therapy*. Robinson.

Levenson, J. S. (2014). Incorporating trauma-informed care into evidence-based sex offender treatment. *Journal of Sexual Aggression*, *20*(1), 9–22. doi:10.1080/13552600.2013.861523

Levenson, J. S. (2017). Trauma-informed social work practice. *Social Work*, *62*(2), 105–113.

Levenson, J. S., & Grady, M. D. (2016). The influence of childhood trauma on sexual violence and sexual deviance in adulthood. *Traumatology*, *22*(2), 94–103. http://dx.doi.org/10.1037/trm0000067

Levenson, J. S., & Socia, K. M. (2015). Adverse childhood experiences and arrest patterns in a sample of sexual offenders. *Journal of Interpersonal Violence*. Advance online publication. http://dx.doi.org/10.1177/0886260515570751

Levenson, J. S., Willis, G. M., & Prescott, D. S. (2014). Adverse childhood experiences in the lives of male sex offenders: Implications for trauma-informed care. *Sexual Abuse*. Advance online publication. http://dx.doi.org/10.1177/1079063214535819

Levenson, J. S., Willis, G. M., & Prescott, D. S. (2016). Adverse childhood experiences in the lives of male sex offenders: Implications for trauma-informed care. *Sexual Abuse*, *28*(4), 340–359.

Levenson, J. S., Willis, G. M., & Prescott, D. S. (2017). *Trauma-informed care: Transforming treatment for people who have sexually abused*. Safer Society Press.

Levenson, J. S., Willis, G. M., & Vicencio, C. P. (2017). Obstacles to help-seeking for sexual offenders: Implications for prevention of sexual abuse. *Journal of Child Sexual Abuse*, *26*(2), 99–120.

Lin, I. M., Tai, L. Y., & Fan, S. Y. (2014). Breathing at a rate of 5.5 breaths per minute with equal inhalation-to-exhalation ratio increases heart rate variability. *International Journal of Psychophysiology*, *91*(3), 206–211.

Lösel, F., & Schmucker, M. (2005). The effectiveness of treatment of sexual offenders: A comprehensive meta-analysis. *Journal of Experimental Criminology*, *1*, 117–146.

Lussier, P., Leclerc, B., Cale, J., & Proulx, J. (2007). Developmental pathways of deviance in sexual aggressors. *Criminal Justice and Behavior, 34*, 1441–1462.

Mann, R. E. (2004). Innovations in sex offender treatment. *Journal of Sexual Aggression, 10*(2), 141–152.

Mann, R., Hanson, R. K., & Thornton, D. (2010). Assessing risk for sexual recidivism: Some proposals on the nature of psychologically meaningful risk factors. *Sexual Abuse: A Journal of Research and Treatment, 22*, 191–217.

Marquis, J. N. (1970). Orgasmic reconditioning: Changing sexual object choice through controlled masturbation fantasy. *Journal of Behavior Therapy and Experimental Psychiatry, 1*, 263–271.

Marques, J. N., Wiederanders, M., Day, D. M., Nelson, C., & van Ommeren, A. (2005). Effects of a relapse prevention program on sexual recidivism: Final results from California's sex offender treatment and evaluation project. *Sexual Abuse: A Journal of Research and Treatment, 17*(1), 79–107.

Marshall, W. L., & Barbaree, H. E. (1990). An integrated theory of the etiology of sexual offending. In W. L. Marshall, D. R. Laws, & H. E. Barbaree (Eds.), *Handbook of sexual assault: Issues, theories, and treatment of the offender* (pp. 257–275). Plenum Press.

Maruna, S. (2001). *Making good: How ex-convicts reform and rebuild their lives*. Washington, DC: American Psychological Association Books.

McGrath, R. J., Cumming, G. F., Burchard, B. L., Zeoli, S., & Ellerby, L. (2009). Current practices and emerging trends in sexual abuser management. In *The Safer Society 2009 North American Survey*. The Safer Society Press.

McGuire, R. J., Carlisle, J. M., & Young, B. G. (1965). Sexual deviation as conditional behaviour: A hypothesis. *Behaviour Research and Therapy, 2*, 185–190.

Merrick, M. T., Ports, K. A., Ford, D. C., Afifi, T. O., Gershoff, E. T., & Grogan-Kaylor, A. (2017). Unpacking the impact of adverse childhood experiences on adult mental health. *Child Abuse & Neglect, 69*, 10–19.

Mews, A., Di Bella, L., & Purver, M. (2017). *Impact evaluation of the prison-based core sex offender treatment programme*. Ministry of Justice Analytical Series. Ministry of Justice, London, England.

Ó Ciardha, C., & Ward, T. (2013). Theories of cognitive distortions in sexual offending: What the current research tells us. *Trauma, Violence, & Abuse, 14*(1), 5–21. https://doi.org/10.1177/1524838012467856

Pavlov, I. P. (1928). *Lectures on conditioned reflexes*. W. H. Gantt (trans.). Allen and Unwin.

Puszkiewicz, K. L., & Stinson, J. D. (2019). Pathways to delinquent and sex offending behavior: The role of childhood adversity and environmental context in a treatment sample of male adolescents. *Child abuse & neglect, 98*, 104–184.

Reavis, J. A., Looman, J., Franco, K. A., & Rojas, B. (2013). Adverse childhood experiences and adult criminality: How long must we live before we possess our own lives? *The Permanente Journal, 17*(2), 44.

Ribeiro da Silva, D., Rijo, D., Salekin, R. T., Paulo, M., Miguel, M., & Gilbert, P. (2020). Clinical change in psychopathic traits after the PSYCHOPATHY.COMP program: Preliminary findings of a controlled trial with male detained youth. *Journal of Experimental Criminology.* https://doi.org/10.1007/s11292-020-09418-x

Rogers, C. R. (1957). The necessary and sufficient conditions of therapeutic personality change. *Journal of Consulting and Clinical Psychology, 21*, 95–103.

Salter, A. C. (1988). *Treating child sex offenders and their victims: A practical guide.* Sage Publications.

Schmucker, M., & Lösel, F. (2015). The effects of sexual offender treatment on recidivism: An international meta-analysis of sound quality evaluations. *Journal of Experimental Criminology, 11*(4), 597–630.

Schmucker, M., & Lösel, F. (2017). *Sexual offender treatment for reducing recidivism among convicted sex offenders: A systematic review and meta-analysis.* Campbell Systematic Reviews, No. 8.

Shahar, B., Doron, G., & Szepsenwol, O. (2015). Childhood maltreatment, shame-proneness and self-criticism in social anxiety disorder: A sequential mediational model. *Clinical Psychology & Psychotherapy, 22*(6), 570–579.

Skinner, B. F. (1953). *Science and human behavior.* Simon and Schuster.com.

Strine, T. W., Dube, S. R., Edwards, V. J., Prehn, A. W., Rasmussen, S., Wagenfeld, M., . . . & Croft, J. B. (2012). Associations between adverse childhood experiences, psychological distress, and adult alcohol problems. *American Journal of Health Behavior, 36*(3), 408–423.

Tangney, J. P., & Fischer, K. W. (1995). Shame and guilt in interpersonal relationship. Self-concious emotions: The psychology of shame, guilt, embarrassment and pride, 1. Guilford Press.

Tangney, J. P., Stuewig, J., & Hafez, L. (2011). Shame, guilt and remorse: Implications for offender populations. *Journal of Forensic Psychiatry & Psychology, 1; 22*(5), 706–723. doi:10.1080/14789949.2011.617541.

Taylor, J. (2017). Compassion focussed working in secure forensic care. *Journal of Criminological Research, Policy and Practice.*

Taylor, J., Akerman, G., & Hocken, K. (2020). Cultivating compassion focussed practice for those who have committed sexual offences. In H. Swaby, B. Winder, R. Lievesley, K. Hocken, N. Blagden, & P. Banyard (Eds.), *Sexaul crime and trauma.* Palgrave Macmillan.

Thorndike, E. L. (1905). *The elements of psychology.* A. G. Seiler.

Topitzes, J., Mersky, J. P., & Reynolds, A. J. (2011). Child maltreatment and offending behavior: Gender-specific effects and pathways. *Criminal Justice and Behavior, 38*(5), 492–510.

Tyler, K. A., Johnson, K. A., & Brownridge, D. A. (2008). A longitudinal study of the effects of child maltreatment on later outcomes among high-risk adolescents. *Journal of Youth and Adolescence, 37*(5), 506–521.

Varese, F., Smeets, F., Drukker, M., Lieverse, R., Lataster, T., Viechtbauer, W., . . . & Bentall, R. P. (2012). Childhood adversities increase the risk of psychosis: A meta-analysis of patient-control, prospective-and cross-sectional cohort studies. *Schizophrenia Bulletin, 38*(4), 661–671.

Walton, J. S. (2019). The evolutionary basis of belonging: Its relevance to denial of offending and labelling those who offend. *The Journal of Forensic Practice, 21*(4), 202–211.

Walton, J. S., & Hocken, K. (2020). Compassion and acceptance as interventions for paraphilic disorders and sexual offending behaviour. In G. Akerman, D. Perkins, & R. Bartels (Eds.), *Assessing and managing problematic sexual interests, a practitioner's guide.* Routledge. ISBN 9780367254186.

Ward, T. (2002). Good lives and the rehabilitation of offenders: Promises and problems. *Aggression and Violent Behavior, 7*(5), 513–528.

Ward, T., & Hudson, S. M. (2001). Finkelhor's precondition model of child sexual abuse: A critique. *Psychology, Crime and Law, 7,* 291–307.

Ward, T., & Siegert, R. J. (2002). Toward a comprehensive theory of child sexual abuse: A theory knitting perspective. *Psychology, Crime and Law, 8*(4), 319–351.

Ward, T., & Willis, G. (2013). Sex offender research. *The Wiley-Blackwell handbook of legal and ethical aspects of sex offender treatment and management,* 5194, 97.

Waxman, R., Fenton, M. C., Skodol, A. E., Grant, B. F., & Hasin, D. (2014). Childhood maltreatment and personality disorders in the USA: Specificity of effects and the impact of gender. *Personality and Mental Health, 8*(1), 30–41.

Willis, G. M., Ward, T., & Levenson, J. (2014). The Good Lives Model (GLM): An evaluation of GLM operationalization in North American treatment programs. *Sexual Abuse: A Journal of Research and Treatment, 26,* 58–81.

Wolff, N., & Shi, J. (2012). Childhood and adult trauma experiences of incarcerated persons and their relationship to adult behavioral health problems and treatment. *International Journal of Environmental Research and Public Health, 9*(5), 1908–1926.

Wu, P., Bird, H. R., Liu, X., Duarte, C. S., Fuller, C., Fan, B., ... & Canino, G. J. (2010). Trauma, posttraumatic stress symptoms, and alcohol-use initiation in children. *Journal of Studies on Alcohol and Drugs, 71*(3), 326–334.

10
Mindfulness for individuals with a violent and/or sexual conviction

Rachael Lee

Introduction

To date, approaches in the UK criminal justice system for addressing and reducing the risk of reoffending in those who have committed sexual and/or violent offences have largely taken a cognitive behavioural approach and aligned themselves with the risk, need and responsivity (RNR) model (see Andrews & Bonta, 2010). Such approaches sit within what is termed a 'second wave' approach to offender rehabilitation, whereby therapists have encouraged individuals to focus on deliberately and consciously trying to control and modify individual cognitions that are relevant to their offending. Within Her Majesty's Prison and Probation Service (HMPPS), a variety of offending behaviour programmes, accredited by the Correctional Services Accreditation and Advice Panel (CSAAP), have been developed in the past two to three decades, centred around the key criminogenic factors linked with sexual and violent offending. More recent developments to the programmes have included a focus on the factors known to promote desistance, as well as those that are risk factors for recidivism, and this has largely been grounded in the Good Lives Model (GLM) (see Ward & Laws, 2010). In addition, there has been a move away from a confessional approach, whereby participants are required to give a detailed account of their offending, and a recognition that a focus on this approach, as well as developing victim empathy, is not a necessary requirement to reduce the risk of recidivism (Mann, Hanson & Thornton, 2010).

The need for effective interventions with those who commit sexual and violent offences is of paramount importance. Such individuals often receive lengthy custodial sentences and are required to demonstrate that they have reduced their risk sufficiently in order to satisfy the parole board that they no longer pose such

DOI: 10.4324/9780429262074-10

a risk to the public that they warrant further detention. The most recent UK government proven reconviction rate for those who commit violent offences (against the person) was 25.8% (for the period April 2018 to March 2019), indicating that although efforts are made to address risk areas and strengthen the factors that will help them to desist, this may not always be effective. For the same period, the reconviction rate for those who committed sexual offences was 12.7%. Although reconviction rates (according to the Risk Matrix 2000) for those convicted of sexual offences is low, ranging between 0.6% and 7.2% at the two-year follow-up and 0.7% and 9.0% at the four-year follow-up (Barnett, Wakeling & Howard, 2010), there is still much scrutiny around the provision of risk reduction strategies for this population. This focus has been even more pertinent since the publication of research exploring the effectiveness of the Core Sex Offender Treatment Programme (SOTP), the main offending behaviour approach for those convicted of sexual offences (Mews, Di Bella & Purver, 2017). This study indicated that 10% of those who had completed the Core SOTP were reconvicted or cautioned for a further sexual offence, compared to 8% of those in the comparison group. The publication of this research coincided with the development of a revised suite of accredited offending behaviour programmes within HMPPS which has adopted a broader biopsychosocial model of change, as well as drawing on influences from what is termed the 'third wave' within its therapeutic approach (Walton, Ramsey, Cunningham & Henfrey, 2017).

Although most current approaches delivered within HMPPS still have their foundations in a second wave approach (largely a cognitive behavioural therapy [CBT] approach), there is a growing empirical support, and therefore appetite, to incorporate approaches from the 'third and fourth wave approach', which centre on acceptance and developing awareness of the present moment (Shonin, Van Gordon, Slade & Griffiths, 2013) and advocating a non-judgemental approach to one's thoughts, feelings and behaviours (Bayles, Blossom & Apsche, 2014). This chapter will focus on mindfulness, one type of intervention amongst the 'third and fourth wave approach' (Hayes, Follette & Linehan, 2004), and focus on how it can be applied to the adult male population with convictions for sexual and/ or violent offences. Although the use of mindfulness in forensic settings is relatively recent, the chapter proposes that it may be helpful in a number of ways. Firstly, it may help individuals bring into their awareness the processes involved in the onset of negative mood states. There is a well-established link between negative mood states and offence-related behaviour (Looman, 1995; McKibben, Proulx & Lusignan, 1994; Pithers, Marques, Gibatt & Marlatt, 1983). Secondly, the use of mindfulness techniques may aid individuals in tolerating and accepting thoughts, feelings and physiological sensations which might act as triggers, for example, to offence-related sexual behaviours or aggressive behaviours. Thirdly, mindfulness techniques may help individuals develop insight and to 'accept', for example, their personal offence-related sexual thoughts and feelings, which can increase the potential for acting out, or indeed the role of violent or sexual ideation, which can precipitate some offending behaviour. This could be achieved through, amongst other ways, mindful observation of thoughts and thought defusion techniques to reduce offence-related sexual arousal (Singh et al., 2010; Worling, 2012).

What is mindfulness?

Although the use of mindfulness is relatively new in Western cultures, it has been used in Eastern cultures for hundreds of years, in particular within the Buddhist faith. Mindfulness involves 'paying attention in a particular way: on purpose, in the present moment and non-judgementally' (Kabat-Zinn, 1994, p. 4). The emphasis is on seeing things as they are without trying to change them and accepting them with curiosity and in a non-judgemental way. A primary method of bringing about mindfulness is through different forms of meditation, essentially sitting quietly and observing one's experiences, not creating or modifying them (Eberth & Sedlmeier, 2012). Baer (2003) proposes that such meditation can be used to attend to internal experiences, such as bodily sensations, thoughts and emotions, or external aspects of the environment, such as sights and sounds (Kabat-Zinn, 1994; Linehan, 1993a).

Over the past 30 years, mindfulness training has been incorporated into hospital clinics and community settings offering pain management and stress reduction programmes (Melbourne Academic Mindfulness Interest Group, 2006). It is also a central component of dialectical behaviour therapy (DBT) (Linehan, 1993b) and of acceptance and commitment therapy (ACT) (Hayes, Strosahl & Wilson, 1999; Hayes et al., 2004). Howells, Tennant, Day and Elmer (2010) propose that the goal of these interventions differs from second wave approaches in that there is a move away from assisting individuals to control and change particular thoughts or emotions to that of encouraging them to observe and accept them. The aim of mindfulness is therefore to change the attentional and cognitive processes, rather than the content of the thoughts themselves (Orsillo, Roemer, Lerner & Tull, 2004). In achieving this, the individual is less emotion driven and has greater choice about whether to act upon their thoughts, feelings and physiological sensations (Chambers, Gullone & Allen, 2009). Such approaches may complement CBT in a number of ways. Firstly, when the individual is tempted to react quickly to consciously intervene or change a thought or behaviour (Fehrer, 2002); secondly when a physiological sensation, emotional response or thought about something is so strong that it leads to sense of a loss of control over behaviour (Goleman, 1995); and thirdly, when the individual lacks the self-reflective capacity to apply the intervention that they have been undertaking (Wright, Day & Howells, 2009).

A number of models of mindfulness have been proposed (see Bishop et al., 2004; Hölzel et al., 2011a), and what is common to all models of mindfulness is the concept of acceptance. Follette, Palm and Hall (2004) suggest that acceptance has three processes:

1   observation of psychological events
2   letting go of the desire to alter these events
3   differentiating actual events from the psychological experiences that are evoked by outside events.

In this way, acceptance is thought to facilitate the process of defusion, whereby the individual separates oneself from one's thoughts (Orsillo et al., 2004). It is important to note that acceptance is not about viewing a situation in a positive way. Rather, mindfulness is about simply noticing the present moment, without judgement of whether that moment is positive or negative. This chapter will now consider how mindfulness might be beneficial for individuals with sexual and/or violent convictions who may or may not have a diagnosable mental health condition.

How does mindfulness work?

For some, being 'mindful' can happen naturally; however, for others it requires training in order for these states to be frequent and sustained (Howells et al., 2010). There is general agreement that practice is essential to see the benefits of mindfulness, and most mindfulness-based programmes require participants to practice regularly, i.e. most days (Kabat-Zinn et al., 1992; Teasdale et al., 2000). If practiced regularly, it is thought to bring with it a number of benefits. Several studies have shown that mindfulness has a measurable impact on brain functioning, specifically that mindfulness can alter levels of neural activity in the pre-frontal cortex and the amygdala (Chiesa & Serretti, 2010; Davidson et al., 2003). Singh et al. (2007a) point out that how mindfulness relates to changes in behaviour is still an empirical question.

Mindfulness is also thought to bring with it physical benefits. For example, through the use of slow, deep, rhythmic breathing, these techniques can affect heart rate variability (HRV), specifically the magnitude of fluctuations in the interval between successive beats of the heart (Thayer & Brosschot, 2005). In turn, this may be activating a type of autonomic nervous system response, which Porges calls the ventral vagal social engagement system. Polyvagal theory (Porges, 1995) is a model which relates autonomic function to social, emotional and communication behaviours (Porges, 2007). It proposes that where the development of the vagal system in early life is in some way disrupted, neural regulation of physiological states is compromised, potentially resulting in difficulties with self-soothing (Porges & Furman, 2011). Changes in heart rate caused by mindful breathing patterns may improve vagal functioning and, in turn, bring a variety of benefits, including good emotional control and a strong physiological ability to recover from stressors (Johnsen et al., 2003; Dishman et al., 2000); psychological, cognitive and emotional flexibility; greater socio-affective competence; and improved emotional regulation (Gillespie, Mitchell, Fisher & Beech, 2012). These effects allow the individual to achieve greater acceptance of threatening thoughts, more resilient coping, reduced emotional reactivity and increased self-compassion. This in turn is thought to lead to a greater sense of happiness, optimism and connectedness to others. Gillespie et al. (2012) therefore argue that by practicing such controlled breathing techniques and increasing pre-frontal control over the amygdala, this could lead to improved emotional control and self-regulation. Within this chapter, I will discuss more on the physiological changes arising from practicing mindfulness and the potential for this to help a person when they struggle to regulate their urges to act aggressively or violently or in a sexually harmful manner.

The application of mindfulness in clinical and forensic settings

Mindfulness practice is widely accepted, and there is growing empirical support for the benefits of mindfulness-based approaches to assist with a variety of psychological issues within clinical and forensic psychiatric hospital settings. For example, higher levels of mindfulness have been related to more positive affect, life satisfaction, self-esteem and optimism and less negative affect and rumination (Brown & Ryan, 2003; Schroevers & Brandsma, 2010; Collard, Avny & Boniwell, 2008). It has also been found to positively influence physical health, including reduced blood pressure and cortisol levels (Carlson, Speca, Faris & Patel, 2007), reducing stress, anxiety and depression (see Segal, Williams & Teasdale., 2002; Dimidjian, Kleiber & Segal, 2010) and ruminative thinking (Chambers, Chuen Yee Lo & Allen, 2008; Ramel, Goldin, Carmona & McQuaid, 2004).

Mindfulness-based cognitive therapy (MBCT) has been identified as an effective intervention for recurrent depression by the National Institute of Clinical Excellence (NICE) in the UK (Kuyken et al., 2008). MBCT may have particular benefits for those who have experienced major depressive episodes because such patients are especially prone to engage in ruminative thinking (Teasdale, Segal & Williams, 2003). Through the practice of mindfulness exercises, such as the body scan, simple yoga-based movement exercises and prolonged periods of sitting meditation, patients learn to be more accepting of intense bodily sensations and emotional discomfort. Being able to be with and accept one's internal experiences slows down internal processes, providing greater cognitive capacity to notice unhelpful patterns of thinking, which perhaps perpetuate poor mental well-being, such as depression-related rumination. Mindfulness-based practice also helps a person emotionally uncouple themselves from the content of negative thoughts, enabling them to disengage from these thoughts and redirect their attention (Piet & Hougaard, 2011). Whilst the content of the thought may be different from those in people with chronic depression, the underlying psychological processes of rumination, being overwhelmed by intense physiological sensations and strong emotions, are comparable for those who have committed violent and/or sexual offences. In principle, therefore, mindfulness or MBCT may help ameliorate some of these cognitive and emotional patterns that are associated with risk of offending (Day, 2009).

Research demonstrating the effectiveness of mindfulness-based approaches in prison settings is less prevalent and more limited than that which exists in relation to wider clinical populations. Mindfulness-based programmes have shown promise in relation to working with a variety of mental health needs found in correctional populations, including decreasing the avoidance of negative emotional states and improving self-regulation (Dafoe & Stermac, 2013). Mindfulness has been used successfully for a number of years in prisons internationally, and various studies emerging from the North American prison system suggest mindfulness can help prisoners develop greater emotional intelligence and self-regulation abilities (Upaya Institute & Zen Centre, 2010). Self-report studies have also shown that prisoners who participate in meditation programmes report less alcohol and drug use, reduced psychiatric symptoms and increased feelings of optimism (Bowen et al., 2006). Mindfulness is also a core component of DBT, which has been used in prisons and forensic psychiatric hospitals treating undercontrolled conditions, such as borderline and antisocial personality disorder (Bohus et al., 2000; Howells et al., 2010; Wix, 2003). A systematic review by Shonin et al. (2013) concluded that participating in mindfulness and Buddhist-derived interventions (BDIs) in prison settings led to significant improvements across key criminogenic variables. Auty, Cope and Liebling (2017) indicated a small increase in the psychological well-being of participants who participated in yoga or meditation programmes in prison, as well as a small improvement in their behavioural functioning (with a larger effect size demonstrated for the former compared to the latter). A narrative literature review by Himelstein (2011) similarly identified therapeutic benefits from meditation-based interventions in prison settings.

Theoretically, mindfulness-based interventions appear to address a number of factors associated with increased risk of violent and/or sexual offending. Early adopters of specific mindfulness-based interventions in forensic settings have provided some empirical evidence to suggest that it may be a useful intervention. However, efficacy studies which are tightly controlled are lacking, and group-based effectiveness studies evaluating mindfulness-based programmes suffer from major methodological weaknesses (Shonin et al., 2013). Howells (2010) proposes that the most positive outcome studies are small-scale, controlled, single-case studies (review by Singh, Lancioni, Wahler, Winton & Singh, 2008a), and those that are larger lack rigorous control groups. Based on expert opinion papers, systematic reviews and empirical research, it can be concluded that mindfulness-based interventions have been tried, with some success, in a range of forensic contexts. MBCT is recommended in NICE guidelines as a suitable intervention for mental health conditions which are widespread amongst the prison population. It seems viable to conclude that mindfulness may be a useful intervention for people with a violent and/or sexual conviction, with an expectation that it would enhance well-being and may address some attentional and cognitive biases, as well as emotional processing factors associated with an elevated risk of re-offending.

The application of mindfulness with violent offending

Understanding first what factors elevate the potential for someone to display violent behaviour is critical in being able to understand how mindfulness might play a role in mitigating this risk. Walton et al. (2017) outline the key criminogenic factors for violent behaviour that might respond to mindfulness techniques. These include attitudes supportive of violence (Douglas, Hart, Webster & Belfrage, 2013), grievance and anger, as well as a tendency to ruminate in a hostile way (Mann et al., 2010), impulsivity (Hanson & Morton-Bourgon, 2004) and poor emotional control (Norlander & Eckhardt, 2005). In particular, difficulties in emotional functioning appear to be a key area of need for those who have committed violent offences (Gillespie, Garofalo & Velotti, 2018; Garofalo, Gillespie & Velotti, 2019).

Based on this understanding of what factors play a role in the commission of violence, there are differing views about the associated mechanisms underlying the use of mindfulness to reduce aggression. Howells et al. (2010) argue that mindfulness could have the potential to address a number of psychological processes and states that are relevant to risk of recidivism. Firstly, negative affective states (Day, 2009), secondly self-control breakdown leading to impulsivity (Farrington, 2000) and thirdly anger (Novaco, 2007). Mindfulness may help to reduce aggression through increasing self-control (Barnes, Brown, Kruusemark, Campbell & Rogge, 2007) or through inducing selflessness, a connection with others and developing compassion (Heppner et al., 2008). Mindfulness may also promote better cognitive functioning and flexibility or decrease the use of behaviour which is more automatic (habitual) and impulsive. Alternatively, it may improve mood and self-regulation or induce relaxation (Gillespie, 2015; Borders, Earleywine & Jajodia, 2010).

Emotion regulation, in particular, as a mechanism by which mindful meditation might be effective has received support by others (Baer, 2003; Bishop et al., 2004; Dafoe & Stermac, 2013; Tangney, Dobbins, Stuewig & Schrader, 2017; Garofalo et al., 2019). This could be through, for example, reducing feelings of anger, improving control over aggressive urges or perhaps increasing acceptance around situations that trigger aggression (Garofalo, Velotti & Zavattini, 2018). A number of authors have proposed that mindfulness interventions which specifically reduce rumination may also improve emotion regulation linked with increased risk of aggression (Auty et al., 2017; Borders et al., 2010). Rumination can exacerbate angry mood and increase hostility, and when confronted by a perceived threat, can lead to a stronger physiological reaction, culminating in aggression. Logically, then, mindfulness may help to stop or prevent the activation of hostile thoughts and feelings by keeping a person grounded in the present moment, thus preventing ruminative thinking. The use of mindfulness to reduce such aggression has been examined in a number of studies with both forensic and non-forensic populations (see Zarling, Lawrence & Marchman, 2015; Singh et al., 2003; Singh et al., 2007a, 2007b, 2008b).

Although these findings may tentatively direct us to the ways in which mindfulness practice might help to reduce aggressive tendencies, a more significant issue is that the research only demonstrates a link between the use of mindfulness and decreased rumination, rather than showing *how* this reduces violent behaviour. Our understanding of this issue can be furthered by considering research which explores the neurological and physiological impact of practicing mindfulness. Reviews of neuroimaging research have revealed significantly reduced structure and function in pre-frontal regions of the brain in anti-social individuals (e.g. Yang & Raine, 2009). Similarly, areas associated with aggression, particularly impulsive acts, are located in the pre-frontal context (Bassarath, 2001), and in a review of the literature on the neural mechanisms of emotion regulation, Davidson, Putman and Larson (2000) concluded that impulsive aggression and violence arise as a consequence of dysfunction in neural circuits involving the pre-frontal cortex, amygdala and anterior cingulate cortex. As mentioned earlier, a number of studies have shown that mindfulness can alter levels of activity in the pre-frontal cortex and limbic structures of the brain, which are involved in emotion such as the amygdala (e.g. Chiesa & Serretti, 2010; Hölzel et al., 2011b).

Gillespie (2015) explains that the neural circuits activated during mindfulness may be similar to those activated when using the cognitive reappraisal strategy for emotion regulation and that there may therefore be considerable overlap in the regions of the brain underlying both emotion regulation and mindfulness meditation. Morley (2018) also explains that meditation has been shown to increase grey matter in the brain regions associated with self-regulation and emotional control (Luders, Toga, Lepore & Gaser, 2009). In addition, it is thought to lead to greater connectivity in something called the default mode network (DMN) (Jang et al., 2011), an important brain network associated with self-awareness (Andrews-Hanna, Reidler, Sepulcre, Poulin & Buckner, 2010), self-concept (Gusnard, Akbudak, Shulman & Raichle, 2001) and emotional processing (Maddock, Garrett & Buonocore, 2003). Morley (2018) hypothesises that perhaps meditation increases the neurological capacity to self-regulate, promotes greater self-awareness, helps process emotions more effectively and reduces impulsive behaviour.

In summary, further research is needed into the benefits of mindfulness for people who have a violent conviction. Whilst the intention in delivering mindfulness is to reduce risk and enhance well-being, mindfulness may also have a 'dark side' (Tangney et al., 2017). Tangney et al. (2017) demonstrated a relationship between greater levels of mindfulness, specifically in relation to a 'non-judgement stance to self, and greater levels of criminogenic cognitions'. In other words, the more participants were skilled at lowering self-criticism, the stronger their thoughts were that supported offending. Tangney et al. proposed that individuals may therefore need some level of self-criticism against one's own thoughts and actions to help promote desistance from offending. They highlighted the implications for mindfulness-based treatments within the criminal justice system and that these could actually increase the risk of recidivism rather than reduce it. Garofalo et al. (2019) dispute this finding, and as well as discussing the conceptual and methodological limitations of the study, also emphasise the adaptive benefits of adopting a non-judgemental stance as opposed to those which might promote criminal or anti-social behaviour. In a conceptual replication of the Tangney et al. (2017) study, they examined the mindfulness facets separately to provide a more nuanced explanation of the relationship between mindfulness, emotion regulation and aggression. They demonstrated an association between impairments in mindfulness and emotion regulation and aggressive tendencies, and therefore support the suggestion that mindfulness-based treatments, and those that aim to develop emotion regulation, may help to protect against aggression. It is clear, however, that given inconsistency in some findings, it cannot be concluded definitively that the use of mindfulness-based interventions that aim to enhance emotion regulation will necessarily reduce someone's risk of committing a violent offence. Indeed, it may be iatrogenic if the outcome of the intervention is primarily about risk reduction.

The application of mindfulness to sexual offending

Howells (2010) suggested that mindfulness may provide an alternative therapeutic intervention to traditional cognitive behavioural interventions for those who commit sexual offences, and he argues that advances in forensic practice should include the introduction of mindfulness techniques. As has been outlined already in this chapter, mindfulness may impact on a number of criminogenic areas; this in turn may help to reduce the risk of committing a sexual offence. In a study exploring the effectiveness of a four-session mindfulness-based intervention for men who have committed a sexual offence, Byrne, Bogue, Ega and Lonergan (2016) concluded the intervention was effective in decreasing the characteristics of alexithymia (the inability to identify and describe emotions in the self) and increasing psychological mindedness. Whilst the study showed improvement in labelling emotions, unsurprisingly, this very brief intervention did not reveal any significant changes in emotion regulation skills, and there was no follow-up period to see if the gains were retained after treatment.

A small number of additional studies have concluded that mindfulness shows promise as an intervention for sexual-related matters. For example, Murray (2005) examined the efficacy of an eight-week mindfulness meditation pro-gramme in reducing the use of sex as a coping strategy in college males and adjudicated men convicted of sexual offences. The treated group showed a significant increase in their belief that they could tolerate negative emotion compared to the control group, and the treatment group also showed a signifi-cant decrease in avoidant coping compared to the control group. However, this attitudinal expression of wanting to do something different did not translate into approach coping, and use of sex in times of distress did not differ signifi-cantly from the control group. In a later study, Dafoe (2011) explored the use of mindfulness meditation with ten prisoners convicted of a sexual offence at a correctional institution in Ontario. Participants engaged in a one-off, ten-minute session of mindfulness meditation, and although most reported that this was a positive experience, a number noted negative experiences when they undertook the mindfulness meditation such as anxiety or troublesome previous memories and that this affected their ability to concentrate and relax. It was concluded that for some, meditation may actually increase the prevalence of negative thoughts or emotions, suggesting that careful consideration would be needed when applying the use of mindfulness within a treatment approach for those with sexual convictions. Singh et al. (2010) explored the effectiveness of various self-regulation techniques with three adult men with sexual convictions with intellectual disabilities and showed tentatively that mindful observation of thoughts can reduce offence-related sexual arousal. Singh et al. (2010) found that participants were the least successful in managing offence-related sexual arousal when they used their own self-control techniques, slightly more effective when using 'meditation on the soles of the feet' and most effective with 'mind-ful observation of thoughts', with all three participants reporting a reduction in deviant sexual arousal as a result of using mindful observation of thoughts. This involved learning techniques to enable participants to disengage from their thoughts by drawing on a number of mindfulness techniques, including focusing on their breath, observing their thoughts and picturing their thoughts as clouds passing through their awareness. The aim of these techniques was to accept and defuse the thoughts without attempting to push them away. Worling (2012) proposes that mindfulness-based cognitive therapy could be particularly useful if incorporated into treatment for individuals who have very intense and enduring offence-related sexual interests, as it may help such individuals learn to notice their offence-related sexual thoughts or urges without judgment or evaluation and to monitor their thoughts, feelings and bodily responses without acting on them. In this way, offence-related sexual arousal is neither acted upon nor suppressed. Rather, it is simply noticed by the individual and experienced until it eventually subsides. As with the majority of studies exploring the effectiveness of mindfulness outlined in this chapter, there were a number of methodological limitations to this study, such as a small sample size, no comparison group and no follow-up assessments. Finally, mindfulness-based procedures warrant further consideration when planning treatment for those who have committed sexual offences; however, it is unlikely to be a standalone intervention. Rather, mindfulness is likely to be part of a larger intervention which aims to not only increase insight but develop skills to help the person do something different. Trauma-sensitive mindfulness may also be more appropriate, given the high levels of post-traumatic stress disorder (PTSD) and complex trauma noted amongst people sexual convictions.

The use of mindfulness within UK-accredited offending behaviour programmes

Within the Healthy Sex Programme (HSP), and within the wider suite of HMPPS-accredited interventions, the use of mindfulness techniques is termed 'Here and Now'. 'Here and Now' is taught through mindful breathing or more simple observation, as well as using mindfulness techniques to help individuals with the acceptance of aggressive, distressing or other risky thoughts and feelings. Whilst HSP and other HMPPS interventions are yet to be evaluated through outcome studies, anecdotal evidence from the providers of these programmes highlights some experiences of incorporating mindfulness meditation in the treatment intervention. Facilitators have reported that the use of 'Here and Now' has assisted participants to **engage more effectively in the session**:

> We had a group member walk out of a session. After giving the individual time to cool down I went to see him . . . where he was struggling to concentrate. . . . I noticed that he was unable to follow our conversation. I asked him to sit down on a chair and be aware of his breathing, taking big slow breathes in and out.

Once this was complete we had a conversation which flowed a lot better and he was able to repeat what was being said, enabling me to check his understanding.

Facilitators have also explained how Here and Now can **help participants with general emotion regulation**:

I encouraged him to work towards his positive goal in the practise of reducing his non-sexual arousal level and being able to focus on the 'here and now'. . . . He was able to verbalise that he was thinking about his heart rate, the breaths moving from his chest to his mouth and the feeling of his body on the floor

as well as the more complex issue of **managing high emotional or physical arousal**:

I supported a resident (convicted of sexual offences) who presented with persistent emotional difficulties. . . . He'd regularly attend sessions finding his emotions difficult to manage. . . . He agreed to engage in 'here and now' practice, rating his levels of emotions before and after each practice. . . . The individual reported that his emotions were reduced and he felt able to accept his feelings more readily, noting that 'everyone has bad days'

and **letting go of unhelpful thoughts**:

They describe the benefits of imagining a peaceful setting and genuine pleasure from letting go of their unhelpful thoughts. They've reflected on achieving a sense of composure and acceptance of their thoughts, an acknowledgement of being more than just their thoughts and for the short-term at least being at peace.

The anecdotal information from facilitators also indicates how **different approaches might be needed for different people**:

I guess in my experience from delivering here and now exercises for the last 10 years the primary violent offenders prefer the physical 'here and now' exercises, whereas primary sexual offenders with higher than average IQ prefer the mental focus of leaves on a stream.

as well as an interesting insight into the challenges of introducing mindfulness practice into forensic settings, in particular the **environmental factors that could be critical in ensuring the success of teaching 'here and now'**:

To be honest I didn't see a massive difference in the guys and I think that had mostly to do with the environment there. It's basically a category B remand prison, so as you can understand it wasn't the best. However, a couple of the guys that were quite into Mindfulness did say that the appreciation list was a wakeup call but it's something they would forget completely once released.

This anecdotal evaluation of the Here and Now skills suggests that, for some, mindfulness-based practice may be a useful distress tolerance or crisis management skill, permitting the person to downregulate sufficiently to engage in conversations and be more compassionate to themselves and others. However, capacity to engage in self-initiated use of these skills, whether in the moment or outside of the treatment room, seems to be difficult for some of the people learning the Here and Now skill. Repetitive practice (both during and following the completion of the HSP) is integral to maximising the benefits of mindfulness and engendering sustained behavioural change. A more systematic evaluation of the Here and Now skill is needed, and clearly a follow-up period post-treatment will be essential to see if the skills taught in the programme are being generalised into everyday living.

Conclusion

The evidence presented in this chapter would suggest that the incorporation of mindfulness methods into existing treatment approaches shows emerging prom-ise and could be beneficial for some people who have committed sexual and/or violent offences. It is recommended, however, that caution is exercised, given the possible adverse effects of mindfulness. Mindfulness is not for everyone, and for some may elevate risk-related issues, e.g. negative thoughts and emotional arousal. Care is also needed in considering who might benefit from a mindfulness-based intervention, given the heterogeneity within offence groups and the high levels of trauma noted with forensic populations. Where mindfulness has been used with people who commit violent and/or sexual offences, in many cases, it is one technique taught as part of a wider treatment approach, which is often still CBT in nature. This makes it very difficult to evaluate outcomes specifically related to mindfulness, and subsequently there is a lack of sound empirical support for its use. Existing studies suffer from a range of methodological problems, such as a lack of an adequate control group or non-randomisation of research conditions, small and/or unrepresentative samples, differing and inadequate outcome measures or appropriate measures of mindfulness, including those that rely on self-report or that are not valid for forensic settings (Gillespie, 2015; Howells et al., 2010), short follow-up periods and a lack of control of confounding factors. They also use a broad range of mindfulness-based interventions, which are not comparable in length or content. The effect sizes across studies ranges from small to large, with the most methodologically robust (i.e. using a randomised control trial) showing the smallest effect sizes, as might be expected. In addition, the research does not conclusively demonstrate that increased levels of mindfulness mediate the positive outcomes demonstrated, as opposed to other uncontrolled factors. A further challenge that is likely to be faced within criminal justice settings is how to embed the use of such approaches within the wider system, given the cultural underpinnings (i.e. Eastern philosophies) of mindfulness and its foundations in a deeper and more sophisticated philosophical, spiritual and psychological system (Brazier, 2003; Rosch, 2007).

The mechanisms by which mindfulness techniques might be useful for a forensic population are not yet fully understood; therefore, further research is needed to theorise the mechanisms which bring about the changes observed, as well as to establish more clearly what the benefits of mindfulness are. There is an emerging collection of studies which indicate a variety of benefits, including those that relate to general well-being, those that could lead to improved custodial behaviour and, if able to impact on the criminogenic factors known to be associated with sexual and violent offending, those that might reduce the risk of violent or sexual recidivism. Whilst it is highly unlikely that mindfulness on its own will impact significantly on recidivism rates, it is important, as with any forensic intervention, that any evaluation consider the outcome of reducing harm to others, as well as improved emotional well-being for the person with a conviction.

References

Andrews, D. A., & Bonta, J. (2010). *The psychology of criminal conduct*. Routledge.

Andrews-Hanna, J. R., Reidler, J. S., Sepulcre, J., Poulin, R., & Buckner, R. L. (2010). Functional-anatomic fractionation of the brain's default network. *Neuron, 65*(4), 550–562.

Auty, K. M., Cope, A., & Liebling, Al. (2017). A systematic review and meta-analysis of yoga and mindfulness meditation in prison: Effects on psychological well-being and behavioural functioning. *International Journal of Offender Therapy and Comparative Criminology, 61*(6), 689–710.

Baer, R. A. (2003). Mindfulness training as a clinical intervention: A conceptual and empirical review. *Clinical Psychology: Science and Practice, 10*(2), 125–143.

Barnes, S., Brown, K. W., Kruusemark, E., Campbell, W. K., & Rogge, R. D. (2007). The role of mindfulness in romantic relationship satisfaction and responses to relationship stress. *Journal of Marital Family Therapy, 33*, 483–500.

Barnett, G. D., Wakeling, H. C., & Howard, P. D. (2010, October). An examination of the predictive validity of the Risk Matrix 2000 in England and Wales. *Sexual Abuse: A Journal of Research and Treatment*, 1–28.

Bassarath, L. (2001). Neuroimaging studies of antisocial behaviour. *Canadian Journal of Psychiatry, 46*(8), 728–732.

Bayles, C., Blossom, P., & Apsche, J. (2014). A brief review and update of mode deactivation therapy. *International Journal of Behavioural Consultation and Therapy, 9*(1), 46–48.

Bishop, S. R., Lau, M., Shapiro, S., Carlson, L., Anderson, N. D., Carmody, J., & Devins, G. (2004). Mindfulness: A proposed operational definition. *Clinical Psychology: Science and Practice, 11*(3), 230–241.

Bohus, M., Haaf, B., Stiglmayr, C., Pohl, U., Böhme, R., & Linehan, M. (2000). Evaluation of inpatient dialectical-behavioral therapy for borderline personality disorder: A prospective study. *Behaviour Research and Therapy*, *38*(9), 875–887.

Borders, A., Earleywine, M., & Jajodia, A. (2010). Could mindfulness decrease anger, hostility, and aggression by decreasing rumination? *Aggressive Behavior*, *36*, 28–44.

Bowen, S., Witkiewitz, K., Dillworth, T. M., Chawla, N., Simpson, T. L., Ostafin, B. D., et al. (2006). Mindfulness meditation and substance use in an incarcerated population. *Psychology of Addictive Behaviors*, *20*(3), 343–347.

Brazier, C. (2003). *Buddhist psychology*. Constable and Robinson.

Brown, K. W., & Ryan, R. M. (2003). The benefits of being present: Mindfulness and its role in psychological well-being. *Journal of Personality and Social Psychology*, *84*, 822–848.

Byrne, G., Bogue, J., Ega, R., & Lonergan, E. (2016). Identifying and describing emotions: Measuring the effectiveness of a brief alexithmyia-specific, intervention for a sex offender population. *Sexual Abuse: A Journal of Research and Treatment*, *28*(7), 599–619.

Carlson, L. E., Speca, M., Faris, P., & Patel, K. D. (2007). One year pre-post intervention follow-up of psychological, immune, endocrine and blood pressure outcomes of mindfulness-based stress reduction (MBSR) in breast and prostate cancer outpatients. *Brain, Behavior, and Immunity*, *21*, 1038–1049.

Chambers, R., Chuen Yee Lo, B., & Allen, N. B. (2008). The impact of intensive mindfulness training on attentional control, cognitive style, and affect. *Cognitive Therapy and Research*, *32*, 303–322.

Chambers, R., Gullone, E., & Allen, N. B. (2009). Mindful emotion regulation: An integrative review. *Clinical Psychology Review*, *29*, 560–572.

Chiesa, A., & Serretti, A. (2010). A systematic review of neurobiological and clinical features of mindfulness meditations. *Psychological Medicine*, *40*, 1239–1252.

Collard, P., Avny, N., & Boniwell, I. (2008). Teaching Mindfulness Based Cognitive Therapy (MBCT) to students: The effects of MBCT on the levels of mindfulness and subjective well-being. *Counselling Psychology Quarterly*, *21*(4), 323–336.

Dafoe, T. (2011). *Mindfulness meditation: A new approach to working with sexual offenders*. Unpublished master's thesis. University of Toronto, America.

Dafoe, T., & Stermac, L. (2013). Mindfulness meditation as an adjunct approach to treatment within the correctional system. *Journal of Offender Rehabilitation*, *52*, 198–216.

Davidson, R. J., Kabat-Zinn, J., Schumacher, J., Rosenkranz, M., Muller, D., Santorelli, S., Urbanowski, F., Harrington, A., Bonus, K., & Sheridan, J. F. (2003). Alternations in brain and immune function produced by mindfulness meditation. *Psychosomatic Medicine*, *65*, 564–570.

Davidson, R. J., Putman, K. M., & Larson, C. L. (2000). Dysfunction in the neural circuitry of emotion regulation: A possible prelude to violence. *Science*, *289*, 591–594.

Day, A. (2009). Offender emotion and self-regulation: Implications for offender rehabilitation programming. *Psychology, Crime and Law, 15*, 119–130.

Dimidjian, S., Kleiber, B. V., & Segal, S. V. (2010). Mindfulness-based cognitive therapy. In N. Kazantzis, M. A. Reinecke, & A. Freeman (Eds.), *Cognitive behavioural theories in clinical practice* (pp. 307–331). Guilford.

Dishman, R. K., Nakamura, Y., Garcia, M. E., Thompson, R. W., Dunn, A. L., & Blair, S. N. (2000). Heart rate variability, trait anxiety, and perceived stress among physically fit men and women. *International Journal of Psychophysiology, 37*, 121–133.

Douglas, K. S., Hart, S. D., Webster, C. D., & Belfrage, H. (2013). *HCR-20v3: Assessing risk for violence: User guide*. Mental Health, Law, and Policy Institute, Simon Fraser University.

Eberth, J., & Sedlmeier, P. (2012). The effects of mindfulness meditation: A meta-analysis. *Mindfulness, 3*, 174–189.

Farrington, C. J. (2000). Individual differences and offending. In M. Tonry (Ed.), *The handbook fo crime and punishment* (pp. 241–268). Oxford University Press.

Fehrer, F. C. (2002). *The awareness response: A transpersonal approach to reducing maladaptive emotional reactivity*. Unpublished doctoral dissertation. Institute of Transpersonal Psychology, Palo Alto, CA.

Follette, V. M., Palm, K. M., & Hall, M. L. R. (2004). Acceptance, mindfulness, and trauma. In S. C. Hayes, V. M. Follette, & M. M. Linehan (Eds.), *Mindfulness and acceptance: Expanding the cognitive-behavioral tradition* (pp. 192–208). Guilford.

Garofalo, C., Gillespie, S. M., & Velotti, P. (2019). Emotion regulation mediates relationships between mindfulness facets and aggression dimensions. *Aggressive Behaviour*, 1–12.

Garofalo, C., Velotti, P., & Zavattini, G. C. (2018). Emotion regulation and aggression: The incremental contribution of alexithymia, impulsivity, and emotion dysregulation facets. *Psychology of Violence, 8*(4), 470–483.

Gillespie, S. M. (2015). Mindfulness meditation as a tool for increasing emotion regulation and reducing violence. *Prison Service Journal, 221*, 47–50.

Gillespie, S. M., Garofalo, C., & Velotti, P. (2018). Emotion regulation, mindfulness, and alexithymia: Specific or general impairments in sexual, violent, and homicide offenders? *Journal of Criminal Justice, 58*, 56–66.

Gillespie, S. M., Mitchell, I. J., Fisher, D., & Beech, A. R. (2012). Treating disturbed emotional regulation in sexual offenders: The potential applications of mindful self-regulation and controlled breathing techniques. *Aggression and Violent Behaviour, 17*, 333–343.

Goleman, D. (1995). *Emotional intelligence*. Bantam.

Gusnard, D. A., Akbudak, E., Shulman, G. L., & Raichle, M. E. (2001). Medial pre-frontal cortex and self-referential mental activity: Relation to a default mode of brain function. *Proceedings of the National Academy of the Sciences of the United States of America, 98*(7), 4259–4264.

Hanson, R. K., & Morton-Bourgon, K. E. (2004). *Predictors of sexual recidivism: An updated meta-analysis* (Corrections Research User Report No. 2004–02). Public Safety and Emergency Preparedness Canada.

Hayes, A. M., & Feldman, G. (2004). Clarifying the construct of mindfulness in the context of emotion regulation and the process of change in therapy. *Clinical Psychology: Science and Practice, 11*, 255–262.

Hayes, S. C., Follette, V. M., & Linehan, M. M. (2004). *Mindfulness and acceptance: Expanding the cognitive behavioural tradition.* Guildford Press.

Hayes, S. C., Strosahl, K. D., & Wilson, K. G. (1999). *Acceptance and commitment therapy: An experiential approach to behaviour chance.* New York: Guilford Press. In Harris, R. (2009). *ACT made simple: An easy to read primer on acceptance and commitment therapy.* New Harbinger Publications, Inc.

Heppner, W. L., Kernis, M. H., Lakey, C. E., Campbell, W. K., Goldman, B. M., Davis, P. J., & Cascio, E. V. (2008). Mindfulness as a means of reducing aggressive behaviour: Dispositional and situational evidence. *Aggressive Behaviour, 34*, 486–496.

Himelstein, S. (2011). Meditation research: The state of the art in correctional settings. *International Journal of Offender Therapy and Comparative Criminology, 55*(4), 646–661.

Hölzel, B. K., Carmody, J., Vangel, M., Congleton, C., Yerramsetti, S. M., Gard, T., & Lazar, S. W. (2011b). Mindfulness practices leads to increases in regional brain gray matter density. *Psychiatry Research, 191*(1), 36–43.

Hölzel, B. K., Lazar, S. W., Gard, T., Schuman-Olivier, Z., Vago, D. R., & Ott, U. (2011a). How does mindfulness meditation work? Proposing mechanisms of action from a conceptual and neural perspective. *Perspectives on Psychological Science, 6*(6), 537–559.

Howells, K. (2010). The "third wave" of cognitive-behavioural therapy and forensic practise. *Criminal Behaviour and Mental Health, 20*, 251–256.

Howells, K., Tennant, A., Day, A., & Elmer, R. (2010). Mindfulness in forensic mental health: Does it have a role? *Mindfulness, 1*, 4–9.

Jang, J. H., Jung, W. H., Kand, D. H., Byun, M. S., Kwon, S. J., Choi, C. H., & Kwon, J. S. (2011). Increased default mode network connectivity associated with meditation. *Neuroscience Letters, 487*(3), 358–362.

Johnsen, B. H., Thayer, J. F., Laberg, J. C., Wormnes, B., Raadal, M., Skaret, E., et al. (2003). Attentional and physiological characteristics of patients with dental anxiety. *Journal of Anxiety Disorders, 17*, 75–87.

Kabat-Zinn, J. (1994). *Wherever you go, there you are: Mindfulness meditation in everyday life.* Hyperion.

Kabat-Zinn, J., Massion, M. D., Kristeller, J., Peterson, L. G., Fletcher, K. E., Pbert, L., et al. (1992). Effectiveness of a meditation-based stress reduction program in the treatment of anxiety disorders. *American Journal of Psychiatry, 149*, 936–943.

Kuyken, W., Byfors, S., Taylor, R. S., Watkins, E., Holden, E., White, K., Barrett, B., Byng, R., Evans, A., Mullan, E., & Teasdale, J. D. (2008). Mindfulness-based cognitive therapy to prevent relapse in recurrent depression. *Journal of Consulting and Clinical Psychology, 76*, 966–978.

Linehan, M. M. (1993a). *Skills training manual for treating borderline personality disorder.* Guildford Press.

Linehan, M. M. (1993b). *Cognitive-behavioural treatment of borderline personality disorder.* Guilford Press.

Looman, J. (1995). Sexual fantasies of child molesters. *Canadian Journal of Behavioral Science, 27*(3), 321–332.

Luders, E., Toga, A. W., Lepore, N., & Gaser, C. (2009). The underlying anatomical correlates of long-term meditation: Larger hippocampul and frontal volumes of gray matter. *NeuroImage, 45*(3), 672–678.

Maddock, R. J., Garrett, A. S., & Buonocore, M. H. (2003). Posterior cingulate cortex activation by emotional words: fMRI evidence from a valence decision task. *Human Brain Mapping, 18*(1), 30–41.

Mann, R. E., Hanson, R. K., & Thornton, D. (2010). Assessing risk for sexual recidivism: Some proposals on the nature of psychologically meaningful risk factors. *Sexual Abuse: A Journal of Research and Treatment, 22*(2), 191–217.

McKibben, A., Proulx, J., & Lusignan, R. (1994). Relationships between conflict, affect and deviant sexual behaviors in rapists and paedophiles. *Behavior Research and Therapy, 32*, 571–575.

Melbourne Academic Mindfulness Interest Group. (2006). Mindfulness-based psychotherapies: A review of conceptual foundations, empirical evidence and practical considerations. *Australian and New Zealand Journal of Psychiatry, 40*, 285–294.

Mews, A., Di Bella, L., & Purver. (2017). *Impact evaluation of the prison-based Core Sex Offender Treatment Programme.* Ministry of Justice Analytical Series.

Morley, R. H. (2018). The impact of mindfulness meditation and self-compassion on criminal impulsivity in a prisoner sample. *Journal of Policy and Criminal Psychology, 33*(2), 118–122.

Murray, R. L. (2005). The efficacy of a mindfulness-based intervention in a decreasing the avoidant coping strategies of sex offenders and college males. *Dissertation Abstracts International: Section B: The Sciences and Engineering, 65*(10), 5414.

Norlander, B., & Eckhardt, C. (2005). Anger, hostility, and male perpetrators of intimate partner violence: A meta-analytic review. *Clinical Psychology Review, 25*, 119–152.

Novaco, R. W. (2007). Anger dysregulation. In T. A. Cavell & K. T. Malcolm (Eds.), *Anger, aggression and interventions for interpersonal violence* (pp. 3–54). Erlbaum.

Orsillo, S. M., Roemer, L., Lerner, J. B., & Tull, M. T. (2004). Acceptance, mindfulness and cognitive-behavioural therapy: Comparisons, contrasts and application to anxiety. In S.C.

Piet, J., & Hougaard, E. (2011). *The effect of mindfulness-based cognitive therapy for prevention of relapse in recurrent major depressive disorder: A systematic review and meta-analysis.*

Pithers, W. D., Marques, J. K., Gibat, C. C., & Marlatt, G. A. (1983). Relapse prevention: A self-control model of treatment and maintenance of change for sexual aggressives. In J. Greer & I. R. Stuart (Eds.), *The sexual aggressor: Current perspective on treatment.* Van Nostrand Reinhold.

Porges, S. W. (1995). Orienting in a defensive world: Mammalian modifications of our evolutionary heritage: A Polyvagal theory. *Psychophysiology, 32,* 301–318.

Porges, S. W. (2007). The Polyvagal perspective. *Biological Psychology, 74*(2), 116–143.

Porges, S. W., & Furman, S. A. (2011). The early development of the autonomic nervous system provides a neural platform for social behaviour: A Polyvagal perspective. *Infant Child Development, 20*(1), 106–118.

Ramel, W., Goldin, P. R., Carmona, P. E., & McQuaid, J. R. (2004). The effects of mindfulness meditation on cognitive processes and affect in patients with past depression. *Cognitive Therapy and Research, 28*(4), 433–455.

Rosch, E. (2007). More than mindfulness: When you have a tiger by the tail, let it eat you. *Psychological Inquiry, 18,* 258–264.

Schroevers, M. J., & Brandsma, R. (2010). Is learning mindfulness associated with improved affect after mindfulness-based cognitive therapy? *British Journal of Psychology, 101,* 95–107.

Segal, Z. V., Williams, J. M. G., & Teasdale, J. (2002). *Mindfulness-based cognitive therapy for depression: A new approach to preventing relapse.* Guilford.

Shonin, E., Van Gordon, W., Slade, K., & Griffiths, M. D. (2013). Mindfulness and other Buddhist-derived interventions in correctional settings: A systematic review. *Aggression and Violent Behaviour, 18*(3), 365–372.

Singh, N. N., Lancioni, G. E., Wahler, R. G., Winton, A. S. W., & Singh, J. (2008a). Mindfulness approaches in cognitive behavioural therapy. *Behavioural and Cognitive Psychotherapy, 36,* 1–8.

Singh, N. N., Lancioni, G. E., Winton, A. S. W., Adkins, A. D., Singh, J., & Singh, A. N. (2007b). Mindfulness training assists individuals with moderate mental retardation to maintain their community placements. *Behavior Modification, 31,* 800–814.

Singh, N. N., Lancioni, G. E., Winton, A. S. W., Adkins, A. D., Wahler, R. G., Sabaawi, M., et al. (2007a). Individuals with mental illness can control their aggressive behaviour through mindfulness training. *Behavior Modification, 31*(3), 313–328.

Singh, N. N., Lancioni, G. E., Winton, A. S. W., Singh, A. N., Adkins, A. D., & Singh, J. (2008b). Clinical and benefit-cost outcomes of teaching a mindfulness-based procedure to adult offenders with intellectual disabilities. *Behavior Modification*, *32*(5), 622–637.

Singh, N. N., Lancioni, G. E., Winton, A. S. W., Singh, A. N., Adkins, A. D., & Singh, J. (2010). Can adult offenders with intellectual disabilities use mindfulness-based procedures to control their deviant sexual arousal? *Psychology, Crime and Law*, 1–15, iFirst article.

Singh, N. N., Wahler, R. G., Adkins, A. D., Myers, R. E., & The Mindfulness Research Group. (2003). Soles of the feet: A mindfulness-based self control intervention for aggression by an individual with mild mental retardation and mental illness. *Research in Development Disabilities*, *24*, 158–169.

Tangney, J. P., Dobbins, A. E., Stuewig, J. B., & Schrader, S. W. (2017). Is there a dark side to mindfulness? Relation of mindfulness to criminogenic cognitions. *Personality and Social Psychology Bulletin*, *43*(10), 1415–1426.

Teasdale, J. D., Segal, Z. V., & Williams, J. M. G. (2003). Mindfulness training and problem formulation. *Clinical Psychology Science and Practice*, *10*, 157–160.

Teasdale, J. D., Segal, Z. V., Williams, J. M. G., Ridgeway, V. A., Soulsby, J. M., & Lau, M. A. (2000). Prevention of relapse/recurrence in major depression by mindfulness-based cognitive therapy. *Journal of Consulting and Clinical Psychology*, *68*(4), 615–623.

Thayer, J. F., & Brosschot, J. F. (2005). Psychosomatics and psychopathology: Looking up and down from the brain. *Psychoneuroendocrinology*, *30*, 1050–1058.

Upaya Institute and Zen Centre. (2010). *Upaya in action: Prison outreach project*. Retrieved from www.upaya.org/action/prisonprogram.php

Walton, J. S., Ramsay, L., Cunningham, C., & Henfrey, S. (2017). New directions: Integrating a biopsychosocial approach in the design and delivery of programs for high risk services users in Her Majesty's Prison and Probation Service. *Advancing Corrections: Journal of the International Corrections and Prison Association*, *3*, 21–47.

Ward, T., & Laws, D. R. (2010). Desistance from sex offending: Motivating change, enriching practice. *International Journal of Forensic Mental Health*, *9*, 11–23.

Wix, S. (2003). Dialectical behaviour therapy observed. *British Journal of Forensic Practice*, *5*(2), 3–7.

Worling, J. (2012). The assessment and treatment of deviant sexual arousal with adolescents who have offended sexually. *Journal of Sexual Aggression: An International, Interdisciplinary Forum for Research, Theory and Practice*, *18*(1), 36–63.

Wright, S., Day, A., & Howells, K. (2009). Mindfulness and the treatment of anger problems. *Aggression and Violent Behavior*, *14*, 396–401.

Yang, Y., & Raine, A. (2009). Prefrontal structural and functional brain imaging findings in antisocial, violent, and psychopathic individuals: A meta-analysis. *Psychiatry Research*, *174*(2), 81–88.

Zarling, A., Lawrence, E., & Marchman, J. (2015). A randomized controlled trial of acceptance and commitment therapy for aggressive behaviour. *Journal of Consulting and Clinical Psychology*, *83*, 199–212.

11

Apollo

An intervention to improve psychological
flexibility for young people displaying
sexually harmful behaviour

Victoria Hodierne, Kerensa Hocken,
and Imogen Byrne

Introduction

The Safer Living Foundation (SLF) charity (saferlivingfoundation.org) was
formed in 2014 by professionals from a range of disciplines working in the field
of sexual offending to provide services that reduce the perpetration of sexual
harm. The charity was formed with the intention of setting up a Circles of Support and Accountability (CoSA) project. CoSA originated from Canada and was
designed as means of offering community support to help people with sexual
convictions reintegrate into the community and to keep them accountable for
their actions (Elliott et al., 2018). The international success of this model has
shown very promising results in its ability to reduce recidivism (Duwe, 2018).
One characteristic of CoSA is that it typically begins once an individual has been
released from prison. However, the majority of the SLF's trustees worked in a
prison setting and had observed that many individuals with sexual convictions
found the transition from prison to the community (i.e. on release) difficult
(Saunders, 2020).

Through care processes for those being released from prison are in place in most
cases via the criminal justice system (CJS), such as the probation service. These
services manage risk by ensuring restrictions are in place and are adhered to, and
many offer offence-focused rehabilitation work. However, in many cases, the
needs of those leaving prison fall beyond risk management and include the need
for practical, social and emotional support, particularly at the release point, which

DOI: 10.4324/9780429262074-11

feels overwhelming for many. Hence, the SLF charity set up the first CoSA project to begin in prison to ensure that close working relationships between the individual and the volunteers working with them are in place before release. This project has shown promising results (see, for example, Kitson-Boyce, Blagden, Winder & Dillon, 2019). The SLF has since started other initiatives which aim to reduce sexual harm perpetration. These include a traditional model CoSA starting in the community and a Young People's CoSA. Following the successful implementation of the CoSA projects, the SLF set up two further projects in response to service gaps: a group-based therapy service for adults to prevent first-time sexual offending (see Chapter 9 of this book for detail) and a service for young people at risk of, or having committed, sexually harmful behaviour. In this chapter, we discuss the latter project, known as Apollo. This project commenced in 2019, and we will outline the development, first 18 months and evaluation plan of Apollo.

Background

Young People's Circles of Support and Accountability

The Apollo project is the second of the SLF's Young People's projects and follows the Young People's CoSA (YPCoSA) for those showing sexually harmful behaviour. As with other CoSA projects, YPCoSA aims to reduce reoffending by improving young people's emotional well-being through decreasing social isolation. One of the key aims, therefore, is for the young person to become engaged with safe, age-appropriate hobbies that they will be able to continue once the support of the YPCoSA has come to an end. Through this, it is hoped the young person will be able to develop confidence, social skills, a sense of belonging to a wider community and a positive, pro-social identity.

The ongoing evaluation of YPCoSA indicates that the project was achieving the intended outcomes for young people, as evidenced by a reduction in risk factors of reoffending measured by psychometric scales administered before, during and after the project. For example, there was an observed increase in self-esteem, a reduction in social and emotional loneliness and a decrease in favourable attitudes towards offending from pre-project to midway for a number of individuals. These trends were consolidated with analysis of interviews with individuals involved with YPCoSA, including the young people, their caregivers, their volunteers and the coordinator (Blagden, Winder, Byrne, Berti & Penford, manuscript in progress).

Although YPCoSA met the needs of some young people, there were a number of referrals which were unsuitable for YPCoSA. Primarily these referrals were for young people showing sexually harmful behaviour who were already engaged in various hobbies and activities and had appropriate, pro-social caregiver support. As the needs of these young people were beyond social isolation or lack of pro-social hobbies, their needs could not be met through YPCoSA.

Other services

Services are available for young people who have shown sexually harmful behaviour and who have needs in areas other than social support. Where a mental health need is identified, support is available through the NHS Child and Adolescent Mental Health Services (CAMHS; www.nhs.uk/using-the-nhs/nhs-services/mental-health-services/child-and-adolescent-mental-health-services-camhs/). If there is a need for protective factors (such as suitable parental supervision), some Children's Social Care teams are able to offer interventions, and if a young person receives a conviction, they may be able to access interventions in custody or through the local Youth Justice Service. Where these criteria are not met, other regional services can offer support, such as the National Society for the Prevention of Cruelty to Children's Turn the Page programme (a manualised cognitive behavioural [CBT] intervention; https://learning.nspcc.org.uk/services-children-families/turn-the-page) or the residential services offered by Glebe House Residential Children's Home (www.ftctrust.org.uk/glebe.php). These services, however, are only available in certain areas of the UK, and the SLF is not aware of any services offered in Nottinghamshire or Derbyshire for young people that do not meet the threshold for statutory agency involvement.

A new project focussed on unmet needs

As a consequence of these service gaps, YPCoSA received many referrals for young people who were ineligible for any other service but who nevertheless needed support for sexually harmful behaviour. There was clearly a need for a service for young people that went beyond support but did not require intensive intervention. Common themes in the referrals unsuitable for YPCoSA were the presence of pro-social peers and interests but difficulties with identifying, coping with and communicating emotions, developing a pro-social sense of identity, understanding sexual urges or managing impulsivity. These needs were not deemed severe enough to qualify for entry into services such as CAMHS but were present to the degree that professionals had concerns about risk of further harmful sexual behaviour.

This unmet need led to the birth of Apollo, a service for young people who needed skills for managing emotions, urges and developing a pro-social identity. In designing Apollo, the community volunteer model of CoSA was retained, primarily because it does not signal 'treatment' or an 'offender' label, an important element in building a pro-social identity (Willis, 2018). The Apollo project is a structured intervention led by community volunteers which helps young people to build the skills necessary for emotional and identity management via improvement in their psychological flexibility skills.

Psychological flexibility

Psychological flexibility is considered to be important to human flourishing and is defined as 'the ability to contact the present moment more fully as a conscious human being, and to change or persist in behaviour when doing so serves valued ends' (Hayes, Luoma, Bond, Masuda & Lillis, 2006, p. 8). Research in the field of human distress suggests that the source of distress and problematic behaviour is its antithesis: psychological inflexibility. Psychological inflexibility can be understood as 'a pattern in which behaviour is excessively controlled by one's thoughts, feeling and other internal experiences, or to avoid these experiences, at the expense of more effective and meaningful actions' (Levin et al., 2014, p. 156). Psychological inflexibility is a transdiagnostic phenomenon in that it does not explain just one type of problem (such as depression) but can explain many different presentations of human suffering, so it transcends diagnostic labels to propose a shared underlying mechanism. The explanatory power of psychological inflexibility goes beyond mental ill health to any behaviour that causes distress such as overeating or persistent pain (Levin et al., 2014). Therefore a means of addressing human suffering is to improve psychological flexibility.

Some models of intervention explicitly train psychological flexibility, with the most well-known being acceptance and commitment therapy (said as one word: ACT; Hayes et al., 2011). ACT is a form of CBT that falls into what is referred to as the 'third wave' generation of CBT (Hayes, 2004). The first wave of CBT is the behavioural approach (e.g. Pavlov, 1928), followed by cognitive therapy (e.g. Beck, 1976), with these two being combined to form second wave CBT, or what is more commonly known as CBT. CBT takes a mechanistic approach to understanding human suffering that sees distress as a problem resulting from something having 'gone wrong' within a person's thinking. The therapeutic aim of CBT is to correct or minimise the problem, typically by changing the faulty thinking pattern linked to the distress, yielding improvements in behaviour (Granthan & Cowtan, 2015). The majority of interventions for sexual offending are CBT based (Schmucker & Lösel, 2017).

Third wave therapies adopt a different philosophy for conceptualising human distress, seeing it not as a problem that needs to be eliminated but as a human response to context (e.g. life experiences, situations). The therapeutic aim is not to change thoughts and feelings, but to improve psychological flexibility so that people are able to live with their distress and behave in accordance with their values (Hayes, 2004). This is consistent with the Good Lives Model (GLM, Ward, 2002) of rehabilitation which emphasises the importance of developing strengths and capabilities for meeting human needs rather than eradicating problematic factors. The messaging made explicit in ACT is that people are not bad, useless or wrong because of the problems they are experiencing, and they are not defined by their internal experiences (thoughts, feelings, urges, memories) (Hayes et al., 2006). This latter point is particularly relevant to work with those who commit sexually harmful behaviour, where the development of a pro-social, non-offending identity is critical to desistance (Willis, 2018).

ACT conceptualises six characteristics of psychological inflexibility. These characteristics are not a problem in and of themselves, but it is the degree to which they restrict quality of life that they can become a problem. The therapeutic aim of ACT is to increase psychological flexibility via values-consistent living and skill development such that people can live rich, full and meaningful lives (Harris, 2008).

1   *Cognitive fusion* is the belief that thoughts are fact and represent reality. We 'fuse' with thoughts and get pulled along by them, by acting on them unquestionably. Psychological flexibility (or *defusion*) is to recognise that thoughts are not reality and involves the ability to step back from thoughts, observe them and question them.

2   *Experiential avoidance* is the avoidance of internal experiences (thoughts, feelings, sensations and memories) that feel uncomfortable and can lead to attempts to suppress or fight them. Psychological flexibility is *acceptance*, an openness to all internal experiences without trying to change them, but at the same time behaving effectively.

3   *Dominance of past and future* is an over-focus on ruminating or worrying about what will or has happened. Psychological flexibility is *present-moment contact*, bringing awareness to the here and now, noticing our experience as they happen.

4   *Attachment to a conceptualised self* is the belief that thoughts and feelings define our identity and involves behaving unquestionably in accordance with that identity (e.g. 'I have sexual thoughts about children, therefore I'm a paedophile'). Psychological flexibility is the recognition that thoughts and feelings do not define our identity and is closely linked to *defusion* since it involves the ability to observe thinking. This is known as *self as context*.

5   *Lack of contact and clarity with values* is not being aware of or invested in what is important or meaningful in life. Psychological flexibility is *contact and clarity with values* and is about knowing what values are important to us and what we want to stand for in life. Values are used to guide behaviour.

6   *Avoidance behaviour* is avoidance of unpleasant experiences, which ends up being or leading to a problematic behaviour (fear of intimacy leads to avoidance of relationships). Psychological flexibility is *committed action* – value-based actions that lead a person to behave in ways that accord with what is important to them in life.

Some of the skills taught to train psychological flexibility include developing abilities for paying attention and present-moment awareness, sometimes via mindfulness, and being able to notice internal events (thoughts, feelings, memories, urges) and metaphorically 'stand back' from these rather than getting caught up with them. This allows people the freedom to live their lives according to what is important to them (values) in the presence of difficult thoughts and feelings, removing the need to 'battle' with them.

The characteristics of psychological flexibility have been implicated as being areas that are subject to intervention, yielding empirically measurable gains in mental wellness and quality of life (Hofmann & Hayes, 2019). ACT has growing and convincing evidence for its ability to ease mental suffering in a variety of mental health problems (e.g. A–Tjak et al., 2015) and is recognised by the American Psychological Association (https://div12.org/psychological-treatments/) as having strong or modest support as an intervention for chronic pain, mixed anxiety, depression, obsessive compulsive disorder (OCD) and anxiety. Very small-scale research shows positive outcomes for ACT and problematic sexual behaviour in the form of compulsive pornography use (Crosby & Twohig, 2016). ACT is gradually being considered as having utility working with forensic populations (Amrod & Hayes, 2013; Zarling, Bannon & Berta, 2017), and Walton and Hocken (2020) suggest it could be one promising approach to working with harmful sexual interests.

Although there are a number of methodological weaknesses with the research, such as small sample sizes and a lack of randomised designs (Swain, Hancock, Dixon & Bowman, 2015), use of ACT with young people has shown promising results for improving emotion regulation problems, including OCD (Armstrong, Morrison & Twohig, 2013), and depression (Livheim et al., 2015). A further appeal of ACT is that it is not confined to use by therapists or the therapeutic context, but has broad-based application, for example, in education, health and social care and sports performance (Levin, Twohig & Krafft, 2020).

ACT has been specifically adapted for use with young people using the DNA-V model. DNA-V was created by Hayes and Ciarrochi (2015a) and described in their book *The Thriving Adolescent*. It built upon their work using ACT with adolescents as presented in their self-help workbook *Get Out of Your Mind and Into Your Life for Teens* (Ciarrochi, Hayes & Bailey, 2012). The philosophy behind DNA-V is to take the key principles of ACT and present them in a way that is more accessible to young people. DNA-V is the model that Apollo uses to help young people build their skills for psychological flexibility.

ACT for young people: DNA-V

DNA-V stands for *discoverer, noticer, advisor* and *values*. The core concept is that *discoverer, noticer* and *advisor* are skills that all human beings possess and that strengthening these skills and learning to use them appropriately will improve psychological flexibility and help us move in the direction of our chosen *values*. Table 11.1 provides a summary of these concepts and examples of related behaviours.

Table 11.1 Discoverer, noticer and advisor skills

Skill	Examples of unskilled behaviours	Examples of skilled behaviours
Discoverer – learning through discovery; trying things out for ourselves and finding out what works	Repeating behaviours that are ineffective or taking uninformed, impulsive actions	Taking informed risks and reflecting on the effectiveness of one's actions
Noticer – awareness of both the inside world (feelings and emotions) and the outside world	Avoiding unpleasant feelings, difficulty in recognising or labelling emotions and automatically reacting to physical sensations	Focusing on internal or external experiences as appropriate, being aware of and identifying feelings and sensations and willingness to experience emotions without reacting to them or trying to control them
Advisor – using our knowledge of the world to make evaluations, judgements and predictions	Accepting thoughts as facts, not questioning the helpfulness of our beliefs and getting caught up in worrying and rumination	Recognising thoughts as thoughts, evaluating whether a belief is helpful or unhelpful and recognising that attempts to control our thoughts and feelings are often ineffective

The concept of the *discoverer* in DNA-V is similar to that of committed action in ACT, *noticer* to acceptance and contact with the present moment and *advisor* to cognitive defusion and contact with the present moment. Conceptualising our different skills as *discover*, *noticer* and *advisor* also serves as a simple defusion exercise in and of itself because it frames thinking as something we can observe, and if we can observe it, we are not it.

Values

As in the ACT model described earlier, *values* form an essential part of DNA-V. The concept of *values* can be challenging to understand and to define. The description given by Hayes and Ciarrochi (2015) is summarised in Table 11.2.

Table 11.2 The meaning of the term *values* as used in DNA-V

Principle	Explanation
A value is chosen	Young people must decide for themselves what they wish to care about based on what is important to them personally.
A value is a quality of action	*Values* are linked to behaviours in that young people can choose whether or not to perform them in any given moment. They are not something which a person can hold, lose or gain, but a metaphorical direction of travel in the journey of life.
A value is not an outcome	A young person can choose their own behaviour, but they cannot often control what happens as a result of that behaviour. Valued actions might make a desired outcome more likely, but it is not guaranteed.
A value is not a goal	Goals are specific targets that can be achieved, whereas *values* are focussed on continuous behaviour. Goals can be useful for helping young people live according to their *values*.
A value is constructed from language and interactions with the world	What a young person cares about can only be based on their life experiences so far, and they should not be expected to describe that in the same terms as a professional.
Discussion of *values* is held lightly	The words a young person uses to describe what matters to them should be based on what is useful, not what is true. Actions are more important than words.

Principle	Explanation
Values are dynamic	The things that matter most to a young person will change as they grow up and throughout their lives. They may also be context specific.
A value is intrinsically reinforcing	Engaging in valued behaviour might not always be easy, but it feels good to the young person to behave in that way, regardless of the outcome.

Self context and social context

Two further concepts which form an essential part of the DNA-V model are the *self context* and the *social context*. As with ACT, DNA-V is grounded in the idea that it is necessary to understand context before it is possible to understand behaviour, as the same behaviour can serve different goals depending on the circumstances.

The concept of the *social context* recognises that we live in a world where we influence and are influenced by others, including teachers, classmates and family members. It also encourages us to apply our *discoverer*, *noticer* and *advisor* skills to understanding others' behaviour. The self, meanwhile, is a context that many people do not often consider. The *self context* recognises that we are not defined by our thoughts, feelings, behaviours or *values*, but rather that all

Context changes meaning

For a simplistic example, consider the *behaviour* of a young person shouting at a classmate.

In the *context* of a ball game where the young person is attempting to attract the attention of a teammate, this behaviour would be considered socially acceptable.

In the *context* of the classmate having accidentally bumped into the young person in the dinner queue, this behaviour would be considered socially unacceptable. By understanding the young person's social learning (including relationships with their caregivers and the classmate) and *self context*, it is possible to understand how this behaviour might have been intended to move the young person towards a valued goal (such as asserting bodily autonomy) in the moment.

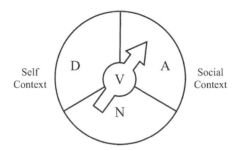

Figure 11.1 DNA-V model represented as a disc

these things and more make up our identity. *Self context* is therefore essentially the same the ACT process of 'self as context'. The *self context* and *social context* combined recognise how our view of ourselves and of others influences our behaviour.

The DNA-V model is often represented as a disc, shown in Figure 11.1. The main part of the disc is divided into segments labelled *discoverer, noticer* and *advisor*, representing these skills in one person. *Values* are represented as a compass-like arrow reflecting the idea of *values* as the direction we choose to move in. The disc is surrounded by the words *self context* and *social context*, placing the young person's *discoverer, noticer, advisor* and *values* in the context of their internal and external world.

The role of autonomy

The DNA-V approach explicitly rejects the idea of supporting young people who have problems by telling them they need to follow the rules set out for them by the adults in their lives (Hayes & Ciarrochi, 2015). Adolescence in mammals is a time of experimentation and risk taking (Macri, Adriani, Chiarotti & Laviola, 2002), and studies have found that young people are more likely to engage with healthier habits if they perceive them as autonomy-assertive and consistent with their existing strongly held *values* (Bryan et al., 2016). Moreover, self-determination theory identifies all human beings as having a need for autonomy, with autonomous individuals showing greater ownership of past experiences (Weinstein, 2017) and negative (e.g. shameful) characteristics in themselves (Weinstein et al., 2011). Instead of resisting adolescents' desire for autonomy, the DNA-V approach embraces it, encouraging young people to discover for themselves who they would like to be (Hayes & Ciarrochi, 2015). With Apollo, it is hoped that this focus on autonomy will support young people in taking responsibility for their harmful sexual behaviour, accepting such behaviour as one part of their personal history and integrated identity and engaging in healthier behaviours in the service of their own personal *values*.

Intervention model for young people at risk of sexual harmful behaviour

Apollo ethos

The project was named after the Greek sun god Apollo. As inscribed on the Temple of Apollo at Delphi, young people engaged with this project are supported to 'know thyself', and in Jungian analysis the sun has associations with both individuation (having a sense of oneself as distinct from others) and integration (a balancing of the different elements of a person's self). The name Apollo was therefore chosen to represent the ethos of this project.

A strengths-based approach

Many young people referred to the SLF experience adults as setting and enforcing rules focussed on their previous sexually harmful behaviour. Whilst this is a necessary and inevitable consequence of their sexually harmful behaviour, it also serves as a near-constant reminder of what they have done wrong. Research with adults who commit sexual offences shows that effective change is more likely to happen if risk management strategies are used in conjunction with strength-based approaches, so that individuals can grow the skills and capacities for a fulfilling life (Ward, 2002). Similarly, it has been argued that effective interventions for young people with sexually harmful behaviour should take a whole-person approach aimed at promoting growth and resilience in line with healthy adolescent development. Such developmental approaches suggest that work with young people should focus on goals, including the young person's ability to self-regulate and engage with adaptive, pro-social problem-solving (Creeden, 2013).

Young people are aware that harmful sexual behaviour is why SLF is working with them, and several have identified help with managing harmful sexual behaviour as their motivation for engaging with the project. In all cases, the young person's previous harmful sexual behaviour is contextualised as one part of their past behaviour rather than their sole identifying characteristic. This is consistent with the wider SLF philosophy, which seeks to avoid labelling those the charity supports as 'sex offenders'; it is felt that this could create fusion with the term as an identity and therefore inhibit the development of a pro-social identity and the person's belief in their ability to choose their future behaviour (Willis, 2018). With regard to young people in particular, research shows that adolescents who have committed a sexual offence are more likely to commit another non-sexual offence than a sexual offence (Carpentier, Leclerc & Proulx, 2011; Waite et al., 2005). The Apollo project therefore focuses on building strengths for pro-social living in a general sense rather than focusing excessively on the incidents of harmful sexual behaviour, as this is believed to be counter-productive and risks increased fusion with a 'sex offender' identity that is already unlikely to persist into adult life. All projects take their inspiration from the GLM (Ward, 2002) that views a person's well-being and the reduction in their risk of further offending as inextricably linked.

Apollo and DNA-V

Apollo was created for young people who had shown sexually harmful behaviour and who had needs in relation to managing emotions and urges and developing a pro-social identity. It is believed that DNA-V is likely to support the needs of these young people by:

- Helping them develop a pro-social sense of identity through:
  - Identifying what matters to them in their lives and what sort of person they want to be (their *values*).
  - Exploring the effectiveness of past behaviours (including harmful sexual behaviours) in achieving this and testing the effectiveness of new behaviours (a *discoverer* skill).
- Supporting them in living more in accordance with their *values* by:
  - Learning to defuse from unhelpful *advisor* thoughts that act as a barrier to living in accordance with their *values*.
  - Strengthening their ability to identify, cope with and communicate emotions through strengthening *noticer* skills.
  - Developing skills in identifying and managing impulsivity and sexual urges through strengthening *noticer* and *discoverer* skills.

As a tool for developing psychological flexibility, it is hoped that DNA-V will show similar effectiveness to ACT in improving mental wellness and quality of life (Hofmann & Hayes, 2019) and managing problematic sexual behaviour (Crosby & Twohig, 2016).

Referrals

Any professional or caregiver who is concerned about a young person showing harmful sexual behaviour may make a referral to the SLF. Referrals are accepted for any young person of any gender who:

- Is aged 12 to 17 years (inclusive) at the time of referral.
- Is living in (or being released to live in) Nottinghamshire or Derbyshire areas, including city centres (referrals from outside of these areas are considered on a case-by-case basis).
- Has shown sexually harmful behaviour (including but not limited to behaviour which has resulted in them receiving a caution or conviction for a sexual offence).
- Needs support in managing their sexual thoughts, feelings or behaviours.
- Is willing to engage voluntarily with the SLF.

The SLF will accept referrals for young people who are maintaining their innocence of any harmful sexual behaviour. It is accepted that denial is a normal response to fear of rejection (Ware & Blagden, 2016); therefore this is not considered to be a barrier, provided a young person is willing to accept support in line with the aims of the individual projects. Between February 2019 and August 2020, the combined SLF Young People's projects received 91 referrals, an average of 1.2 referrals per week. Approximately half of these referrals were from social care teams (including child protection teams, family services and assessment teams), and approximately one-third were from police staff. The remainder were from NHS teams (including CAMHS), other specialist harmful sexual behaviour services, criminal justice agencies (including the Youth Justice and Probation Services), schools and the young person's caregiver.

The referral and assessment process is outlined in Figure 11.2. Referrals are screened by paid project coordinators based on:

- The nature and persistence of the harmful sexual behaviour – in some cases, the 12- to 18-month interventions offered by SLF Young People's projects would be a disproportionate response and other interventions (such as advice from a caregiver or a school nurse) would be more appropriate.
- The young person's unmet needs – including the presence or absence of pro-social peers and interests and the involvement of other agencies (such as CAMHS).

The coordinator will meet individually with the young person to complete the Needs and Resources profile (a semi-structured interview produced by the

Figure 11.2 Referral and assessment process for Young People's projects referrals

SLF to assess the young person's social needs and independent living skills) and Avoidance and Fusion Questionnaire for Youth (assessment of psychological flexibility – AFQ-Y; Greco, Murrell & Coyne, 2005). Based on these assessments and the information gathered about the young person, the coordinator will make a clinical judgement on whether the young person is most likely to benefit from YPCoSA (greater need for pro-social peers and interests) or Apollo (greater need for psychological flexibility), or if they are unlikely to benefit from either.

Apollo structure

A summary of the Apollo intervention structure is provided in Figure 11.3. The support provided to young people by the Apollo project is divided into three stages:

- Stage one (introduction) – The young person is introduced to the DNA-V model and supported in identifying their areas of strength and development.
- Stage two (intervention) – The young person is supported in developing their DNA skills and engagement with *values* in line with the needs identified during stage one.
- Stage three (consolidation) – No new work is completed, and the young person is supported in reflecting on how they are applying the skills they have learnt.

Psychometric assessments are completed at the end of stage one and approximately every 12 weeks during stages two and three. Various measures are used to evaluate the impact of Apollo on young people's well-being and attitudes, and the AFQ-Y is also used by the coordinator to monitor the young person's development of psychological flexibility. Psychometric assessments are discussed in more detail in the 'Evaluation' section later.

Throughout this process, young people are expected to engage fully with sessions and practice applying the skills between sessions, for example, by taking steps towards a personal goal or noticing when they have self-critical thoughts. Real-world practice of DNA-V skills is essential, as young people cannot be expected to change their behaviour if they only engage in different behaviours in session and not the real-world contexts in which they have had problems in the past (Hayes & Ciarrochi, 2015a).

Each young person in Apollo is supported by two or three Apollo-trained volunteers. All SLF volunteers must complete two days of SLF volunteer core training, including work on interpersonal skills, personal boundaries, consent, the Sexual Offences Act 2003, prison interventions and their terminology, safeguarding and risk escalation and the CoSA format used by some SLF projects. Additionally, Apollo volunteers must complete ten hours of Apollo-specific training delivered by the coordinator over four sessions and provide proof of completing an online safeguarding course (or equivalent). This equips them with a basic understanding of DNA-V in general and how this is applied in the Apollo model specifically.

Before meeting the young person, the volunteers participate in group supervision with the coordinator, and additional group supervision takes place throughout their work with the young person. Through this volunteers are encouraged to identify what they need in order to become increasingly competent in the model and take responsibility for developing this.

During stages two and three, the volunteers meet with the young person independently of the coordinator but never one-to-one. The SLF is aware that volunteers are generous in offering their time and energy to help young people and that few are trained mental health professionals. For these reasons it is felt that expecting or permitting one-to-one meetings between the volunteers and the young person would place responsibilities on the volunteers that go beyond their training and what is reasonable to expect for unpaid work. The requirement to have a minimum of two volunteers present also provides an additional layer of oversight, as volunteers are able to monitor each other to ensure compliance with the Apollo model and SLF safeguarding procedures.

Stage one: introduction

The young people in Apollo spend a number of sessions working with the project coordinator and their volunteers. The aim of stage one is for all members of the team (the young person, the coordinator and the volunteers) to get to know each other and for the young person to become familiar with the DNA-V model and how this relates to their own experiences. Alongside the young person's

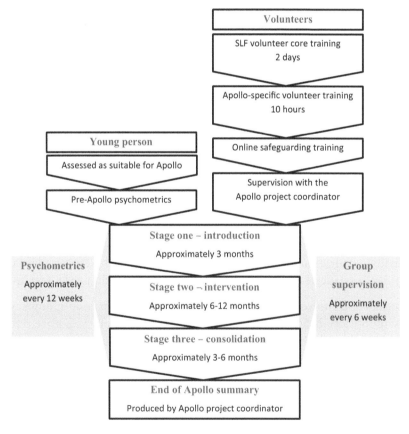

Figure 11.3 Apollo intervention structure

learning from sessions, group supervision allows the coordinator and volunteers to discuss their own observations of the young person's DNA skills, understanding of and engagement with their *values* and their *self* and *social context*. This allows the coordinator and volunteers to support the young person in identifying their own strengths and treatment needs. Consequently, work in stage two can be focussed on the skills the young person most needs to develop, utilising the strengths which they already possess. A case example of how this is used with young people in Apollo is shown in Figure 11.3.

Young people typically spend around three months on stage one of Apollo, with sessions taking place once every two weeks; however, there is significant individual variation. This is due to the diversity of the young people on Apollo in terms of age (between 12 and 18 years), motivation to attend and engage with sessions and cognitive functioning (including attention span and ability to understand the concepts or retain learning between sessions).

Stage two: intervention

During stage two, the volunteers support the young person in strengthening skills related to the areas of DNA-V that the team identified as in need of development. This could include, for example:

- Practicing evaluating the effectiveness of their behaviours in moving them towards their *values* (a *discoverer* skill).
- Strengthening emotional awareness (a *noticer* skill) through an exercise commonly known as a body scan, where attention is directed to notice sensations within the body.
- Broadening the young person's self-concept by exploring encouraging, critical and neutral *advisor* statements.

Periodically the team will review the young person's progress and identify whether they have any outstanding needs. The team work together to agree when the young person is ready to move to the next stage, usually when they are confident in their knowledge of DNA-V and applying the skills consistently in real life.

Each young person is expected to spend around 6 to 12 months in stage two of Apollo depending on their individual needs. During this stage, sessions take place every one to two weeks.

In some cases the end of stage one review, taking into account the views of all members of the team, has identified that the young person's level of outstanding need is low. Typically, the young person will rate themselves highly in terms of how effectively they use their skills and engage with their *values* and not identify any areas needing significant improvement. The rest of the team feels that the young person has a fair understanding of the DNA-V areas and that this assessment is an accurate assessment, often supported by the end of stage one AFQ-Y indicating there is no longer a significant need in relation to psychological flexibility. In these instances, further intervention may be beneficial but completing stage two as outlined earlier would be excessive. Consideration may be given to the young person completing low-intensity work as stage two, either continuing with their volunteer team or working one-to-one with the coordinator. Low-intensity sessions take place once every four weeks.

Regardless of how the young person is completing stage two, there is scope at this point to include specific sex and relationships education work. Exactly what material is delivered depends on the young person's needs, as agreed between the young person, their caregiver, the coordinator and any relevant professionals. Sex and relationships work can include understanding sexual development and urges, consent and the law, pornography, role models or any other relevant material. Young people are supported to apply the skills from DNA-V to sexual thoughts and urges, so they are not distressed by them and they are able to regulate them such that they do not behave in harmful ways.

Stage three: consolidation

Stage three is intended to provide a period of consolidation. During this time the young person will meet with their volunteers and/or the coordinator less frequently and will not cover any new material. Instead, sessions will be focussed on checking in with the young person on how they are applying their DNA-V skills in the real world, if they need support in maintaining their skills and how they are working towards their goals.

The young person's work with Apollo will come to an end once the team agree that the young person is using the skills they have developed consistently and effectively in the real world. This could include, for example, being able to spot when they are getting caught up in self-critical *advisor* thoughts, using *noticer* skills to take a step back and using *discoverer* skills to try a new behaviour to take them towards their *values*. Young people are expected to spend three to six months on stage three of Apollo, with sessions taking place once every four weeks.

At any point during stage three a young person can move back to stage two if any additional intervention needs are identified.

End of Apollo

Any young person who has completed at least stage one will receive an end-of-Apollo summary. This is a brief summary of their learning in relation to DNA-V (both the general principles and their own personal *discoverer, noticer, advisor* and *values*) and any sex and relationships work, as well as recommendations for how they can continue to build on their learning after their work with Apollo is finished (for example, by practicing specific exercises or working towards personal goals). This summary is provided to the young person, their caregiver and any relevant professionals such as social workers.

If a young person leaves Apollo before the end of stage one, no summary is produced. The coordinator will contact any relevant professionals to provide a short summary of the young person's engagement and the reasons for disengagement, if known. Young people who disengage can be re-referred to SLF Young People's projects at any point before their 18th birthday.

Case example: 'Josh'

Josh is a 14-year-old male referred to SLF Young People's projects after receiving a Youth Conditional Caution for sexually assaulting his 11-year-old sister, 'Grace', in the family home. The coordinator's observations about Josh from stage one of Apollo are summarised in Figure 11.4.

In this example, Josh already has a good understanding of what matters most to him (his *values*) and he has shown some limited willingness to try new behaviours (*discoverer*). Other professionals have commented that they view his reluctance to attend after-school meetings as resistance and are focussed on the possible consequences for Josh of refusing to engage (e.g. he will be perceived as non-compliant and therefore a higher risk of further harmful sexual behaviour, and any future incidents could result in a custodial sentence). The Apollo approach is to instead focus on the motivation for this behaviour. As an adolescent, autonomy is important to Josh, and he has identified caring about having fun and having freedom, so he does not see attending compulsory meetings in his own time as fitting with his *values*. To improve his engagement with these meetings, the Apollo team might try exploring ways in which *choosing* to attend these meetings could contribute to his *value* of having freedom in the long-term (professionals will trust him more and therefore be less restrictive) and his *value* of caring for his family in the short-term (he knows they are upset about what happens, so engaging with the meetings would show them he cares about their feelings).

DNA-V area	Observations
Discoverer	Proactively seeks out new hobbies and interests – recently started a band with his friends at school during lunch break Avoids trying new behaviours outside of routine – e.g. starting a new after-school club or talking to professionals after school Repeats ineffective strategies for coping with boredom – tries to relieve boredom by scrolling through social media even though this does not result in him feeling less bored
Noticer	Limited emotional vocabulary – happy, sad, angry Possibly mislabels other emotions as anger – e.g. anxious, scared, let down Has expressed a desire to 'get rid' of sadness
Advisor	Accepts self-critical thoughts as facts – e.g. 'I'm stupid' Tendency towards rumination Reports 'getting lost in my head' as a problem – focussing on things he is worried might happen gets in the way of things that are important to him, e.g. distracts him from school work, which leads to behaviour warnings (impacts entitlement to end-of-year privileges) and reinforces 'I'm disruptive' self view
Values	Being a good friend (including listening to others' problems and sharing), caring for my family, having fun, having freedom
Self view	'I'm disruptive' 'My parents shouldn't spend time and money on me because I only waste it'
Social view	'Other people think I am bad, but my friends care about me'

Figure 11.4 Case example of DNA-V formulation for 'Josh'

By the end of stage one, Josh had started to talk about the day of the harmful sexual behaviour incident, identifying that he felt bored and angry. Further exploration would be required once he had developed his understanding of his own thoughts and feelings. At this stage, the coordinator thought that Josh's harmful sexual behaviour may have been an unskilled *discoverer* attempt to cope with the anger he reported feeling (or another emotion mislabelled as anger) and that grievance thinking may have played a role (if there was something in particular he was angry about that day).

At the end of stage one, the team agreed that work during the next stage would focus on strengthening Josh's ability to:

- Identify and label emotions (inside *noticer*).
- Shift his focus from his thoughts (particularly when ruminating) to the physical world (outside *noticer*).
- Defuse from self-critical and grievance-related thoughts (*advisor*).

Specific sex and relationships education work would focus on sexual development (including understanding puberty and developmentally appropriate sexual behaviours), consent and managing sexual urges (inside *noticer*). Josh's willingness to try new behaviours could be developed by identifying how he feels strengthening these areas would help him be a good friend and family member, have fun and lead to greater freedom.

Josh understood the work on consent very well, but during the work on sexual development, it became apparent that he did not realise that having sexual urges and being interested in experimenting sexually with same-age peers was developmentally normal for a young person his age. This discussion helped him to understand that whilst his harmful sexual behaviour was unhealthy (due to the lack of consent, the age difference and his relationship to Grace), in a different context (e.g. a consenting, same-age peer), this same behaviour would be considered safe and healthy. Through this Josh was able to let go of a *self view* he had developed that 'I am broken and wrong' and develop the more flexible *advisor* statement: 'I did something wrong'.

Josh also opened up about using masturbation to cope with feelings of anger, as he found it relaxing. The team supported him in using his *discoverer* skills to explore how effective this was, and he understood that whilst masturbation was safe and healthy, it was unhelpful to rely on it for stress relief. From here Josh was willing to explore new ways of using his *noticer* skills to responding to both unwanted emotions and sexual urges in a more helpful way.

An exercise focussed on emotional memories was used to help Josh explore some of the bodily sensations he experienced in relation to times when he had felt 'angry'. He was able to identify that some were similar whilst others were different, and using a diagram showing different words for emotions, he now labelled some as 'unfair' and 'ignored' instead. Josh shared that whilst he cared about Grace, these feelings sometimes showed up in relation to her, as he felt his parents expected too much from him and sometimes paid her more attention than him.

Josh explained that on the day of the harmful sexual behaviour incident, these feelings were particularly strong. Earlier that day Grace had broken one of his video games discs when she stepped on it, and their parents had told Josh it was his fault for leaving it on the floor. He had said that he wanted Grace to pay for a replacement, but his parents said this was 'silly' and that he should save up his pocket money instead. Josh ruminated on thoughts about how he had been treated unfairly and Grace 'owed' him for the game. Combined with his previous strategy of using sexual behaviour to cope with 'anger', this led to Josh acting out sexually against her.

Through discussion with the team Josh was able to see that fairness was also an important value for him and that his behaviour had been intended to move him towards this value and away from feelings of 'anger' and thoughts that his parents were right, which reinforced his *self view* that he wasted the money his parents spent on him. He shared that he felt bad immediately afterwards and that his behaviour had not been effective in taking him towards his goals. Recognising this increased Josh's motivation to apply what he had been learning about responding to emotions and sexual urges and also increased his willingness try defusing from ruminating thoughts instead of getting caught up in them.

The team supported Josh in shifting his focus from whether an *advisor* thought was true or untrue to whether it was helpful or unhelpful in taking him towards his *values*. He was able to see that whilst it might be true that he was being treated unfairly in a given situation, for example, it might not be helpful to focus on these thoughts if it was getting in the way of him having fun with his friends or caring for his family. From here Josh was willing to practise different ways of defusing from these thoughts.

By the end of Apollo, Josh had:

- Understood what parts of his sexual behaviour were healthy or unhealthy.
- Identified how his unhelpful *advisor* thoughts and attempts to avoid emotions contributed to his harmful sexual behaviour.
- Developed *noticer* skills to help him respond to difficult emotions and manage problematic masturbation, including simple mindfulness exercises focussed on his breathing.
- Increased his understanding of his personal *values* to include fairness and being trustworthy.
- Expanded his social view to better reflect his values, including *advisor* statements such as 'no one is perfect, everyone makes mistakes sometimes'.
- Developed skills in defusing from unhelpful *advisor* thoughts, including imagining these thoughts being said by a cartoon character.
- Used his *discoverer* skills to try new ways of living according to his *values* and evaluate their effectiveness.
- Committed to repeating helpful behaviours that were in line with his *values* and which expanded his *self view* to include more positive self-concepts, including 'I am a caring person', for example, offering to help his parents and being patient and forgiving if Grace said or did something he did not like by mistake.

Progress

At the time of writing, two young people have completed the Apollo project. Five young people are currently engaged with the project, with one completing stage one, two completing stage two with volunteers and two completing stage two one-to-one with the coordinator. To date, seven young people have discontinued work with the project: four during the first stage, two at the end of stage one and one during the third stage:

- One young person had a change of caregiver and unexpectedly moved outside of the area in which SLF Young People's projects operate and is now too far away for the work to continue.
- One young person did not feel that Apollo would be helpful to him, and his caregiver was unsuccessful in persuading him to continue to the end of stage one.
- One young person and his caregiver felt the working relationship with the coordinator had broken down irretrievably.
- One young person discontinued contact with the coordinator, and his caregiver was unable to provide a reason.
- One young person felt that he had achieved his goal by the end of stage one and was unwilling to continue to low-intensity stage two.
- One young person and his caregiver did not feel that Apollo would be helpful to him having completed stage one.
- One young person unexpectedly moved outside of the area in which SLF Young People's projects operate during stage three and was unwilling to complete the final stage remotely.

Challenges

For many young people in Apollo, sessions take place at their education provision, whilst for others sessions have taken place in community locations. Identifying suitable community venues (including during school holidays for young people who normally meet at their place of education) has sometimes proved challenging owing to the needs for locations to be within travelling distance for young people, offer sufficient privacy for the work, be willing for work with this client group to take place on the premises and avoid any scheduling conflicts which could pose safeguarding concerns. In some cases, identifying a suitable venue has caused considerable delay to a young person's progress through Apollo.

All young people currently engaged with stage two of Apollo have completed stage one one-to-one with the SLF Apollo coordinator. It was observed that after becoming familiar with the coordinator over a period of weeks, some young people were reluctant to progress to working with the volunteers instead, and as noted earlier, one of the young people who disengaged identified a breakdown in his working relationship with the coordinator as his reason for leaving the project. Additionally, where there has been a delay in identifying suitable volunteers, this has caused disruption to the young person's engagement with Apollo. For these reasons, the decision was made to change the model so that young people would start working with their volunteers at the start of stage one.

Difficulties in recruiting and retaining suitable volunteers to work with young people on Apollo has been a major challenge, with only a small number of the SLF's active volunteers having completed Apollo volunteer training. The ability of volunteers to travel to work with a young person has also been an issue. Work is ongoing to establish the reasons for the low uptake of Apollo training by SLF volunteers and to improve SLF volunteer diversity.

Strengths

Overall young people appear to respond well to the Apollo model. They generally find the concepts easy to understand and apply to their own lives, and initial observations by the coordinator suggest improvements in psychological flexibility as young people progress through Apollo. Anecdotally, volunteers who have completed Apollo training report finding the skills and principles useful in their own lives.

Evaluation

There is limited research into effective interventions aimed at young people who display harmful sexual behaviour. Hackett (2014) suggests interventions ought to be goal-oriented, structured and teach specific skills to help adolescents manage their thoughts, feelings and behaviour. A holistic approach such as this is more likely to address the wider social and adolescent-focussed needs associated with anti-social behaviour change (Letourneau et al., 2009).

It is paramount that interventions are monitored for evaluation purposes to inform learning and evidence-based best practice. Conducting a process and outcome evaluation is an effective way to achieve this. The process evaluation begins at project start and continues during its lifetime and is; concerned with how the project is being implemented (Public Health England, 2018a). The outcome evaluation commences on service-user engagement, evidencing any impact (Public Health England, 2018b). Grimshaw (2008) concurs that monitoring service inputs, delivery processes, service outputs and service user outcomes is the framework upon which an evaluation concerned with the treatment of young people who have displayed harmful sexual behaviour should be structured.

Academics from the Sexual Offences Crime and Misconduct Research Unit (SOCAMRU), based at Nottingham Trent University (NTU), were granted ethical approval to evaluate the Apollo project. The research takes a convergent mixed-methods design; quantitative and qualitative data are collected, which is hypothesised to allow for a comprehensive understanding of this niche intervention (Creswell & Clark, 2007).

The quantitative strand aims to determine the psychological impact of the Apollo project on its young people. A battery of psychometrics is administered before, during and after the project and measures a number of intervention outcomes relevant to young people's lives, including risk factors of reoffending (Grimshaw, 2008).

Measures and analysis

As the model is based on improving psychological flexibility, this is a key outcome measure. The AFQ-Y (Greco et al., 2005) is administered to gauge the responsivity of the young people to the DNA-V model during their time on the Apollo project (Hayes & Ciarrochi, 2015b). The SLF also wants to explore the impact of Apollo on typical risk factors associated with sexual offending by young people in order to understand the change mechanisms. Therefore, psychological constructs, including mental well-being, social and emotional loneliness and self-esteem, are monitored throughout the project, as well as attitudes towards crime. Table 11.3 presents further details about the quantitative measures used.

Numeric data are statistically analysed to assess individual and group change over time. The Reliable Change Index (RCI; Jacobson & Truax, 1991) is also calculated. The RCI is a ratio intended to assess whether the difference between pre- and post-intervention scores is clinically significant (Guhn, Forer & Zumbo, 2014).

Qualitative interviews

The qualitative strand of the evaluation aims to explore the experience of being involved with the Apollo project. Semi-structured interviews will be conducted with individuals involved with the project, including young people, their primary caregivers, volunteers and the project coordinator. The interview schedules are concerned with personal journeys, perceived impact of the intervention, any positives or pitfalls and recommendations for the future.

Challenges

Generally, participant engagement with the evaluation has been consistent, attributed to an understanding that the evaluation contributes to the running of

Table 11.3 Psychometric measures used in the Apollo evaluation

Measure	Description
Avoidance and Fusion Questionnaire for Youth (Greco et al., 2005)	A 17-item child-report scale measuring psychological inflexibility as caused by cognitive fusion and experiential avoidance.
Warwick Edinburgh Mental Well-Being Scale (Tennant et al., 2007)	A 14-item positively worded scale measuring aspects of mental health.
Social and Emotional Loneliness Scale for Adults – Short (DiTommaso, Brannen & Best, 2004)	A 15-item scale comprising three subscales measuring romantic, family and social loneliness.
Rosenberg Self-Esteem Scale (Rosenberg, 1965)	A 10-item scale that measures the qualities participants self-attribute.
Crime-PICS II (Frude, Honess & Maguire, 1994)	A two-part scale with the first assessing offending-related attitudes and the second measuring life problems associated with crime.
Youth Dynamic Risk Review (YDRR)	The YDRR was adapted from the Juvenile Sex Offender Assessment Protocol-II (Prentky & Righthand, 2003) and measures dynamic risk levels associated with sexual offending.

the project and continuation of support for other young people. However, some feedback has included confusion around the wording of reverse-scored items and first-person language. Young people have reported to struggle with phrasing that they would not use to describe their experiences, e.g. 'I have been feeling interested in other people' (WEMWBS; Tennant et al., 2007).

Trends in the literature suggest methodological issues in evaluating interventions for adolescent forensic populations, including small sample sizes, short follow-up periods, attrition and low engagement (Townsend et al., 2010; Carl, Schmucker & Lösel, 2020). Carl et al. (2020) found that low initial motivation, low engagement and a younger age were predictors of service attrition. Whilst the age range of the Apollo sample (12 to 17 years) is reflective of Carl et al.'s (2020) sample (15 to 21 years), the initial motivation of Apollo service-users is characterised as high, as participation is voluntary.

Application of findings

Results from this evaluation are expected to allow for a comparison of existing interventions against the Apollo project. A comparison of models can be used to provide evidence of what works best in reducing the risk of young people displaying escalated harmful sexual behaviours. The evaluation is ongoing, with updates made available via the SLF website (http://saferlivingfoundation.org/). Dissemination via presentation, research webinars and papers to peer-reviewed journals has also commenced.

Conclusion

The Apollo project is an innovative response to meet the needs of a group of young people to reduce sexual offending risk who otherwise have no access to formal support services. It is a supportive intervention that takes the benefits of community volunteer support combined with individual needs assessment to provide a structured process to develop psychological flexibility. The experience so far is that subjectively, participants are gaining from their involvement in Apollo, but it is too early for formal evaluation outcomes.

The evidence for the role of psychological (in)flexibility as a causal mechanism for human distress and problematic behaviour is growing, although there has been little attention given to its role in offending behaviour. We hope to contribute to the evidence base with the evaluation of this project and examine and understand the role psychological flexibility may have both as a causal mechanism for offending and as means of intervention for offending.

References

A-Tjak, J. G., Davis, M. L., Morina, N., Powers, M. B., Smits, J. A., & Emmelkamp, P. M. (2015). A meta-analysis of the efficacy of acceptance and commitment therapy for clinically relevant mental and physical health problems. *Psychotherapy and Psychosomatics, 84*(1), 30–36.

Amrod, J., & Hayes, S. C. (2013). ACT for the incarcerated. In R. Tafrate & D. Mitchell (Eds.), *Forensic CBT: A handbook for clinical practice* (pp. 43–65). Wiley-Blackwell.

Armstrong, A. B., Morrison, K. L., & Twohig, M. P. (2013). *Journal of Cognitive Psychotherapy, 27*(2), 175–190.

Beck, A. T. (1976). *Cognitive therapy and the emotional disorders.* International Universities Press.

Bryan, C. J., Yeager, D. S., Hinojosa, C. P., Chabot, A., Bergen, H., Kawamura, M., & Steubing, F. (2016). Harnessing adolescent values to motivate healthier eating.

Proceedings of the National Academy of Sciences of the United States of America, 113(39), 10830–10835. https://doi.org/10.1073/pnas.1604586113

Carl, L. C., Schmucker, M., & Lösel, F. (2020). Predicting attrition and engagement in the treatment of young offenders. *International Journal of Offender Therapy and Comparative Criminology, 64*(4), 355–374.

Carpentier, J., Leclerc, B., & Proulx, J. (2011). Juvenile sexual offenders: Correlates of onset, variety, and desistance of criminal behavior. *Criminal Justice and Behavior, 38*(8), 854–873. https://doi.org/10.1177/0093854811407730

Ciarrochi, J. V., Hayes, L. L., & Bailey, A. (2012). *Get out of your mind and into your life for teens, a guide to living an extraordinary life.* New Harbinger Publications.

Creeden, K. (2013). Taking a developmental approach to treating juvenile sexual behavior problems. *International Journal of Behavioral Consultation and Therapy, 8*(3–4), 12–16. http://dx.doi.org/10.1037/h010097

Creswell, J. W., & Clark, V. L. P. (2007). *Designing and conducting mixed methods research.* John Wiley.

Crosby, J., & Twohig, M. P. (2016). Acceptance and commitment therapy for problematic internet pornography use: A randomized trial. *Behavior Therapy, 47*, 355–366.

DiTommaso, E., Brannen, C., & Best, L. A. (2004). Measurement and validity characteristics of the short version of the social and emotional loneliness scale for adults. *Educational and Psychological Measurement, 64*(1), 99–119.

Duwe, G. (2018). Can circles of support and accountability (CoSA) significantly reduce sexual recidivism? Results from a randomized controlled trial in Minnesota. *Journal of Experimental Criminology, 14*(4), 463–484. doi:10.1007/s11292-018-9325-7

Elliott, H., Hocken, K., Lievesley, R., Blagden, N., Winder, B., & Banyard, P. (Eds.). (2018). *Sexual crime and circles of support and accountability.* Springer.

Frude, N., Honess, T. M., & Maguire, M. (1994). *Crime-PICS II: A psychometric tool for measuring attitude change in probation clients.* Michael and Associates.

Granthan, P., & Cowtan, C. (2015). *Third wave CBT therapies brief literature review.* SDS Seminars Ltd. www.skillsdevelopment.co.uk

Greco, L. A., Murrell, A. R., & Coyne, L. W. (2005). *Avoidance and fusion questionnaire for youth.* Retrieved from www.contextualpsychology.org.

Grimshaw, R. (2008). *Young people who sexually abuse.* Retrieved from www.crimeandjustice.org.uk/sites/crimeandjustice.org.uk/files/Young_People_who_Sexually_Abuse.pdf

Guhn, M., Forer, B., & Zumbo, B. D. (2014). Reliable change index. In A. C. Michalos (Eds.), *Encyclopedia of quality of life and well-being research.* Springer.

Hackett, S. (2014). *Children and young people with harmful sexual behaviours.* Research in Practice.

Harris, R. (2008). *The happiness trap: How to stop struggling and start living.* Trumpete.

Hayes, S. C. (2004). Acceptance and commitment therapy, relational frame theory, and the third wave of behavioral and cognitive therapies. *Behavior Therapy*, *35*, 639–665.

Hayes, L. L., & Ciarrochi, J. V. (2015a). *The thriving adolescent: Using acceptance and commitment therapy and positive psychology to help teens manage emotions, achieve goals, and build connection*. Oakland: New Harbinger Publications.

Hayes, L. L., & Ciarrochi, J. (2015b). Using acceptance and commitment therapy to help young people develop and grow to their full potential. In B. Kirkcaldy (Ed.), *Promoting psychological well-being in children and families*. London: Palgrave Macmillan. https://doi.org/10.1057/9781137479969_7

Hayes, S. C., Luoma, J., Bond, F., Masuda, A., & Lillis, J. (2006). Acceptance and commitment therapy: Model, processes, and outcomes. *Behaviour Research and Therapy*, *44*(1), 1–25.

Hayes, S. C., Strosahl, K. D., & Wilson, K. G. (2011). *Acceptance and commitment therapy: The process and practice of mindful change* (2nd ed.). The Guilford Press.

Hofmann, S. G., & Hayes, S. C. (2019). The future of intervention science: Process-based therapy. *Clinical Psychological Science*, *7*(1), 37–50. https://doi.org/10.1177/2167702618772296

Jacobson, N. S., & Truax, P. (1991). Clinical significance: A statistical approach to defining meaningful change in psychotherapy research. *Journal of Clinical and Consulting Psychology*, *59*, 12–19.

Kitson-Boyce, R., Blagden, N., Winder, B., & Dillon, G. (2019). Supporting desistance through ambiguous practice: What can be learnt from the first prison-based model of CoSA in England and Wales? *Journal of Forensic Psychology: Research and Practice. 19*(2), 186–209. doi:10.1080/24732850.2019.1571362

Letourneau, E. J., Henggeler, S. W., McCart, M. R., Borduin, C. M., Schewe, P. A., & Armstrong, K. S. (2013). Two-year follow-up of a randomized effectiveness trial evaluating MST for juveniles who sexually offend. *Journal of Family Psychology*, *27*(6), 978.

Levin, M. E., MacLane, C., Daflos, S., Seeley, J. R., Hayes, S. C., & Biglan, B. (2014). Examining psychological inflexibility as a transdiagnostic process across psychological disorders. *Journal of Contextual Behavioral Science*, *3*(3). doi:10.1016/j.jcbs.2014.06.003

Levin, M. E., Twohig, M. P., & Krafft, J. (2020). *Innovations in acceptance and commitment therapy: Clinical advancements and applications in ACT*. New Harbinger Publications.

Livheim, F., Hayes, L., Ghaderi, A., Magnusdottir, T., Högfeldt, A., Rowse, J., Turner, S., Hayes, S. C., & Tengström, A. (2015). The effectiveness of acceptance and commitment therapy for adolescent mental health: Swedish and Australian pilot outcomes. *Journal of Child and Family Studies*, *24*, 1016–1030. https://doi.org/10.1007/s10826-014-9912-9

Macri, S., Adriani, W., Chiarotti, F., & Laviola, G. (2002). Risk taking exploration of a plus-maze is greater in adolescent than in a juvenile or adult mice. *Animal Behaviour*, *64*(4), 541–546. https://doi.org/10.1006/anbe.2002.4004

Pavlov, I. P. (1928). Lectures on conditioned reflexes: Twenty-five years of objective study of the higher nervous activity (behaviour) of animals. (W. H. Gantt, Trans.). Liverwright Publishing Corporation. https://doi.org/10.1037/11081-000

Prentky, R., & Righthand, S. (2003). *Juvenile Sex Offender Assessment Protocol-II (J-SOAP-II) manual.* Washington, DC: US Department of Justice, Office of Justice Programs, Office of Juvenile Justice and Delinquency Prevention.

Public Health England. (2018a). *Guidance: Process evaluation.* Retrieved from www.gov.uk/government/publications/evaluation-in-health-and-well-being-overview/process-evaluation

Public Health England. (2018b). *Guidance: Outcome evaluation.* Retrieved from www.gov.uk/government/publications/evaluation-in-health-and-well-being-overview/outcome-evaluation

Rosenberg, M. (1965). Rosenberg self-esteem scale (RSE). *Acceptance and Commitment Therapy: Measures Package, 61*(52).

Saunders, L. (2020). *"It felt like falling off a cliff": The transition of people convicted of sexual offences from prison to the community.* Doctorate of Philosophy. The University of Nottingham.

Schmucker, M., & Lösel, F. (2017). Sexual offender treatment for reducing recidivism among convicted sex offenders: A systematic review and meta-analysis. *Campbell Systematic Reviews, 13*(1), 1–75.

Swain, J., Hancock, K., Dixon, A., & Bowman, J. (2015). Acceptance and commitment therapy for children: A systematic review of intervention studies. *Journal of Contextual Behavioral Sciences, 4*(2), 73–85.

Tennant, R., Hiller, L., Fishwick, R., Platt, S., Joseph, S., Weich, S., . . . & Stewart-Brown, S. (2007). The Warwick-Edinburgh mental well-being scale (WEMWBS): Development and UK validation. *Health and Quality of Life Outcomes, 5*(1), 63.

Townsend, E., Walker, D. M., Sargeant, S., Vostanis, P., Hawton, K., Stocker, O., & Sithole, J. (2010). Systematic review and meta-analysis of interventions relevant for young offenders with mood disorders, anxiety disorders, or self-harm. *Journal of Adolescence, 33*(1), 9–20.

Waite, D., Keller, A., McGarvey, E. L., Wieckowski, E., Pinkerton, R., & Brown, G. L. (2005). Juvenile sex offender re-arrest rates for sexual, violent nonsexual and property crimes: A 10-year follow-up. *Sexual Abuse, 17*(3), 313–331. https://doi.org/10.1177/107906320501700305

Walton, J. S., & Hocken, K. (2020). Compassion and acceptance as interventions for paraphilic disorders and sexual offending behaviour. In G. Akerman, D. Perkins, & R. Bartels (Eds.), *Assessing and managing problematic sexual interests, a practitioner's guide.* New York: Routledge. ISBN 9780367254186.

Ward, T. (2002). Good lives and the rehabilitation of sexual offenders: Promises and problems. *Aggression and Violent Behavior, 7,* 513–528.

Ware, J., & Blagden, N. (2016). Responding to categorical denial, refusal, and treatment drop-out. In D. P. Boer (Ed.), *The Wiley handbook on the theories, assessment and treatment of sexual offending*. Wiley. doi:10.1002/9781118574003.wattso076

Weinstein, N., Deci, E. L., & Ryan, R. M. (2011). Motivational determinants of integrating positive and negative past identities. *Journal of Personality and Social Psychology*, *100*(3), 527. Retrieved from https://ntu.idm.oclc.org/login?url=www.proquest.com/docview/854948040?accountid=14693

Weinstein, N., Legate, N., Ryan, W. S., Sedikides, C., & Cozzolino, P. J. (2017). Autonomy support for conflictual and stigmatized identities: Effects on ownership and psychological health. *Journal of Counseling Psychology*, *64*(5), 584–599. https://ntu.idm.oclc.org/login?url=www.proquest.com/docview/1898069481?accountid=14693. doi: http://dx.doi.org/10.1037/cou0000224

Willis, G. M. (2018). Why call someone by what we don't want them to be? The ethics of labelling in forensic/correctional psychology. *Psychology, Crime & Law*. doi:10.1080/1068316X.2017.1421640

Zarling, A., Bannon, S. M., & Berta, (2017). Evaluation of acceptance and commitment therapy for domestic violence offenders. *Psychology of Violence*. doi:10.1037/vio0000097

Index

internet pornography 58, 116
interpersonal 72
intervention(s): individually tailored 8;
    meditation-based 225; mindfulness-based
    225, 226, 228, 232; prison-based 177, 182;
    rehabilitative 149; RO DBT 95
intimacy 55, 57, 94, 97, 109, 115, 118, 119,
    175, 246; lack of 175
intimate partner violence 93
isolation 12, 174, 176, 201, 242, 243

Jungian analysis 251

Kaplan-Meier estimator 44
killing, mass 93

LANCOVA analysis 40, 42
learning disability 109
life satisfaction 224
lip-reading 171
loneliness 152, 175, 201, 242, 265, 266
longitudinal studies 91, 92

macho culture 4
maladaptation 2, 3,90, 92, 95, 147–149, 152,
    193, 211
maladaptive overcontrol 90, 92, 95
maltreatment 173, 195
maps: me 77; we 77
master status 151
masturbation 50, 51, 55, 56, 59, 60, 114, 189,
    261, 262
meditation 222, 224, 225, 227–230
mental health: in-reach 13; problems in UK
    prisons 7
mindfulness 61, 96, 109, 202, 205, 220–233,
    246, 262; training 222
mindfulness-based approaches 224, 225
mindfulness-based cognitive therapy (MBCT)
    224–226, 230
mindfulness-based practice 225, 231
mindfulness-based programmes 223, 225,
    226
minimisation 142–146, 153, 181, 190
mistreatment 195
modus operandi 146

National Health Service (NHS) 9–14, 16–18,
    176, 243, 253
National Institute for Health and Care
    Excellence (NICE) 16, 224, 226

neurodevelopmental 113, 115, 117, 118;
    correlates 113
neurohormonal 112
neuroimaging 113, 227
neutralisations 150
NHS Child and Adolescent Mental Health
    Services 243
NHS treatment values 9
nonconsenting 110

obsessive compulsive disorder 74, 246
offence paralleling behaviour 49
offending 2, 108, 175, 181, 189, 226, 228, 230
offending behaviour 2, 175, 230; in deaf
    populations 175; programmes 2, 230
omnipotence 50
Offenders with Personality Disorder Pathway
    (OPDP) 12, 14, 17
open systems 71
operant conditioning 55, 112, 189
operationalisation 76
Over- and Under-control Trait Measure
    (OUT'M) 97
overcontrol(led) 3, 90–97

paedophilia 10–113, 115, 117, 151, 153, 201,
    245
paedophilic disorder 110
paraphilia 109–118, 120, 121, 197, 202:
    biopsychosocial processes underlying 112;
    long leather boots 113
paraphilic disorder 110
Pavlov, I. P. 113, 189, 244
personality disorder 9–14, 16, 74, 94, 95, 97,
    172, 194, 225; diagnosis 97
phallometric testing 111
polyvagal theory 223
pornography 50, 58, 59, 116, 117, 246, 258
positive reinforcement 113, 114
post baseline 40
power dynamic 77, 148, 149
practice(s)/practicing 1, 13, 16, 17, 28, 37,
    48, 53, 54, 55, 56, 57, 59, 60, 61, 67, 69,
    75, 77, 81, 83, 91, 109, 119, 122, 141–143,
    154, 170, 176–178, 205, 224, 231, 227,
    257, 259, 262
practitioners 1, 2,6, 15, 58, 95, 146, 192, 196,
    210
pre-frontal cortex 223, 227
premeditation 143
proactive 5, 79, 83, 196